Agroforestry and Watershed Management: An Interloked System

Agroforestry and Watershed Management: An Interloked System

Ajay Mukherjee

RANDOM

RANDOM PUBLICATIONS

NEW DELHI (INDIA)

Agroforestry and Watershed Management: An Interloked System

ISBN 978-93-5111-825-1

Published in 2016 in India by

RANDOM PUBLICATIONS

4376-A/4B, Gali Murari Lal, Ansari Road
New Delhi-110 002
Phone : +9111-43580356, 011-23289044, 011-43142548
e-mail: sales@randompublications.com,
info@randompublications.com, randomexports@gmail.com

Reprinted 2026

Type Setting by : Friends Media, Delhi-110089

Preface

Agroforestry is an activity that combines production on the same plot of land, from annual agricultural activities (such as crops and pasture) and from delayed long-term production by trees (for example timber and services). This is obtained either by planting trees on agricultural land or by cropping (for example after thinning) on forested land. Plots that combine arable intercrops with forestry trees are silvoarable plots, while wooded plots with pasture under the tree canopy are known as silvopastoral plots.

Agroforestry practices are intentional combinations of trees with crops and/or livestock which involve intensive management of the interactions between the components as an integrated agroecosystem. These four key characteristics - intentional, intensive, interactive and integrated - are the essence of agroforestry and are what distinguish it from other farming or forestry practices.

Agroforestry provides a different land use option, compared with traditional arable and forestry systems. It makes use of the complementarity between trees and crops, so that the available resources can be more effectively exploited. It is a practice that respects the environment and has an obvious landscape benefit. Efficient, modern versions of agroforestry have been developed, that are adapted to the constraints imposed by mechanisation. The agroforestry plot remains productive for the farmer and generates continuous revenue, which is not the case when arable land is exclusively reforested. Agroforestry allows for the diversification of farm activity and makes better use of environmental resources. Agroforestry has interesting advantages from three different perspectives.

Watershed is defined as a geohydrological unit draining to a common point by a system of drains. All lands on earth are part of one watershed or other. The problems of watershed management are often exacerbated by a relative lack of observational information concerning water, in its various positions in the environment. In this new century of complexity and conflicts, water mangers will have to confront a confusing arena. To achieve success in this field, technological skills together with public cooperation is very essential.

The book will be useful both as a text book for the students of the agroforestry as well as a compendium of the foresters and scientists. The prose is quite simple and readable without any ambiguity in meaning.

*– **Author***

Contents

1

Agroforestry

Agroforestry is an activity that combines production on the same plot of land, from annual agricultural activities (such as crops and pasture) and from delayed long-term production by trees (for example timber and services). This is obtained either by planting trees on agricultural land or by cropping (for example after thinning) on forested land. Plots that combine arable intercrops with forestry trees are silvoarable plots, while wooded plots with pasture under the tree canopy are known as silvopastoral plots.

IMPORTANCE OF AGROFORESTRY

Agroforestry provides goods and services to the farmer. The main service roles include soil conservation, creation of a favourable microclimate, and societal benefits through the multitude of traditional roles that trees play in many civilizations. Other service roles include nitrogen fixation (although nitrogen-fixing plants do not enrich the soil if most of the fixed N is removed from the site, as in the case of fodder); increased water retention capacity of the soil due to frequent loosening of the topsoil layer; and substantial reduction of weed competition when crops are tended. There are several products from multipurpose trees, and these can be used for subsistence or income generation, helping farmers to diversify production and so reduce risk. Agroforestry practices seek to address the problem of deforestation and to achieve a positive ecological interaction between the components of the system and the environment (especially the microclimate). At present, the problem of deforestation is intensifying, with trees being cut down at a faster rate than they are being replaced. Moreover, the demand for fuelwood and other tree products is rising as population increases. Deforestation may also lead to loss of habitat for wildlife, and eventually to their extinction and hence loss of national heritage; to shortages of forest products such as timber, poles, firewood, charcoal and medicines; and ultimately to environmental degradation and erosion of genetic resources. In Mbale decreased fodder availability due to restricted access to forests led to a decrease in number of animals owned by households.

FARMING PRACTICES

Farming practices have to change if the land is to continue producing food for the ever-increasing population, for example continuous cultivation of the same fields leads to a decline in the productivity of the land and monoculture farming, coupled with the use of chemical fertilizers and pesticides, has an adverse ecological effect.Agroforestry can prevent a decline in soil fertility and productivity, which is an added motivation for practising it. Furthermore, the productivity of many tree products is superior on farms, as opposed to natural wooded land, because of farmer management (F. Place, pers. comm. 2002).

Trees and shrubs are an important source of nutrition for livestock. Fodder trees (browse or top feed), are an effective insurance against seasonal feed shortages. They are used to supplement the quantity and quality of basal feeds such as grasses and crop residues. Fodder trees are less affected by dry conditions, owing to their extensive root systems and longer life spans. Incorporation of trees and shrubs for fodder in smallholder farming and intensive systems is gaining ground in Uganda.

Use of Agroforestry Systems

Calliandra has been introduced in farming systems as a multi-purpose shrub. There are many reasons for growing it on one's farm. These include 1) fuelwood, 2) stabilising soils and water conservation structures, 3) soil fertility improvement, 4) fodder supplement for ruminant livestock, 5) secondary production (bee forage, stakes for climbing beans and tomatoes), and 6) income generation through sale of wood, fodder and seed. Calliandra also provides several secondary products. It flowers prolifically and is a favoured source of nectar for honeybees. The honey produced is considered to be of high quality, with a bittersweet flavour. Processed into leaf meal, it has shown promise as a protein source for livestock.

Importance of Agroforestry Systems on Livelihoods

The economic viability of agroforestry systems has to be considered with regard to the benefits they can provide to farmers in Uganda. Calliandra can increase nutrient availability, improve crop output or, as fodder, increase milk production and so contribute to food security. Food insecurity is of major concern to Ugandans, as it is an important indicator of poverty. Smallholder production of food crops has been declining. Uganda has a high rate of infant stunting and mortality. Food insecurity, and particularly the inability of the smallholder sector to maintain or increase levels of food output, has been attributed to serious shortages of arable land, the low levels of technology practised by most smallholders and weaknesses in the delivery of agricultural and forestry services. Incorporation of Calliandra in the farming system can contribute towards reversal of these negative trends through its many uses in the farming system.

Use as a Fodder

Calliandra leaf material contains 17-28 per cent crude protein (dry matter basis) and can be used for dairy feed supplementation. Its use as a supplement to basal feeds, which in Uganda consist mainly of Napier and other grasses and crop residues, increases the overall protein content of the fodder ration and thereby increases milk production. Calliandra improves milk production of both dairy cattle and dairy goats.

In on-farm experiments with dairy cows under East African conditions, 3 kg of fresh Calliandra leaves provided a similar response in milk yield and butter per cent to 1 kg of commercial concentrate, increasing milk production by roughly 0.75 litre under farm conditions, although response varied depending on such factors as the cow's health and the quality of its basal diet. However, in a separate on-station experiment with sheep and goats, when concentrate or Calliandra was used in the same relative proportions as a supplement to Napier grass (without additional concentrate), the concentrate gave significantly better animal performance than Calliandra.

A cow needs to be fed roughly 6 kg of fresh leaves every day, while a goat needs about 0.7 kg. Increased milk production improves the nutritional status of households by increasing the proportion of milk in the diet. For those households that sell milk, income increases; and if prices become lower as a result of increased supply, poorer households also become able to afford to buy milk. Calliandra can also be fed to other types of livestock such as sheep, rabbits and chicken, which are more affordable to poorer households (although care must be taken with non-ruminants to feed Calliandra in small amounts, to avoid problems with toxicity due to tannins). Other feeds with high levels of condensed tannins are known to have anthelmintic (de-worming) properties.

To harvest 6 kg of fresh leaves every day on a sustained yield one needs to plant about 500 Calliandra trees at a spacing of 0.5 m (1.5 ft), making 250 m (800 ft) of hedge. Tuwei *et al* (2003) reported annual forage (leaf biomass production) yields of Calliandra of 13-15 t/ha/year (DM) in Embu, Kenya. The economic benefits of supplementation with Calliandra. In the first year, a small investment by farmers was required in planting labour and purchase of seedlings. This amounted to US $ 7.00 for the 500 shrubs needed. Supplementary feeding of 6 kg of fresh Calliandra fodder on a daily basis to a diary cow through a 10 month lactation period gave a net benefit of up to Ug shs 230,100 (US $ 122.32) per cow per year, beginning in the second year. This is as a result of increased milk production, assuming an increase of 10 per cent over base milk yields. Feeding 2 kg dry Calliandra day^{-1} as a supplement throughout the lactation period increased milk production by about 450 kg yr^{-1}.

BUDGET ECONOMIC ANALYSIS

In the same study, partial budget economic analysis showed that by feeding Calliandra as a substitute, the farmer saved money that would otherwise have been spent on buying and transporting 730 kg of dairy meal during the year. In the partial budget, assessing Calliandra as a substitute for dairy meal, incremental benefits per year after the first year were over 14 times higher than incremental costs. The net benefits per cow per year during years 2-5 were Ug shs 266,500 (US $ 141.68). In other words using Calliandra increased farmers' annual income by about US $ 120-142 per cow per year. These figures are based on the substitution rates (of Calliandra for concentrate) determined by the study of Paterson *et al.* (1996). Tree legume leaves are commonly fed to improve the utilisation of low quality grasses and crop residues in tropical areas. For example, goats in Zambia maintained on poor quality pasture hay lost weight (-20g/day), but gained weight (24g/day) when provided with supplements of Calliandra (140g DM/day). Similarly, Palmer and Ibrahim (1996) found that increasing levels (0 to 35 per cent DM) of fresh Calliandra leaves in a diet of low quality hay increased the live weight gain of sheep from -27g to 52g/day.

Studies in Australia and Indonesia in the early 1990s suggested that forage of Calliandra had higher nutritive value when fed fresh. When leaf material of Calliandra was fed fresh to sheep, voluntary intake was 59g dry matter/kg $W^{0.75}$ ($W^{0.75}$ is the metabolic weight of the animal), but for dried leaves it was only 37g dry matter/kg $W^{0.75}$. More recent research, however, suggests that there is usually no significant negative effect of drying on animal production.

Positive Effects on Animal Nutrition

For non-ruminants, the high tannin content of Calliandra results in less positive effects on animal nutrition than is achieved with ruminants. Supplementation of poultry feed with Calliandra tends to increase feed intake and reduce egg production, although at low levels of supplementation yolk colour is improved. Calliandra is a source of carotene, which is used to maintain yolk colour in commercially produced eggs. Inclusion rates of Calliandra in poultry diet greater than 5 per cent decreased the number of eggs produced per chicken. Yolk colour was markedly improved at 5 per cent level and it was concluded that 5 per cent Calliandra leaves was the maximum level of inclusion consistent with the maintenance of production.

CHALLENGES FOR SUSTAINABLE ARID ZONE AGROFORESTRY

Agroforestry has been followed since time immemorial for sustainable livelihood in the arid zone, but in the recent past some changes have occurred, due to which the need is being felt to develop agroforestry systems, which may be able to meet the requirements of sustainable livelihood in the future.

HEAVY BIOTIC PRESSURE

Chalcolithic and Iron Age maps of the Indian subcontinent suggest that human occupation of the current Thar Desert region was thin during these earlier ages, and that populations depended upon hunting and limited pastoralism. From the analysis of available census records, the population of the Thar Desert region registered an increase of 490 per cent from 1901 to 1991. The present population of the Thar is about 40 million.

Decennial variation in population from 1901 to 1991 in the Thar showed a growth rate of 186 per cent (between 1901 and 1971) as compared with 132 per cent for the whole country. The population growth rate for the decades 1971-1981 and 1981-1991 were 36.7 per cent and 30.7 per cent, respectively. The population density is quite high compared with the global average of 6-8 persons/km^2 for arid zones. The major factor responsible for such phenomenal growth of population in the Thar is a wide gap between birth and death rates. Moreover, social values favour large families and positive sanctions for fertility outnumber negative ones.

Cropping on Marginal Lands

Of the total area of the Thar, only 1.3 per cent is now under forest cover. The net cultivated area increased by 54.1 per cent from 1915 to the early 1980s. This trend in cultivated area increase has further accelerated during the past decade (the 1990s), having increased by 11.7 per cent compared with the amount in the early 1980s. As a consequence of this, barren, cultivable and uncultivable wastelands, permanent pastures, and fallow land have declined substantially. There was a significant decline in grazing land area as marginal lands were brought under cultivation in recent years (the late 1990s). Because of low and erratic precipitation, restricted to a very short period, only one crop, the kharif (monsoon) season crop, is sown each year in most of the Thar.

The common crops are pearl millet, cluster bean, green gram, moth bean and sesame. In the arid zone of peninsular India, in addition to these crops, sorghum, maize pigeon pea and other coarse millets are also grown.

It has been observed that the agricultural holdings during late medieval times were only one fifth of those found today. By 1951, much of the potential agricultural land was brought under plow, and the trend since then in already established agricultural tracts has been intensification of farming, and the expansion of agriculture into new lands that may be considered environmentally marginal. Mechanized field operations (use of tractors) not only increase soil erosion but also reduces the naturally regenerated population of various useful species.

Unsustainable Development Policies

With the advancement of science and technology, efforts have also been made to enhance production in the arid zone. Some of the technologies like sand dune stabilisation, wind-breaks and agri-horticulture have produced good results because they are developed in synergism with nature (ecosystem) and natives (people and vegetation).

But some other technologies imported from less environmentally stressed areas have proven to be unsustainable. For example use of tractors adversely affected the natural regeneration of native trees like Prosopis cineraria, and increases wind erosion. Irrigation with waters from the Indira Gandhi canal network has caused problems of water logging and, secondary salinization. Several exotic species either become invasive, like Prosopis juliflora, or didn't prove economically productive, like Faidherbia albida, jojaba etc. The overall impact of these imported technologies, along with high biotic pressure and a fragmented approach to desertification control, can now be observed in terms of loss of biodiversity, increasing desertification, and other adverse impacts. It is now imperative to think broadly and plan holistically for the future of arid zone agroforestry, the basis of sustainable livelihood in the arid zone. Throughout the arid zones, there is no dearth of problems, but rapidly increasing desertification (some call it land degradation) is a worldwide problem. Land degradation appears to be more of a descriptive term than desertification, as it better describes the process of wind and water erosion, soil salinization, and loss of vegetation cover. It helps in clarifying relationships among climate, topography, soil structure, land use, hydrology, and vegetation. Throughout the arid zones of the world, the major factor responsible for land degradation is soil degradation.

At the world scale, the GLASSOD database indicates that in arid zones, more than 60 per cent of soil degradation is caused by wind erosion, with human-induced water erosion accounting for 8 per cent of the phenomenon. At the global level, 349.6 million hectares of land in arid zones are characterised by a light to moderate degree of soil degradation, and 42.9 million hectares have strong to extreme soil degradation.

Besides wind and water erosion, over-grazing, high magnitude agricultural degradation activities, over exploitation of vegetation for domestic use, *e.g.* for fuel, and faulty land use are other factors responsible for ever increasing land degradation in arid zones.

The links between land or soil degradation and vegetation in arid zones are complex. Vegetation and soils display differing resilience to disturbance. Although in arid zones vegetation communities can be readily disturbed and degraded, recovery rates are very slow in comparison with those of other ecoclimatic conditions. Vegetation in arid zones is highty sensitive to natural climatic variability. Decreased production and an ability to lie dormant are two strategies displayed by arid zone plants for survival at times of moisture deficiency. Although an adequate database is not available, two useful relationships between soil degradation and vegetation can be determined. First, vegetation cover may help to indicate the vulnerability of a particular habitat to soil degradation, and second, vegetation cover or community type or plant species may indicate that soil degradation.

THE ADVANTAGES OF AGROFORESTRY

Agroforestry provides a different land use option, compared with traditional arable and forestry systems. It makes use of the complementarity between trees and crops, so that the available resources can be more effectively exploited. It is a practice that respects the environment and has an obvious landscape benefit. Efficient, modern versions of agroforestry have been developed, that are adapted to the constraints imposed by mechanisation. The agroforestry plot remains productive for the farmer and generates continuous revenue, which is not the case when arable land is exclusively reforested. Agroforestry allows for the diversification of farm activity and makes better use of environmental resources. Agroforestry has interesting advantages from three different perspectives.

FROM THE ARABLE PERSPECTIVE

Diversification of the activities of arable farmers, with the building-up of an inheritance of valuable trees, without disrupting the revenue from those plots which have been planted. Protection of intercrops and animals by the trees, which have a windbreak effect, providing shelter from the sun, from the rain, from the wind, holding the soil in place, and stimulating soil microfauna and microflora

Recovery of some of the leached or drained nutrients by the deep roots of the trees; enrichment of the soil organic matter by tree litter and by the dead roots of the trees. Possibility of combining the interest of the owner (for an inheritance of wood) and the farm (for access to cultivated land). Possible remuneration for the arable farmer for looking after the trees

An alternative to full reforestation of arable land, permitting the continuation of arable activity on land whose arable potential is therefore conserved. The tree component can be reversed, the plot stays "clean" (free from scrub) and is easy to destump when the trees are clear felled (the stumps are in lines and few in number). In silvopastoral plots, fodder units can be available at different dates compared to full cropped plots, extending the grazing calender.

From the Forestry Perspective

Acceleration of the diameter growth of the trees by wide spacing (+80 per cent over 6 years in the majority of the experimental plantations). Reduction of the capital cost of the plantation, by reducing the number of trees planted with no commercial future. A large reduction in the maintenance costs of the plantation, due to the presence of the intercrops. Improvement in the quality of wood produced (wide regular rings, suited to the needs of industry), because the trees are not subjected to cycles of competition and thinning.

Guaranteed follow-up and tree care due to the arable intercropping activity. In particular, protection against the risk of fire in susceptible areas, with pastoralism or with intercrops like vine or winter cereals (clear bare ground in summer after stubble ploughing). Agroforestry plantations on arable land allow the development of a quality wood resource that complements, rather then competes with, the products from traditionally exploited forests. It is especially important to produce wood that can substitute for tropical sawlogs, which will soon decline in availability and quality. The areas concerned will remain small in terms of their absolute value, but the production of wood from them could become a critical input to the European wood supply network. Tree species that are little used in forestry, but are of high value, could be grown in agroforestry systems: service trees, pear trees, common sorbs, walnut trees, wild cherry trees, maple trees, tulip trees, paulownias, etc...

From the Environmental Perspective

Improvement to the development of natural resources: the total wood and arable production from an agroforestry plot is greater than the separate production obtained by an arable-forest separate cropping pattern on the same area of land. This effect results from the stimulation of complementarity between trees and crops on agroforestry plots. Thus, weeds, which are spontaneously present in young forestry plantations are replaced by harvested crops or pasture; maintenance is less costly and environmental resources are better used. Better control of cultivated areas of land: by substituting for arable plots, the agroforestry plots contributes to diminishing the cultivated area of land. The intensification of environmental resource use by agroforestry systems is not resulting in more crop products.

Creation of original landscapes that are attractive, open and favour recreational activities. Agroforestry plots have a truly innovative landscaping potential, and would improve the public image of farmers to society. This will be particularly the case in very sparsely wooded areas, where plots are developed by planting arable land, and in very heavily wooded areas, where plots are developed by thinning the existing forest.

Counteract the greenhouse effect: constitution of an effective system for carbon sequestration, by combining the maintenance of the stock of organic material in the soil (the case especially with meadows), and the superimposition of a net fixing wooded layer. Protection of soil and water, in particular in sensitive areas. Improvement of biodiversity, especially by the abundance of "edge effects". This in particular, permits a synergistic improvement, by favouring the habitat of game. The integrated protection of crops by their association with trees, chosen to stimulate the hyperparasite (parasites of parasites) population of crops, is a promising way forwards. These favourable characteristics are as coherent with the many objectives of the laws guiding agriculture and forestry, as they are with the directing principles of the Common Agricultural Policy.

SCIENTIFIC APPROACH TO AGROFORESTRY

A scientific approach to agroforestry has only been developed in the past twenty years, with technologies intended to address land use conflicts and/or developmental and environmental problems. All agroforestry systems including those with Calliandra have benefits and opportunities as well as costs and constraints.

In order to demonstrate to decision-makers the possible repercussions or trade-offs that result from alternative courses of action in implementing one agroforestry system over the other (or not implementing it at all), economic analysis is used. Such economic examination of alternative agroforestry systems can assist decision-making by offering a common monetary standard of measurement between alternatives. In the case of the individual farmer, economic analysis can help to ascertain whether or not agroforestry can increase productivity and farm income, and improve livelihoods in relation to traditional land-use agricultural activities. From a macro-economic perspective, economic analysis can show the expected economic outcomes of agroforestry interventions, to determine whether the net contribution to society can justify the expenditures incurred.

WIDE RANGE OF CLIMATIC AND SOIL CONDITIONS

Calliandra tolerates a wide range of climatic and soil conditions, but is affected negatively by frost and acidic soils. The plant is not tolerant of low oxygen tensions in waterlogged situations and does not grow well on poorly drained calcareous soils. Calliandra is a fast-growing tree, which can provide economic and environmental benefits in a short time (nine months to two years) making it easily acceptable to farmers. It can be grown in different niches on the farm: farmers in Uganda prefer to plant it on boundaries and soil conservation structures.

Good management reduces its competition with other crops for above- and below-ground resources. Calliandra has been widely promoted in Uganda by various organisations such as ICRAF-FORRI (NARO) since 1988, and by NGOs such as Heifer Project International (HPI) and its intermediaries operating in 25 districts, Send-a-Cow (23 districts), Africa 2000, Vi-Agroforestry Project (in 2 districts, since 1992), World Vision (22 districts with 1-3 sub-counties in each district) and the Uganda Land Management Project (in four districts). The various organisations cover up to 80 per cent of the country where there are farming households, however the proportion of farmers reached varies widely in the districts of operation, from three to fifteen percent.

The ICRAF-FORRI Agroforestry Research and Development Project had its initial focus in Kabale, in the Kigezi Highlands, and later expanded to Mukono District on the Lakeshore belt of Lake Victoria. The aim of the project is to improve livelihoods and ecosystem functions through the diversification of agroforestry systems. In Kabale and Mukono, farmers use Calliandra fodder in zero grazing (cut-and-carry) systems. It is estimated that 700,000 Calliandra seedlings have been planted every season since 1998 in Kabale District.

Calliandra is also widely promoted in other parts of Uganda by other agencies. For example, Vi-Agroforestry Project has been distributing seed to farmers in Masaka and Rakai Districts for the last ten years: in 2001 alone, a total of 1,574 kg was distributed while in 2002 it was 1,197 kg and in 2003 the total amount distributed increased to 2,309 kg (information from Vi organisation records and staff). In Uganda, there are regular feed shortages and droughts and therefore under such conditions subsistence feeding, mainly poor quality grasses and crop residues results in reduced live weight and low productivity of livestock.

The severe nutritional limitations are further associated with delayed age at first calving, increased interval between parturitions, increased non-productive life of animals and herd wastage. Therefore, during times of feed shortages, foliage from shrubs and trees such as Calliandra have a great value as they supply dietary nitrogen.

Problem Statement

Many development projects are financed with public funds and a significant proportion fail to achieve their main objectives. It is therefore essential to assess the potential and actual impacts of research and development initiatives. The great majority of agroforestry research to date has concentrated on the biological and physical factors that affect productivity rather than the economic and environmental value of agroforestry. There is a serious lack of reliable information, based on actual farm conditions, about the economic benefits and costs inherent in many agroforestry systems. The cost of production of Calliandra seedlings and the costs and benefits of its use as fodder for supplementation and substitution, as well as other impacts experienced under farm conditions, were the main focus of this study.

Although a number of farmers have adopted Calliandra in Kabale, the enormous potential benefits of Calliandra and other trees for smallholders still remain largely unrealised in both the study districts (Kabale and Mukono) due to the low numbers of trees planted per farmer, for example, in Kabale, adopting farmers have planted an average of 320 trees, yet the recommended number for feeding a dairy cow throughout the year is 500 trees.

Secondly, there is lack of knowledge among farmers on how to use and manage the species.

There are also many other outstanding questions. For example, who depends on planting of Calliandra? Are they rich or poor? Male or female? How does the use of Calliandra in agroforestry systems affect the incomes and welfare of farmers, especially the poor? The study was an attempt to answer these socio-economic questions and to quantify the actual, and determine the potential, socio-economic impact of Calliandra on farmers' household welfare in Mukono and Kabale Districts.

SEVERAL IMPORTANT OF JUSTIFICATIONS

There are several important justifications for this study:

1. Several of the agroforestry systems that have been tested using on-farm trials in Mukono and Kabale have shown positive results in terms of biophysical aspects and productivity increases at the plot level. However, little is known about the socio-economic impacts at the household level. For instance, observations made elsewhere (in Masaka and Rakai Districts) by Vi agroforestry staff and Mukasa (2003) have shown that farmers have complained about stiff Calliandra competition with bananas.
2. There is a lack of information on (a) the financial returns over time, (b) the labour requirements, and (c) the opportunity costs of land and crop yield for Calliandra-based agroforestry systems. Therefore, the profitability of agroforestry systems based on Calliandra, towards poverty alleviation, are unknown. Early adoption of technologies is mainly by well-off farmers, so the technology may have had little impact on the poorer farmers in the community. This study tried to fill this information gap by applying economic analysis both to primary data collected from farmers in the field, and to existing experimental data on the contribution of Calliandra.
3. There is little information on whether the incorporation of Calliandra in farming systems has contributed to environmental protection through planting, managing or changing land and other resource use practices. The study assessed the current and potential socio-economic and environmental impacts of Calliandra, as perceived by the farmers.
4. The generation of technologies that meet the needs of users is a necessary condition for the success of agricultural research. Only if farmers use the technologies developed through agricultural research, can research make an ultimate impact on the key goals of poverty

alleviation, conservation of natural resources, and food security. Since not all outputs from research do indeed fully meet the needs of users, ongoing assessment of the use and impact of research provides crucial information. Moreover, even where innovations achieve widespread adoption and impact, they may not meet the needs of all farmers. In such cases, studies of adoption and impact can supply crucial information on the patterns of adoption, identifying who is by-passed by an innovation.

5. In Uganda, political support for agroforestry's contribution to the Plan for Modernisation of Agriculture (PMA) requires that the cost effectiveness of various agroforestry technologies be demonstrated at the farm level. This study attempted to generate evidence that Calliandra-based agroforestry systems are cost effectiveness and that Calliandra has a role to play in the realisation of the goal of the PMA, *i.e.* 'eradication of poverty through profitable, sustainable and dynamic agricultural and agro-industrial sector'. Impact assessment is an essential requirement for achieving sustainable development. By integrating the economic, environmental and social dimensions of development into policy and project processes, it assists in advancing international and national development targets for long term sustainability.

Overall Objective

The overall objective of the study is to determine the potential and current socio-economic and farmers' perceived environmental impacts of Calliandra at the plot, household and community levels.

Specific Objectives

The specific objectives are:

- To determine the primary reasons for planting and primary benefits derived from Calliandra;
- To assess the cost of Calliandra seedling production and the costs, returns, and economic impact of Calliandra use as fodder;
- To establish farmers' own perceptions of the economic and environmental impacts of Calliandra.

Hypotheses Objectives

In line with the specific study objectives, the following hypotheses were made:

- Calliandra is a useful tree and meets the needs of farmers, although the primary reasons for its initial planting may be different from the primary uses at the time of utilisation;

- The economic benefits derived from establishment, management and use of Calliandra for fodder, outweigh the costs incurred in its establishment, management and use;
- There are more farmers who have experienced positive economic, social and environmental impacts of Calliandra than those who have experienced negative ones.

LIMITATIONS TO ENVIRONMENTAL IMPACTS

Environmental impacts could not be quantified. The data rely on farmers' perceptions, which were, however, cross-checked with secondary data from studies done elsewhere.

Analysis of Assumptions

It was deemed necessary to make assumptions about data collected and its analysis and the following assumptions were made:

- Selection of farmers for the study is representative of study area.
- The data are accurate and reliable.
- The tools used for data collection are accurate.

Scope of the Study

The study aims to assess the impact of Calliandra-based agroforestry systems, most of which have been tested by ICRAF/AFRENA in Kabale and Mukono Districts. In these districts, the focus is on sites at which there has been longer exposure to the Calliandra-based technologies.

In Mukono, the study focuses on fodder banks (the main use for which Calliandra has been promoted in this area), while in Kabale the focus is on hedgerows (contour hedges), fodder banks and rotational woodlots.

FUNCTIONS OF AGROFORESTRY BIODIVERSITY

Throughout the world human communities have played a central role in shaping nature's diversity and its associated functions. Biological diversity has contributed in many ways to the development of human culture, and mankind has in turn influenced biological diversity.

As an example, gourds (*Lagenaria siceraria* and *Luffa spp.*) show tremendous varietal diversity and have been selected for a multitude of use and functions, including containers, pipes, scrubbers, floats, musical instruments, penis sheaths, ornaments and food. Plants and animals, both wild and cultivated, have been combined in complex and diverse agroecosystems in terrestrial and aquatic environments. At the broader landscape level, recent scientific evidence suggests that virtually every part of the globe-from boreal forests to the humid tropics-has been inhabited, modified and managed for millennia. Over time, human influence has shaped the expression of agricultural biodiversity at the genetic, species, ecosystem and landscape levels. The present paper is a contribution to the FAO/Netherlands Conference on the "Multifunctional Character of Agriculture and Land-MFCAL" that will take place in Maastricht, The Netherlands, in September 1999. This background paper focuses on the relationships between agricultural biodiversity and the functions of agro-ecosystems at different spatial and temporal scales.

Selected examples are used to highlight the multiple functions of agricultural biodiversity and its links with rural livelihoods in a range of ecological and economic settings. The paper is divided into three parts.

Part one draws from the MFCAL approach, and in particular focuses on the contribution made by agricultural biodiversity to 1) food and livelihood security 2) production and environmental sustainability and 3) rural development. Part two identifies the forces which impact on agricultural biodiversity. Part three concludes by outlining some of the policy and institutional reforms needed to sustain agricultural biodiversity and agro-ecosystem functions.

THE MFCAL APPROACH

The MFCAL Approach provides the overall referential framework for this paper. The approach recognises that the first and foremost role of agriculture remains the production of food. It stresses however, that agriculture and related land use activity can also deliver a wide range of non-food goods and services, influence the natural resource system, shape social and cultural systems and can contribute significantly to economic growth. The approach also focuses on the trade-offs and synergies that can exist between these different functions.

The first dimension of the multifunctional character of agriculture and related land use concerns food production and the contribution that this makes to food security.

Food security has been defined by FAO as a situation in which all people at all times have physical and economic access to sufficient, safe and nutritious food to meet their dietary needs and food preferences for an active and healthy life. There are three dimensions implicit in this definition: availability, stability and access.

Adequate food availability means that, on average, sufficient food supplies should be available to meet consumption needs. Stability refers to minimising the probability that, in difficult years or seasons, food consumption might fall below consumption requirements. Access to food draws attention to the fact that, even with bountiful supplies, many people still go hungry because they are poor and unable to produce or purchase the food they need. In addition if food needs are met through exploiting non-renewable natural resources or degrading the environment there is no guarantee of food security in the longer-term.

Current concerns for food security stem from both the unacceptability of current levels of food insecure people (at least 800million people) and the recognition that agriculture will have to feed an increasing human population, forecast to reach 8 000 million by 2020, of whom 6 700 million will be in developing countries. In most developing countries, the majority of the poor live in rural areas and depend on agriculture for their livelihoods. Expanding food production to feed this increasing population, while alleviating poverty through gainful employment in agriculture, is a formidable challenge.

In addition to food production and the vital contribution that it makes to food security, the MFCAL Approach recognises three further broad functions 1) environmental 2) economic 3) social.

The Environmental Function. Agriculture and related land use can have beneficial or harmful effects on the environment. The MFCAL approach can help to identify opportunities to optimise the linkages between agriculture and the biological and physical properties of the natural environment. The environmental function of the MFCAL Approach is relevant to a number of critical global environmental problems including biodiversity, climate change, desertification, water quality and availability, and pollution.

The Economic Function. Agriculture remains a principal force in sustaining the operation and growth of the whole economy, even in highly industrialised countries. Valuation of the various economic functions requires assessment of short, medium and long-term benefits. Important determinants of the economic function include the complexity and maturity of market development and the level of institutional development.

The Social Function. Both the maintenance and continuing dynamism of rural communities are basic to sustaining agro-ecology and improving the quality of life (and indeed, to assuring the very survival) of rural residents, particularly of the young. On another level, the capitalisation of local knowledge and the forging of relationships between local and external sources of expertise, information and advice are fundamental to the future of existing rural communities. Social viability includes maintenance of cultural heritage: for we know that in many instances, societies still identify strongly with their historical origins in agrarian communities and rural lifestyles.

2

Agroforestry and Farming Systems

AGRO-FORESTRY; ADDING TREES TO FARMING SYSTEMS

It is relatively new to think of farming systems as including trees, or to plant trees with farming systems in mind. As recently as 1982, for example, a major study of farming systems made no mention of trees except as an "off-farm" source of fuel [1]. At the same time, most tree planting projects were assuming that farmers would grow woodlots on marginal land far from their crops.

Ideas are rapidly changing. A more recent study of African farming systems gives considerable attention to trees, especially in long sections devoted to soil conservation and the improvement of soil fertility 2. Simultaneously, social foresters have begun to give urgent attention to activities such as Niger's Maggia Valley Project, which planted windbreaks to protect farm La id from wind erosion. The convergence is not yet perfect: there are still foresters who seldom think of farms, and agronomists who seldom think of trees.

Nonetheless, there is increasing agreement on the need to grow trees within farming systems, or even to conceive of a wider range of plants and animal mix in order to create a sustainable, productive farming system: for example, to a maize monoculture might be added Leucaena leucocephala, bananas, sisal, groundnuts, small livestock, pigeon peas, cowpeas, mangos, yams, Cassia siamea, or Acacia albida. Properly arranged, these would serve to add nitrogen and humus to the soil, prevent erosion, fence off the garden, and provide food, fruit, poles and firewood for consumption and for sale. Since the soil would be automatically replenished with nutrients and organic material, such a system could continue indefinitely.

Conceived in this way, agro-forestry is a land use strategy that would: (a) increase the output of food and other products on a given unit of land; (b) ensure that increases in output were stable and sustainable; and (c) raise farmers' cash incomes.

It is noteworthy that these are exactly the conditions necessary for greater food security in developing countries.

AGRO-FORESTRY TECHNIQUES

Many of today's agro-forestry techniques will be adaptations of traditional practices. However, non-traditional problems are raised by the decline of shifting cultivation, growing pressure on land, and rapid deforestation.

For example, there is new need for fast-growing, nitrogen-fixing tree species suitable for different ecological zones. In addition, ways must be found to compress larger numbers of trees, animals, and food crops on intensively managed farming systems. Intensive research is still required in this field.

SCATTERED FARM TREES

One agro-forestry intervention is simply to increase the number of trees or shrubs scattered among crops or pastures and along farm boundaries. These trees may have value greater than any crops they displace (as can be true of fruit trees). Alternatively, the trees may actually enhance the productivity of crops and pasturage by replenishing soils and helping to reduce erosion. For example, millet and sorghum may increase their yields by 50-100 per cent when planted directly under Acacia albida. Often, trees can be planted that will serve multiple purposes; Leucaena leucocephala, for example, can be used for poles, firewood, fodder and soil enrichment. Scattering trees across the farm will not by itself meet all domestic needs for tree products or ensure sustainable agriculture. However, this kind of agro-forestry action is most likely to make immediate sense to farmers. Benefits are diverse and in line with felt needs. New species can be introduced cautiously and cried alongside proven ones. Risks are minimized. In a number of countries, this approach is now the principal way in which agro-forestry ideas are being introduced.

Improved Fallows

Another technique that can be introduced without making radical changes in the farming systems is the improvement of fallows.

This is required by the fact that fallow periods in many areas have been substantially shortened. As a result, only shallow-rooted grasses of little value to the soil establish themselves naturally before crops must again be planted. The usefulness of short fallows can be greatly improved by planting green manure crops such as Desmodium and Tephrosia spp., Lupinus mutabilis, Dolichos, Indogofera, etc. In addition to improving the soil, such crops may yield livestock feed or food for human consumption. It is worth noting that fallows can be improved without the use of "trees". Nonetheless, this kind of action falls directly within the scope of agro-forestry as defined here.

Alley Cropping

A much more complex agro-forestry technique is alley cropping, as developed by the International Institute for Tropical Agriculture (IITA). This involves the growing of crops between closely-spaced lines of trees or shrubs, usually legumes. To prevent competition with crops for light and water, the trees are regularly cut back and are kept pruned during the growing season. Larger cuttings are available for firewood. Leaves and twigs are spread as mulch among the crops. This mulch replenishes the soil with humus and nutrients, as well as providing a barrier against erosion. Among the tree species found to work best in IITA's trial plots are Leucaena Leucocephala and Gliricidia sepium.

The details of alley cropping systems will vary. For example, herbicides may be applied (as IITA does), or weeding may be done by hand. Mulch may be spread before the crops are planted (as at IITA) or afterwards (as farmers have tried with mulching in northern Cameroon). Trees may be cut at ground level (as at IITA), or just the branches may be lopped off (as farmers do on Mount Kenya, leaving a bare pole that does not shade the crops). The appropriate combination of techniques in a given area will depend en such factors as the availability of labour for mulching and weeding, the presence of pests Chat might be spread by mulching, specific crops to be grown, and the farmers' willingness to make large changes in farming practice.

Mulching

Mulch may also be used outside of alley cropping systems to protect or rehabilitate land. For example, the application of branch mulch helps restore nutrients to the soil, reduces erosion by breaking the impact of falling raindrops, and encourages water infiltration by slowing run-off and making the soil more porous.

Buffer Strips

Strips of vegetation planted along the contour lines of slops can serve as "buffers" against water erosion. Perennial grasses have long been used for this purpose in many countries. In more complicated systems, buffer strips may include grasses, fodder legumes, trees and shrubs. In such cases, the strip can yield mulch, forage, fruit and fuelwood, as well as controlling erosion.

Terracing

On gentle slopes, water erosion may be prevented through buffer strips and mulching. Where slopes are more severe, however, construction of terraces may also be necessary. This job will be made simpler if buffer strips are included in the form of dense vegetation planted along the risers and edges of each terrace. If this is done, a much smaller earth structure will be required to control run-off than would the case with conventional, "naked" terraces.

Windbreaks

Planting lines of trees to break the wind sweeping across open land can prevent erosion and slow the evaporation of moisture from the soil. Species can be chosen that will also yield fodder, poles or firewood. Individual farmers may act to protect land by planting trees on the windward boundaries of their farms. More ambitious schemes seek to control wind erosion over much larger areas.

For example, a CARE project in Niger's Maggia Valley established 250 km of windbreaks in seven years. These consisted of staggered, double rows of trees, primarily Azidirachta indica and Acacia scorpioides, planted across the valley at 100-metre intervals. Roughly 2,500 hectares of farmland were protected in this way. Initial indications are that millet production has been increased by 15 per cent above yields on comparable, unprotected land.

In contrast to most agro-forestry techniques, large-scale windbreak schemes necessarily involve whole communities. This raises delicate issues in terms of sacrifices (whose land will be pre-empted for planting the trees?) and benefits (whose land will be best protected from the wind, and who will get such by-products as fodder and firewood?). Social analysis will obviously play an important role in this kind of project.

Live Fencing

Many of the trees and crops in an agro-forestry system are vulnerable Co being eaten or trampled by livestock. Farmers will try to keep the animals away from the plants.

However, adequate supervision of the animals may be Coo time-consuming, and wire or metal fencing too expensive. To solve this problem, farmers can plant "live fences" in the form of tightly spaced lines of species such as Prosopis juliflora. Acacia scorpioides, or Euphorbia spp.

Woodlots

Farm woodlots have often been promoted to provide firewood, either for domestic consumption or for sale. As far as domestic consumption is concerned, it will sometimes be appropriate for a family to plant such a woodlot on marginal land. However, recent estimates suggest that household firewood needs may be harvested from as few as 50-100 trees. This is most likely to be true if the trees are scattered around a farm rather than packed into a woodlot, where yields per tree are lower. Any serious agro-forestry scheme would include several times that number of trees as part of windbreaks, buffer strips, or scattered farm plantings. Under these conditions, there would be little need for a separate woodlot to produce fuel. The growing of firewood for sale will usually be less attractive. Almost everywhere in developing countries, farm-gate prices of firewood are extremely low. Under these conditions, any attempt at firewood farming will lose money, either in absolute terms or relative to alternative uses of the same land. Where woodlots are established, these are most likely to be for production of high-value outputs such as building poles or timber, although markets for such commodities are limited.

Project Components

The exact nature of any agro-forestry project will depend on the results of the rural appraisal outlined above. However, it is safe to assume Chat most projects will involve some form of research, demonstration, on-farm trials, extension, and monitoring and evaluation.

Research

Research must be done on the impact of including trees and other agro-forestry plants within farming systems. Both exotic and local agro-forestry species should be tried. Harvesting regimes should be designed to provide the products that people actually want, as determined by rural appraisals. Since many agro-forestry species grow slowly, research on these issues is a long-term endeavour.

However, it may also be a long-term endeavour to convince large numbers of people to adopt complete agro-forestry systems. If research is begun immediately, results may therefore be known at just the point when people are looking seriously for proven techniques.

Demonstration

Even while research is still underway, it will be possible to demonstrate basic agro-forestry practices whose results are relatively well understood: for example, windbreaks; scattered plantings of Acacia albida, Leucaena spp., and fruit trees; live fencing; etc. Demonstration areas should incorporate crops, trees, and harvesting regimes that are consistent with local practices and desires.

Management of these areas should be flexible, with species and techniques added or subtracted as they prove more or less convincing. An important part of this work would be to demonstrate agro-forestry plots alongside fields planted in traditional ways. This would allow farmers and other visitors to see quickly the differences made by agro-forestry techniques.

On-farm Trials

The ultimate test of an agro-forestry system is its performance on farmers' fields. At the farm level, results (and perceptions of results) may be very different from findings on research or demonstration plots. Agro-forestry projects will therefore need to sponsor on-farm trials of the most promising techniques. To be useful, these trials should as much as possible be conceived and evaluated by the farmers who are to carry them out. This implies the participation of farmers who are already fairly conscious of agro-forestry relationships. Results would be used to modify research and demonstration programmes, as well as to determine the agro-forestry message to be passed on by extension services.

Extension

The first extension job is to teach the extension agents themselves about interactions among trees, land, and food. Then, guidelines would be provided on how to evaluate farming systems, so that agents could guess what interventions might be appropriate under specific local conditions. Much information for this teaching programme would come from rural appraisals. Once the extension agents understood agro-forestry concepts, they could begin to introduce promising species and ideas. This would be done gradually, starting with straightforward techniques such as boundary plantings of fruit and leguminous pole trees. More complex techniques would be channelled through the system after being proved successful during on-farm trials.

Monitoring and Evaluation

Monitoring will be extremely complex, requiring measurement of yields (of both crops and trees) in very different places: research plots, demonstration areas, farmers' fields. These data are needed to assess the actual impact of various agro-forestry techniques. Equally important is to determine farmers' responses to agro-forestry. This should be judged by the number of farmers who become involved, and by what they say about their experiences.

National and Local Institutions

Each agro-forestry project would require a multi-disciplinary implementing group. A social scientist would be needed to conduct rural appraisals, to help design on-farm trials and extension messages, and to monitor project activities in terms of farmers' reactions and socio-economic results. The research programme would require joint effort by an agronomist, a forester, and an animal husbandry expert. An agro-forestry extension officer would supervise the communications support system, in collaboration with the national extension service. Additional technical and extension staff would be based at out-stations to run agro-forestry demonstrations and on-farm trials.

If the process is functioning properly, participation of farmers is guaranteed throughout. The original choice of research priorities and extension messages builds on the situation and attitudes of farmers. Farmer's' groups are identified or created to carry out on-farm trials and participate in other activities. Monitoring gives voice to farmers as the project proceeds. At the end, farmers are asked to help evaluate what has happened. Of course, this participation will not happen automatically; vigilance must be maintained to ensure that the farmer's point of view remains at the project's heart. Ideally, all of this work would be centred within the ministry already responsible for farmers and farming systems. It might prove desirable, therefore, to create an agro-forestry "cell" within the ministry of agriculture or rural development, made up of the kinds of professionals specified above. In many countries, there exist non-governmental organisations (NGOs) that have close and continuing relationships with distinct groups of farmers. Some of these NGOs will already have experimented with tree-planting, generally as a means of meeting family needs for wood energy. Within an agro-forestry project, these NGOs could play an important role by carrying out demonstration activities and on-farm trials. However, close links would have to be maintained with the government, which presumably would retain primary responsibility for research and extension.

FOREST FARMING

Forest farming is the cultivation of high-value specialty crops under a forest canopy that is intentionally modified or maintained to provide shade levels and habitat that favour growth and enhance production levels. Forest farming encompasses a range of cultivated systems from introducing plants into the understory of a timber stand to modifying forest stands to enhance the marketability and sustainable production of existing plants.

Forest farming is a type of agroforestry practice characterized by the "four I's": intentional, integrated, intensive and interactive. Agroforestry is a land management system that combines trees with crops or livestock, or both, on the same piece of land. It focuses on increasing benefits to the landowner as well as maintaining forest integrity and environmental health. The practice involves cultivating non-timber forest products or niche crops, some of which, such as ginseng or shiitake mushrooms, can have high market value.

Non-timber forest products (NTFPs) are plants, parts of plants, fungi, and other biological materials harvested from within and on the edges of natural, manipulated, or disturbed forests. Examples of crops are ginseng, shiitake mushrooms, decorative ferns, and pine straw. Products typically fit into the following categories: edible, medicinal and dietary supplements, floral or decorative, or specialty wood-based products.

PRINCIPLES

Forest farming principles constitute an ecological approach to forest management. Forest resources are judiciously used while biodiversity and wildlife habitat are conserved. Forest farms have the potential to restore ecological balance to fragmented second growth forests through intentional manipulation to create the desired forest ecosystem.

In some instances, the intentional introduction of species for botanicals, medicinals, food or decorative products is accomplished using existing forests. The tree cover, soil type, water supply, land form and other site characteristics determine what species will thrive. Developing an understanding of species/site relationships as well as understanding the site limitations is necessary to utilize these resources for production needs, while conserving adequate resources for the long-term health of the forest.

Apart from the environmental benefits, forest farming can increase the economic value of forest property and provide short- and long-term benefits to the landowner. Forest farming provides economic return from intact forest ecosystems, but timber sales can remain part of the long-term management strategy.

Methods

Forest farming methods may include: Intensive, yet careful thinning of overstocked, suppressed tree stands; multiple integrated entries to accomplish thinning so that systemic shock is minimized; and interactive management to maintain a cross-section of healthy trees and shrubs of all ages and species. Physical disturbance to the surrounding area should be minimized. The following are forest farming techniques described in the Agroforestry Training Manual produced by the Center for Agroforestry at the University of Missouri.

Level of management required

1. Forest gardening is the most intensive of forest farming methods. In addition to thinning the overstory, this method involves clearing the understory of undesirable vegetation and other practices that are closely related to agronomy (tillage, fertilization, weeding, and control of disease and insects and wildlife management). Due to input levels, this method often produces lower valued products compared to other methods. Forest gardens take advantage of the vertical levels of light availability and space under the forest canopy so that more than one crop can be grown at once if desired.
2. Wild-simulated seeks to maintain a natural growing environment, yet enriches local NTFP populations to create an abundant renewable supply of the products. Minimal disturbance and natural growing conditions ensure products will be similar in appearance and quality of those harvested from the wild. Rather than till, practitioners often rake leaves to expose soil, sow seed directly onto the ground, and then cover with leaves again. Since this method produces NTFPs that closely resemble wild plants; they often command a higher price than NTFPs produced using the forest gardening method.
3. Forest tending involves adjusting tree crown density to manipulate light levels that favour natural reproduction of desirable NTFPs. This low intensity management approach does not involve supplemental planting to increase populations of desired NTFPs.
4. Wildcrafting is the harvesting of naturally growing NTFPs. It is not considered a forest farming practice since there is no human

involvement in the plant's establishment and maintenance. However, wildcrafters often take steps to protect NTFPs with future harvests in mind. It becomes agroforestry once forest thinnings, or other inputs, are applied to sustain or maintain plant populations that might otherwise succumb to successional changes in the forest. The most important difference between forest farming and wildcrafting is that forest farming intentionally produces NTFPS, whereas wildcrafting seeks and gathers from naturally growing NTFPs.

FARM FORESTRY—A WIN-WIN SITUATION

Farm forestry or social forestry is a silent movement sweeping across parts of rural India which has the potential of creating another green revolution. Simply put, farm forestry is aboutcorporates promoting cultivation of trees as a crop by small farmers. Farm forestry was initially promoted as a NABARD assisted project during 1987-95. Now the paper industry is using this tool effectively to get its raw material without harming forests and at the same time generating income and employment for the farmers. This helps the environment, thecorporates and the poor at the same time, which is a rare proposition.

The Need

As nearly 50 to 60 per cent of the paper mills in the world are wood based, forests have a very important role to play in this industry. Forests account for nearly 30 per cent of the world's land surface. The shrinking forest area (due to the increasing population and use of wood for various applications) is a cause of concern for everyone. The paper industry accounts for nearly 12 per cent of the world's wood harvest (including the harvest for fuel purpose). If the wood harvest for industrial purpose alone is considered, the paper industry accounts for nearly one fourth of the total industrial consumption. Forest cover in India is much lower than the world average, and an increasing rate of population promises that the pressure on forests will increase manifold and reach unsustainable levels.

The Solution

To meet the increasing need for raw material without harming the environment, some large paper companies have turned to farm forestry. Companies are working with NGOs to identify poor households in rural and tribal areas owning wastelands and organizing them into self-supporting groups. These groups are provided with good planting stock of pulpwood species and other local species that meet domestic, fodder, fuel and nutrition requirements. They are also provided with technical and financial assistance and an assured buy-back of wood. Technical assistance includes services like land development, planting of saplings and plantation maintenance.

Farmers plant trees on their land as a crop or on the periphery of their farmland as an additional source of income. A project in Andhra Pradesh has even gone a step further where the government is ensuring access to land for the poor. Some of this land is completely scrub, lying unutilized for generations. This project has also brought about pooling of the small land holdings of the poor to form land banks.

Bio-technology comes in handy

Companies are using biotechnology to leverage the development of high yielding clones of pulpwood species as well as to create desirable characteristics in such trees. For instance, one clone developed by ITC has a root system that does not go beyond 1.5 meters in depth, thus minimizing access to precious ground water. Some clones have productivity rates six to nine times those of conventional seedlings and some are site-specific clones adapted to problematic alkaline and saline soils.

Micro benefits for the backward

Farm forestry has a substantial employment generation potential and this is a huge positive for a populous country like India with high unemployment rates. A significant part of the land under such projects is wasteland owned by marginal farmers, many in tribal areas. This project increases incomes of poor households in some of the most backward districts of the country. ITC alone has created around 3 lakh jobs through its farm forestry project, which had covered around 29,000 hectares of land by 2004. Ballarpur Industries Limited (BILT) and JK Paper had also covered 21,900 hectares and 27,000 hectares of land respectively under their farm forestry programmes till 2004.

There are macro benefits as well

Apart from increasing the forest cover, farm forestry reduces pressure on public forests by providing fuel wood to poor households from their plantations. It also contributes to in-situ moisture conservation, reduction in air pollution, groundwater recharge and reduction in top-soil losses. Depleted soil is also enriched due to leaf-litter from plantations. This might lead to a decline in fertilizer and pesticide consumption in the future, thus reducing the pollution of groundwater sources. Over the years, this alternative source of employment and income for a section of the marginal landless farmers and ofVadgam, a small village in Gujarat, has resulted in a positive change for them, through a partial disintegration of negative social patterns of traditional land ownership. Since it is difficult to find employment, the villagers rely on their land, however small and unproductive it may be. They find work as agricultural labourers only during the peak season and remain without work for several months of the year. Thus, they require both secure employment and regular income to keep out of the clutches of money-lenders.

Economic benefits

To top it all, farm forestry programmes have huge carbon sequestering potential, thus creating additional economic benefits in the form of carbon credits (*refer I-Mag issue Sep 2005 "Demystifying Carbon Credits"*). According to an estimate, ITC's plantations alone have the potential to sequester 18 lakhtonnes of carbon, reducing 67 lakh tonnes of carbon dioxide, thus creating a carbon credit value of ₹ 25 crores per annum approximately. However, it needs to be ensured that the economic benefits of these carbon credits accrue to the farmers who own the land, rather than to the corporates driving the initiative. This will be a bonus for small and marginal farmers of the country, 40 percent of them living below the poverty line.

Challenges

The corporates would have to disseminate information about the benefits of land pooling for marginal and scattered land holdings, which might not be readily accepted by the farmers. The cost benefit analysis for the corporates themselves might also not favour such an undertaking unless the benefits of carbon credits, conformance to environment regulations are factored in.

FARMING SYSTEMS APPROACH TO DEVELOPMENT

Details concerning the characteristics and methodology of the FSD approach, as developed by the Farm Management and Production Economics Service of FAO, are available elsewhere. Thus, the following discussion represents only a brief summary. The primary objective of FSD is to improve the well-being of individual farming families by increasing the overall productivity of the farming system in the context of both the private and societal goals, given the constraints and potentials imposed by the factors that determine the existing farming system. It is based on the development principles of improving productivity, increasing profitability, ensuring sustainability, and guaranteeing an equitable distribution of the results of production,

The farm household is the principal system and focus of FSD and consists of three basic subsystems, which are closely interlinked and interactive: the household, the farm, and off-farm activities. The two major categories of activities or thrusts of FSD, both of which involve intensive interaction with farmers? are:

- Farming Systems Analysis. This involves studying, together with the farmers the natural (*i.e.*, technical) and socio-economic (*i.e.*, human) environments in which farm households operate. The aim is to identify the constraints limiting farm productivity and production and hindering improvement in the welfare of the farm households themselves. Potential solutions to these problems are identified, and the results of this analysis, formulated as suggestions for further action then are passed on to the relevant 'actors'. These could include researchers, extension and support service staff, and/or policy makers.

- Farming Systems Planning, Monitoring, and Evaluation. These involve testing, monitoring, and evaluating improvements on-farm, with the direct involvement of farmers. Examples of such activities include those regarding proposed technological improvements, proposed revisions in farm plans, and improvements in support services and farm-level impact of proposed policy changes. Those improvements thought to be potentially useful then are disseminated to other farmers via the extension service. Prior to this stage, it may be necessary to negotiate adjustments in the policy/support services that will facilitate the dissemination and adoption of the improvement. After dissemination, it is of primary importance to monitor and evaluate the adoption rate of the proposed improvements by the farming community. This provides an indication of the actual value of the improvement being disseminated.
- Many individuals in the last 15 to 20 years have written extensively to clarity the concepts of the farming systems, particularly with respect to the development of relevant improved technologies. There are many ways of presenting a diagram involving the application of farming systems methodology to research (*i.e.*, technology development). One such way of emphasizing the technical research aspects of FSD. There are four fundamental stages in the FSD approach.
- The Descriptive or Diagnostic Stage, in which the actual farming system is examined in the context of the 'total, environment — to identify constraints farmers face and to determine the potential flexibility in the farming system in terms of timing, unused resources, etc. An effort also is made to understand the goals and motivation of farmers that may affect their efforts to improve the farming system, The following sequence of activities is usually undertaken:
  - After deciding on the location of the work, start-up activities include reviewing secondary sources of information, making the necessary contacts, assembling the professional team, and making logistical arrangements,
  - Farming families are classified tentatively into homogeneous groups. The farming families within each group or domain usually practice the same farming system(s), face the same constraints, and have the same potential solution(s) to their problems. This tentative classification can be modified as additional information becomes available.
  - An informal exploratory diagnosis or survey is undertaken to

obtain a qualitative understanding of the determinants of the existing farming systems (*i.e.*, both biophysical and socioeconomic). At the same time, efforts are made with farmers to ascertain the constraints, flexibility, and potential opportunities in the farming systems they are using currently.

- Sometimes a verification survey involving a structured formal survey, suitable for statistical analysis, is undertaken to quantitatively confirm insights obtained in the exploratory diagnosis. It also can be used to provide a database for farm and development planning, policy analysis, monitoring, and evaluation.

• The Design Stage, in which a range of strategies is identified that are thought to be relevant in dealing with the constraints determined in the descriptive or diagnostic stage.

The usual sequence of activities involves the following:

- Together with the farmers, the constraints are ranked according to their severity, and potential solutions are identified after determining what flexibility exists in the farming systems currently practiced. Information for designing such strategies (*i.e.*, particularly relating to technological issues) comes from experiment station work, researcher managed and researcher implemented (RMRI) type work on farmers' fields, and from other farmers.
- An evaluation is made of the proposed solutions before putting them into practice. These solutions can be technological or institutional in nature. A number of analytical techniques can be used to evaluate the potential technical feasibility? economic viability, social acceptability, and ecological sustainability of the proposed solutions before they are put into practice. One or more of the proposed solutions are selected for actual evaluation on-farm.

• The Testing and Implementation Stage, in which one or more promising strategies, arising from the design stage, are examined and evaluated under term conditions to determine their suitability for producing desirable and acceptable changes in the existing farming system.

Activities at this stage involve the following:

- On-farm testing or evaluation with farmers determining how well the potential improvements fit into the system, whether or not they are acceptable to farming households, and what modification may be needed to make them acceptable. In terms of technological issues, this stage conventionally has consisted of two steps:

- Researcher managed but farmer implemented (RMFI) tests to establish whether previously determined technical relationships are altered by farmers' management of non-treatment variables.
- Farmer managed and implemented (FMFI) tests, when the team is confident that technical relationships will hold but needs to evaluate the proposed technologies under local socio-economic circumstances. In addition to the on-farm evaluation of the proposed technologies, evaluations also can be made of the proposed farm plans and of proposed changes in support systems and/or policies.
- Positive results of such evaluations provide justification for the FSD team to advocate further action. The tested technologies can be disseminated through the extension service to other similar farming households, The same applies to the farm plans that have been tested successfully. Favourable test results for proposed changes in support services and/or policies provide valuable farm-level information on necessary programme or policy adjustments (*e.g.*, in extension, marketing inputs and products, pricing policy, credit, etc).

• The Dissemination and Impact Evaluation Stage, in which the strategies that were identified and screened during the design and testing stages are extended to farmers. In terms of activities at this stage, impact/adoption studies can be very important. These potentially can be very useful, not only in giving some idea of the impact of, for example, agricultural research, but also in giving some idea of future priorities for agricultural researchers and indicating what adjustments are required in the policy/support systems to ensure better rates of adoption. Thus, through monitoring and evaluating the impact and rate of adoption of the changes that have been implemented and proposed/tested earlier, it is potentially possible to provide some indication of further desirable activities by both researchers and planners.

There are often no clear boundaries between the various stages, Design activity, for example, may begin before the descriptive and diagnostic stages and may continue into the testing stage, as promising alternatives emerge from RMFI trials.

Similarly, testing by farmers may mark the beginning of dissemination activities.

Also, going through all stages may not always be necessary. FSD team confidence in transferability during design/planning activities can sometimes mean going straight to FMFI work or even to recommendation/dissemination activities.

Thus, the process of FSD is recognized as being dynamic and iterative, with linkages in both directions between farmers, researchers, extension staff and policy/support service staff, The iterative characteristic can improve the efficiency of the development process by providing a means of identifying and fine tuning improved technologies for a specific location-that is, climatic situation, soil type, and/or farmer resource base.

FARMING AS A BUSINESS

Farming has not usually been considered a business. The diversity of the duties of the farmer, the area over which the operations of the farm extend and the complexity of the records required, combine in making difficult the organization of the details of farming into business form. The successful financial operation of a farm presents quite as complex problems and calls for at least as much business ability and judgement as is required in operating a store with the same investment.

Farming, therefore, should be considered as a business, and the man who can produce his crops and products at the lowest cost and sell them at the highest price, investing the proceeds to the best advantage, should be considered the best farm manager. The man who knows the details of the cost of production and operation, and whose records show the profitable and unprofitable lines of production, thus enabling him to eliminate those that do not yield a profit, may be counted as the best business man.

A farmer should know the elements of soil fertility. He must understand the principles of the movement of soil water, and the action of soil bacteria. He should understand the nature of plant growth and be familiear with varieties and species of plants and with the effect of one crop on the crop following. He must also be familiar with animals and their habits and know how to feed and care for them. In addition, he must know how to buy and sell to advantage, make contracts, and plan his buildings and his farm so as to necessitate a light expenditure for labour, also that he may distribute his labour to advantage over the various farm enterprises. And he should know how to keep accounts. The farmer in organizing his business could well follow the example of the merchant. The merchant first takes an inventory of his stock. He studies the demand for his goods, both present and prospective. He notes the supply, the cost, and the demand for each article. He calculates the labour required to operate his business and such other items of expense are considered as may be legitimately charged against the business. He regulates his purchases and his prices according to the cost of securing his goods and putting them on the market. In conducting a large store business, it is customary to organize it into departments, putting some competent person in charge of each department and having the labour and accounting charges so systematized and recorded as to show the profit or loss from each department and from the business as a whole.

The farmer should likewise take an inventory of his capital, stock, and equipment. He should consider the type of farming to which the soil and climate are adapted. He should consider the fertility of the soil and the demand that will be made upon it by the crops grown. He should consider, in connection with the soil fertility, the sources from which it may be renewed and at what cost. He must study the markets, the transportation, and the demand for such crops as he grows; also the cost of producing each of the crops and the probable net profit that will be returned. His labour likewise should be charged against the various crops or enterprises and distributed to the best advantage.

In studying the problems of farm organizations, interest on investment, taxes, insurance, and other expense must be included as they affect the financial result. As in a large store business, it is frequently necessary to organize the large farm into departments, keeping accounts with the dairy, with the swine, the grain crops, the garden, and other similar enterprises. Where the business is large enough, it is well to put an expert in charge of each large branch or group of enterprises, thus enabling one to use cheaper labour for performing the work or making the labour more effective by closer supervision.

Where the farming is conducted as an organized business, and accounts are kept with the various lines of work, it is possible at the end of the year, to make a business statement which will show which lines have been profitable. The manager then can change his methods or drop out those lines that prove to be unprofitable and the business as a whole may be put on a better basis.

Investment

The investment of money in land, buildings, and equipment demands careful consideration. It is possible to pay so much for a farm that it will be impossible to produce sufficient revenue to meet the expense of operation and to pay a normal rate of interest on the money invested. This is particularly true where low-priced products are produced. A farm may be highly productive but so located that it will be impossible to market the produce on a profit bearing basis. One should study closely the market facilities of the neighbourhood and raise supplies which can be successfully marketed locally, or which can be transported to a market that pays well for such produce. Unless the produce of the farm is well related to the market, the farm is likely to be operated at a loss.

Proportion in Real Estate

It is a mistake for one to invest all of his capital in the real estate itself. Sufficient capital should be reserved for operating the farm. The hunger for land has induced many farmers to buy more land that they can equip and operate well. Such farmers are said to be land poor. They would secure greater profit from a medium sized farm, well tilled and managed, than from a large one which is insufficiently equipped and poorly operated. Rarely should more than 50 or 60 per cent of the capital be tied up in the land. The size of the farm and the amount of equipment are closely related to the possible profits. A farm of forty or eighty acres devoted to diversified crops and live stock, cannot be so economically equipped per acre as a larger farm. The investment per acre in machinery will be higher as the cost will be spread over fewer acres than the machinery has capacity to handle. Investment in other equipment will also be correspondingly high. Often the labour on such a farm is not fully employed and loss results from inactivity of labour and equipment. A medium to large sized farm, when well organized, fully equipped, and with sufficient capital reserved to operate it well, will pay a much better labour income than a small farm.

Proportion of Investment in Machinery

Investments in machinery are worthy of quite as much consideration as investments in land. Machinery is looked upon as one of the means of reducing the cost of production. The wise use of machinery saves time and labour and enables the farmer to handle large acreages. In this light, the use of ample machinery is wise. The fact remains, however, that investments in machinery are often poorly made and that many farmers are embarrassed by debts for machinery. Frequently, farmers purchase machinery because it is fashionable or because a neighbor has it, rather than because carefully made calculations show that a certain machine can be used profitably.

A safe rule is to buy no machine until carefully made calculations show that the cost of production of a certain crop or product will be reduced sufficiently by the purchase to cover the cost of the machine. That machinery investments can be studied from a business standpoint is quite plain. The following example, showing the relative cost of cutting corn with a machine versus cutting by hand, will illustrate:

The original cost of a corn binder is $125. The annual depreciation, as shown by statistical records covering ten years' work with farmers in Minnesota, is $12.50. The interest on the investment at the average value of the binder throughout its life will be $4.12. Repairs, shelter, and insurance will cost $2 annually. The total annual cost for the use of the binder, therefore, will be $18.62. If only twenty acres of corn are grown each year, the annual cost an acre for the corn binder will be $.93. The cost of cutting corn would be as follows: It will be noted that a twenty-acre corn field can be more economically harvested by hand where labour is available. On a ten-acre field, the difference in expense would be still greater in favour of the hand harvesting, as the cost of machinery per acre would be doubled. The scarcity of labour, however, and the necessity of harvesting corn quickly to save it from frost, would often warrant the expenditure for the machine, even though it does slightly raise the cost of harvesting per acre. The greater the acreage, the more useful the machine becomes in harvesting, and the less the expense per acre for machinery use. Calculations similar to this should be made before purchasing a machine for any purpose. If it can be shown that the cost of performing the labour may be reduced by the machine, and that the labour can be performed in a more satisfactory and efficient manner with the use of it, then the purchase may be warranted. In many cases, however, calculation will show that the purchase is not warranted and that it would be better to hire labour and rent the machine, or to buy in partnership with some one else.

Cost of Motive Power

Another factor that should receive consideration is the cost of motive power in use on the farm. Horses usually furnish the farm motive power, though tractors are used to advantage in some cases. Auto trucks and automobiles can often be used to advantage in marketing dairy, fruit and garden products and the cost of using them, when it can be ascertained, should be compared with the cost of horse power. It costs from $40 to $100 per year to keep a work horse, depending on the locality and on the price of feed stuffs; also on the work that the horse does. The average cost a year of keeping a horse in Minnesota for the years 1904 to 1907, varied from $75.07 at Halstad, to $90.40 at Northfield.* Often a large number of horses are kept because the farm has been devoted to grain raising and the horses are needed at seeding and harvest times. They run in the pasture during the summer and are idle during the winter months. They must be fed and cared for during this time. The money invested in them would be drawing interest if invested somewhere else. Farmers should reduce the horses kept to the number actually required to do the work, unless the surplus are colts growing in value as one of the market products of the farm. The work of a farm can often be lessened by adopting a good crop rotation and using such crops as do not demand large amounts of horse labour at the same time. In this way a farm of 160 to 240 acres can often be worked with four to six horses, whereas eight to ten are frequently kept. The support of two or three extra horses per year would amount to $200 to $250 and is an item well worth saving.

Investment in Buildings

Investment in buildings, fences, and other items of equipment should be considered in the same business-like way. A barn costing $4,000 and providing shelter for forty head of cattle would carry with it an annual cost of $440. This annual cost is made up from the interest on the investment, insurance, depreciation, paint, and repairs. It will be about 11 per cent on the total investment. If the same forty cattle could be housed in a barn costing $2000 the total annual cost would be only $220, charging the same interest and expense rates as in the first instance, and assuming that the rate of depreciation would be the same. While the $4000 barn would undoubtedly be a better barn, it would not add to the production of the cows housed, unless it was much more comfortable. It would not add to the net profit from the investment unless the labour of doing the chores and caring for the cows would be considerably reduced by greater convenience. The cost of horse barns, swine barns, and other buildings can be similarly calculated. One should not erect a building unless it is going to add to the efficiency of the live stock, shelter hay or machinery, or lessen the labour of doing the chores. It is wiser to invest money in drainage or in better tillage of the soil, than to invest it in buildings that shelter unproductive stock, or that add nothing to the earning power of the farm.

Cost of Labour

The employment, organization and direction of labour demands considerable study. The value of a good farm manager lies quite as much in his abilitiy so to select and direct labour as to yield a profit, as it does in his ability to drive a good bargain or sell his crops well. The only reason for employing labour is to increase the product and consequent profit. If a farmer can, by employing a man eight months in the year at $40 per month, increase the product of his farm by $500, he will be warranted in employing the labour. If, however, the $320 invested in labour should yield an increase of only $200 in the products of the farm, employment would be at a loss.

The Factors of Production

Three primary factors are necessary in agricultural production. These are capital, land, and labour. The adjustment of these three factors is an important part of the business of the farm owner or manager, and determines largely the profits that may be made from the individual farm.

Capital, as commonly understood, includes the money value represented in the investment of the farm property, no matter what the form may be. Implements, live stock, teams, buildings, and other articles of equipment, are each a part of the capital of the farm. Cash for operating is also included.

Land represents the larger part of capital on most farms, and demands special consideration because the amount of land available for agricultural purposes is limited. Farmers have for this reason, regarded it wise to secure large quantities in localities where it was cheap, anticipating a rise in value. Location and demand for land in particular sections has led to much speculation, and land values fluctuate frequently.

The proportionate investment in each of the three forms,—circulating capital, land, and labour—bears a vital relation to the profits possible from the farm, and must be given the most careful consideration by the person who is buying and equipping a farm.

Capital Classified

There are two forms of capital in common use. They are known as fixed or invested capital, and circulating or working capital. The fixed capital properly includes all forms of permanent equipment, such as investment in land, buildings, implements, teams, and other articles that are used continuously. In land it includes the natural value and the value of the improvements that have been made upon it. Picking stones from a rough section of land adds to its value and increases the capital invested. Clearing trees from the land has the same effect. Wells, drainage, roads, fences, and other forms of improvement which are permanent and which become part of the land, also add to the natural value and become a part of the fixed capital.

Buildings also are looked upon as part of the fixed capital. Strictly speaking, only those buildings which add to the producing power of the farm should be included in the capital invested in the farm. The dwelling house, while commonly added to the investment in the farm, is really intended for the personal use of the farmer and his family.

Except in so far as it shelters the help employed on the farm, it can add but little to the returns from it.

So far as making a statement of the business of the farm is concerned, it would be better were the farm-house inventoried separately from the other buildings and regarded as a personal expense to the farmer, just as the house of the banker in the city is separated from the business of the bank. All other buildings including silos, corn cribs, granaries, and buildings for sheltering the stock and necessary in conducting the farm business, should be included in the inventoried capital of the farm.

Equipment in the way of teams for work purposes; implements; live stock, such as cows, brood sows, sheep and poultry, that are kept for live stock products, are all a part of the permanent equipment, since they are permanently employed and if sold are replaced by other animals for the same purpose. The circulating or working capital, includes such items of equipment as are frequently changing. Seed grain, household and farm supplies that are immediately used or marketed, live stock, such as fattening steers, and money for hired labour, are examples of circulating capital. The classificiation intends that the term "circulating capital" shall include only those items that are used once and disappear. If sold for cash, the cash may be invested in other forms of working capital which in turn disappear. Needless to say, the amount of working or circulating capital varies greatly in accordance with the type of business done, with the market, and with the tastes of the farmer. No rule can be given for the exact adjustment of capital for these reasons.

Production Limited by the Deficient Factor

It is a common experience that the production on a farm is limited by the minimum amount of the one deficient factor. Difficulty is experienced in securing profitable production on a limited land area. In such a case, labour will not be fully employed or the equipment cannot be used effectively. On the other hand, a large land area and large equipment cannot be used to advantage without a plentiful supply of labour. Again, neither land nor labour can be used to the best advantage if the equipment is inadequate. It therefore stands to reason that these three factors must be carefully considered and proportioned in accordance with the needs of the business.

In purchasing and organizing a farm with limited capital, it is believed best to make the investment in about the following proportions:

- 45% for land investment
- 20% in buildings, provided they are to shelter productive live stock or market products;
- 22% in work animals and live stock;
- 8% in implements and tools;
- 5% reserved as working capital.

In buying a farm and equipping it with new machinery, the land investment will run lower than above indicated and the implements and tools investment will run higher. The machinery, however, will depreciate in value while the land is more likely to increase in value. As the farm becomes older and the land is improved, the proportion of investments will gradually change. On old farms near city markets, the machinery investment may become comparatively insignificant. The proportionate investment will necessarily vary with the type of farming followed. In the highly intensified forms of farming much more will be invested in live stock. H. W. Mumford, in Bailey's Cyclopedia of Agriculture, gives a table showing the investment on a live stock farm in Illinois, from which it is calculated that there is invested in land and buildings, 60 per cent; in machinery, 4 per cent; in live stock, including horses, 30 per cent; and in labour, 5 per cent.

THE CONSTRUCTION AND MANAGEMENT OF DRYLAND FARMING SYSTEMS

Richard's studies on the rice-growing zones of Sierra Leone suggested that shifting rice cultivators attempt to "hitch a ride upon, rather than to override and forcibly control, processes observed in 'nature'". In carving out a farm from the forest, Mende farmers employ their detailed agro-ecological knowledge, seldom needing to create enduring and managed landscapes in order to grow their crops. They work with, and help preserve, ecological diversity. This image appears in other studies of West African farming systems which stress improvisational skill, and the success of local agricultural techniques.

Richards suggests that this process of 'hitching a ride' upon ecological systems emerges from his own observations. Little of such a 'performance' is preplanned - rather, crop mixes and farming operations are strung together and modified with inventiveness and opportunism. He stresses the practical, everyday problem-solving abilities of rice cultivators, and his work is regarded as a benchmark in the recovery of an overdue assertion of the populist argument that directly challenges 'top-down' models of rural development and agricultural research. The implication is that successive attempts by colonial regimes and agricultural research organisations to 'improve' African agriculture have failed to appreciate how farmer performances are adapted to environmental and labour constraints.

My worry is that further north in dryland regions like the Central Plateau, 'hitching a ride' in its less productive agro-ecologies is unlikely to be as successful. Forms of indigenous knowledge, technologies, institutions and ecological characteristics differ, soil fertility is usually poor, and thus different labour inputs and techniques are required. In northern Burkina Faso it has become less and less common to see traditional long-fallow agriculture practiced, even where population densities are relatively modest; the availability of good quality land for farming is declining. Dryland farming in the Sahel requires farmers to marshal labour, apply it to often limited land, and to invest scarce capital, to obtain what are sometimes meagre harvests from unyielding or exhausted soil.

A young male farmer in the Mossi regions of Burkina Faso must "build" his farm, from the moment he leaves the family plot and commences cultivation on his own account, in order to meet regular subsistence needs through the years. As Chris Reij has suggested for the Mossi of Yatenga region, it appears that, where fertile land is scarce, young men lacking private land access and income may choose to "carve out" a farm from the barren, crusted soils of marginal zipelle land previously abandoned to agriculture.

These actions require not the clearing of vegetation from rich soils before cultivation, as in the Sierra Leone case - but the painstaking construction of planting pits by men and women, and the collection and transport of manure to the site; compost, manure or local rock phosphate is thrown into the pits in order to restore some basic fertility to the rooting zone and to encourage termite activity. Reij suggests the treatment of 1ha of land - barely enough to nourish a farmer and a small family for a season - may take up to 100 person-days of backbreaking labour. Similar examples of highly intensive regenerative schemes can be found in other Sahelian regions, like southwest and central Niger, where degraded land is now being traded for its unrealised productive potential and considerable investments are being made in reclamation by various conservation techniques. Frequently, planting pits are supplemented by diguettes, to aid the infiltration of scarce run-off and brake the erosion of topsoil. This process of land rehabilitation - increasingly common since now encouraged by some of the numerous extension services and development projects - has much in common with the laborious process of building a house for one's own occupation.

The metaphor is an interesting one, although we should be wary of overextending it; explanatory metaphors also have power to generate a certain form of thinking and to exclude or marginalise others. They do, however, allow us to 'ground' our analyses in the real world. A family wishing to build a home must make many hard decisions about its location, its cost, its dimensions, and its design. Many possible variables, from personal preferences to financial constraints and difficulties encountered over land rights and access, may influence the final outcome of such an endeavor. Like the farmer, the builder must assemble scarce resources, call in favours, and set aside time. A farm, as Richards points out, is never 'finished'.

But the actions required to farm in dryland regions are much like those involved in the process of local house construction. The house builder must undertake a certain amount of initial work to raise the roof of a house; equally, the farmer will never obtain his or her first harvest from a formerly unproductive or low-yielding plot without sizeable initial investments of time and labour. This metaphor of 'building' is not designed to usurp a visualisation of dryland farming as rich in the 'performance elements' noted by Richards. Rather, my intention is to highlight the need to consider the structured and planned elements of dryland farming alongside the myriad performances, and processes of experimentation, enacted by farmers. It is this revised perspective, not the abstract metaphor itself which matters.

Once constructed, a dwelling benefits its inhabitants in two distinct ways, which can be referred to as material and symbolic.

- *The Material: Satisfaction and basic needs*. A home offers security; a base where the regular activities of the day are performed and where one can both work and relax. It is tinkered with, adapted, repaired and maintained not just to please neighbourhood gossips, but to maintain the household's own needs for warmth (or shade), protection from the elements and shelter. It is a lived environment which slips into unconscious acceptance, like a favourite pair of well-worn shoes. A 'home builder' is someone who creates a home for the pleasure of doing so, using skills learned through trial, error and experience, and reaps his/her rewards through the pleasure of living within this personally structured environment. He/she feels pride.
- *The Symbolic: Status and appearance*. A dwelling is an expression of ones' persona: it says who the owner is, as well as telling the observer something about the social and economic status of its occupiers. It is filled with personal objects, embellishments and decorated in a style which sets it apart from one's neighbours. It is "lived in". It is a place to offer hospitality, to teach offspring the basics of household management and how they themselves must behave when they set up home themselves. Over the year, specific tasks must be carried

out both to maintain appearances and to prepare for seasonal weather conditions. Leaving the compound upswept, or a hole in the roof unrepaired after a storm, invites neighbourly censure.

Mossi efforts to reclaim degraded or less fertile land can be likened to the builder preparing a site, staking boundaries, wheeling and dealing to procure the necessary materials, and then keeping costs down by doing the bulk of the work him/herself. Tapping affective kin networks or friendships, he/she might perhaps borrow or rent a donkey cart, picks and shovels from a friend.

Unlike the case of the shifting cultivator in the Sierra Leone rice farming zone, this young Mossi farmer's goal is not to steal a living on a plot destined to return to the natural forest from which it came - rather, the savings that went into his (or her) initial investment demands the farmer secures a return from his/her labour in terms of adequate food crop yields for several seasons.

In so-doing, a successfully reclaimed and productive field may inspire admiration and perhaps jealously from his/her peers. Those who 'build' their own habitats in this way will tailor them to their own requirements and generally wish to stay put for quite a while.

The builder's knowledge comes from multiple sources (including development projects and extension workers), and it is impossible to freeze it in time or space for documentation and classification. My own fieldwork in a region of the Central Plateau revealed a staggering range of traditional agricultural practices and erosion control techniques among Mossi, Yarsé and Peulh cultivators.

These include the construction of bunds and barriers from sticks, andropogon grasses and stones, micro-variations in planting densities and spacing taking into account soil fertility and water supply, these of millet-stalk or straw mulches to encourage termite activity in hardened soils, and selective cutting of forest areas to encourage natural regeneration of certain woody species. Larger-scale, labour-intensive practices such as the digging of zai, the construction of extensive diguettes (more appropriate for the reclamation of very unproductive land), and growing use of compost pits, are techniques promoted by project and extension services, and were rarely practiced in their present form before the arrival of volunteer services and NGOs in the late 1970s.

Chris Reij dates the first improved zai techniques to the late 1970s; the first 'digue filtrante' (permeable rock dam) on the Central Plateau is thought to date from 1981/2 and was initiated by a French volunteer in Rissiam, Bam. Today, such techniques are widespread, and are learned not just from project personnel, but also from other farmers.

The presence of soil and water conservation techniques is evidence that Mossi farmers are engaged in carving out new agro-ecologies necessary to coax tired soils back into productive use; they are building for the future with new materials.

3

Agroforestry and Forest Management

As stated above, the prevalent form of forest management in arid lands is agroforestry, which is concerned with the management of trees and shrubs for conservation and sustainable development. Agroforestry in arid lands differs in many ways from the timber forestry practiced in moist tropical and other temperate ecosystems and in many cases its applications are broader in their scope. These applications include production of wood for fuel and poles; horticultural practices for fruit and nut production; range management for fodder and forage production; forestry to modify microclimate for improved agricultural crop production; and protection forestry on land susceptible to wind and water erosion.

Many rural people combine these applications of agroforestry with other land uses linked to their needs and social values. The value of forestry in the arid zone is difficult to evaluate in monetary terms. Arid zone agroforestry therefore needs to be understood broadly as management of trees and shrubs to improve the livelihood and quality of life for rural people in the arid environment. It is in this diverse context that policy developemnt must take place if sustainable development of forest resources in the arid zone is to be achieved.

Agroforestry is being followed traditionally in the arid zone to minimize the risk of drought and sustain life in climatic adversities. Several need-based systems have developed traditionally and some have been improved or incorporated in recent times.

ARID ZONE AGROFORESTRY

Drylands cover more than 60 per cent of the earth's surface. Arid zones are described as a part of the drylands, and have the most severe edapho-climatic conditions. The major distinguishing feature for defining and for planning for the arid zone is the low rainfall (below 500mm or Aridity Index <0.20) with more than 50 per cent inter-annual variability. This makes a great difference in terms of the nature of the ecosystem, the socio-economic environment and the challenges for sustainability. High wind and solar regimes further increase the effect of rainfall variability and the whole complex makes a fragile ecosystem in which small disturbances may cause great loss to the sustainability, which are sometimes irreversible. The hot arid zones of the world are economically and environmentally disadvantaged, with unique problems.

The ecosystems of these zones are highly fragile with large risks that cause severe impediments to development programmes. Of the total land area in the world, arid zones cover 18.8 per cent. The hyper-arid zones account for 22.3 per cent of the total arid zones. These arid zones are diverse in terms of climate, soils, vegetation, animals, and the lifestyles and activities of the people. Little but variability in rainfall and the presence of distinctive periods of drought are the characteristics of the arid tropics. Often, the terms drought and aridity are used incorrectly. A drought is a departure from average or normal conditions in which shortage of water adversely impacts on the functioning of ecosystems, and the resident population of people, whereas aridity refers to the average conditions of limited rainfall and water supplies, not to the departures there from. In general, arid zones are characterised by pastoralism and little farming but there are always exceptions. Arid zones are found in almost all the continents of the world. In North America, arid zones are found in the southern US and Mexico, and in South America they are located in Brazil, Argentina, Chile, and in some other countries. In Africa, substantial parts of Saharan Africa, Ethiopia, and Namibia, are classed as arid environments. The hot arid regions of India lie between 24° and 29° N latitude, and 70° and 76° E longitude, covering an area of 31.70 million hectares, and involving seven states: Rajasthan, Gujarat, Punjab, Haryana, Andhra Pradesh, Karnataka, and Maharashtra. In total, 11.8 per cent of the country is under a hot arid environment. The arid regions of Rajasthan, Gujarat, Punjab, and Haryana together constitute the Great Indian Desert, better known as the Thar Desert, which accounts for 89.6 per cent of the total hot arid regions of India, and constitutes the principal hot arid zone of the country.

Table. Distribution of arid regions in different states of India.

State(s) (10^6 hectares)	**Area total**	**Percent of**
Rajasthan	19.61	61.0
Gujarat	06.22	19.6
Punjab and Haryana	02.73	09.0
Andhra Pradesh	02.15	07.0
Karnataka	00.86	03.0
Maharastra	00.13	0.4
Total	31.70	100

In arid zones, vegetation is typically sparse, and is comprised of perennial and annual grasses, other herbaceous plants, shrubs and small trees. The native plant species have adaptations that enable them to reproduce, grow and survive in the most inhospitable edapho-climatic conditions. Some plants have evolved special root systems, while others have unique leaf characteristics that allow them to withstand prolonged periods of drought. The number of tree species is very limited in arid zones, and in general, they are very slow growing due to limitations of environmental conditions, but nowhere in the world are they are so intricately associated with the life of human beings.

To evade or minimize the adverse affects of frequent droughts, the native peoples in arid zones have often developed production systems in which woody perennials have a very important role, both from a productivity as well as a resource conservation point of view. Their centuries-old experiences, under diverse socioeconomic and cultural conditions, were passed from generation to generation and people have established well-contained systems of production (silivipastoral/agrisilvicultural/agrisilvipastoral/livestock husbandry) that accrue maximum benefits from their woody components. When arid zones have been looked at from the perspective of forestry development, the focus has been on the management of trees and shrubs that are either native to a particular arid zone, or have been introduced, especially for conservation purposes.

However, concern for trees and forests has increased in arid zones as it has in many other regions in recent years. This concern has been fuelled mostly by the disappearance of large areas of woodlands and trees from such fragile ecosystems in many countries of world. In the arid zone, closed forests are seldom available. In India, traditional animal husbandry and agroforestry practices have been used to manage parklands, rangelands, reserved silvipastures near holy places, lay farming, and run-off farming (traditional watershed management). Trees are managed mainly for their non-wood forest products (NWFP) and their environmental services. Animals are an essential part of the production system. The whole system has been traditionally developed to spread the risk of drought in diversified components and efficient utilisation of scarcely available natural resources.

FUTURE DIRECTIONS FOR ARID ZONE AGROFORESTRY

Every ecosystem has some buffering capacity that enables it to remain unchanged for some time if it is overexploited.

While this applies to the arid zone, its fragile nature limits its buffering capacity. Thus, for a few decades the shortcomings of policy were not observed but as the buffering capacity is gradually being eroded, the indicators of unsustainability as a whole, *e.g.* decreasing natural resources, deforestation and desertification, become visible. For fragile ecosystems, like those that occur in arid zones, one thing needs to be recognised by policy makers and scientists, that is; sustainability of agroforestry in the arid zone depends on the degree of synergism with '3Ns' *i.e.* Nature, Native vegetation and Native people.

Some of the future directions for arid zone agroforestry need to focus on the evaluation, improvement and encouragement of sustainable traditional agroforestry systems, exploring the possibilities of natural regeneration/ rehabilitation of arid zone ecosystems, NWFPs as the basis of sustainable livelihood, rethinking of research priorities, and policy improvement. Evaluation, improvement and encouragement of sustainable traditional agroforestry systems that have been developed for centuries in harmony with nature. Agroforestry systems have been developed and used in this region since time immemorial. This may be because the inhabitants of this region found that no other option was sustainable aside from conserving and harvesting whatever nature is giving. The present forms of traditional agroforestry developed over the centuries through the experiments of earlier generations in all types of climatic variations. The validation of their sustainability is very difficult to establish by conducting short-term experiments lasting only 5-6 years. Thus, there is immense possibility for evaluation, improvement and encouragement of these traditional agroforestry systems.

Exploiting the possibilities of natural regeneration/rehabilitation of arid zone/arid zone agroforestry as an alternative to failed plantation/rehabilitation strategies. It is a mechanism of restoration or maintenance of ecosystems by nature that trees produce numerous seeds. A small part of this seed population is sufficient to replace the loss of plant population due to various factors. Human beings propagate the plants artificially to compensate for what they harvested form the natural vegetation or to get a higher quantity of the natural products. Those needed in large quantities have already been domesticated, *e.g.* food crops, fruit trees etc. Still a large number of natural species are wild or depend on natural regeneration. Trees in agroforestry may fall under this category. Natural regeneration as well as artificial tree establishing technologies works comparatively better in humid and irrigated areas. In the arid zone, due to climatological, physiological and sociological reasons artificial establishment has not achieved the required success. The need for domestication and technology development for sustainable harvesting and value addition for non-wood forest products (NWFPs). Unlike the humid or sub-humid regions where trees are typically grown for timber, the trees are grown in this arid region mainly for non-wood forest products (NWFPs). In the arid zone closed forests are seldom available and agroforestry has been followed since time immemorial in which peoplc conserve and manage whatever seeds of native tree species like Prosopis cineraria and Zizyphus numularia germinate in the crop field or on the common land. After the establishment of trees only annual lopping of branches is done which provides precious fodder during scarcity/drought. Taking the example of P. cineraria, this tree is found in this region at densities ranging from 40 to 120 trees/ha.

This we can say is the natural forest in common or private lands otherwise no dense forest is found as in the high rainfall areas. People lop the branches of this tree in the month of December and it becomes lush green in the month of

May-June when no other fodder is available. Simultaneously, pods develop which are used as vegetables. Similarly other tree species provide fodder, pods, fruits etc. The interesting thing is that, during drought when annual crops fail, the yield of NWFPs does not decrease drastically, thus trees provide food security during drought. Besides some trees produce other products like gum, resins, edible/non-edible oils etc. which increase the income of the marginal farmers who are in the majority in this region.

The services provided by the trees in hot arid regions are equally important for moderating the climate. Cultivated in the form of shelterbelts, they reduce wind erosion and conserve soil and water.

In agroforestry systems, trees reduce the solar heat load on crops and also decrease wind speed and soil temperature, conserve soil moisture, increase biological activities in the soil and thereby improve the microenvironment for crops. The yield of crops grown under P. cineraria is generally higher than sole crops, knowing this fact agroforestry has been followed in this region for centuries. The edapho-climatic conditions in this region are so harsh that every tree improves the environment, it may be at micro level, yet its impact is visible. The other important NWFPs in these arid areas are plants with medicinal values. Due to climatic specialty there are medicinal plants which are either endemic to this region or their quality deteriorate if they are grow/found in higher rainfall areas.

Research Priorities: Considering the social and ecological demands, policy on agroforestry research also needs to be prioritized. Some of the possible priorities are-In-situ rainwater conservation for tree establishment and for agroforestry more generally.

Water is the most limiting factor for productivity and sustainability in the arid zone. As described earlier, the effect of bringing additional water through canals or ground water has been the cause of unsustainability in the ecosystem. Thus the only possibility remains the conservation of rainwater. Trees are the keystone of arid zone conservation and once trees are established the other conservation processes start automatically *e.g.* rainwater conservation, development of vegetation cover etc.. Further research is required on:

(i) Development of in-situ rainwater conservation techniques that require less labour and maintenance;

(ii) Development of plant-based water absorbing/retaining materials;

(iii) Initiatives for widespread adoption of rainwater conservation techniques;

(iv) Improvement in traditional water harvesting systems;

(v) Development of simplified windbreak establishment techniques.

Improvement of Policy: There are some important aspects on which improvement of policy is needed for creating a more congenial environment for development. These include:

Increased international funding for arid-zone research and development. The arid regions of the world in general suffer from a vicious cycle of low productivity, a low level of investment and as result, poverty. Greater priority is given at the international level for funding of projects and programmes related to timber forestry and rainforest management, perhaps because these activities contribute more to international trade. Very limited funds aimed at combating desertification are available to the arid lands.

Forestry and agroforestry activities in arid regions no doubt contribute less to international trade but they provide substantially support to the livelihood of people in these climatically less favoured regions.

There is a need to rationalize these priorities and for the international community to give due importance to the non-tradable benefits of forestry/ agroforestry, which are otherwise the basis of sustainability and livelihood. Suggested areas for increased investment in the arid zone are as follows:

(i) *Organic farming in virgin arid lands*. The philosophy of the traditional systems was to work in synergism with nature and use locally available natural resources. High input agriculture (HIA) on the other hand is only sustainable with assured input supply, *e.g.* irrigation, fertilizers etc, which is not always possible in drylands. Thus the chances of failure are much greater than in traditional systems during drought. Also due to less use of synthetic chemicals in the past, these lands are comparatively free from the residues of such chemicals. Hence organic farming, based on traditional systems and conservation of local natural resources can be one area for investment without much effort. Organic farming of NWFPs can be the first choice for investment.

(ii) *Eco-tourism*. Investment in eco-tourism can prove to be a large income generator in the arid lands. Increasing numbers of people are spending increasing amounts of time and money enjoying the unique resources of these arid land environments, *e.g.* spectacular scenic beauty, diverse wildlife population, relatively clean air and other amenities such as large open spaces. Investment in the forestry sector can be in amenity plantations, desert parks, buffer strips, roadside plantations and green belts can be economically as well as environmentally beneficial for the arid zone.

Exploring the potential of arid zone agroforestry as a tool for solving environmental problems.

Conservation of Biodiversity: Biodiversity is the essential safety mechanism of any ecosystem and as the arid zone is considered to be fragile in nature the importance of conservation of biodiversity is further increased. Because of biotic interference and developmental activities, not only is the population of various species reduced but also their natural habitats have been destroyed. Thus the easiest way to save these species is ex-situ conservation with protection. This is possible through arid zone agroforestry, in which all types of plants *e.g.* trees, shrubs, climbers etc can be accommodated, combining conservation with domestication for increased production.

Desertification Control: Desertification is the result of exploitation of arid zone ecosystems beyond their carrying capacity. The carrying capacity of the arid lands is inherently low thus they are highly prone to desertification. Through soil and water conservation and sustainable management of vegetation, the carrying capacity of natural resources can be enhanced.

Various arid zone agroforestry models, *e.g.* wind breaks, sand dune stabilization, silvi-pasture, agri-horticulture etc. can be appropriate for soil and water conservation in arid lands, and the productivity of lands suffering form desertification can be enhanced and in this way desertification can be controlled. Arid lands can be considered simulated desertified drylands for planning of desertification control. This can be important for preventive strategies for drylands rather than to control desertification after the process starts. Any technology or strategy that is found suitable to increase the productivity of arid lands, would give better results if applied to the desertification-prone drylands because they have a better environment than the arid lands. Assessing the potential of arid zones as carbon sinks. In addition to their other benefits, trees on farms or in pastures also store carbon. Arid lands cover almost one forth of the earth's surface and any effort to increase tree populations substantially contributes to their value as carbon sinks. Due to their perennial nature and high root turnover, grasses can also prove to be a good carbon sink. Silvipasture systems are prevalent in most of the arid zone and when both the tree and grass components are properly managed, an increase in net carbon storage can be achieved. The arid lands are prone to desertification and trees and shrubs can be grown on these lands to prevent further soil degradation and to produce biofuel. These trees also enhance soil organic carbon content and thereby increase soil carbon storage. About 104 million ha land area in the world is affected by strong and extreme soil erosion.

SUSTAINABLE FOREST MANAGEMENT

Criteria, indicators and standards for sustainable forest management and for SFM are important market based water demand management tools that foresters can use for improving the water application and water productivity elements in WC&DM. The organised industry has adopted the Forest Industry Environmental Guidelines for Conservation of Commercial Plantations in South Africa, which include water management measures.

WATER MANAGEMENT PLANS

The National Water Policy requires sectoral management plans. These are to incorporate into the WC&DM Strategies. This section outlines the requirements for the water management plans in the forestry sector. Water management plans may be formulated at three scales. The first would be for the forest management unit (FMU), *i.e.* as defined in the National Forest Act as "an area of land on all or part of which there is forest and which is managed as an integrated unit". The second would be for a Water User Association comprising of several owners of forest management units within a Water Management Area. The third would be for the sector as a whole. What follows are requirements for plans at the level of FMU. Plans at the other levels can be built from these guidelines.

These requirements are built upon the "Environmental Guidelines for Conservation Management of Commercial Plantations in South Africa" (second edition, in press), and the minimum standards for forest certification according to the Forestry Stewardship Council (FSC) as applied in South Africa. These have been enhanced to take account of the requirements of national water policy. South Africa has adopted principles of sustainable forest management (SFM), which are in harmony with international principles, and which are incorporated in the National Forests Act. These will guide the development and regulation of criteria, indicators, and standards of SFM in South Africa.

Forest management requires as standard practice the development of detailed forest management plans for each forest management unit. These plans deal in detail with the full cycle of forest production, from seedling through final harvest, as well as overall environmental management of the FMU. The Environmental Guidelines for Conservation Management of Commercial Plantations in South Africa stipulate an inclusive set of environmental guidelines that should be followed in forest management planning. The FSC also sets standards to which the plans and their execution must comply if the FMU is to be certified as sustainably managed. The incentive for certification is strong, since a grower wishing to sell forest produce to a processor who exports, needs such a certificate.

Thus, water management planning on the FMU must be an integral part of the sustainable forest management plan for a FMU. Whether or not the water management plan is adequate must be judged by the overall adequacy of the forest management plant itself. Generally, the certification of a forest can be taken as an adequate test of the water management plan if clear standards are available, since the first requirement of certification is compliance with all relevant laws.

WATER AUDITS IN THE WATER MANAGEMENT PLAN

The first section of the water management plan must consist of a documented audit of the water resource of the FMU. This audit must be based upon the best available information, such as the recorder water balance (precipitation and run-off), flow regime, and water quality regime of the catchments or parts of catchment included in the FMU, or the best predictions from appropriate hydrological models. The audit must also include an assessment of the relevant elements of the current management plan for the FMU.

The documented audit must contain at least the following:

- A quantification of the water balance of the FMU under natural conditions, *i.e.* as it would have been without afforestation, under natural vegetation, during the period since afforestation, together with the flow-duration curve after afforestation.
- A quantification of the water balance and flow-duration curve after afforestation.
- The same for the water quality regime, and an assessment of how this departs from the resource-quality objectives for the river reach fed by the FMU, as set out in the DWAF Resource-Directed Measures.
- From all this, an assessment of current water use, allocation efficiency, application efficiency, and productive efficiency.
- An assessment of the compliance of the water management elements of the forest management plan to accepted minimum standards.

Management Goals and Objectives

The water management plan must contain a statement of overall goal and of contributory objectives, in terms of mean annual run-off, the flow-duration curve, and water quality objectives, as well as management standards. These goals must take account of normal climatic variation and predicted climate change.

Elements of Water Management

The principles that apply here come from the National Forest Act, the National Water Act, and the National Environmental Management Act, and are summarised in the Environmental Guidelines for Conservation Management of Commercial Plantations in South Africa. The South African Forestry Industry is committed to Integrated Environmental Management to ensure that:

- Development takes place in the most economic and environmentally acceptable way;
- Resources are managed in a manner which will ensure the sustainability of the forestry enterprise; and
- The people on which the Industry depends may work in safety and live under conditions of acceptable quality.

Principles of Sustainable Forest Management (SFM)

The National Forests Act of 1998 contains the following six principles to guide SFM:

- Maintain the resource base

- Maintain the sustained yield of goods and services
- Maintain biodiversity
- Wise use of water
- Optimise the socio-economic impacts of forestry
- Develop supportive institutional frameworks and policy

The Environmental Guidelines for Conservation Management of Commercial Plantations in South Africa recognises the following as some of the values that could be associated with the above Principles of SFM:

Soil

- Soil quality
- Soil quantity
- Nutrient status

Water

- Water quality
- Water quantity
- Wetland habitat

Biodiversity

- Species diversity
- Ecosystem function
- Important species

Forest Health

- Protection against pests
- Protection against diseases
- Protection against fire

These form the framework for detailed guidelines on several aspects of environmental management on the FMU, including the following:

- fire protection: adequate and appropriate fire management strategies are imperative to ensure that the forest resource, together with its ecological and other associated values, are protected
- Site/species matching: to ensure optimum yields, quality and economic benefits, the requirements of the species should be matched to the characteristics of the site
- Avoiding monoculture landscapes: monocultures pose a risk in terms of disease and fire, which are heightened when single clones are utilised; If monocultures are unavoidable, a variety of age classes is a suggested improvement for reduction of risk and to improve the general aesthetics.
- Weed potential

- Water use efficiency: efficient species, clones and management regimes should be favoured
- Wetland protection.
- harvesting system: The environment should determine the type of harvesting system to be used. In choosing the most appropriate system, terrain, weather, extraction routes, timetables and yarding sites should be considered: detailed guidelines for environmental protection are applicable

roads: the exposed surfaces of roads are the main source of sedimentation in the plantation environment; by restricting this disturbance as much as possible, this impact and the loss of productive land can be reduced: detailed guidelines for environmental protection are applicable.

MANAGING FORESTS FOR CLEANER WATER FOR URBAN POPULATIONS

Access to clean water is one of the most fundamental of human rights, but currently more than one billion city-dwelling people lack access to clean water. Generally it is not because water supplies are insufficient. Rather, this crisis is due to an inability to organize supply properly to meet demand. This failure is particularly frustrating in that nature contains the necessary mechanisms to provide clean, healthy water, including the filtering effect provided by healthy forests in watersheds. Yet in many parts of the world environmental mismanagement has led to a critical shortage of freshwater.

This article highlights how some of the largest cities in the world are able to supply sufficient freshwater to their inhabitants at least in part through the protection of forests. It identifies some key policy initiatives that could help reduce the vast number of people whose lives are dominated by the daily search for clean and safe water.

SUPPLY AND DEMAND

Water is, in theory, a quintessentially renewable resource. Water covers most of the world's surface, and over much of the world it falls unbidden from the skies. Yet because of the carelessness and profligacy with which water resources have been used, the speed of human population growth and the increasing demands for water, the provision of adequate, safe supplies of water is now a major source of concern, expense and even international tension.

The poorest members of society, unable to afford safe water, suffer the greatest impacts. One in five people in the developing world lives without a reliable water supply. Lack of clean water has dire short- and long-term health impacts including increased infant mortality and impaired ability to work, which reduce industrial productivity and put pressure on already overstretched health services. On the other hand, access to clean water can have dramatic positive health impacts. For instance, it is estimated that when clean water is available the risk of early death is reduced by 23 percent in Uganda and 30 percent in Cameroon (UNDP, 2006). Today, around half the world's population lives in towns and cities, and of these people one-third live without clean water or adequate sanitation (United Nations Human Settlement Programme, 2003). Municipal authorities have a variety of ways of supplying drinking-water, depending on where they are located, the resources available, social and political issues and the willingness of the population to conserve water. Most cities rely on the collection and diversion of existing surface and underground freshwater sources. Only minor amounts, on the global scale, are extracted directly from rainwater or from the seas. Until recently, the main focus of efforts to improve urban water supply has been within the cities themselves, including better distribution systems, treatment plants and sewage disposal. However, many authorities are now increasingly looking at land management systems that can help maintain pure water at the source.

WATER QUANTITY, QUALITY AND REGULARITY

People have settled historically in areas rich with natural resources, and today most of the world's population lives downstream of forested watersheds (Reid, 2001). Societies have created strong cultural links with forests, and it is widely assumed that forests help to maintain a constant supply of good-quality water. Conversely, loss of forests has been blamed for problems ranging from flooding to aridity.

In fact, the hydrological role of forests remains a subject of debate. Some of the common assumptions about the benefits that forests bring are wrong in most situations; for example, most forests do not increase water flow in a catchment (in fact the reverse is often the case), nor do they necessarily control flooding. On the other hand, some positive benefits, including particularly their potential to supply relatively pure water, are frequently overlooked. Impacts of forests are influenced by many factors including the age and species of the trees, the amount of watershed under forest, soil, climate and forest management practices. A meta-study conducted for the World Wide Fund for Nature (WWF) on the role of forest protection in drinking-water provision (Dudley and Stolton, 2003), including a survey of more than 100 of the world's most populous cities, revealed – as described below – a clear link between forests and the quality of water coming out of a catchment, a much more sporadic link between forests and the quantity of water available and a variable link between forests and the constancy of flow.

Quality

Forested watersheds generally offer higher-quality water than watersheds under alternative land uses, if only because virtually all the alternatives –

agriculture, industry and settlement – are likely to increase the amounts of pollutants entering headwaters. Quality can also be higher because forests sometimes help to regulate soil erosion and reduce sediment load, although the extent and significance of this function will vary. Undisturbed forest with understorey, leaf litter and organically enriched soil is the best watershed land cover for minimizing erosion by water. While forests are less able to control some contaminants (the human parasite *Giardia lamblia,* for example), in most cases the presence of forests can substantially reduce the need for treatment for drinking-water and thus radically reduce costs of supplying water.

Where municipalities have protected forests for their water resources, quality issues have generally been the primary motivation. In Tokyo, Japan, for example, the Metropolitan Government Bureau of Waterworks manages the forest in the upper reaches of the Tama River to increase the capacity to recharge water resources, to prevent reservoir sedimentation, to increase the forest's water purification capacity and to conserve the natural environment. In Sydney, Australia, the Catchment Authority manages about one-quarter of the catchment as a buffer zone to stop nutrients and other substances that could affect the quality of water from entering storage areas.

Quantity

The situation with regard to the flow of water from catchments is more complex. Despite years of catchment experiments, the precise interactions between different tree species and ages, different soil types and management regimes are still often poorly understood, making accurate predictions difficult. In contrast with popular assumptions, many studies suggest that in both very humid and very dry forests evaporation is likely to be greater from forests than from land covered with other types of vegetation; thus less water flows from forested catchments than, for example, from grassland or crops (Calder, 2000). The evidence seems to suggest, however, that cloud forests (Bruijnzeel, 1990) and some older natural forests (such as old*Eucalyptus* forests) can increase net water flow. Some cities factor management of these forests into plans for maintaining adequate water supplies.

Regularity

Constancy of flow is as important as total quantity, in terms of both maintenance of dry-season flow and absence of flooding during periods of heavy rain. Here opinion remains divided, as examples of very different responses can be found. In some cases dry-season flow is depressed by the presence of trees, while in other cases it is increased. Natural forests and plantations have different effects, but again these do not show a constant trend. In very general terms, forests often help to regulate relatively minor floods but are seldom able to prevent occasional, very major floods. Flooded forests – both lowland forests such as the Várzea forests of the Amazon and swamps in the uplands – have a more definite role in regulating water supply. However, the debate about the role of forests in maintaining constancy of water flow continues; a recently published study suggests that natural forests have a larger role in flood prevention than has generally been argued of late (Bradshaw *et al.*, 2007).

URBAN SUPPLY

The contributions of forests in providing clean water depend to a large extent on individual conditions, tree species and age, soil types, climate, management regimes and needs from the catchment. It is therefore perhaps not surprising that information on best practices for policy-makers remains scarce and models for predicting responses in individual catchments are at best approximate. Towns and cities are faced with a bewildering diversity of opinions on which to make hard financial and politically charged decisions about their water supply. Yet many of the world's biggest cities are choosing to rely at least in part on forested areas to help maintain water supplies.

The meta-study described above (Dudley and Stolton, 2003) indicated that about one-third (33 of 105) of the world's largest cities obtained a significant proportion of their drinking-water directly from forested protected areas. At least five other cities in the review obtained water from sources originating in distant protected forested watersheds, and eight more obtained water from forests managed in a way that gave priority to their functions in providing water. In a number of cases there is also good evidence that forests help maintain water flow – for example in Melbourne, Australia and in some cities fed by cloud forests such as the Caribbean National Forest in Puerto Rico. However in some other cases where cities have been protecting forests specifically to maintain water supplies, there is little hard evidence that forest protection has this effect.

Many municipalities (although certainly not all) cite maintenance of a pure water supply as a reason for introducing forest protection or reforestation. In the United States, all states are required under federal law to have a Source Water Assessment, which promotes the idea that protecting drinking-water at the source is the most effective way of preventing drinking-water contamination (NRDC, 2003).

The city of New York is famous for its use of protected forests to maintain its high-quality water supply. This approach was supported by popular vote in part because it was a cheaper option than building more treatment plants. Other cities in the United States also rely on forested catchments. Around 85 percent of San Francisco's drinking-water comes from the Hetch Hetchy watershed in Yosemite National Park. In Seattle, Washington, the primary sources of water are the Cedar River watershed and the South Fork Tolt watershed, which together serve a population of 1.2 million people with unfiltered drinking-water.

MANAGING FORESTS FOR WATER

Forests offer a range of options for water provision, depending on their type, location and age and on what users need. Cities may choose a number of different forest management options, including protection, sustainable management and, where necessary, restoration.

Those responsible for water supply and forest management are faced with a number of questions: about whether forested watersheds offer real benefits for water supply; if they do, how much forest is required to gain these benefits; and how forests in watersheds can best be managed to protect water supplies. In most cases decisions will need to be taken in a context of competing demands on land, so that management for water will have to be balanced and traded off with other uses.

The following questions all need to be answered before any decisions are made about forests managed for water.

- *What are the most pressing needs regarding water supply?* Are the pressures on water supply primarily driven by the need to get enough water, or a constant supply of water, or is the priority more to do with water quality? What quality issues are most important? For example, sediment will be most important for hydropower, whereas pollutants such as agrochemicals will also be of concern for drinking-water.
- *How is vegetation in the catchment likely to affect water quality and flow?* This needs specialist analysis, although some general points can be made. For example, cloud forests are likely to increase water, some old natural forests may also increase flow, and young forests and plantations are likely to decrease flow. Individual cases need to be assessed, depending on soil, climate, forest types and age, and management regime.
- *What is the land use?* Current status is important, but so are recent changes and likely future trends. Answering these three questions will help to determine what natural vegetation (and perhaps other land uses) in the catchment offers in terms of water supply and whether future changes are likely to increase benefits or create problems. With this information, more strategic analysis can help to plan optimum management interventions:
- *What other demands are there on land in the catchment and how much might be available for water management?*Are other pressures on land likely to improve or degrade water? How much land is available, partially or completely, for water management? Can current land uses be improved from the perspective of the water from the catchment? What impacts would these changes have for local people and what

are their needs and wishes? Can catchment areas also be used for other land uses, such as recreation or biodiversity conservation?

- *What are realistic management options?* Present and future management options should be analysed, including establishment and maintenance of protected areas, forest restoration and other forms of land use.

The analysis should tell whether the presence of forests can help supply the water required from the catchment and provide the information needed to make informed choices about a landscape mosaic that will fulfil both water needs and other needs from the watershed.

VALUING FORESTS

In many cases the economic case for managing ecosystem services can provide the impetus for sustainable forest management. A team of researchers from the United States, Argentina and the Netherlands put an average price tag of US$33 trillion per year on global fundamental ecosystem services, which are usually taken for granted because they are free. Water regulation and supply was estimated to be worth US$2.3 trillion (Costanza *et al.*, 1997). At the national level, the economic value of the water storage function of China's forests is estimated as 7.5 trillion yuan (approximately US$1 trillion), three times the value of the wood in those forests. Another study calculated that the presence of forest on Mount Kenya saved Kenya's economy more than US$20 million by protecting the catchment for two of the country's main river systems, the Tana and the Ewaso Ngiro (Emerton, 2001).

The issue for policy-makers is how to translate these values to help support particular types of land management. One reason why it has proved so difficult to halt and reverse global forest loss is that those who manage forests typically receive little or no compensation for the services that forests generate for others and hence have little incentive to manage them sustainably. Even when areas are protected, values such as water provision are often not recognized by the users. Owing to the serious financial difficulties faced by protected areas in Venezuela, in 1999 the Instituto Nacional de Parques(INPARQUES), the State agency for protected areas, considered charging water companies for the direct services they obtain from these areas (including the three protected areas that are the source of water for the country's capital, Caracas). However, until now this initiative has not been further developed (Courau, 2003).

Recognition of this issue has encouraged the development of systems in which land users are paid for the environmental services that they generate through management. The central principle of the "payment for environmental services" (PES) approach is that those who provide environmental services should be compensated for doing so from those who receive the services. Projects using water resources as a springboard for PES schemes have mainly been developed in Latin America, but interest is quickening throughout the world. In Quito, Ecuador, for example, water companies are helping to pay for the management of protected areas that are the source for much of the capital's drinking-water.

PARTICIPATORY FOREST MANAGEMENT APPROACH

PAST ACTIVITIES

Forest extension activities were formally launched in the country in the year of 1964 with the establishment of two forest extension divisions at Dhaka and Rajshahi and later two divisions at Comilla and Jessore. It was really a very small programme and the activities were confined only to establish nursery in the districts headquarter and raised seedling and sell the same to individuals and organizations. The location of this programme was so urbanized and limited that it only partially served the needs of the effluent town dwellers only.

Betagi-pomora Comunity Forestry Project

The first community forestry programme in the country, started at Betagi and Pomora mouza (village) under the district of Chittagong in the year of 1979 with the personnal initiative of Prof. A. Alim, renowned forester and Prof. Dr. Mohammed Yunus, founder of Gramen Bank. Initially the project covered 160 ha of Government denuded hilly land at Betagi and with 83 landless participants from adjacent community and subsequently extend over another 205 ha of Government owned denuded hilly land at Pomora with another batch of 243 landless (families) participants. Under this programme each landless participant was provided with 1.62 ha of land for growing tree and hoticultural crops with technical and financial assistance from the Forest Department. This community programme has given the landless an identity of their own and a sense of direction in life. But this model has not been replicated in the other areas due to lack of initiative of the Forest Department as well as the Government.

Rehabilitation of Jhumia Families

Another project was undertaken by the Forest Department in the Hill tract areas to establish plantation through rehabilitation of Jhumia families in 1980. Main objectives of the programme were (i) to rehabilitate tribal families in the Unclassed State Forest(USF) lands along with rehabilitation of denuded USP land; (ii) to introduce a sustainable agroforestry production system; (iii) to improve the socio-economic condition of the tribal people and (iv) to motivate tribal people in development of forestry.

Under this programme each family was allocated 2.02 ha of USF land for growing agricultural crops (over 1.20 ha), raising plantation (0.80 ha) and for house construction (0.20 ha). The rehabilitated families were given land use rights and were allowed to enjoy 100% benefits accrued to those lands.

The participants were given input support for growing agriculture, horticulture and forestry crops and cash support for house construction. This programme continues for quite a long period of time but could not sustain mainly because of nomadic character of the tribal groups.

Another reason of failure was that the families were rehabilitated in clustered villages without considering their cultural and religious values. Thus in most of the cases it was found that the families have left the area.

A parallel programme was also initiated by the Chittagong Hill Tract Development Board in which Forest Department was responsible for implementation of afforestation component where Cittagong Hill Tract Development Board was responsible for the rehabilitation component. This programme was also not found so much responsive to hilly people except for some plantation establishment.

Development of Community Forests Project

The activities of the first phase of this project began in 1981 and were completed in 1987 in seven greater districts of the North-Western zone of the country.

The main components of the project were:

- Strip plantations along roads and highways, railways, canal sides, district and Union Parishad roads, totalling about 4,000 km.
- Fuelwood plantation on 4800 ha of depleted Government land on participatory concept.
- Agroforestry demonstration farms over 120 ha also with participatory concept.
- Replenishment of depleted homestead wood lots in 4,650 villages.
- Training of Forest Department Personnel and Village leaders.

Development of Forest Extension Services (1980-1987)

Development of Forest Extension Services (Phase II) began in 1980 with the Government funding and subsequently amalgamated in some areas (*i.e.* North-North West district) with Asian Development Bank funded Community Forestry Project. The main activities under this programme were:

- afforestation in some 3100 villages.
- roadside tree planting along 3600 km of primary highways and roads and about 600 km of Union Parishad roads.
- production of 49 million seedlings for distribution.

Thana Afforestation and Nursery Development Project

This project is a follow-up of Development of Community Forestry Project and Forest Extension Project and has been designed primarily to: (i) increase the production of biomass fuels and (ii) enhance the institutional capability of FD and local administration in implementing a self-sustaining nationwide social forestry programme. In order to increase the production of biomass fuel and to arrest the depletion of tree resources, the project envisaged to develop tree resources base through planting of depleted sal forest as well as brining all suitable and available land in the rural areas under tree cover with active participation of the rural poor of the locality.

Originally the project was to be implemented by the Forest Department and former Thana Parishad during the period of 1987 to 1994. But in 1992 Government decided that the all project activities were to be implemented by Forest department alone. The major components of the project were:

1. Establishment of plantation over 20,225 ha depleted Sal forest areas.
2. Development of agroforestry over 4,200 ha in the Sal forest lands.
3. Raising strip plantation on 17,272 km along Road and highway, Railways, Embankment and Feeder Roads.
4. Raising 1,282 ha plantation in the land outside the BWDB.
5. Planting 7.017 million seedlings at the premises of different education, religious and social institutions
6. Establishment of 345 nurseries at Thana headquarters.
7. Raising of 10.618 million seedling for distribution to public.
8. Training of some 76,000 people of different levels.

Here this may be mentioned that at the last stage of the project implementation, the Government has found that this was quite impossible to protect the strip plantation and also impossible to trained 76,000 people by the Forest Department alone. The Government invited NGOs to participate in this programme for successful implementation. PROSHIKA, POUSH, GRAMMEN BANK and other NGOs came forward to help the Government for successful completion of the project; NGOs employed their group members to protect the strip plantation and ADAB came forward to train people at different levels with the help of its member organisations.

The above plantation activities were carried out with the direct participation of the local people with the help of the NGOs by executing benefit sharing agreement.

Coastal Greenbelt Project

Another project financed by Asian Development Bank is under implementation in the Coastal region of Bangladesh. The main objective of the project is to create a vegetative belt all along the coast to save the lives and properties of the people living in the coastal areas from devastated cyclone and tidal surges which occur very frequently in those areas. All of the activities of this project are also being carried out following participatory approach. In this project also the participants have been selected among the poor people living in the adjacent areas by involving NGO and a pre-designed benefit sharing agreements also being executed with the participants to protect their rights over plantations and to ensure benefit expected to be received out of the plantation.

Agroforestry Research Project

Pilot Agroforestry Research and Demonstration was implemented by the FD in the Sal forest areas. The project had been developed precisely to design/develop agroforestry modules which is environmentally feasible, socio-economically acceptable enhance tree and crop production at the same time to uplift the socio-economic condition of the participants. The project aimed at using 120 ha of encroached Sal Forest land of Dhaka, Mymenshing and Tangail Forest Division to develop suitable participatory plantation models.

Food Assisted Social Forestry Programme

The World Food Programme assisted the Government to develop Social Forestry as a national programme and the Government incorporated WFP assisted social forestry programme in its annual development plan from 1998. Poverty alleviation, economic rehabilitation of rural poor especially the destitute women of the society by engaging them in forestry activities, social uplift of rural poor and environmental improvement are the main objectives of this project. Historically this programme was conceived in the country since 1989 on pilot basis allocating in kind resources (Wheat) to a limited number of NGOs for raising strip plantation along roads, embankments, Highways etc. in rural areas following the participatory mechanism. In implementing this programme FD was involved later on to provide technical guidance to the NGOs and other GOB agencies. At present probably this is the largest Participatory Forestry Programme in Bangladesh. From 1990, 100 NGOs are involved in this programme and at present about 60 NGOs are continuing with the programme. Commencing from 1990 up to 1998 about 31 million trees were planted involving 0.062 million people directly and 0.62 million people indirectly. The programme has created employment to the tune of 68 million man days. This programme is being implemented by the NGOs through contractual benefit sharing among participating poor men & women 60%, NGOs 10%, the rest land owners.

PARTICIPATION IN THE PARTICIPATORY FOREST MANAGEMENT

The inclusion of communities in the management of state-owned or formerly stateowned forest resources has become increasingly common in the last 25 years. Almost all countries in Africa, and many in Asia, are promoting the participation of rural communities in the management and utilisation of natural forests and woodlands through some form of Participatory Forest

Management (PFM). Many countries have now developed, or are in the process of developing, changes to national policies and legislation that institutionalise PFM.

In Bangladesh the history of NGO involvement in the field of development is not very old. After liberation, NGO started their activities through relief and rehabilitation of the war victims. During mid-seventies, NGO switched over to the socio-economic development of the rural poor, and at present there are thousands of NGOs most of whose mandate is to organise rural poor and provide awareness, education, skill training and various support services including credit to enhance participation of landless poor in the development process towards self reliance. On the basis of the networking throughout the country the NGO can be classified into two levels; (i) local and (ii) National. At present more then 100 NGOs both local and National are implementing social forestry programme in Bangladesh. It is not possible to enlist activities of all the NGOs involved in the Social forestry programme in the country. The participatory forestry activities of some of the NGOs are highlighted here who are playing pioneer role in this field.

BRAC:The Bangladesh Rural Advancement Committee (BRAC) has been established in 1972 and this is the largest NGO in Bangladesh. BRAC has six categories of projects/ programmes in broad sense among which Social Forestry falls within rural development programme. The Social/ Participatory forestry has three components; (a) Nursery establishment; (b) Plantation and (c) Establishment of agroforestry. They claim that they have assisted their women members in raising more then 225 homestead nurseries and 100 large nurseries with a combined production capacity of a million seedlings of fruits and forest seedlings. They have established 200 mulberry nurseries with the production capacity of 2 million seedlings. Social afforestation programme of BRAC is WFP assisted which has been commenced from 1989 and till now it is going on. Most of the plantation under this programme has been established along the strips. Up to this time about 33.72 million seedling have been planted over an area of 33,700 km strips along road, railway and embankment. This programme involves about 670,000 participants of which 80% are women.

PROSHIKA:Proshika-A centre for human development is one of the largest NGO in Bangladesh. The Social Forestry Programme of Proshika is a systematic intervention effort to enhance afforestation in the country and to make a case that the poor are the best managers and protectors of forest resources if they are granted usufruct rights on these resources. Proshika has introduced its group members in social forestry activities and provided them with credit and technical support, which contributed significantly to their self-sufficiency.

The main components of social forestry programme of Proshika are; i) Homestead plantation; ii) Strip and block plantation; iii) Natural Forest protection, and iv) Nursery establishment. Proshika has planted 71 million seedlings which covered along 8,887 km strips, 37,662 areas of block plantation which included natural Sal forest protection throughout the country. One of the most significant contributor of Proshika to the development areana is the introduction of the concept of participatory forest management for natural forest protection. Proshika has successfully involved the forest dwellers in the Sal forest areas of Kaliakoir, Mirzapur, Shakhipur and Shreepur thanas under district of Tangail and Gazipur for the protection of coppice Sal forest by involving group members of Proshika. It has already been proved that when poor people surviving on the forest resources are organised, trained and granted usufruct rights, they present on enormous human potential needed for afforestation and forest protection.

RDRS:The Rangpur-Dinajpur Rural Services operating in 28 thanas of greater Rangpur and Dinajpur districts covering 28 thanas. It is the largest International Integrated Rural Development NGOs operating in Northern Bangladesh for more than two decades. Its entry point in forestry was through road side plantation in 1977. Initially, seedling were protected with bamboo cages.

Situation has been changed a lot nowadays and protection of seedlings with bamboo cage has become a part of history. Besides strip plantation, they also extend their tree plantation programme in homestead, institutional grounds as well as raising of local nurseries. With the assistance of WFP they have planted about 10.66 million trees under their participatory afforestation programme.

TMSS:It stands for Thangamara Mohila Sabuj Sangha. It is an NGO exclusively meant for women. Although, it was initiated in 1976, its presence was visible only since 1965. This NGO believes in the concept of simple living and high thinking. TMSS was also involved in the social forestry programme particularly in the Northern districts of Bangladesh. The organisation has been implementing both road side and farm forestry with assistance from the WFP and Swiss Development Corporation (SDC) respectively.

POUSH:Another NGO has been engaged in planting in the private lands also by persuading the owner farmers in Baroibari, Kaliakoir thana with the food aid from WFP. Its activities in the forestry field are limited to strip plantations and it plans to expand its programme extensively. Target groups of POUSH are mostly landless destitute, widow and divorced women. POUSH also happens to be the first of its kind to get involved in participatory forestry in the hill district of Bandarban

PROBLEMS AND PROSPECTS OF PARTICIPATORY FOREST MANAGEMENT

Considering the demand and supply situation for forest products to meet the economic and environmental needs, no one can deny the need of people's participation in forestry. Probably there is no second answer except participatory forestry in developing, managing, and protecting the country's forest land and the forest resource. But there are numbers of issues remain unresolved. As a technical department, Forest Department is playing pioneer role in implementing and popularising Participatory Forestry in the country. Up to this time Forest Department is managed by the professional foresters who have educational background only in managing traditional forests and who do not consider people as development partners. Participatory Forestry, if we recollect the Chinese proverb, needs mental development managers towards the people.

Realisation has started among the planners, policy makers, administrators and Senior managers to involve people in forestry development activities. But up to this time Government has failed to adopt real Participatory Forestry programme to address the basic need of the peoples.

Mobilisation of the people in participatory forestry programme is another bottleneck of the Forest Department who has not had the machinery to reach the community people. NGOs who work at the grassroots level have developed their own expert to mobilise people and ensure their participation in any development programmes as partner. So NGO should be involved in the implementation of the participatory forestry programme where Forest Department should confine their activities only in technical aspect.

In the context of Bangladesh, the scarcity of land is a most vital problem. On the other hand, Forest Department controlling over 16% of the total land area of the country is still hesitant to allow Participatory Forestry in reserved forest areas. According to FD, it should be confined only in public and private lands beyond reserved forest areas through these are devoid of trees. The Participatory Forestry is being practiced in marginal lands which are under administration control of other Government departments. Recently, due to pressure from planners and donor communities, Forest Department has allowed to practice participatory forestry in Sal Forest areas. Tenure of the contract was found as a bottleneck for implementing Participatory Forestry. Forest Department allowed rights of participants over these lands for a period of seven years, but there was a strong desire, that this tenure should more and at least for rotation period, so that participants can manage and protect trees till harvesting.

A negative attitude was also observed among the Foresters to involve women in forestry activities. They viewed that activities of women should be confined in the areas where there is a locality apprehending the social problems. But in participatory forestry both men and women should be treated equally.

4

Components of Agroforestry System

INTRODUCTION

The significance of agroforestry as a land use system has been highlighted extensively in recent years. Among the many favourable attributes of agroforestry is its suitability for degraded land. In India, the area of land that belongs to this category is considerable. Commonly known as wastelands, the total area of such land in the country is variously estimated at less than 70 million to more than 170 million ha. Even to allow the low end of this range to remain idle is ill-affordable to the country as the pressure on natural resources is immense. A systematic approach is necessary to rehabilitate wastelands because they are a national wealth remaining underutilised. Agroforestry is a potential alternative suggested by many for the rehabilitation of wastelands. Their current fertility status is such that the probability of success of annual cropping systems is low whereas agroforestry has a reasonable chance to succeed. Along with the material harvests from the perennial component, soil fertility improvement is a benefit of agroforestry. Thus, fertility restoration is a key objective of agroforestry.

Meeting the energy needs of a rapidly-growing economy is another matter of apprehension for India. Issues associated with conventional petroleum energy are fluctuating global prices, depletion of reserves, dependence on imports and environmental pollution. Understandably, efforts have been intensified to identify alternative sources of energy. Biodiesel has emerged as one of thc promising options and production of its raw material, oilseeds, is now gaining wide publicity. Although all oils can be used, edible oils as a source for biodiesel production have to be ruled out because they are required for cooking and food purposes. Therefore, non-edible oils are the premier raw material for biodiesel production in India. Seeds rich in these oils are mostly produced by perennial species. Hence these trees are referred to as Tree-Borne Oilseed Species (TBOS) and they produce Tree-Borne Oilseeds (TBOs).

Production of TBOs on wastelands meets the twin objectives of rehabilitation of a vital natural resource and obtaining an energy substitute.

This is a highly appealing combination because it includes a number of ecological and economic benefits. Establishment of agroforestry systems with TBOS on vast areas of barren or scrub land as well as less fertile farm land will change the rural landscape and bring with it many environmental benefits. Environmentally, the gains can be in the form of reduced erosion, improved micro-environment for intercrops, enhanced soil fertility, production of raw material for less polluting biofuel and by-products for various uses. The economic benefits being highlighted are increased rural income, reduction in expenses on petroleum imports and energy at lower cost.

Although there are definite advantages in promoting TBOS-based agroforestry on barren wastelands and marginal farmland, achieving the desired outcome is not easy. The major constraint, in this regard, is the lack of accurate information about TBOS, their cultivation practices, potential yields and income. In the absence of reliable sources on the topic, interested growers have to rely on whatever information that comes their way. Unfortunately, most promotional literature available at present tends to exaggerate the returns and understate the efforts required to succeed. In the wake of the publicity jatropha and other TBOS are receiving, there is a proliferation in the number of stakeholders. Unfortunately, a majority of them are misled by promoters who are overenthusiastic or are taking advantage of the prevailing euphoria. At stake are the feasibility of agroforestry as a production system and the suitability of TBOS as a source of energy. Among the many issues to be addressed is the need for a systematic effort to develop and disseminate appropriate production packages so that an excellent opportunity is not lost.

MEANING OF AGRO-FORESTRY

Agro-forestry is an old concept. Trees, crops and animals have traditionally been raised together on small farms throughout the World. This concept first derived in the temperate zone due to the small family farms, as a result trees, crops and animals become separately managed on a large scale in modern agriculture and forestry. In India also we exploited our natural resources and adopted this sectorial policy.

In our country the functional allocation on land is 46.4% for Agriculture and 22.7% area for forestry is not sufficient for meeting the multi ferrous requirement of growing population for food, fodder and fuel and other raw materials. The only answer appears to be to integrate the land used for agriculture and forestry in such a way as to maximize production of foods and services for diverse requirements rural communities. Modern Agro-forestry establishes a symbiosis among agricultural crops tree species and livestock rising. In other words, these are complementary and beneficial to each other.

In short conventionally there had been separation between Agriculture and Silviculture. From immemorial on a limited scale a combination of food crops and forest crops had been adopted in land management by the farmers throughout the world, however due to steep rise in the demand for fuel wood and food, due to increase of population, present and early and urgent necessity to adopt the scientific approach on a large scale to the dual system of production or co-existence of forestry and farm council of research for FAO set Agroforestry in 1878 and it is a landmark in history in Agro-forestry. Growing of forest crops along with food grains in dual system has been extensively being adopted world over by the farmer.

Agro-forestry is defined as an efficient, integrated and sustainable land use system that combines Agricultural crops, Forest corps and/ or Livestock together on the unit of farmland at the same time or in sequential manner. In an Agroforestry there are both ecological and economical interactions between the various components.

Agro-forestry is collective name for land used systems involving trees combined with crops and/ or animals on the same unit of land.

It combines production of multiple outputs with protection of resources.

It places emphasis on the use of multiple indigenous trees and shrubs.

It is particularly suitable for low input conditions and fragile environment.

It is structurally and functionally more complex than mono culture (single crop culture) the cycle of Agroforestry system is always more than one year.

OBJECTIVE OF AGRO-FORESTRY

- To manage land efficiently so that its productivity is increased and restored.
- To use available resources efficiently and economically
- To generate employment opportunities for rural peoples.
- To provide raw material for small cottage industries in rural areas.
- To raise the supply of fuel in the rural areas at convenient distance for consumer. In India 70 million tons of dried cow dung is used every year, which can be diverted for natural organic fertilizer moreover undue pressure is on traditional forest for obtaining fuel wood.
- Agro-forestry aims to raise the supply for small timber used by villages for agricultural implements, house construction and other domestic purposes. In this way Agroforestry can meet this requirement of the rural population and reduce pressure on forest.
- One of the main objectives of Agroforestry is to raise the production of food crops, legumes and tuber to meet the rapidly growing food requirements of the Indian population.
- Agroforestry aims at promoting production of, vegetables, pulses, milk and meat. Thus it can raise the Nutritional value of food, which is urgently, require for mankind in our country. Average Indian gets 2000 calories when 3000 calories require per day.

- Agro-forestry programme helps in obtaining an ecological balance in rural areas and thus it may be consider a matter of great significance for a country like India.
- Preservation of humidity in cultivable lands and check soil erosion. Increase productivity of land. In drought prone areas Agroforestry reduces insecurity of the agriculture; in such areas the dual system of production of tree and grasses ensures stability with productivity of land.
- Supply of fodder for vast population of livestock. For proper feeding to livestock increase supply of fodder is urgently required. Large supply of milk and meat is achieved from livestock and poultry when fodder and feeding is proper.

LIMITATIONS OF AGRO-FORESTRY

Agro-Forestry Does Have Certain Negative Aspects

- Possible competition of trees with food crops for space, sunlight, moisture and nutrient which may reduce crop yield.
- Damage to food crops during harvesting of trees.
- Potential of trees is serving as hosts to insects and birds.
- Rapid regeneration of profile trees may displace food crops and take over entire fields.

Through skilled management practices any or all these aspects can be controlled.

For example, once it is known that trees complete with food crops and may reduce food yields, it is easy to adopt some of the following strategies.

- Select legume trees that have small or light crowns so that sunlight will reach the food crops.
- Select trees that are deep-rooted so that they will also absorb moisture and nutrients from the deeper subsoil.
- Space the trees further apart to reduce their competitive effect on the food crop.

SOCIO-ECONOMIC ASPECT OF AGROFORESTRY

- Requirement for more labor inputs, which may cause search at times in other farm activation.
- Competition between food or fore crops which could cause aggregate field, to be grown than those of single crop.
- Longer period required for trees to grow to mature and acquire an economic value.
- Resistance by farmers to displace food crops with trees especially where land is scarce.

CLASSIFICATION OF AGRO-FORESTRY SYSTEM

Different types of Agroforestry systems exist in different parts of the world. These systems are highly diverse and complex in character and functions. To evaluate understand and seek to improve them requires their classification into different categories. Several criteria can be used in classifying them, but the most common include the system's structure, functions, and socio-economic scale of management and ecological spread. According to Nair (1987), Agro-forestry systems can be classified according to following sets of criteria.

Structural Basis

Consider the composition of the components; specially refer including spatial admixture of the woody component, vertical stratification or the component mix and temporal arrangement of different components.

Functional Basis

This is based on the major function or role of the system; mainly of the woody components (This can be productive or protective).

Socio-Economic Basis

Consider the level of inputs or management (low input, high input) or intensity/scale or management and commercial goals.

Ecological Basis

Take into account the environmental conditions on the assumption that certain types of systems can be more appropriate for certain ecological conditions.

CLASSIFICATION OF STRUCTURAL BASIS AGRO-FORESTRY SYSTEM

In these systems the type of component and their arrangement are important.

On the basis of structure, Agroforestry systems can be grouped into two categories

- Nature of components
- Arrangement of components.

Nature of Components

- Agri-silvicultural Systems
- Silvipastoral Systems
- Agro Slivipastoral Systems
- Other Systems

Arrangement of Components

- Spatial Arrangement
- Temporal Arrangement

SYSTEMS

Modern agroforestry systems are classified according to the components present – trees with crops are referred to as silvoarable, trees and animals as silvopastoral, and trees with crops and animals as agro-silvopastoral. Two specialised systems include entomoforestry (trees with insects e.g. honey bees or silk moths) and aquaforestry (trees with fish e.g. mangroves or trees round ponds so leaf litter enriches the water for fish production).

Agroforestry systems have traditionally been important elements of temperate regions around the world, evolving from shifting cultivation towardsmore settled systems involving agriculture, woodland grazing and silvopasture, with fertility transfer from woodlands to cultivated land via manure. In the UK, traditional agroforestry systems include wood pastures such as the New Forest, browsing of acorns and beech mast (pannage), parklands, pollarding, orchard grazing and hedgerows.

Modern agroforestry in the UK is mostly still at the experimental stage, with a number of trial sites established across the UK during the late 1980's, including a network of six silvopastoral systems set up by the UK Agroforestry Research Forum (now the Farm Woodland Forum).

There are only a few examples of organic agroforestry farms in the UK. The Organic Research Centre currently carries out research at three sites: Wakelyns Agroforestry in Suffolk; Sheepdrove Organic Farm, Berkshire; and Whitehall Farm, Cambridgeshire.

AGROFORESTRY SYSTEM COMPONENTS

Agroforestry systems can be made up of many different woody components (as well as the livestock and crop components)

- Alley cropping - rows of trees (either standards or coppice) in between alleys of crops or pasture.
- Hedges
- Shelter belts
- Trees and woodland round riparian zones
- All types of woodland areas – coppice woodland, woodland with standards, and coppice woodlands with standards
- Orchards
- Grazed woodland
- Trees in pasture
- Pollards

In an agroforestry system all woody components should be fully integrated into the agricultural production system. The woody components should have a beneficial ecological impact on the land and other system components (i.e. livestock and crops).

Through management, it should also be possible to gain an economic profit from the woody components either directly by selling products, or indirectly from the woody components having a beneficial effect on other system components (i.e. the shelterbelt producing higher yielding crops or sheep)

Furthermore for an Eco-Agroforestry approach, diversity should exist on all levels of the system.

- Within species diversity of trees, crops and livestock
- Diversity of tree, crops and livestock species
- Diversity of system components at the landscape level

BENEFITS

Trees in agroforestry systems modify microclimatic conditions including temperature, water vapour content of air and wind speed, which can have beneficial effects on crop growth and animal welfare.

Additionally a wide range of other services can be provided including:

- Soil management
- Weed control
- Natural fencing
- Carbon sequestration
- Nutrient recycling

By minimising nutrient losses and maximising internal cycling of nutrients, and by enhancing pest and disease control, agroforestry systems reduce the need for agrochemical inputs.

Agroforestry has a further role in protecting the environment and providing a number of ecosystem services, such benefits include:

- Regulation of soil, water and air quality
- Enhancement of biodiversity
- Climate change mitigation and adaptation

PRODUCTS

Agroforestry systems support the production of a wide range of products including:

- Food
- Fuel
- Timber
- Fodder and forage
- Fibre
- Gums and resins
- Thatching and hedging materials
- Gardening materials
- Medicinal products
- Craft products
- Recreation
- Ecological services

The stack of photos shows a short rotation coppice/potato silvorable system at Wakelyns agroforestry. The short rotation hazel coppice is for energy, from field to wood chip boiler.

These products can impact the local economy through increasing;

- Economic stability
- Diversification of local products and economies
- Diversification of rural skills

- Improved food and fuel security
- Improvements to the cultural and natural environment
- Landscape diversification

BASIC ELEMENTS OF A SYSTEM

A system may have many elements. The six basic elements of any system are:

- Boundary
- Structure
- Function
- State
- Hierarchy
- Type

A system has a boundary. This clearly defines what remains inside (endogenous) and what remains outside (exogenous). Understanding a system means knowing how the endogenous pans relate to each other and how they independently and holistically relate to the exogenous environment. Boundaries can be real or imaginary.

A system has structure. This refers to how the pans relate to each other in terms of space and time. In other words, structure signifies spatial and temporal arrangements.

A system has function. This refers to input-output relationships. A function is a process in which inputs are introduced, managed, and convened into outputs within a time spectrum, in order to achieve desired objectives or goals.

A system also has state. For example, a steady state system is one that does not experience any change in structure or function within a given period. This would not be the case in a system that is just being developed, or a system experiencing a declining state of resources or productivity. Both endogenous and exogenous factors can cause changes in the state of the system.

There is a hierarchy of interrelated and interdependent systems. For example, a human being system is pan of a household system, which is pan of community system, which is part of a regional system, which is pan of a nation, which in turn is part of a community of nations. This means that the analysis of any system in this hierarchy must take cognizance of the influence of higher and lower-order systems. For example, one cannot fully understand an individual person's behavior without understanding the household and community of which he or she is part.

Furthermore, there is the question of how generally or specifically a system is defined. One could describe and analyze a human being system, for example, at a general level such that it applies to all human beings on earth, or at a very detailed level such that each person is, in fact, a different system. Thus the choice of the precise level in this hierarchy is critical for systems definition and analysis.

Basically, there are two types of systems: mechanistic and purposeful. In the former, behavior is predictable as the system does not determine its own goals, rather it reacts to predetermined stimuli (e.g., a computer or an airplane). A purposeful system determines its own goals and the ways to achieve them (e.g., an animal, household or nation).

APPLICATION TO AGRICULTURE AND AGROFORESTRY

There are many uses of systems terminology in agriculture, such as ecozone system, land use system, farming system, cropping system, livestock system, agroforestry system. Let us develop one of which is in common use today, the farming system, and refer to it to explain others.

Farming Systems

Most experts agree to a definition of a farming system as a combination of crops, livestock, and trees, managed in diverse spatial and temporal arrangements, subject to biophysical and socioeconomic conditions, to satisfy the household's objectives and priorities. Such a system can be described, first, in terms of structure. Literally, structure is what one sees on a farm and where each component is located in relation to the others: boundary, buildings, crops, animals, etc. Often the structure of a farming system is subject to seasonal variations within or across years particularly with respect to the temporal arrangement of annual crops.

A farming system can also be described functionally. This is a qualitative representation, indicating the endogenous interactions among production systems and the household, and also the exogenous interactions with the environment. It is imperative to quantify these interactions in order to understand how well this system is managed and how well it is meeting the household's objectives as well as to Identify its constraints.

Other Systems

Cropping and Livestock Systems: A structural description of the crop component alone, that is to say the cropping system of a farming system. The different cropping patterns are managed with respect to spatial and temporal arrangements. A functional description of the livestock component. It identifies the specific contributions of various livestock species to the household and to other components of a farming system.

Agroforestry systems: The presence of trees on external and internal boundaries, cropland, homestead plots or on any other available niche of farmland, defines the agroforestry systems structurally. There are several agroforestry systems on this farming system, and each can be described functional, i.e., in terms of inputs used and outputs generated. The structural and functional considerations which can be used to define and analyze agroforestry systems. However, it is essential to remember that any agroforestry system can be subdivided into other systems and is a part of larger systems.

Land-use systems: What is a land-use system? Each system identified thus far can be described and analyzed with emphasis on how land as an essential resource is being used and managed by. the household in the farming system or in any production system.

The land-use systems analysis could comprise:

- Household priorities and objectives,
- Land-use intensity, namely, units of inputs or labor per hectare,
- Levels of management,
- Productivity levels and potentials, and
- Disposal and use of outputs.

Similarly, one could analyze systems defined on the basis of other crucial factors such as labor, household information, or market participation. It is all a question of the desired focus or emphasis for understanding a given farming system or its parts.

Ecozone System: One usually wants to study farming systems within a larger system, e.g., an ecozone system. The latter could be defined on the basis of homogeneous characteristics such as altitude, climate, topography, soil type, or vegetation; or, alternatively, on the basis of specific farming and/or production systems which reflect to a large extent what is feasible in terms of the above agroecological determinants.

The analysis at this level can be conducted as follows: If one studies many farming systems in a particular ecozone, one notices common patterns with respect to structural and/or functional characteristics which provide a logical basis for classifying farming systems. A general definition criteria (e.g., systems with maize and cattle), will encompass a greater number of farms, while a more specific definition criteria (e.g., systems with specific management and yield levels of maize), will contain a lesser number of farms.

SYSTEMS ANALYSIS

Systems analysis aims at comparing one system with others or assessing the comparative performance of the same system over different periods of time. The performance of a system depends to a large extent how its components interact, both structurally and functionally.

To analyze a system one should use assessment criteria based on the relationship between structural and functional components of the system. Farming systems in tropical environments are typically characterized by multiple combinations of structural and functional interactions and therefore it is important to identify such interactions and to quantify their positive and negative effects.

Table.Qualitative assessment of livestock roles in a farming system

Role	Cattle	Goats	Sheep	Donkeys	Pigs	Poultry	Wildlife
Food							
Meat	X	XXX	X			XXX	XX
Milk	XX	X					
Egg						XXX	
Traction							
Land prep	XXX			XXX			
Cultivation	X						
Transport	XX			XXX			
Manure/Fert.	XXX	X	X			X	
Storage							
Food Supply		XXX	X		X	XXX	
Capitalization		XXX	X	X			
Seasonal feed excesses	XXX	XXX	X		X	XX	
Weed and	X	X					
Bush Control							XX
Cultural Needs							
Contract agreement	XXX	XX					
Rituals	XXX	XXX				X	
Ornamentation	X	X					XX
Sports/Recreation	X	X					X

X = Weak XX = Moderate XXX = Strong

System Assessment Criteria

Three useful indicators of performance for a system are:

- Management intensity, which is measured as an input/input ratio. For example, amount of fertilizer/ha, or labor input/ha.
- Productivity, which is measured as an output/input ratio, For example, yield/ha, or yield/livestock unit.
- Profitability, which is measured as output value/input. For example, net benefit invested or net benefit/ha.

Other indicators include those related to the physical resource status, such as soil fertility and structure, or vegetation cover. The criteria are calculated for a given time period, usually a season or year. If one studies how and why these indicators vary over the medium term (2 - 5 years) or the long term (5 - 15 years), then one can assess whether the system in question is stable and sustainable. Thus, sustainability of a system can be ascertained by studying long-term trends in the indicators of physical resource status, management intensity, productivity, and profitability.

Analytical Steps

In a general sense, systems analysis means an explicit consideration of system objectives, interplay of endogenous components and factors, and interaction/linkages with exogenous systems; the analysis Uses the time factor as an important variable. On the basis of the preceding sections, the systems analysis process can be broken into a series of steps, each answering one of the following key questions:

Present Performance of the System

- What is the structure of the system(s)? The structural components refer to basic resources such as edaphic, biotic, abiotic, or economic resources. Structural assessment involves a specification of boundary and spatial, as well as temporal arrangements of physical components; this is Usually done on a qualitative and/or quantitative basis.
- What is the function of the system(s)? The functional components refer to management resources, viz, input levels used, technological and economic input, and output levels achieved, both in physical and/or economic terms. Functional assessment involves a description of inputs (use of labor, cash inputs, information), outputs (food, feed, materials) and their disposal (home consumption, sale), and the timing of when these events occur. Management and performance analysis is needed here, including quantitative analysis. Biophysical as well as socioeconomic criteria should be used for functional assessment over a given period such as 1, 2, or 5 years.
- What is the state of the system? Answering this requires analysis of trends with respect to changes in the basic structure and/or functions of the system. Stability and sustainability are important considerations in this step.

In all these investigations, the influence of risk and uncertainty factors (e.g., climate price structure, human emergencies) should not be underestimated, especially in agriculture-based systems.

Future Improvements

The above questions seek information on the present performance of the systems.

If the task is to improve the system, then one must ask a set of additional questions:

- What are the objectives of the system manager(s) (e.g., farmer and household). And how do those objectives match up with present system performance? It should be noted that, although the manager's objectives and priorities for the system may not acceptable to all, they can be ascertained and recorded accurately.
- What are the positive and negative effects on the system of the present component structures and/or functions? How could they be modified or replaced to achieve higher levels of performance? Any

proposed interventions must to be appropriate and acceptable to the manager(s).

- What are the positive and negative effects on the system of exogenous factors, and what should be done about these factors to move the system in the desired direction?
- If endogenous and/or exogenous changes should be carried out, what adjustments of structure and/or function are required by the system manager to successfully implement the proposed changes? Are they feasible technically, managerially, and economically?

The primary focus analysis of system performance is the identification of constraints and key opportunities for improvement. This leads to a better understanding of the type of changes to structure and function that would be required to make the system perform as expected by its manger(s) - whether fine-tuning, incremental changes, or major changes.

SYSTEMS AND INTERDISCIPLINARY RESEARCH

Research with a systems approach is used in almost all biophysical disciplines, such as ecology, genetics, soil science, husbandry, pathology, and engineering, as well as in social science disciplines including economics, sociology, anthropology, and political science. However, there is a major difference in the conceptual framework and analytical methods used by natural scientists, as compared to social scientists. For the former, research typically deals with plants, organisms, and animals under "controlled" conditions, while for the latter, research deals with people in their "natural" habitat where "controls" can be exercised only through analytical methods. In this respect, each discipline in the natural and social sciences has different tools for studying and improving land-use production systems. An interdisciplinary, systems approach is often used in research on land-use systems, whether homogenous or mixed systems. Research to improve any of the land-use systems, would require interaction among scientists from the different disciplines. Particularly in the case of mixed systems, interdisciplinary research can be quite complex and challenging. To be effective, team interaction should be based on a consensus on the systems analysis process and on the specific contribution to be made by each discipline to the overall research strategy. Productive interdisciplinary research requires a leader or leaders possessing expertise in systems analysis, orientation to client farmer needs, technical know-how, and team management skills.

CLASSIFICATION OF AGROFORESTRY SYSTEMS

Agroforestry systems can be classified in different ways using structural and functional considerations. One common classification of agroforestry includes agrosilvopastoral, silvopastoral or agrosilviculture systems, which can be further sub-divided depending on specific arrangements and/or functions.

Table.Types of Land-Use Systems.

Type of System	Examples of Components
Homogenous Systems	
Monocropping systems,	Maize, wheat, rice.
Mono-animal systems	Cattle, sheep, poultry.
Mono-tree systems	Timber plantations, woodlots.
Mixed Systems	
Crop-crop	Maize/cassava, maize/beans.
Animal-animal	Cattle/goat, cattle/poultry.
Crop-animal	Maize/cattle, cereals/poultry/household waste.
Crop-tree	Alley farming, mixed intercropping, boundary tree
planting.	
Animal-tree	Alley grazing, fodder tree banks.
Crop-animal-tree	Homegardens, alley farming with Livestock.

Another classification divides agroforestry systems into "mainly agrosilvicultural" (i.e., trees with crops), "mainly or partly silvopastoral" (i.e., trees with pasture and livestock) "tree-component predominant", and "other components present". This scheme recognizes further subdivision according to structural or functional considerations. This particular classification is probably best suited for analysis of the potentials of agroforestry.

More recently, with a view to reviewing and synthesizing the state-of-the-art in agroforestry research and development for an annual ICRAF three-week course, the author and a lecturing team adopted the classification.

Table.An Example of the Classification of Agroforestry Systems.

1. Mainly Agrosilvicultural (trees with crops)

Rotational:

- Planted tree fallow
  - Taungya
    Spatial mixed
- Trees on cropland
- Plantation crop combination
  - with upper-storey trees
  - with lower-storey
  - tree/shrubs crops
  - with herbaceous crops

  Tree gardens:
  - multistorey tree gardens
  - home gardensSpatial
    zoned;Alley farming
    Boundary planting

  Trees for soil conservation:
  - barrier hedges
  - on grass barrier steps
  - on bunds, etc.
  - on terraces
- Windbreaks and shelterbelts

- Biomass transfer

2. Mainly or partly Silvopastoral (trees with pastures and livestock)

Spatial mixed:

- Trees on rangeland or pastures
- Plantation crops with pastures

Spatial zoned:

- Live fences
  - mainly barrier function
  - multipurpose. Fodder banks

3. Trees Component Predominant

- Woodlots with multipurpose management
- Reclamation forestry leading to production:
  - on eroded land
  - on salinized land
  - on moving sands

4. Other Components Present and Special Aspects

- Apiculture with forestry
- Aquaforestry (trees with fisheries)
- Trees in water management
- Irrigated agroforestry

Table.A Second Example of the Classification of Agroforestry Systems

1. Alley Farming (hedgerow intercropping)
2. Crops under tree cover
3. Pastures and animals under tree cover
4. Agroforests (live fencing, boundary planting, windbreaks, shelterbelts)
5. Sequential technologies (shifting cultivation, taungya, improved fallow)
6. Other technologies (aquaculture and apiculture with trees)

Structural criteria are readily applicable in classifying agroforestry systems. In contrast, the use of functional criteria to classify agroforestry systems is uncommon. The science of agroforestry is not yet sufficiently advanced in the analysis of technology management and performance to define useful functional criteria for system classification. The occasional exceptions include, for example, speaking of alley farming for soil fertility improvement or for fodder production, or indicating how a farming system's output is to be disposed of (e.g., for home consumption, cash generation, or both). The key task at present is to determine the most appropriate criteria to apply in classifying agroforestry systems. The choicc of classification depends on its intended use of the classification. For purposes of technology development, the chosen classification should provide a useful framework for guiding research and assessing research progress.

SCOPE OF AGRO-FORESTRY IN INDIA

There is tremendous scope for Agroforestry because India has achieved self-sufficiency in food production. Now its attention is becoming more focused on the ecological problems and shortage of fuel, fodder and other outputs as well as unemployment.

Agroforestry has vast scope in meeting this requirement through multipurpose tree species as:

- Large area is available in the form of farm boundaries, bunds, waste lands where this system can be adopted
- This system permits the growing suitable tree species in the field where most annual crops are growing well
- By growing trees and crops on Agricultural or forest land, Resources are utilized efficiently
- System has potential generate employment.
- Provides raw material for the cottage industries
- Helps in maintaining ecological balance
- Soil and water conservation, soil improvement.
- Helps in meeting various needs of growing population.

SYSTEMS

Agroforestry is a traditional practice among farmers in India. The practices adopted may not be well-defined systems like those evolved scientifically in recent times. Nevertheless, they too have followed the same principles and realised the benefits. A comprehensive description of all these practices and systems is found in the documentation of Tejwani (1994). There are many traditional agroforestry systems in practice in arid regions of India. Presence of *Acacia nilotica* and *Dalbergia sissoo* is very common in northern parts of the country. In the humid tropical areas along the south-western coast, systems which combine several perennial species are a common occurrence. The inclusion of several spice crops in these intensively-managed systems makes them highly remunerative.

TBOS have not been a key component of any traditional agroforestry system and often they may not have been established deliberately by farmers. The exception is jatropha, which is established by farmers as a live fence. This requires planting them in a row at close spacing. Other species like *Pongamia pinnata*, *Madhuca* species and *Calophyllum inophyllum* probably came up as wildlings and were retained by farmers. Their presence is usually limited to a few trees in the middle of crop fields or along the borders. Oilseed production is not the intention of retaining these trees and they are mostly there for service functions like providing shade and protection as fence.

Agroforestry technology development has been an active programme in the country for many years. In recent years, several agroforestry systems have been successfully introduced and accepted by farmers in India. Systems based on poplar (*Populus deltoides*) in the north-western region of the country are highly intensive and are suitable for irrigated conditions. An agri-horti-forestry system - where the component species are horticultural crops like mango and cashew, annuals as intercrops and multipurpose trees along the border of the farm - has gained acceptance in Maharashtra and Gujarat (Mahajan *et al.*, 2001). Additionally, there are many innovative farmers who have developed or modified existing agroforestry systems to suit local conditions. TBOS can fit into most of these systems, contributing positively towards the overall productivity and farm income.

LIMITATIONS

Wastelands belonging to farmers that can be brought under TBOS is available in plenty. The present production levels of some marginal farmlands are so low that farmers will be happy to try out alternative crops. Therefore, land availability for oilseed production is unlikely to be a constraint. The vital resource that will determine the area eventually brought under oilseed production is water. Although most TBOS are hardy, they will still require adequate water to produce satisfactory yields. Because priority allocation of available water would be for food production, oilseed production has to be concentrated on land where competition for water does not occur.

TREE-BORNE OILSEED SPECIES

Seeds of many tree species contain high levels of oil and their use for bioenergy generation has been a topic of interest for long. Those popularly known as TBOS are *Jatropha curcus* (jatropha or ratanjyot), *Pongamia pinnata* (pongamia or karanj), *Madhuca latifolia* and *M. indica* (mahua), *Calophyllum inophyllum* (undi), *Azadirachta indica* (neem) and *Simarouba glauca* (simarouba). Simarouba has been studied to standardise various aspects of it cultivation. It is not a very familiar species in India. It produces edible oil and probably requires relatively better growing conditions compared to others in this group. Mahua oil is also edible and is used by tribal communities. Undi probably has the highest seed oil content among these species, but its major limitation appears to be the restricted environmental niche of sandy soil with humid environment. Moreover, mahua and undi are very slow-growing species and hence may not fit into an agroforestry system. Neem has recognition more for its pesticidal uses than seed oil. Thus, the list narrows down to jatropha, pongamia and neem. Jatropha appears to be the frontrunner at present.

There are several reasons for the greater interest in jatropha. It already has a domestication record as research on it has been carried out in India and other countries. Seed oil characteristics of jatropha are superior to others for biodiesel production. Besides its faster growing attribute when compared to most other TBOS, it also has the ideal size for agroforestry. Thus, jatropha has emerged as the premier TBOS. Unlike most other perennial species, jatropha has a shorter gestation period and regular seed harvests are possible within four years of establishment. Being a small tree with a lax canopy, it is ideally suited for small farm agroforestry systems. Its natural distribution throughout

India is indicative of its adaptation to diverse agro-climatic conditions. Farmers are also familiar with jatropha as a hardy fence plant that can survive with very little inputs or management. These advantages notwithstanding, it should not be assumed that jatropha can succeed under any condition.

Another advantage of jatropha is the properties of its oil for biodiesel production. Its low free fatty acid content, almost similar to edible oils, makes it ideal for transesterification and the oil to biodiesel conversion ratio is higher than in other non-edible oils. A higher ratio means better profit margins and hence jatropha oil is a more desirable raw material than others. Combustion studies have also shown jatropha biodiesel to be superior to others as its emissions are less polluting. Pongamia has its own merits as a TBOS. Rural communities in India are familiar with this species because its oil has been used traditionally for lighting lamps in households. It grows well in most parts of the country. A particular merit of this species is its ability to withstand both waterlogging and extreme drought conditions. In dry areas, it is one of the few species remaining green during the summer season. Its ability to fix atmospheric nitrogen is another advantage of this species. Domestication work on this species to identify elite genotypes and standardise cultivation practices is still at an early stage. Because this species is native to India, most of the information related to its use as an economically important plant and contribution to scientific knowledge has to be generated locally.

Neem is a species that combines two environment-friendly themes of current interest in the form of biopesticide and biodiesel. It is a hardy species that not only suvives, but produces reasonable quantities of seed in all types of environments. Of particular significance is its ability to grow on saline soils. Its wood is of reasonably good quality timber that can be used for making farm implements and construction purposes. It can also combine well with many annual crops as well as small trees like jatropha in agroforestry systems.

PROSPECT OF AGROFORESTRY IN INDIA

Trees and forests were always considered as an integral part of the Indian culture. The ancient scriptures and historical records amply support this. The best of Indian culture was born in the forests. The Aryan civilization was started in our forests and our Rishis who evolved the Hindu religion, lived in forests in complete harmony with nature. The ashrams were the centers which harmonized agriculture and pasture with trees, animals and birds. It was widely believed that destruction of forests and cutting of trees created famine conditions, where as planting and maintaining trees were regarded as noble acts. In fact, so much has been written in our ancient literature that individuals on their own agricultural fields were doing planting tree in ancient times.

Gradually, during recent periods because of increasing population and huge gap between demand and supply, forests were ruthlessly exploited to meet the increasing demand of fuel, fodder and timber. To overcome this huge burden upon our existing forests, some alternative steps have to be taken to meet the increasing demand of forest produce i.e. production of such items have to be carried outside the forest areas as well. Hence, in the light of ever increasing demand, concept of multiple use of land with multipurpose tree species has become immensely important. In this context, agro forestry, which is a form of multiple land/use system, should be adopted and encouraged.

The reasons for higher production under agro forestry system include:

- Greater efficiency of tree species for photosynthesis.
- Improved soil structure and fertility with increasing effects on crop yield.
- Reduce losses from soil erosion and more closed cycling of organic matter and nutrients.
- Creating better micro climatic conditions for the growth of agricultural crops.

AGROFORESTRY: CONCEPT AND DEFINITION

Agro forestry is not a new system or concept. The practice is very old, but the term is definitely new. Agro forestry means practice of agriculture and forestry on the same piece of land. Bene et al. (1977) defined agro forestry as a sustainable management system for land that increases overall production, combines agricultural crops and animals simultaneously. Nair (1979) defines agro forestry as a land use system that integrates trees, crops and animals in a way that is scientifically sound, ecologically desirable, practically feasible and socially acceptable to the farmers. Another widely used definition given by the International Center for Research in Agro forestry (ICRAF) Nairobi, Kenya, that, "agro forestry is a collective name for all land use systems and practices where woody perennials are deliberately grown on the same land management unit as agricultural crops or animals in some form of spatial arrangement or temporal sequence" (Nair, 1983).

Benefical Effect of Agroforestry

Higher yields of crops have been observed in forest-influenced soils than in ordinary soils. In the Tarai area of Uttar Pradesh, Taungya cultivators harvested higher yields of crops such as maize, wheat, pulses etc. without fertilizer. Approximately, 20% higher yields of grains and wood have been reported in agro forestry areas of Haryana and western Uttar Pradesh than from pure agriculture. Experiments conducted at IGFRI, Jhansi indicate that the total yield of fodder is more when fodder grasses are grown with fodder trees than pure fodder grass cultivation. Leucaena leucocephala intercropped with agricultural crops and fodder grasses increase the total yield of food grains, fodder and fuel. Nitrogen fixing trees grown in the agro forestry systems are capable of fixing about 50 -100 Kg

N/ha/year. Experience in Punjab, Haryana, Uttar Pradesh, Gujarat and some parts of the southern states indicate that a tree and agriculture crop production system is more productive. The total production and value of fuel, fodder and small timber in degraded lands are reported to be many times more than the coarse grains usually produced on them. Sanchez (1987) stated that, " appropriate agro forestry systems improve soils physical properties, maintain soil organic matter and promote nutrient cycling". Nitrogen fixing trees are mentioned as one of the most promising component of agro forestry system. The leaf litter after decomposition forms humus, releases nutrients and improves various soil properties, it also reduces the fertilizer needs.

Growing of trees and fodder crops (including fodder trees) is more economical, particularly on marginal lands. Observations taken in hot arid and semi-arid areas of Rajasthan indicate that marginal lands are incapable of sustaining stable and dynamic cultivation of agricultural crops. Silvipasture consisting of growing trees such as Prosopis, Albizia, Zizyphus and Acacia species may provide many times more returns per unit of land than agriculture under such conditions. Eucalyptus in agro forestry has been found to be more profitable than pure agriculture in Haryana. Populus deltoides increases the farm return by 50% in Tarai region of Uttar Pradesh.

AGROFORESTRY IN UTTAR PRADESH

After creation of Uttaranchal state in the year 2000, the tree cover in Uttar Pradesh has reduced to only 4.46% where as, the State Forest Policy 1998 envisaged that one third of the total geographical area should come under forest/ tree cover. Hence, agro forestry is now the only option to increase the desired tree cover of 33%. In Uttar Pradesh, practices of agro forestry vary considerably according to the agro climatic zones, socioeconomic conditions and site-specific tree species.

The benefits of agro forestry is better understood by the farmers in western region of the state, this may be attributed, to the assured market of agroforestry produce because of flourishing wood based industries in the region. Eucalyptus and Poplar are preferred species in the western region, whereas, Shisham and Teak is preferred species in eastern region. Fruit trees also have considerable share of agro forestry particularly in western part of the state.

Hence, to workout suitable agro forestry models with preferred timber, fodder, fuel and fruit tree species for different agro climatic zones of U.P. a state level workshop was conducted by the research circle of U.P. forest department at Kanpur. The aim of the workshop was to bring together different workers including forest officers, scientists, subject matter specialists and NGOs working in the field of agro forestry at different places. Suitable recommendations for tree-crop combinations in four different agro climatic zones of the state viz. tarai region, western plain gangetic region, eastern plain gangetic region and vindhya and bundelkhand region have been made. The outcome of the workshop held on dated 5-6th May 2001 was published and circulated under Lab to Land leaflet series entitled "Significance and use of Agro forestry System".

The tangible and intangible benefits of agro forestry as suggested in the leaflet are mentioned below:

- To meet the demand of fuel, fodder and timber for the increasing population.
- To reduce the biotic pressure on existing forests.
- To obtain maximum output in terms of yield from the same piece of land.
- To develop wasteland/ degraded lands by planting suitable tree species with agricultural crops.
- To reduce the environmental pollution by planting tree species.
- To reduce soil erosion.
- To increase the soil fertility by planting nitrogen fixing tree species.
- To create availability of raw material for wood based industries.
- To create opportunity of employment to local people and to increase the return in terms of money by increased crop production.

AGROFORESTRY PROMOTION

The National Agriculture Policy, (2000) clearly states, "Agriculture has become a relatively unrewarding profession due to generally unfavorable price regime and low value addition, causing abandoning of farming and increasing migration from rural areas." Hence the Policy stresses, "Farmers will be encouraged to take up farm/agro-forestry for higher income generation by evolving technology, extension and credit support packages and removing constraints to development of agro forestry".

Rural people have been practicing tree planting in their farms and homesteads to meet household requirements of fuel, poles, timber and medicinal plants. With the advent of social forestry, diversification in agriculture was encouraged to generate high income and minimize risks in cropping enterprises.

Planning Commission, GOI, 2001 for promoting agro forestry, has recommended the following: -

- Rather than having a uniform strategy for the whole country, commercial agro forestry should be adopted in irrigated districts of the country.
- A separate strategy should be developed for rain fed areas for environmental security, sustainable agriculture (production and economy) and food accessibility.
- Suitable species for commercial agro forestry may include Acacia nilotica, Bamboo species, Casuarina equisetifolia, Eucalyptus species,

Populus deltoides and Prosopis cineraria for different climatic, edaphic and agricultural conditions.

- Specific institutes have been identified for tree improvement and development of clones of specified species.
- Corporate private sector may be encouraged to take up research and development in tree improvement, development of better clones and micro and macro propagation of quality planting material.
- About 100 NGOs may be identified to carry out clonal propagation of seedlings for distribution to farmers at appropriate price and carrying out extension work. Extension activities should include organizing farmers, providing them training in planting techniques, protection measures and other silvicultural operations.
- Technological development to diversify usage of agro forestry species will help to ensure a ready market; for example bamboo is getting rediscovered as a potential raw-material for the development of bamboo composites suitable for use in place of wood and wood composites.
- Bamboo technology mission should be started keeping in view the impending gregarious flowering, followed by mass mortality of bamboo, forest fire famine and insurgency. Circumstances warrant formulation of emergency plans for harvesting and processing of bamboo prior to their flowering.
- As more and more farmers are taking up agro forestry, export - import policies should be modified to encourage agro forestry product marketing.
- A system of market regulation to be put in place, including a mechanism of periodic review in order to protect the interest of both producer and consumer of agro forestry produce.
- A suitable market information system needs to be introduced to inform farmers about major buyers, prevailing prices trends, procedure etc.
- All existing laws executive orders relating to tree felling transport, processing and sale should be amended to facilitate agro forestry.
- Commercial agro forestry may be planned in irrigated districts covering 10 m ha. On annual basis, one million ha should be brought under multipurpose tree species identified by the Task Force. The scheme of NABARD for farm/ agro forestry should be expanded and investment of Rs. 100 crores per year should be ensured.
- It is proposed to cover 18 million ha of rain fed areas on watershed basis under agro forestry for conservation of soil and water and plantation of hardy species such as Eucalyptus, Bamboo and Babul. On annual basis 1.8 million ha is proposed for afforestation under

various schemes of Rural Development, NAEB and 'food for work' scheme. An investment of Rs. 2700 crores will be required on yearly basis.

- Major states may establish Agro forestry Cooperative Federation for increasing bargaining powers of farmers in marketing of agro forestry products.
- Wood based industries should continue supply of quality planting material to farmers and ensure suitable buy-back arrangement.

DESCRIPTIONS OF INDIAN AGROFORESTRY PRACTICES

As suggested in the definition of agroforestry cited above, trees may be integrated with agricultural crops and/or animals either simultaneously or sequentially. Historical accounts indicate that the Indians practiced sequential agroforestry systems on level, alluvial soils where they grew annual crops of corn, squash, and beans, as well as perennial crops of berries. Simultaneous agroforestry systems were practiced on the upland, glacial till soils, where Indians grew perennial crops of berries and nuts, which were harvested by the Indians themselves as well as by the animals they hunted; upland soils also produced crops of fuelwood and other products important to humans and wildlife.

Sequential agroforestry practices, or shifting cultivation, in the Northeast entailed fallow periods for fields during which they would be invaded by grass, herb, shrub, and tree species. Crops of corn, squash, and beans would be grown for 5-10 years. Then the soil would go uncultivated for 10-20 years. Early accounts described these fallow areas as grassy, with berry bushes and small trees. If the fields were burned, as was common, berries such as strawberry, raspberry, and blackberry would often follow the fires. Perennial grass species, particularly little bluestem, would also follow fires. Nitrogen-fixing species such as wild indigo and lespedezas would likewise increase after fires. After a fire, the perennial grasses resprout vigorously from rhizomes which are protected by the soil above them; the hard coatings of leguminous seeds are scarified by the combination of heat and moisture, which promotes their germination.

Exposed mineral soils—resulting from cultivation or intense fires—would often be colonized by light-seeded tree species such as birches and white pine. Day noted that the Indians' name for alluvial areas (the "intervales" of the early records) meant the "places of little pines." Gordon noted that pre-settlement white pine stands existed on areas that had previously been cleared for agriculture. When the Indians decided to clear land for agriculture, they would girdle the trees with axe cuts or build fires at the bases of the trees to girdle them. Corn would be planted among the dead trees, which would later be removed by felling and burning in place. Land that had not grown up to trees could have been cleared by burning the grass and shrubs. An intense fire in early summer would reduce the incidence of resprouting by shrubs and tree saplings. Simultaneous agroforestry practices in the Northeast involved manipulating the forest environment to shift the species composition in the direction of more food-producing shrubs and trees, and to increase the productivities of these species. The chief forest management tool used by the Indians was fire. Bromley and Day cited many of the early accounts describing the presettlement landscape in advancing the theory that large areas of forest land were intentionally burned, chiefly during the months of November and April. The following quotation from Wood is typical of the early accounts:

... for it being the custom of the Indians to burn the wood in *November,* when the grass is withered, and leaves dried, it consumes all the Underwood, and rubbish, which otherwise would overgrow the country, making it unpassable, and spoil their much affected hunting...

The early accounts generally ascribed the purposes of improving travel and hunting to the Indians' burning of the woods. Some later reviews of these accounts put emphasis on the additional purpose of favoring nut trees and berry plants. The early accounts are, in fact, fairly consistent in their indications of the predominance of nut trees in upland forests; the following citations from Day are typical:

In 1607 Captain Gilbert described the trees at a point on the Maine coast—probably Point Elizabeth south of Casco Bay. They were "the most part of them ocke and wallnutt (hickory) growing in a great space assoonder on from the other as in our parks in Ingland and no thickett growing under them". Richmond Island nearby had "fine oaks and nut trees with cleared land and abundance of vines which in their season bear fine grapes."

Fig. A part of Green Hill Park in Worcester.

The relatively thick barks of oak (especially chestnut, black, scarlet, and red oak), shagbark hickory, and American chestnut were able to withstand the heat of periodic low intensity burns. The relatively thin-barked maples, birches, beech, and hemlock would have been limited to the less frequently burned, mesic sites. Since the nut trees are also prolific sprouters from stumps, they would have assured their persistence on sites which were cut for fuelwood or burned intensively. The decay resistance of white oak and American chestnut would have increased their resistance to basal wounds which would have inevitably resulted from periodic burning.

Historical accounts and archaeological discoveries concur on the relative importance of various foods of the presettlement Indians. In addition to the staples of corn and beans, Thomas and Russell emphasized the importance of small fruits and tree nuts in the Indian diet. By floating the contents of refuse pits from an early 17th century Indian settlement in southwestern New Hampshire, Thomas was able to establish their extensive use of berries and nuts. Furthermore, Thomas cited Wright regarding the record of Indian deeds which reserved certain privileges (italics added—KD):

... that they (the Indians) shall have and enjoy all that cottinackeesh, or ground that is now planted; And have liberty to take Fish and Deer, ground nuts,*walnuts, akornes* and sasachiminesh or a kind of pease... (deed for a part of Agawam, MA)

... (the Indians) doth reserve liberty of fishing for ye Indians in ye Rivers of waters and free Liberty to hunt deere or other wild creatures and to gather*walnuts, chesnuts and other nuts* things &c on ye Commons... (deed for a part of Deerfield, MA)

Berries were an important source of vitamin C and sugars, not only in season, but throughout the year in dried form mixed with corn meal. Nuts were an important source of protein and oil, particularly shagbark hickory ("walnuts") and butternuts. Acorns and chestnuts were dried and stored; water mixed with alkaline maple wood ashes would be used to leach the tannic acid from the acorns. Hickory nuts and butternuts would be husked and shelled, or crushed and then boiled to float off an oil emulsion that had a variety of uses. Nut meats or oils would greatly enhance the food value of corn, which by itself is considered a nutritionally poor staple.

ECOLOGICAL ASPECTS OF SHIFTING CULTIVATION

Although fish manures may have been used, the only nutrients known to have been added were the nitrogen fixed by beans, and the minerals released from crop residues by burning. But since the Indians did not practice plowing or cultivating (except very locally in the corn "hills"), the modern problems of soil erosion would have been minimal. Thus, a soil's fertility could have been restored relatively quickly by natural successional processes.

Carmean et al. reported on the improvement in structure and fertility of a soil which had gone from cultivation (and consequent erosion) to pasture to young forest. The improvements were attributed to the actions of root penetration and leaf litter accumulation. Fisher and Stone reported specifically on the increased availability of nitrogen and phosphorous under young conifer plantations:

Despite cumulative net withdrawal into the conifer biomass, soluble forms of both elements were higher near and under the trees.

The mechanism for increasing the available nutrients was not identified although they hypothesized that:

... the conifer rhizosphere can mineralize or otherwise extract some fraction of the soil N and P that was resistant to microbial activity under the previous vegetation of grasses and forbs.

Thus, the "little pines" of the intervals agricultural areas of the Indians would have served the purpose of improving soil fertility in two ways: by the unidentified action of the rhizosphere and by the accumulation of nutrients in the above-ground biomass which could be partially returned to the soil by felling and burning. Young pine stands would also have served as cover for wildlife species such as ruffed grouse, turkey, deer, and bear.

Repeated burning of fallow, grassy areas would reduce diseases of the grasses and shrubs, particularly leaf spot fungi. Fire would also stimulate heavier fruiting of these plants. Sharp stated that grouse populations under fire management were 2-1/2 to 5 times higher than under timber-cutting management for the species, and that:

Evidence from various sources poses the hypothesis that the ruffed grouse is a fire climax species or one that benefits from recurrent fires in its habitats. Its basic or key food plants are fire induced at crucial stages of development such as by stimulating seed germination and seedling establishment, by rejuvenating decadent plants or clones, or by controlling plant diseases.

Other birds, particularly the now extinct passenger pigeon and heath hen, would also have benefited from burning fallow Indian fields for the reasons cited above, and because fire would also destroy some parasites and diseases of the birds. Grouse, heath hen, passenger pigeon, turkey, and other fowl would have been important dietary items in early fall and early spring.

Some of the early accounts of Indian burning practices ascribed another purpose, above—that of eliminating the "vermin". Specific vermin were not indicated, although one reason that the Indians often moved their villages was apparently to avoid fleas and lice which had come to infest a site. Moist conditions are needed for the build-up of inocula for many plant diseases and for the survival of many insects which live on or near the soil surface. Burning would destroy inocula on grasses and shrubs, and would temporarily create drier conditions on and near the ground surface. Some diseases would affect the plants as well as the animals which ate them. Ergot and other fungal poisons affect animals (and humans) which eat infected grassland plants. Burning would also destroy insects and arthropods such as ticks, fleas, chiggers, and lice which live on the ground surface when not parasitizing an animal host. These insects can be particularly damaging when they act as transmitters of internal parasites or diseases of wildlife and humans. A recent outbreak of "Lyme disease" in southern Connecticut has been partially attributed to the increase in the population of deer ticks-which carry the disease and infect humans with it (R. Wyatt, personal communication). Whether this disease existed in pre-settlement times is not known, although the transmitters of the disease existed then and certainly could have carried this or other diseases.

Fire affects organisms living below, as well as above, the soil surface. Ahlgren reviewed the research on how fire affects soil organisms. Increased availability of mineral nutrients, which leach from the ash, improve conditions for the nitrogen-fixing bacteria of the *Azotobacter* and *Clostridium* species. The overall pH of the soil increases for the same reason. Stone reported that these bacteria, as well as blue-green algae, were most likely the organisms responsible for increased levels of available nitrogen in frequently burned soils in the Southeast and in the Coastal Plain.

These increases occurred in several studies, despite the volatization of much of the nitrogen in the accumulated organic layer. Actinomycetes also increase following fires, but are not known to increase available nitrogen. Other soil fauna generally decrease after fire (e.g., earthworms, snails, beetles, mites, collembolans, centipedes, and millipedes). These organisms probably do not significantly affect soil fertility, but they do improve soil porosity and texture.

ECOLOGICAL ASPECTS OF CONTROLLED FOREST BURNING

The term "controlled burning" is used advisedly here, considering the lack of specific information in the early accounts about how the Indians actually managed the fires they set, although Martin cited one account of Indians uprooting the grass around the circumference of an area they intended to burn in order to prevent the fire from running back. Martin stated that "all other early references to Indian burning are unsubstantial" (i.e., unspecific), in making the point that the Indians were not the "irresponsible incendiaries" that some early colonists and some historians claimed them to be. Indeed, it is likely that in their thousands of years of experience with fire the Indians would have learned as much as (if not more than) we know today about how meteorological, vegetational, and topographical factors interact to control the course of a fire.

If the forest fires were set in November or April, as stated in nearly all the early accounts, the soil would have been moist, since these months typically have increased precipitation in the Northeast. Furthermore, during these months very little or no water is being withdrawn from the soil by transpiring vegetation. Thus, a fire would have consumed only the dry grass and some or most of the dry leaves. Intense fires which destroy the organic soil layer or reach the tree crowns would not normally have occurred at these times of year.

Bodies of water such as streams, swamps, lakes, and rivers would have stopped a fire. Rocky ridges or hilltops, where grass and leaves would have been sparse, would also probably have stopped most fires in November or April. For these reasons, most fires probably would have been limited by natural factors to relatively small areas between streams and ridges. If the Indians used methods such as the one described by Martin, above, the areas burned could have been even smaller.

There has been some objection to the general assumption that the Indians' burning in the Northeast was of wide extent, although Raup did not consider the evidence of the early accounts cited by Bromley and Day, and Russell only attempted to call their validity into question. Neither writer produced a coherent theory as to how the pre-settlement landscape could have appeared as described without the agency of fire, particularly the extensive occurrence of grasslands and fire-resistant nut trees. The following parts of this section will indicate ways in which periodic burning of the forest would have benefited the Indians by shifting the species composition towards more food-producing plants and increasing their productivities at the same time. As will be shown, the benefits would have considerably outweighed the liabilities, thereby giving the Indians significant motivation to periodically burn the forests near their settlements.

In addition to the berries and nuts, there were also deer, bear, moose, small mammals, and fowl. All these animals have in common the fact that they depend on foods which are available on or near the ground level: seed from grasses and herbs (especially fowl), berries and shoots from shrubs, nuts from trees, and sprouts from trees (especially deer and moose). All of these foods would be more available in a periodically burned forest. Bendell included the northeastern mammal species of moose, white-tailed deer, black bear, beaver, and hare in his list of fire-followers; on the other hand, marten, squirrel, and fisher were included in his list of species displaced by fire. Of the birds, Bendell stated that turkey, pheasant, quail, grouse, and some water fowl would follow fire, while smaller birds would be displaced:

Many kinds of wildlife are adapted to living in environments created largely by fire. Some of the features of flammable forests and grasslands that may affect wildlife are much growth of vegetation on or near the ground; growth of trees and shrubs in open stands with thick, often stubby branches and twigs; large fruits, seeds, and nuts that may be retained on the plant and protected in serotinous cones or thick shells... Under these conditions we would expect birds and mammals that live as browsers and grazers. There should be a tendency for large size, for this is of advantage where there are large variations in local climate and for other reasons. Large wildlife are possible where they can feed from the ground and in shrubs and trees with open, strong branches. Thus, in fire forest there may be deer and spruce grouse. In relatively fireproof forest, such as hemlocks, there are birds... and mammals that are smaller in size. One is tempted to add another mammal to the list of fire forest species: the human hunter, since he is so closely associated with the other animals of the fire forest.

It would be perfectly natural for a human culture which depended heavily upon hunting and trapping, as did the Indians, to manipulate their environment so as to increase the number of large animals and birds. Larger targets would be easier to hit and would yield a higher return of food for each unit of energy expended in hunting and trapping. In this context, Bendell's thesis would indicate that the Indians should have burned their environment. The Indians, as well as all the other mammals and birds in the fire forest, would thereby have maximized their efficiency of food utilization according to the criteria of Bock and Lynch who found that larger birds (or mammals) are less active than smaller ones and therefore utilize food more efficiently, and that the unit weight of birds (or mammals) is greater on a burned forest site.

One fundamental reason for more efficient and greater food utilization on burned sites is that some of the nutrients which have been tied up in the organic biomass—as live and dead trees, fallen dead branches, and fallen leaves—are released by fire and then become available to other plants which produce fruits and shoots that are eaten by wildlife. Unburned oak-hickory forests in Tennessee and North Carolina have been shown to have amounts of nitrogen and calcium stored in the forest floor which are equal to or greater than the exchangeable amounts in the mineral soil. Low intensity fires would convert most of these nutrients to exchangeable forms after leaching from ash, and they would also oxidize some of the tannins in the oak and hickory leaves which are known to inhibit nitrification. However, some nutrients could be lost to groundwater or streamwater, particularly if burning occurred when the plants were not actively growing. From this point of view, burning in April would have been preferable to November.

Over the long term, controlled burning could reduce the thickness of the soil organic layer, thereby exposing the mineral soil to erosive forces, especially where vegetative cover is less and slopes are steep. On the other hand:

Low intensity fires which leave some litter and a large portion of the humus on the soil surface have little or no effect on surface runoff and erosion.... The most stable forest sites following logging and burning are on level terrain, have deep, well drained soils, have soils that are high in clay content, are on areas with low precipitation surplus, are seral forest types with a favorable growing season after treatment, and have a site history of periodic fires... Thus, it appears that low intensity fires on level or gently sloping sites in April would have significant benefits without harmful side effects. November burns would be less desirable because of potentially higher losses of nutrients to stream water, although in the absence of a thick, insulating layer of organic litter, the ground would tend to freeze earlier, thereby reducing water infiltration and leaching of nutrients. Increased availability of nutrients following fire would increase the productivities of all plants, especially those at or near ground level: little bluestem grassland productivity would increase 20%; blueberry (and presumably other shrubs) would increase production at least a similar amount. Tree productivity would also be increased. Although no studies were found on oak or hickory productivity following fire, one study on red and white pine showed an 18% increase in volume production after 20 years of controlled burning in Connecticut. But, since the Indians would have been interested chiefly in nut production, and since nut production does not necessarily follow trunk volume growth, other ways that fire might affect tree fruiting should be investigated.

Widely spaced trees with full, deep crowns are generally known to produce more fruit (nuts) than trees in closed canopy forest stands. By eliminating or reducing the fire-susceptible birches, maples, beech, hemlock, and weak individuals of other species burning would have created the open stands of oak, hickory, and chestnut of the early accounts. Trees of such an "oak-hickory savannah" (D. Olson, personal communication) would have had full, deep crowns for optimum nut production. Furthermore, the blackened soil would have absorbed heat in the daytime and re-radiated it at night which would have reduced spring frost damage to reproductive tissues: warm air temperatures in late April are known to be crucial to good acorn and hickory nut production. Burning would also have made available significant amounts of potassium, which is known to be very important to the nutrition of nut trees. Finally, scorching of the bark would probably have served the same purpose as partial girdling in blocking the downward translocation of carbohydrates, which is known to be a cause of increased fruiting in some trees.

The forest animals which were most important in the Indians' diet (e.g., deer, bear, moose, turkey) are all heavy consumers of mast when it is available. But these animals, as well as humans, experience intense competition from squirrels and other rodents, birds, insects, and fungi. Ahlgren and Ahlgren, Bendell, and Wright and Bailey stated that squirrels and other rodent populations are much lower in fire forest because removal of their cover (grass and shrubs for mice, voles, etc.) and escape routes (continuous tree canopy for squirrels) would make them more susceptible to predators. However, large nut-eating birds such as jays and crows would probably increase following fire. Some nut tree insect larvae which overwinter in the leaf litter would be destroyed by fire, particularly the hickory shuckworm, oak twig pruner, oak twig girdler, solitary oak leaf miner, and walnut curculio. Since fire would generally disfavor conditions for buildup of fungal inoculum, fallen nuts would probably be less affected in a fire forest. Smoke is also known to have an antimicrobial effect.

The animals that the Indians hunted heavily are all browsers as well as berry and mast-eaters. They all rely on large quantities of succulent grass, forb, and shrub shoots in the spring and early summer. In the fall and winter they require (deer especially) shrub and tree sprouts for browsing. Niering (personal communication) found that oak seedlings nearly doubled following burning, and hypothesized that persistent oak seedlings are stimulated by fire; Swan also found vigorous sprouting from stem-killed oak and northern hardwood saplings. Both Niering and Swan found increased production of succulent grasses and shrubs following fire. Furthermore, Wright and Bailey noted that the nutrient content of grasses, shrubs, and tree seedlings improves for several years following burns.

According to studies in Colorado and California, deer herds in burned forest are at least 2-4 times greater than those in unburned forest. Increased mast, browse, and better nutrient status of these foods have been indicated as the causes. Fire effects on bear, moose, or turkey have not been studied, nor have effects on total wildlife standing biomass been investigated.

It would appear likely that a sort of "coppice with standards" forest would result from less frequent burning. The grass species found on more frequently burned savannah sites would be displaced by tree sprouts and, eventually, saplings, while the overstory of large nut trees would remain. Such a coppice with standards stand was in fact described by an early explorer in Maine:

And surely it did all resemble a stately park, wherein appears some old trees with high withered tops, and other flourishing with living green boughs... the wood in most places, especially on the East side, very thinne, chiefly oke and some small young birch.

If allowed to grow out of the reach of deer, birch or other understory trees could eventually become a crop of fuelwood which could be killed by burning and then left to dry standing. Because of its susceptibility to fire, a birch understory would have been especially appropriate for this type of coppice with standards forestry. Furthermore, birch, like pine, would invade a disturbed site by seeding in from adjacent, undisturbed stands and quickly become established.

The importance of fuelwood to the Indian subsistence strategies has been well documented, although the actual means by which the Indians harvested the wood is unclear. Stone axes were available, but whether they were extensively used for felling and splitting is unknown. Considering the evidence produced by Niering et al., it seems likely that fire-susceptible species like black birch could have been allowed to grow in old fields or nut groves near the villages as indicated above. Fire killing would save the labor of felling and small fire-killed wood, once dried, could be broken into usable lengths by hand. Larger trees, whether fire susceptible or not, would be harder to kill by fire and would require extra labor with tools of questionable effectiveness and durability in order to produce usable-sized pieces of wood. In small to medium sized pole stands (10-20 cm diameter at breast height) of mixed species composition the nut trees would have developed fire resistance, while other trees would still be susceptible; a controlled burn in such a mixed stand would accomplish the dual objective of releasing the nut trees from competition and providing a supply of dead wood for fuel. Areas producing fuelwood as suggested above would have been but one more aspect of a very diverse landscape of fields in various stages of cultivation or fallow succession, plus forest stands variously affected by fire. Diversity would have been imposed by physical features of the environment as well as the Indians' manipulation of it. Since burning in November or April would normally have been somewhat hampered by wet ground conditions, individual burns are likely to have been of limited extent, because of natural water courses and because of seasonally moist soils which would have burned less than during summer or early fall. A soil series map would easily indicate the areas having soils with poor drainage which would be less likely to burn in November or April. Thus, a soils matrix overlain by a land use matrix could show a variety of types of vegetation in various stages of recovery from small burns. The increased diversity of plant species following fire would add another dimension to this picture of diversity.

These factors of diversity—different types of vegetative covers, different ages of covers, and complexity of species within a type of cover—are all regarded as desirable characteristics in wildlife habitat management. Not only do they provide an abundance of food and protection, they also provide different types of cover needed by birds and animals in their various life activities:

Generally a mosaic of seral and climax stages of vegetation that may be created by a series of fires over time in shrub and forest communities is the preferred habitat for the highest diversity and number of wildlife species. Such habitat provides maximum "edge" for feeding, escape, loafing, and nesting. Diversity and maximum edge would be natural results of periodic low-intensity fires, whereas no fire and high intensity fire would result in less diversity and edge. To conclude the discussion of the effects of controlled burning of the forest, several off-site effects require mention. First, any shift in species composition away from trees and toward grass would entail a loss of transpiring leaf surface area, and a consequent increase in water runoff. Second, the amount of nutrients in water leaving a controlled burned watershed will generally be slightly greater than from unburned controls; sediment loading of the streams may also be slightly higher. Effects on stream flora and fauna should be positive from slightly increased nutrient levels, but negative from slightly increased sedimentation. Third, the negative impact of smoke on air quality involves many complicated factors, but if a choice must be made between relatively frequent prescribed fires and infrequent wildfires (which eventually must occur if fuels are allowed to accumulate), then prescribed fires are preferable.

Discussion

The present day oak and white pine types of southern New England described by Bromley can also be found in southern New Hampshire, southern

Maine, New Jersey, southeastern New York, central New York, and eastern Pennsylvania. These types can be characterized as being fire resistant, but not fire adapted. The thick-barked black oak species and shagbark hickory (and in former times, American chestnut) are especially resistant. Bromley believed that in pre-settlement times the oak type also included most of the areas now covered by the pine type. Studies by Oosting and Little and Moore would tend to confirm Bromley's hypothesis: low-intensity fires tend to favor regeneration of oak and hickory and discriminate against pine. Thus, by the use of controlled burning, the Indians could have greatly expanded the extent of the areas that could have naturally tended toward the oak type.

Fire rotation times, or the length of time between fires, have been hypothesized for the oak and pine types:

... fires may have burned at intervals of 3 years or less on the drier forested sites, at 1-year intervals in the grasslands, and at long intervals—100 years or so—on the wetter forested sites, at which times severe fires could have developed during drought periods in certain types...

A three year fire rotation time in the oak-hickory savannah would probably have maintained the type indefinitely. Similarly, a one year fire rotation time would probably have maintained the grasslands indefinitely. If such were the case, the sequential agroforestry practices would not have been very significant in extent, except perhaps on some of the poorly drained grassland soils which might not actually have burned each year. Less frequent burning of the grasslands, or use of fire breaks as indicated by Martin, would have allowed for establishment of tree cover on old fields. In any case, berry production and large bird habitat would have been byproducts of the grass and/or tree-covered fallow fields.

Moist forest sites on long fire rotation times would have added edge and wildlife shelter to the landscape. These areas would have been refuges for the smaller birds and mammals which were not adapted to the grasslands or fire forest, and for larger birds and mammals in hot weather and during winters with deep snow. The hemlock-pine stands typical of these areas would have intercepted snowfall and allowed easier browsing. Areas with deep soils in moist areas would undoubtedly have grown some butternut or black walnut; nuts of the butternut were especially important to the diets of Indians in northern parts of the Northeast.

We will probably never know the actual extent of the fire-adapted oak-hickory savannahs and grasslands that the Indians created where the present day oak and pine types are now found, but their existence cannot be seriously doubted in light of the historical accounts and of modern research on the effects of fire on ecosystems. Periodic low intensity fires in November or April would have increased primary production of vegetable foods for humans and wildlife by 20-100% and would have concentrated the food production within easy feeding reach of large birds and mammals. Competition for these foods from rodents, insects, and fungi would have been reduced. Large birds and mammals (e.g., grouse and deer) would have increased 100 to 400% in the periodically burned forest. The Indians were doubtless very much aware of these beneficial effects of fire, and managed their environment accordingly.

The sustainability of the Indian agroforestry systems is of course open to question. But there seems to be no evidence that serious "leaks" would have developed, in the sense indicated by Harper:

Agriculture deliberately channels energy and mineral resources out of one area into another and in addition it commonly creates "leaks" in otherwise self-maintaining systems.

Since soil would have been exposed to erosive forces only following very infrequent severe burns, and since nutrient losses would have been minimal or non-existent, no leaks of these resources should have occurred. And, obviously, there would have been no inputs (losses) of fossil fuel energy in the form of fertilizers, herbicides, or machinery fuel. The only leaks would have been in the form of the food crops which the Indians harvested from their agro-ecosystems. it is interesting to note in this regard that historical records indicate that the Indian fields were able to produce crops of corn equal to or greater than the settlers' fields —without use of draft animals or plows; these same Indian fields also produced crops of beans and squash which the settlers' fields did not.

PROFILES OF IMPORTANT TBOS

Considered to be a species of high potential for oilseed production, jatropha is an ideal species for wasteland development programmes. It is a small tree of about 6.0 m height belonging to family Euphorbiaceae. Its natural distribution is in Mexico and the Amazon region. It has a short trunk with thick branches spreading into a crown of dark green leaves. The bark is pale brown and the leaves are attached to long petioles. Native to humid zones under arid and semi-arid conditions, jatropha thrives under a wide range of soil and climatic conditions. It grows under annual average rainfall of 480 mm to 2400 mm and its daily average temperature range is 20-28°C. It tolerates extreme temperature conditions as well. It is drought tolerant and can withstand slight frost. Jatropha can grow on almost any site, ranging from gravel, sandy to clayey soils. But its growth form is stunted in highly eroded soils of low fertility and in alkaline soils. It tolerates drought by shedding the leaves. This, however, results in decreased growth. It grows at altitudes ranging from sea level to 1000 m. Jatropha comes into flowering during September to December and fruits mature 2-4 months after flowering. However, in irrigated or high rainfall areas, a main harvest in October and a second harvest in March/April are possible.

Jatropha can be established with seeds or cuttings. Seeds can be sown directly at the onset of the rainy season or seedlings can be raised in polybags and transplanted. Branch cuttings grow vigorously when used as planting material. Cuttings of 45-100 cm in length and 3-4 cm in thickness taken from the base of the stem are the best for vegetative propagation. Plants raised from cuttings start bearing within one year whereas those propagated from seeds bear in 3-4 years. Canopy development by periodic pruning in the first three years is necessary to ensure high yields subsequently. Flowering occurs on one-year old branches. Therefore, after the tree enters the seed production phase, selective pruning must be done after harvesting the crop so that the new flush is mature enough to bear seeds during the next rainy season.

Apart from the use of seed oil for biodiesel production, parts of jatropha have several other uses. The latex, oil, twigs, wood and leaves have medicinal value. Leaves are used as a fumigant for bed bugs. Different parts of jatropha are also used as pesticides. There are reports of leaves being used as a feed for silkworms. A dye extracted from leaves and tender stems is used for colouring cloth and fishing nets. Tender foliage and oil cake of jatropha can be used as organic manure.

Pongamia Pinnata

Pongamia pinnata, belonging to family Leguminosae, was earlier known as *Derris indica* and *Pongamia glabra*. It is a nitrogen fixing tree that produces seeds containing 25-30% oil. It is often planted as an ornamental and shade tree. It is native to India and is receiving a widespread attention at present as a TBOS. Pongamia is a medium-sized tree that generally attains a height of about 8.0 m and a trunk diameter of more than 50 cm. The bark is thin, gray to grayish-brown, and yellow on the inside. The alternate, compound pinnate leaves consist of 5 or 7 leaflets which are arranged in 2 or 3 pairs, and a single terminal leaflet. Pods are elliptical, 3-6 cm long and 2-3 cm wide, thick walled, and usually contain a single seed. Seeds are 10-20 cm long, flat, oblong, and light brown in color.

Pongamia thrives in areas having an annual rainfall ranging from 500 to 2500 mm. In its natural habitat, the maximum temperature exceeds 38°C and the minimum can be as low as 1°C. Mature trees can withstand water logging and slight frost. This species grows in elevations of 1200 m, but in the Himalayan foothills it is not found above 600 m. It can grow on most soil types ranging from stony to sandy to clayey, including dry sands and saline soils. The natural distribution of this species is along coasts and river banks in India and Burma.

The average seed oil content is about 25%, but higher percentages are claimed nowadays because of its use for making biodiesel. The oil is thick and yellow-orange to brown in colour. Traditionally, besides the cooking and lighting uses in rural areas, it was used as a lubricant, water-paint binder, pesticide, and in soap making and tanning industries. The oil is known to have value in folk medicine for the treatment of rheumatism as well as human and animal skin diseases. Wood is beautifully grained and medium to coarse textured, but is not durable as it is susceptible to insect attack and tends to split when sawn. Therefore, it is used as fuelwood and cheap timber. The leaves are not readily eaten by animals, but it has some fodder value in dry areas. Leaves are also used as insect repellent in stored grains. The oilcake has use as poultry feed and also as manure with nematicidal value.

Azadirachta Indica

Azadirachta indica (neem) of family Meliaceae is native to dry forests of South and Southeast Asia. It has been receiving wide publicity because of the pesticidal properties of azadirachtin and other such constituents in its seeds. Neem can also fit into agroforestry systems as it is a multipurpose tree. It is a medium to large tree of about 20 m height. It can grow on a wide range of soils and climatic conditions. Neem grows on all types of soils, but prefers deep clay soils. It can survive on acidic soils as well as those having pH of 10. The temperature range in its native range is between 15-45°C. Best growth of neem is found in areas receiving 750-1000 mm annual rainfall. In India, it grows in tropical dry areas up to an elevation of 1200 m. Neem seed has a very low period of viability and has to be sown within a month after harvest. Stump planting is the best method for neem establishment.

Neem leaves also contain the compounds found in the seed, but their concentration is very low. Therefore, the tree is not totally free of pests. Neem trees usually flower in April and the fruits mature 2-3 months later. The kernel contains about 30-40% oil, which has the same range of uses as that from other TBOS. The seed cakes can also be used as manure. Recent advances in processing technologies can remove the bitter constituents in oil and seedcake and thereby widen their uses. The wood is strong and can be used for furniture, implements and construction. Seed, leaves, bark and fruit pulp have medicinal properties.

Madhuca Species

Madhuca longifolia and *Madhuca indica* belong to family Sapotaceae and are native to India. Although their seed oil is considered to be non-edible, they are used for cooking in tribal areas. The trees are generally decidous, light demanding and reach a height of up to 18 m and a diameter at breast height of 80 cm. The bark is grey to black with vertical cracks. Leaves are oblong shaped with a pinkish tinge and have a wooly underneath. Flowers are pale yellow and the flesh of the fruits is juicy. Fruits are 3-5 cm long and contain 1-4 seeds. Commonly found in dry tropical and sub-tropical regions, mahua is found in areas receiving annual rainfall of 550 to 1500 mm. The temperature extremes it can tolerate are 2-46°C. It can grow in elevations up to 1200 m. This species requires deep loamy or sandy loamy soil with good drainage. It also grows well on shallow, clay and calcareous soil.

Besides the use of oil for cooking, fresh leaves of mahua are eaten as a salad and its ripe fruits are used for fermenting liquor. During periods of fodder scarcity, the foliage is used as fodder. Seeds contain 20-50% oil and the seed cake has use as manure. Mahua oil is also used by rural communities for protection against storage pests. Almost all the parts of mahua tree have medicinal properties. Its reddish brown hardwood is strong and durable, and is used as timber.

Calophyllum Inophyllum

Calophyllum inophyllum is a medium-sized tree that sometimes reaches more than 25 m tall and up to 150 cm in diameter. It is a species for coastal environment. It thrives in areas having an annual rainfall of 750-5000 mm. In its natural habitat, the temperature rang is 7-48°C. This species grows at elevations up to 200 m. Calopyllum is sensitive to frost and fire. It prefers deep soils near the coast and can thrive even on pure sand. Its leaves are elliptical, thick, smooth and polished. Fruits are spherical to ovoid, greyish-green in colour and smooth skinned. Seeds have large cotyledons and the oil content of dry kernels is about 70%.

The fruit is edible; usually it is pickled but care must be taken as it contains toxins. The strong and durable wood is used for boat building, railway sleepers, implements, instruments and construction. Oil has medicinal uses in treating rheumatism, ulcers and skin diseases. The latex is used internally against diarrhoea and externally against skin and eye diseases. Leaves, flowers and seeds are sometimes also used in local medicine.

PRODUCTION POTENTIAL OF KEY TBOS

Promotional efforts make out jatropha to be a wonder crop. Not all the information circulated to highlight its merits is based on hard evidence or actual field observations. Common beliefs, distorted claims and wishful thinking are all part of the information dissemination that jatropha is presently going through. Jatropha can be a success only if its potential is realised as an oilseed crop. The experiences of many who make unrealistic claims are based on observations of jatropha as a plant and not in a cropping situation. Highlighting the advantages of pongamia over jatropha, its proponents present a strong case for this species to be the mainstay for TBO production in the country. Apart from its merit as an indigenous nitrogen-fixing tree, it has certain other favourable traits such as tolerance to waterlogging. However, as in the case of jatropha, not all what is presented can be taken at face value as some of the claims are yet to be substantiated. A few years back neem received the same type of publicity that jatropha is receiving at present. The validity of the claims pertaining to these species is discussed below.

Hardy Species

It is common knowledge that jatropha is a hardy species that can survive under extremely harsh environmental conditions with little or no external inputs and management. Similarly, pongamia survives under exceedingly dry conditions and often appears luxuriant even under the most stressful condition. But mere survival is not what is expected of a crop when it is cultivated for oilseed production. In most farms where it is grown for livefencing, jatropha is planted as a single row. Pongamia and neem grow as scattered single trees or in small patches that probably are better in soil conditions than the neighbouring areas. The presence of trees in a very low population density or growing wild do not necessarily indicate their ability to survive anywhere. Moreover, the hardiness of a species can be ascertained only when it produces repeated high yields for which it is grown. Without evaluating the productivity of these species as plantation crops in diverse agro-climatic conditions for a few years, they cannot be concluded to be hardy species.

Planting Material

The rapid rise in the interest to grow jatropha and pongamia has created a huge demand for seed, seedlings and vegetative propagules. A natural extension of this demand is the emergence of planting material suppliers who claim to have elite varieties of these species. It is not known whether these so-called varieties have undergone performance testing anywhere. The difference in performance observed among three genotypes of jatropha (BAIF, unpublished). Although the local genotype outperformed the others, its superiority can be confirmed only if this performance is repeated in many locations over a period of time. Seed oil content is another parameter about which inflated claims are made. Generally, oil content of jatropha kernel is around 25%, but some researchers have reported twice as much oil in seed collections from natural stands. It is too early to say whether such high oil contents can be achieved in large-scale cultivation. Moreover, oil content by itself is not of value unless it is associated with high yield of seed.

Another issue for consideration is the use of vegetative propagules as planting material. There are nurseries that sell propagules at exorbitant rates with the promise that they will come into seed production early. It is an established fact that propagules from cuttings or grafts of any species start bearing early and show uniform growth. Vegetative propagation has been very successful in plantation crops like tea and rubber, but the recommended clones of those species have undergone testing for long periods under biotic and abiotic stresses. The suitability of vegetative propagules for establishing plantations of TBOS is untested. Until studies are conducted on this aspect, seedlings that have the tap root system may be a safer option for wastelands than propagules with adventitious roots.

Seed and Oil Yield

The most appealing aspect of jatropha for unsuspecting growers is the claim of promoters that a seed yield can be had in the first year itself and eventually when the trees mature in 3-4 years, the yield can be as high as 8.0-10 tons per ha per year. These are highly optimistic projections. Although it is a perennial, jatropha starts flowering in the first year itself and may produce some seeds. Harvesting these seeds is undesirable because the priority for the first three years of establishment of a commercial plantation is to develop the tree canopy. This is achieved by periodic pruning and thinning of branches. During this juvenile phase, flowers that appear should be removed at the bud stage so that vegetative growth continues unaffected. Thus, the information circulated with regard to the time of first commercial harvest and the seed yield at maturity is not unrealistic.

Similarly, yield and age at first seed harvest projected for pongamia are also disputable. Seed production of pongamia will be small for at least six years. There are claims that each pongamia tree will yield a minimum of 20 kg and the per ha production will be more than 10 t. These are highly optimistic expectations and will require fertile land with irrigation and high levels of nutrient application, negating the argument for production of oilseeds on wastelands.

Seed oil content is another parameter about which misleading data is in circulation. There are some claims of more than 50% oil and the economics of production are calculated accordingly. It does not appear that there are varieties or genotypes that can yield such high levels of seed oil when cultivated commercially. Under certain conditions or certain genotypes may be having such levels of seed oil content, but their seed yield may be low. Therefore, seed oil produced per unit area of land, which combines both seed yield and seed oil content, is a more useful indicator of productivity of TBOS.

Inputs

The belief that jatropha, pongamia and other TBOS grow with little or no inputs is also a popular perception and does not apply to commercial cultivation. Repeated harvest of seed in substantial quantities will drain the soil as well as the plant of nutrients and moisture. Unless these are replenished through fertiliser or manure application, seed production cannot continue. Like other crops, these species will also require water to grow and be productive. The seedlings will require irrigation during the first two years in the field. Thereafter, once the root system grows deep and establishes well, it will be able to make use of water held in lower layers of soil. If the water holding capacity of the soil is low, regular irrigation will be necessary for regular seed harvests to be obtained. If the goal is to produce seed on a commercial scale, input supply has to match the crop requirements. Such requirements are usually much higher for trees grown for the purpose of production than those serving the function of live fencing.

Multipurpose Use

All the TBOS are multipurpose in their utility, making them what is desired for agroforestry systems. However, caution is necessary in assessing whether all the uses will be realised at the same time. For example, jatropha has several other uses besides the seed oil. Almost all its parts have medicinal properties and are used in native medicinal preparations. Extracts of its bark can be made into a wax. Tannin or dye can be extracted from leaf and root of jatropha. These characteristics are projected as additional benefits from the multipurpose jatropha tree. In reality, if plant parts are harvested for other purposes, seed yield will be adversely affected. Therefore, commercial cultivation should focus on the seed; periodically pruned branches and fallen leaf litter should be considered as by-products from the jatropha plant. In addition, others like oilseed cake and glycerol will be obtained as by-products of seed processing.

Productive Lifespan

The lifespan of jatropha, according to most literature, is 40-50 years and that of pongamia is more than 80 years. It is possible that trees of these species can survive this long when regular harvests are not taken from them. Growing them as commercial plantation crops will result in regular harvest of seed. In addition, there will be growth stimulation in the form of periodic pruning and application of fertilisers or manures. All these practices will make the tree weaker. Experience with plantation crops like tea and rubber show that even if the trees survive, beyond a particular stage their productivity will decline to such an extent that it will not be economical to retain them. Therefore, it is safer to assume the productive life for jatropha and pongamia to be about 20-30 years.

The foregoing paragraphs clearly show that there are inaccuracies in the information being publicised. The beliefs or claims about jatropha and the actual or likely situation. This is also applicable to other TBOS, particularly pongamia and neem.

PRODUCTION POTENTIAL

Realistic Goals

The manner in which TBO production is promoted at present with exaggerated claims is fraught with the possibility of growers losing interest if the very high expectations are not realised. This has happened in other crops in the past. It is not that these crops failed altogether, but their potential was blown out of proportion and farmers were unhappy with what they eventually realised. Even jatropha went through such an experience when farmers discontinued its commercial cultivation in Maharashtra a few years ago. However, the current situation and the purpose for which it is promoted are totally different, so the chances of its success are greater this time around.

Information to set realistic production targets for TBOS is scanty, but approximate figures are possible for jatropha. Intensive jatropha production on good agricultural land with drip irrigation, high levels of fertilisers or manures and adoption of management practices such as regular pruning may yield 5.0 t per ha or more. However, a farmer getting into jatropha production cannot start off with an expectation of 5.0 t per ha or more. Plantations of this intensive category have been established in recent years, but they are mostly still in their juvenile stage and actual production data is unavailable at present. The other extreme is a below-average land that is managed less intensively to yield about 1.0 t per ha. This level of yield does not hold out much promise for a prospective grower to enter into TBO production. In between these two extremes is the production under average conditions of soil fertility and management. With presently available planting material and technology package, a modest target that has a high probability of attainment is 2.0 t per ha. Therefore, the short to medium-term oilseed production strategy has to target a potential yield of 2.0 t per ha on land of average to marginal productivity.

Although popular literature claims a seed yield advantage of more than 50% for pongamia over jatropha, in the absence of hard evidence, the yield levels of both species have to be assumed to be almost the same. In terms of suitability for agroforestry with annual crops, jatropha with its sparse canopy appears to be more suited. It also responds well to training of the canopy by trimming and pruning (Banerjee, 1989). If the system is a combination of perennials, pongamia is likely to fit in better.

Tbos-Based Agroforestry Systems

The success of any agroforestry system depends to a great extent on the compatibility among the component species. In situations where jatropha or pongamia grows on farmland, a negative effect on the growth of crops growing nearby can be seen. This may not be apparent during the first five years, but becomes pronounced with time. This may be partly overcome in mature trees by canopy management practices like pruning. Studies conducted at BAIF to examine the suitability of jatropha for agroforestry purposes showed that the yield reduction on horse gram and finger millet was negligible during the first four years. In fact, the annual crops seemed to benefit from the sheltering effect of jatropha when there were strong dry winds.

Agroforestry systems can be in the form of:

- Scattered trees,
- Rows or strips of trees and
- Trees in border rows or strips. The ratio of trees to crops in the system can be determined by adjusting the spacing between the trees as well as spacing between rows or strips. The present practice of a single row of jatropha livefencing can be extended to a strip of 3.0-5.0 m. This strip can accommodate 2-3 rows of jatropha or a single row of pongamia. This would effectively mean devoting up to 20% of land to the tree component. This arrangement will take up relatively less land for the tree species while the protection function of the livefence will be strengthened. The outcome of this arrangement would be a loss of about 25% in the yield of the crops in the middle of the field while the fence produces oilseed. Farmers may not opt for this system if the land is fertile because the loss in crop production is unlikely to be compensated by the TBOS in the fence. On the other hand, it can be a favourable alternative for lands where crop yields are low and less reliable.

The other two systems, scattered trees and strips within the cropping area, are also unsuitable for fertile lands because the trees can reduce the crop yields. On such lands, fruit trees may be acceptable as the produce is of high value. But the returns from TBOS are unattractive for farmers to forego existing crops that are proven and more remunerative. Depending upon the fertility, a suitable tree:crop ratio can be decided upon and the tree spacing can be arrived at. If the tree proportion in the system is assumed to be 50%, the jatropha yield, as discussed earlier for average production conditions, will be about 1.0 t per ha. This translates to an income of Rs. 10,000 per ha (2000 kg per ha at the rate of Rs. 5 per kg of seed), which is not appealing enough to attract growers in large numbers. But it is also a fact that present returns from vast areas of wastelands in the country are lower than this amount. Most of these lands belong to small marginal farmers in dry areas who routinely take up cultivation of some crop during the rainy season. Jatropha and pongamia are suitable options for them. There are others who raise crops on a part of their land while the less fertile part usually remains barren. Such land can be brought under TBOS as it requires very little management after establishment and will not be a constraint on farmer's time and resources.

Concluding Remarks

Presently, tree-borne oilseed species, jatropha in particular, find themselves in a rare situation where several factors are in their favour. Those of significance are: the record high prices of petroleum products and the rapid depletion of their global reserves; worsening environmental problems and the emerging stringency in the emission standards of fast-growing economies; the expanse of degraded barren land in India that has to be brought under vegetation for the future common good; an opportunity to earn carbon credits through Clean Development Mechanism while creating rural employment and a non-conventional energy system. Opportunities such as this with so many factors in favour do not come up that often.

Considering the prevailing favourable situation, the biodiesel programme based on TBOS should not be allowed to falter at this stage. A lot is heard about government programmes for their promotion, but there appears to be a lull at implementation level. The non-government efforts tend to be driven by overly optimistic or deliberately exaggerated production levels. TBOS can succeed if promoted through a systematic programme with realistic targets.

AGROFORESTRY PRACTICES AND TECHNOLOGIES

A further evaluation of the organization of these various agroforestry systems shows that an agroforestry system involves extensive application of agroforestry practices, thus forming a significant form of land use in a locality or area, described according to the system's biological composition and arrangement, level of technical management, or socio-economic features. An agroforestry practice, on the other hand, denotes a specific agroforestry combination in a land-management unit, and consists usually of arrangements of agroforestry components in space and/or time. Several such practices are involved in the constitution and maintenance of an agroforestry system.

Although several agroforestry systems have been recorded from around the world, the distinctive agroforestry practices that constitute these systems in various ecoregions and locations are few in number.

The scale of management and extent of adoption of these different practices in any particular system will vary considerably depending upon a number of factors. Any of these practices can become an agroforestry system when it is developed or spread to such an extent in a specific local area so as to form a distinct land utilization type in that area. One essential point to note here is that an agroforestry practice can be found to exist even in a non-agroforestry land-use system. An example is the practice of growing rows of *Sesbania grandiflora* on the bunds of rice paddies in Java, Indonesia. This woody species is harvested for its leaves as green manure, its flowers are eaten as a vegetable, it provides firewood and it adds to the fertility of the soil underneath through biological fixation of atmospheric nitrogen. Thus the woody species interacts ecologically and economically with the crop (rice) production system; in other words, it is an *agroforestry practice* in a crop production system.

Another term that is commonly used in all land use systems including agroforestry is 'technology'; it is usually used in combination with a particular production system or land-use system as the prefix; thus, agricultural technology, wood production technology, agroforestry technology, and so on. The word or suffix 'technology' in this sense indicates an improvement or innovation, usually through scientific intervention, that can be applied with advantage in the management of the system or practice concerned. The inputs that are used for developing such technologies can sometimes be the most significant aspects, and these are called input technologies; e.g., improved varieties of plants, agrochemicals, and so on.

ECOLOGICAL SPREAD OF MAJOR AGROFORESTRY SYSTEMS

Ecological Zones of Agroforestry Significance in the Tropics and Subtropics

The major physical parameters that determine the ecology of a location in the tropics are rainfall (quantity and distribution) and temperature regimes. Altitude also is important because of its influence not only on temperature, but also on land relief characteristics. The FAO Agro-Ecological Zones inventory divides tropics into 'warm', 'moderately cool', 'cool' and 'cold' climates depending on the climatic (mainly temperature) regime during the 'growing period'. These growing periods refer to a few selected agricultural crops (that are seasonal) and therefore do not necessarily reflect the growing periods of perennial species (although it can be argued that the agricultural growing period represents the peak growing seasons of the perennial species also in most cases).

Agroforestry Systems in Lowland Humid and Sub-Humid Tropics

Characterized by hot, humid climates for all or most of the year, and an evergreen or semi-evergreen vegetation, the lowland humid and sub- humid tropics (but referred to as humid tropics) is by far the most important ecological region in terms of the total human population it supports, extent of area and diversity of agroforestry and other land-use systems. Because of the climatic conditions that favour rapid growth of a large number of plant species, various types of agroforestry plant associations can be found in areas with high human population. Various forms of homegardens, plantation crop combinations, and multilayer tree gardens are common in such regions. In areas with low population density, such as the low selvas of Latin America, trees on rangelands and pastures, other silvopastoral systems, improved fallow in shifting cultivation areas, multipurpose tree woodlots, etc., are the major agroforestry systems.

The lowland humid tropics also represents areas under natural rain forests. In such areas, cutting of rain forest at rates much faster than natural or managed regeneration is a common problem. This causes shortening of fallow periods in shifting cultivation cycles and resultant loss of soil productivity and accelerated soil erosion. The potential of appropriate agroforestry systems to combat these problems needs to be exploited in future land-use strategies in this zone.

AGROFORESTRY SYSTEMS IN SEMI-ARID AND ARID TROPICS

Extending over the savanna and Sudano-Sahelian zones of Africa, the cerrado of South America and large areas of the Indian subcontinent, the semi-arid and arid tropics are characterized by one or two wet seasons (Köppen Aw or Aw", respectively) and at least one long dry season. Drought is a hazard in the drier parts of the zone. The main agroforestry systems in this zone also depend on the human population pressure; homegardens and multilayer tree gardens are common in the wetter areas with high population pressure.

But generally speaking, the predominant agroforestry systems in this zone are:

- Various forms of silvopastoral systems;
- Windbreaks and shelterbelts; and
- Multipurpose trees on crop lands, notably *Acacia albida*-based systems in Africa and *Prosopis*-based agrisilvicultural systems in the Indian sub-continent.

Fuelwood shortage is a major problem in most parts of the semi- arid and arid tropics. Agroforestry potentials in fuelwood production are well documented (e.g., Nair, forthcoming). Similarly, desertification and fodder shortage — the other major ecological problems in this zone — could be tackled to some extent through the agroforestry approach.

AGROFORESTRY SYSTEMS IN TROPICAL HIGHLANDS

Approximately 20% of the tropical lands are at elevations from 900 to 1800 m, in about half of the Andean highlands of Central and South America, parts of Venezuela and Brazil, the mountain regions of the Caribbean, many parts of East and Central Africa, the Cameroons, the Deccan Plateau of India and some parts of the southeast Asia mainland. The altitude exceeds 1800 m in about 3% of the tropical area in the Andes, the Ethiopian and Kenyan Highlands, northern Burma and parts of Papua New Guinea. In the subtropical regions, the most important highlands are in the Himalayan region. These highland tropics with significant agroforestry potential are humid or sub-humid, such areas with dry climates being of very low potential.

Land-use problems in the highlands are similar to those in humid or dry lowlands depending on the climate, with the addition that sloping lands and steep terrains make soil erosion an issue of major concern. Moreover, annual temperatures are low in the highlands (for every 100 m increase in elevation in the tropics, there is a decline of 0.6°DC in the mean annual temperature), which affect the growth of certain lowland tropical species.

The main agroforestry systems in tropical highlands are:

- Production systems involving plantation crops such as coffee and tea in commercial as well as smallholder systems;
- Use of woody perennials in soil conservation and soil fertility maintenance;

- Improved fallows; and
- Silvopastoral combinations.

Agro-Ecological Analysis of Existing Agroforestry Systems

The existence of an agroforestry system or practice in a particular area is determined not only by the environmental and agro-ecological factors, but also by socio-economic considerations. In different areas with identical agroclimatic conditions, factors such as human population pressure, availability of labour and other production resources, proximity and accessibility to market sources, etc., are the main determinants of the types and forms of agroforestry systems. Even in the case of systems that are widespread in most ecological and geographical regions such as shifting cultivation and taungya, these systems have very many variants that are specific to certain defined situations. As a general rule, it can be said that while the ecological factors determine the major type of an agroforestry system in a given locality, the complexity of the system and the degree of intensity of its management increase in direct proportion to the population intensity and land productivity of the area. A typical example is the spread of the multi-species, multi-storied homegarden systems. Though found mostly in humid lowlands, the home-gardens are common in pockets of high population density in other ecological regions also. Analysing the structural and functional aspects 10 selected homegarden systems from different ecological regions, Fernandes and Nair (1986) found that although the average size of the homegarden units is less than 0.5 ha, the units are composed of a large number of woody and herbaceous species, carefully structured to form 3-5 vertical canopy strata, and each component having a specific place as well as function in the multispecies complex.

There are some functional aspects of specific agroforestry practices that are emphasized or necessitated in specific agroecological situations. For example, the functional emphasis of agroforestry systems in sloping lands is erosion control and soil conservation; in wind-prone areas, woody species are successfully used in agroforestry practices of shelterbelts and windbreaks; the emphasis is on fuelwood production in areas with fuelwood shortage; there are also specific agroforestry approaches for the reclamation of degraded lands and other waste lands (such as highly eroded lands, areas with high levels of salinity or alkalinity, etc.)

The ecological potential of an area is undoubtedly the prime factor that decides the adoption and spread of specific agroforestry systems in different parts. The preponderance of homegardens and other multi-species mixes in fertile lowlands and high potential areas at one end of the ecological scale and extensive silvopastoralism at the other end, with various systems in between gives a spectrum of agroecological adaptability and spread of various agroforestry systems. The general pattern of the major agroforestry systems in various ecological regions. It does not include all agroforestry systems, nor does it fully portray the relative spread (in terms of areas involved) or the level of management of the various systems. A further step in this direction is to indicate the major known areas of concentration of important agroforestry systems in the tropics and subtropics, i.e., something like a 'map of the agroforestry situation in the tropics and subtropics'.

This 'map' represents areas with relative abundance of specified agroforestry systems, but does not identify localized systems as well as systems whose presence is relatively less significant in an area. For example, as mentioned earlier, 'multipurpose trees on farmlands' can be found in almost all ecological and geographical regions. But there are only a few such systems that make them distinctly unique agroforestry systems. Examples include the arid zone systems involving *Acacia albida* and *Prosopis*. Thus, only some such 'multipurpose trees on farmlands' systems have been studied and/or described in some detail, and thus gone into ICRAF's Agroforestry Systems Inventory (AFSI) data records. The mention of the existence of any of these systems, therefore is mainly an indication that AFSI records are available. Indeed, innumerable location-specific agroforestry systems and practices do exist all over the tropics and subtropics and many of them are important in various ways. But most of them may not often be significant enough in terms of their individual importance in the overall economy and land-use pattern of the area where they exist, and thus may not merit a special mention on such a condensed and abstract global map.

BENEFITS OF AGROFORESTRY SYSTEM

- Environmental benefits
  - Reduction of pressure on natural forests.
  - More efficient recycling of nutrients by deep rooted trees on the site
  - Better protection of ecological systems
  - Reduction of surface run-off, nutrient leaching and soil erosion through impeding effect of tree roots and stems on these processes
  - Improvement of microclimate, such as lowering of soil surface temperature and reduction of evaporation of soil moisture through a combination of mulching and shading
  - Increment in soil nutrients through addition and decomposition of litterfall.
  - Improvement of soil structure through the constant addition of organic matter from decomposed litter.
- Economic benefits
  - Increment in an outputs of food, fuel wood, fodder, fertiliser and timber;

  - Reduction in incidence of total crop failure, which is common to single cropping or monoculture systems
  - Increase in levels of farm income due to improved and sustained productivity
- Social benefits
  - Improvement in rural living standards from sustained employment and higher income
  - Improvement in nutrition and health due to increased quality and diversity of food outputs
  - Stabilization and improvement of communities through elimination of the need to shift sites of farm activities.

5

Sustainable Watershed Management

WATERSHED DEVELOPMENT PROGRAMME (WDP) IN INDIA

A primary reason in favour of Watershed-Based Development in rain-fed region is the enormous cost of major water projects like the under-construction Narmada river-valley project. Hence the Govt. of India lays emphasis on augmenting water resources through small and decentralised projects like the watersheds. In India watershed projects have been undertaken under six major national programmes, *viz.* Drought-Prone Area Programme (DPAP), Desert Development Programme (DDP), National Watershed Development Project for Rainfed Area (NWDPRA), Watershed Development in Shifting Cultivation Areas (WDSCA), Integrated Watershed Development Project (IWDP) and Employment Assurance Scheme (EAS) etc. by three Central Ministries of Govt. of India namely, Ministry of Rural Development (MoRD), Ministry of Agriculture (MoA) Ministry of and Environment and Forestry (MoEF). Significantly, 70 per cent of funds for watershed development in the country are being spent under these six major programmes. In 1999 a common approach was evolved for undertaking of WDP in India.

Several evaluation studies have been undertaken to assess the impact of WDP in rain-fed regions of India. Most of these evaluation studies conducted till date, are based on econometric analysis as baseline information is often very difficult to obtain from the project implementing agency or the funding agency without which meaningful evaluation is impossible. The present study attempts to use tools of Geomatics in consonance with conventional techniques of field survey, soil and water analysis and socio-economic survey for creating baseline information of pre-project period and evaluation of post-project scenario.

INVESTMENTS IN WATERSHED MANAGEMENT

Watershed management seeks to make the best use of soil, water, and vegetation within the constraints of a watershed's agroclimatic and topographic conditions to strengthen the natural resource base (soil, vegetation cover) and to increase agriculture productivity, thereby improving peoples' livelihoods. Watershed management strategies vary. For example, in dry areas, increasing water availability raises potential returns, making the land more attractive to investment; in areas with short, intense rainy seasons, watershed management harvests water in surface reservoirs; and in areas with excess moisture, facilitating safe run-off through contour plowing or drainage systems reduces waterlogging and erosion. New modeling tools coupled with more precise spatial and temporal impacts of land cover and land-use changes on water flows are providing new information to guide managers and policy makers. Investments in technology, social institutions, and markets are frequently needed to maximize the impact of improved watershed management.

Technical investments. Soil conservation, water harvesting, increasing vegetative cover, and safe disposal of excess water are basic watershed management technologies. In dry areas the focus is on water harvesting (capturing rainfall otherwise lost to run-off), whereas in wet areas it is disposal of excess water. In many upland watersheds in seasonally water-scarce areas, upper catchments are often degraded lands used for grazing, gathering firewood, or cultivation (often on unproductive plots). Lower watershed areas typically contain better agricultural land. Harvesting water from the upper catchment areas makes it available for irrigation and other uses downstream.

Social institutions. At the community and national levels, watershed management improvements rely on the development of social institutions for the resource user groups for water, forests, and land, as these groups are key to most watershed programs. The groups also represent social capital formation that can have wide applicability in empowering rural people, enabling them to undertake additional development activities. Such groups must often deal with problems of unequal distribution of benefits in which downstream land users benefit at the expense of upstream land users.

Investment in markets. Sustainable watershed development relies on well-developed markets to give farmers incentives to invest in sustainable production systems, facilitate access to inputs, and increase agricultural productivity. Increasing productivity and decreasing marketing costs lead to increased profitability, which reduces the need for farmers to expand into marginal areas, such as steep slopes. Where market access is poor, watershed projects may need to invest in infrastructure and communications systems to improve access to input and output markets.

WATER REQUIREMENT OF DIFFERENT CROPS

Climate, soil and water are the three basic resources which determine the nature of crops that can be grown successfully in a particular region. An efficient utilisation of these resources is essential for optimum production of food and fibre for human life, feed for cattle and raw materials for industry. Climate determines the suitability of a region as a habitat for different flora and fauna, also the availability of water for production of Crops and other uses.

Under a given set of environmental conditions production of crops is limited by the availability of nutrients and water. Soil provides anchorage for the plants and serves as a reservoir of water and nutrient required by them. Chemical fertilizer can supplement nutrients to poor soil, but there is no substitute of water for production of crops. As the resources are limited an efficient management is of utmost importance for sustaining and increasing agricultural production.

Competing demands of water for domestic use, sanitation, industrial and recreational purposes makes it more essential to maximize the efficiency of water for agricultural production.

Agriculture consumes the largest amount of available water, yet, it uses water less efficiently. If food crisis is to be solved, there is no other alternative than to increase area under irrigation which can be made possible only when we use our present water resources most judiciously for irrigating our agricultural crops.

SOIL, PLANT AND WATER

Soil acts as a reservoir of water for the plants to use through root zone system. When rainfall is inadequate or untimely, application of irrigation water becomes essential for successful growth of crops. The factors influencing plant growth and productivity may be grouped as follows.

Soil Factors

The major soil factors are: soil moisture, texture, structure, density, salinity, fertility, aeration, temperature and drainage.

Plant Factors

The major plant factors are: types of crops, density and depth of rooting, rate of root growth, aerodynamic roughness of the crop, drought tolerance and varietal effects.

Climate Factors

The climatic factors are: sunshine, temperature, humidity, wind and rainfall.

Miscellaneous Factors

Some of the major miscellaneous factors are: soil volume, plant spacing, crop and soil management.

Water is retained around the soil particles and in capillary pores by the forces arising out of surface tension and presence of salts. A plant has to overcome retentive forces to absorb water; from the soil. The upper limit of water retention is limited to the field capacity of the soil. Any amount of water added to soil in excess of field capacity is not going to be retained in the root zone of the crop. When the soil texture is more of the clay content, the field capacity value increases. Time required for draining of the excess water also depends on soil texture. When the amount of water is reduced to a permanent wilting point, at this point or below plants can no longer absorb water and survive. The moisture content between field capacity and permanent wilting point is known as available soil moisture regime for plant growth. Humid conditions enables plants to draw soil moisture almost up to the permanent wilting point. On the other hand in hot and dry conditions, plants may show wilting symptoms in spite of enough available water present in the root zone.

Plants use only about 5 per cent of the total water absorbed for physiological functioning. Most of the water is lost in transpiration and, therefore, it has to be replaced. Water absorption, conduction, translocation and water loss through transpiration are some of the main processes in plant growth. Water absorption by roots is dependent on the supply of water at the root surface and growth of roots in the soil mass. As the soil dries from saturated state, the rate of water movement in the soil decreases rapidly. The root system must expand continuously to provide the plant with sufficient water to replace the transpiration losses through the leaves. The internal water balance in a plant depends on the relative rates of water absorption and loss.

Water stress whether mild, moderate or severe can affect photosynthesis, respiration, growth and reproduction of plant. Water stress at certain critical stages causes more injury to plant growth and productivity. Some plants survive water stress owing to their drought resistant qualities.

Since field capacity and wilting percentage are peculiar to soils, water absorption may be effectively controlled by adopting an effective root zone. Shallow rooted plants like paddy and potato require frequent water application than moderately deep and very deep rooted crops such as wheat, groundnut, maize, sorghum, cotton and sugarcane. Moisture is extracted to a larger extent from the first quarter of the root zone than others. Transpiration is the process by which water vapour from plant leaves enters the atmosphere. Though it is essentially a process of evaporation, it is different from the latter in several aspects. Evaporation from leaves meets with considerable amount of resistance like an open surface.

Evapo-transpiration (ET) is the quantity of water transpired by the plants during their growth, or retained in the plant tissues, plus the moisture evaporated from the surface of the soil and vegetation, *i.e.*, the amount of water between field capacity and wilting point within the root zone become available for ET. This is nothing but the consumptive use (CU) of water by the plants, because water used for metabolic activities is very insignificant (less than 1 per cent of En and, therefore, it denotes use for losses due to ET. Under field conditions, solar radiation supplies the energy for ET process. Wind is also important in removing water vapour from the field.

USE OF WATER BY PLANTS

The kind and the extent of various plant roots largely determine the amount of water required at each irrigation. Roots usually; represent one half or even more of the total weight of the plants.

Water is absorbed mainly through root hairs of the roots near the terminal portion. Root hairs are usually very minute and they can not be seen by naked eye. Several hundred of root hairs may be located on a square millimeter of the root surface. With rapid root growth larger number of root hairs are sent into small soil capillaries and crevices between soil particles contacting and absorbing soil water.

After absorption by the roots, the water moves up the stem of the plant and into the leaves where it is given off as vapour. This loss of water is controlled to a limited extent by openings (stomata) in the leaves. The stomata are capable of opening and closing. There is very close relationship in the opening of stomata, transpiration rate and the soil moisture condition.

WATER REQUIREMENT OF CROPS

The Water Requirement (WR) of crops depends upon retention and transmissivity of water in soil, absorption and transmission within plant, transpiration, effective rainfall, vapour pressure, and energy. WR is that quantity of water regardless of its sources required by a crop in a given period of time for its maturity. It includes losses due to ET or CU plus the losses during the application of irrigation water which may be unavoidable.

Irrigation requirement (IR) of a farm is the sum total of irrigation need for an individual crop in a specified time plus the losses occurring in field distribution such as seepage, percolation etc. Similarly, IR for a command area will constitute the sum of water needs for individual farms plus the loss taking place in the distribution system in that area.

Net irrigation requirement (NIR) is the depth of irrigation water, exclusive of precipitation, carry-over soil moisture or ground water contribution which is required for plant growth. It is that amount of irrigation water which is required to bring the soil moisture of the effective root zone to field capacity (PC). Thus, it is the difference between FC and soil moisture content in the root zone before irrigation.

Irrigation frequency depends on CU of a crop and the amount of available moisture in root zone. Sandy soils must be irrigated more often than fine textured deep soils. In general, irrigation should be given when, about 50 to 60 per cent of the available soil moisture has been used from the root zone. The critical periods during the stages of growth are very important factor. Irrigation period is the number of days that can be allowed for applying one irrigation to a given area during the peak CU period.

The aim of the irrigation schedule should be to obtain maximum yield per unit area. In case of water resources being defined the objective should be to obtain maximum production per unit of water. In heavy soils, depletion of available moisture is at a slower rate and in a lighter soil it is at faster rate. For paddy, it is enough to impound 5 cm of water and recharge to the same level once in four days or when the field comes to a saturation point but before the formation of hairline cracks, whichever is earlier. For maize at 25 per cent depletion of water, irrigation frequency should be once in four days and six days in case of clay soils. Cotton and groundnut requires irrigation once in 10 days in red and 15 days in clay soils when the depletion of available soil moisture is 75 per cent. Other soils which fall in between red and clay loams, may have to be irrigated once in 10 or 15 days at the level of depletion.

GUIDELINES TO EFFICIENT USE OF WATER

The following are some guidelines for improving irrigation practices and efficiencies for different field crops.

- Before irrigating, check the soil moisture in the root zone at several locations and estimate the amount of water require to bring the soil to field capacity. About 2 -3 days after an irrigation, check the soil moisture again. The moisture should be close to field capacity throughout the rooting depth. There should be no dry spots or dry layers in the field.
- Determine the depth of water in centimeters applied to the field during irrigation. For this, the measurement of the stream size and the period of time for which water was delivered to the field are required. Then calculate the depth applied. For sprinkler irrigation multiply the application rate in millimeters per hour by the length of time in hours.
- How does the estimation of the amount of water needed compare with the amount delivered to the field? About what efficiency irrigation was obtained? Note that high efficiency can be secured, but a poor irrigation may result if only a small amount of water is applied on the dry soil.
- During irrigation, see whether the intake opportunity time is about the same throughout the field. When irrigation is done by the border method, does the water-stand about as long at the lower and middle of the field as it does at the upper end?

  If furrows are used, does the water reach the lower end at I about one fourth of the total time that it is on the upper end? Are basins and level borders filled quickly?

- Observe the amount of irrigation water flowing out of the field as waste. A large amount of surface water flowing out from a border indicates that the stream is too large or water has been running into the border strip for a long time. When the water in a well designed border (not a level border) approaches the lower end of the strip, the stream may be reduced or cut off at the upper end. In this way, an even distribution will be obtained with little or no run-off. The stream size must be properly adjusted to the soil intake rate and to the border length if the border is to be evenly irrigated without excessive run-off. If furrow run-off is excessive, the furrow stream should be reduced to about one-third to two- thirds of the initial flow after the water reaches the lower end.

IRRIGATION REQUIREMENT OF CROPS

Several experiments on various crops for their irrigation requirements have highlighted the following results.

Paddy

Paddy is a semi-aquatic plant and covers about 35 per cent of irrigated area in the country. Different varieties have been evolved to suit different regions, season and water availability. Cultural practices like puddling and transplanting reduce percolation losses, weed growth but increase the availability of plant nutrients and regulate soil and water temperatures. It improves photosynthesis in the lower leaves due to reflected light from the water surface. These operations may require about 200 -300 mm of water per hectare. Submergence below 50 mm for low land rice has been found to yield low. Recent researches have shown that continuous submergence throughout the growth period may not maximize the yield. Selective submergence during critical stages (initial tillering, panicle initiation to flowering) would be sufficient to maximize yield and to save water during the monsoon period.

However, during summer, continuous submergence has to be followed for maximum yields, Proper drainage helps to remove the toxic substances and regulate the oxygen supply to the roots. About 15 to 20 days prior to harvest, irrigations are stopped and water is drained to facilitate harvesting operations. A major problem in paddy irrigation is deep percolation losses which is 50 to 75 per cent of water applied. Reduction of deep percolation of water is generally achieved by soil manipulation of three types *viz.* (i) Puddling (ii) compaction, and (iii) sub-surface placement of impermeable materials like bitumin and plastic films. Because of its prohibitive cost and mechanical difficulty, the third option is not practicable at farmers field.

Farmers generally continue to irrigate rice till about 4 -7 days before harvest. A recent study has stated that suspension of last irrigation for 14 -17 days before harvest causes more uniform ripening of the crop and economises 16 cm of irrigation water. However, termination of irrigation 3 weeks before harvest may cause marginal yield decrease, but it will save about 20 cm of irrigation water. The critical stages for irrigation in rice crop are tillering, panicle initiation, flowering and grain filling stage. The irrigation requirement of paddy at different locations are given in table.

Table. Different locations

Sl.No.	Place	Water Requirement (mm)	Irrigation requirement (mm)	Seasons
1	Kharagpur (WB)	1890 2150	1440 N.A	July/Aug/- Nov/Dec. Dec/Jan - Mar/April
2	Cuttack (Orissa)	1300 1190	790 780	June-September Jan- April
3	Bhubaneshwar (Orissa)	1440 1650	780 1630	June-September Sept-Dec
4	Roorkee (U.P)	1620	750	June-October
5	Dhanauri (U.P.)	1630	910	June-October
6	Karnataka	1520	1170	June-October
7	Hyderabad (A.P)	N.A.	780	Mar-June
8	Coimbatore	N.A	1680	N.A. July/Aug Dec/January
9	Chalakudy (Kerala)	N.A	1520	Feb-May
10	Delhi	2400	1600	June-October
11	Ludhiana	N.A.	1240	June-October

Cultivation of Sorghum

Cultivation of sorghum is mostly confined to tropical and subtropical areas in Maharashtra, Madhya Pradesh, Andhra Pradesh, Karnal, Gujarat, Rajasthan, Uttar Pradesh, Tamil Nadu, Punjab and Haryana. Being the third important cereal of the country, the crop is planted in a total area of about 16 million hectares, of which 0.7 million hectares are irrigated. In Punjab, Haryana, Uttar Pradesh and some part of Rajasthan, it is mostly grown for forage rather than grain. The main growing season of the crop extends from March to October. In southern states, it is also taken as a rabi crop during October to February.

Experiments have shown that kharif crop do not require any irrigation, if there is sufficient rain during the season. It is a drought resistant crop and can withstand soil moisture depletion up to 75 per cent. Some. varieties of sorghum are of very short duration, adding to the adaptability, varied soil and water conditions. Seeding, flowering and sometimes milking are the critical stages when the crop is irrigated in case it is raised as irrigated crop.

Maize

Maize is grown both for grain and forage. Maize occupies an area of 5.9 million hectares. It is grown primarily as a kharif crop from March to October in Uttar Pradesh, Bihar, Madhya Pradesh, Punjab, Gujarat, Jammu and Kashmir, Himachal Pradesh, Orissa, Andhra Pradesh, Karnataka, Maharashtra and Haryana. Some also come under rabi crop in the southern, mid-west states and more recently in Bihar, Uttar Pradesh and Punjab. Preliminary studies have shown that rabi crop has a higher judicious water management and is important for improving the productivity of both kharif and rabi crops.

The crop has early vegetative, tasselling and silking stages as critical periods. After dough stage, there is no need of irrigation. The permissible depletion of soil moisture may be 25 per cent in light soils and 50 per cent in sandy loam to loam soils. Some research findings have revealed that crop should not be subjected to excess water- soil submergence during early growth. If the draining out of water in case of heavy rains is delayed, 30 to 60 kg N/ha may be added immediately following drainage to retrieve the yield loss.

Bajra

Bajra is an important millet grown during kharif in warm areas with a seasonal rain of about 15-20 centimeters. It is cultivated on an area of 11.7 million hectares mostly on relatively light textured soils of Rajasthan, Haryana, Punjab, Uttar Pradesh, Kamataka, Gujarat and Tamil Nadu. In most of the areas it is sown with the onset of monsoon and no post-sowing irrigation is applied. However, the crop, particularly the hybrid strains, has been found to respond to irrigation.

Flowering and milking stages are the critical stages of irrigation for bajra crop. The crop gives the optimum yield with irrigation based on 75 per cent depletion of available soil moisture from the top 30 cm layer. Bajra is a drought resistant crop. If there is enough rain, kharif crop does not require irrigation. If there is no rain generally, two irrigations are required, first at flowering stage and second at the milking stage. If moisture is a limiting factor, irrigation should also be done at the time of ear head emergence because it is the most critical stage for moisture stress. Bajra does not tolerate water logging. So, do not allow rain water to remain in the field for more than a few hours. Proper arrangement for draining out of excess water must be made.

Barley

Barley is an important rabi cereal and is also used in brewery industry. It is grown on an area of only 1.75 million hectares in the states of Uttar Pradesh, Madhya Pradesh, Rajasthan, Bihar, Haryana, Punjab and Himachal Pradesh. Its cultivation is preferred to wheat under low fertility, low irrigation and late sown conditions. A few irrigation studies based on growth stages of barley have shown that barley shows favourable response to irrigation particularly if the rainfall is low. Generally, it require two to three irrigations to give good yield. One extra irrigation shall be required to sandy soils. If supply of water is inadequate, its efficiency should be increased by giving irrigation at critical stages of growth. If only one irrigation is available, it should be given near active tillering stage (30 -35 days after sowing). When two irrigations are available, one should be applied at active tillering and the other at flowering stage. On highly saline and sodic soils frequent light irrigation gives better result than few heavy irrigations.

Cotton

Cotton is cultivated primarily as a kharif crop on an area of 8 million hectares of which only 25 per cent is irrigated. Major cotton growing states are Maharashtra, Gujarat. Karnataka, Punjab, Madhya Pradesh, Andhra Pradesh, Rajasthan, Haryana and Tamil Nadu. The crop is sown in the hot months of April and May and is harvested during October to November in north-west and mid- west States and December to January in southern states. It requires more frequent irrigation in the southern states where the weather is warm and long season varieties are grown. In the North-west. cotton generally needs 2 to 5 irrigations depending upon the soil type and amount and distribution of seasonal rains. In drier and ill-distributed rainfall conditions, the crop needs 6 to 8 irrigations with 50 to 75 per cent soil moisture depletion. Delayed irrigation prevents the plants from making excessive vegetative growth. The first irrigation should be given 40-45 days after sowing and subsequent irrigations should be light and be given at an interval of two to three weeks. The crop should not be allowed to suffer from water stress during flowering and fruiting period, other wise excessive shedding of flower buds and young bolls may occur resulting in the loss of yield. Cotton during its early growth is very sensitive to water st3gnation for long periods. Therefore, proper drainage should be done.

Sugarcane

Sugarcane is an important crop of tropical areas. In India. it is grown on an area of about 3.19 m. ha. in Uttar Pradesh, Karnataka, Haryana, Bihar, Punjab, Gujarat and Madhya Pradesh. It is planted during January to March and is harvested after 10 -18 months in different parts of the country. It has a fibrous root system which can penetrate as deep as 2.5 m in well-drained soils devoid of any restricting layer and salinity. Thus, the crop utilises most of the moisture stored in the root -zone. In the major sugarcane growing areas, 2 -3 months dry and hot pre-monsoon period of the growing season is very crucial from the irrigation point of view. During this period the young crop is adversely affected by severe soil moisture deficiency and excessively high soil temperature. In the rainy period, there is little need for irrigation unless the rains are too scanty and erratic. During post- monsoon growth period crop again needs irrigation adequately to meet its evapo-transpiration needs and in some cases to mitigate damage by frost.

The life cycle of sugarcane plant is divided into four distinct phases namely germination phase (from planting to 60th day); formative phase (from 60th to 130th day); grand growth phase (from 130th to 250th day) and maturity phase (250th to 365th day). The water requirement during formative phase and grand growth phase is maximum. Generally under north Indian condition, the water requirement of grand growth phase is met with rain, while the requirement of formative phase (during pre- monsoon period) has to be met through irrigation. The total water requirement for sugarcane varies from 200-300 centimeters. In northern India, autumn cane requires on an average 7 irrigations, 5 before monsoon and 2 after monsoon. Spring planted crops may be irrigated only six times. In drier climate and light soils, the crop may require 8 to 10 irrigations. In each irrigation, 3 acre inch of water should be applied. In Tarai areas, 2 to 3 irrigations before and one irrigation after monsoon are sufficient.

Drainage is also equally important in waterlogged areas. Drain excess water from the sugarcane field if they are flooded during the rainy season. Due to waterlogged condition, the quality of cane deteriorates greatly. Drainage greatly helps in increasing the yield and sucrose content of the cane.

Groundnut

Groundnut is the most important oilseed crop of the country. It is mainly grown in Gujarat, Andhra Pradesh, Tamil Nadu, Maharashtra, Karnataka, Madhya Pradesh, Uttar Pradesh, Orissa, Rajasthan and Punjab. Raised as kharif crop in warm areas of relatively high rainfall, it often suffers from periodic water deficits during long rainless intervals. This occasional moisture deficiency is one of the important factors contributing to low yield of kharif groundnut. Consequently provision of irrigation to groundnut would greatly aid in improving its yield. Even now the farmers of southern states are growing groundnut during rabi as an irrigated crop. Being a rainy season crop, groundnut does not require irrigation. However, if dry spell occurs, irrigation may become necessary. One irrigation should be given at pod development stage. In the southern part of the country where groundnut is grown as rabi crop, 3-4 irrigations are necessary. Give the first irrigation at the start of flowering and subsequent irrigations whenever required during the fruiting period to encourage peg penetration and pod development. The last irrigation before harvesting will facilitate the full recovery of pods from the soil.

Mustard and Rapeseed

India is a major producer of mustard and rapeseed crops. These crops are primarily raised as rainfed crops during the rabi season on an area of 4.38 million hectares in Uttar Pradesh, Rajasthan, Madhya Pradesh, Assam, Haryana, West Bengal, Gujarat, Orissa, Punjab and Bihar. Due to low and uncertain rainfall during their growing season, these crops generally show favourable response to irrigations. It has been told that these crops need 1-4 irrigations, depending upon the soil moisture storage in the profile and the prevailing weather. Pre-bloom and pod filling stages are considered to be critical stages, therefore, irrigations at these stages are beneficial.

Gram

Gram is the most important pulse crop which is grown on an area of 3.5 million hectares mostly as a rainfed rabi crop in Madhya Pradesh, Rajasthan, Uttar Pradesh, Haryana, Maharashtra, Punjab, Karnataka etc. The crop has a deep tap root system and can make an efficient use of the profile-stored water in the well-drained alluvial soils of northern states and retentive clay or clay loam soils of mid-west and southern states. Although, water requirements of the crop are relatively low, it often suffers from periodic water deficits owing to low and uncertain rains in the rabi season. Consequently, the average yield of the rainfed crop is low. With recent advancement in irrigation facilities, a part of rainfed area under gram can be brought under irrigation for improving its yield. Therefore, there is need to conduct studies to determine irrigation requirements of the crop in various agro- climatic region. If irrigation facilities are easily available, give a pre-sowing irrigation which will ensure proper germination and smooth crop growth. If winter rains fail, give one irrigation at pre-flowering stage and one at pod development stage. In no case first irrigation should be given earlier than four weeks after sowing. No irrigation should be given at flowering time. A light irrigaiton should always be given because heavy ones are harmful. Excess of irrigation enhances vegetative growth and depresses the yield.

Potato

Potato is an important vegetable crop which has two growing seasons *viz.*, autumn and spring. Autumn potato is the main crop and sown in September-October and harvested in December- January. The crop requires frequent irrigations for optimum growth. A wet moisture regime is conducive not only for adequate water availability to the crop but also keeps soil strength low which permits better development of tubers.

Potato crop requires frequent and light irrigations at low moisture tension, irrespective of the varieties. This is particularly important with new varieties which produce large sised tubers. It is therefore important to keep the ridges moist but not too wet which may be attained by giving irrigation at regular intervals. Accordingly, the first irrigation should be light and is given 7 -10 days after planting or even earlier depending upon soil moisture content. the subsequent irrigation should be moderate to heavy which should cover 2/3rd to 3/4th height of the ridges. The intervals in subsequent irrigations could be about 15 days in heavy soils and 10 days in light soils. To complete its life cycle, the total water requirement of the crop about is 25 acre inch. Over-flooding results in soil compaction of the ridges which results into the poor aeration and poor tuber development. The crop should be given light irrigation if the frost is expected. The most critical stages for irrigation in potato are germination, stolon formation followed by earthing, tuber bulking which coincide 10 -12, 30 -35 and 55 -60 days after sowing. Moisture stress at these stages results in drastic reduction of tuber yields.

METHODOLOGY OF EVALUATE WATERSHEDS DEVELOPMENT

The methodology was applied to evaluate watersheds developed in the Telengana region of AP which forms a part of the semi-arid and dry-sub-humid agro-ecological region of India. Five watersheds located in Telengana region in the districts of Rangareddy (RR) and Nalgonda were studied.

The present chapter describes the evaluation of WSD in one of the villages, Pamana in Chevella Mandal in RR district. While over 5000 ha area around Chevella township was developed as model watershed in 1985, Pamana village/ watershed (78°7'30"E & 17°16'45"N) was developed within Chevella Mandal under DPAP programme in 1999. Under the WDP, ten check-dams were constructed in two micro-watersheds (MWS, catchment of first-order stream) in a planned manner.

The study of a treated and another untreated micro-watershed in Pamana provided interesting results. The village has a total area of 1010 ha with 300 farm households. Land holding size range from 0.5-4 ha although a majority of land holding size is lesser than 1 ha. A large majority of them are un-irrigated. Soil is essentially black belonging to Vertisols. Earlier, paddy cultivation was dominant wherever irrigation was available, however, with initiation of WDP, cash crops *viz.*, cotton, tomato, carrot, coriander, onion, sugarcane, garlic and maize, besides flowers like Marigold, Jasmine, Chrysanthemums and Aster, have been introduced.

In accordance with new guidelines for implementation of WSD in participatory mode, a Watershed Committee was formed in the village consisting of stakeholders (farmers belonging to the respective watersheds). Seed money was sanctioned to the village administration (Gram Panchayat) and the Department of Agriculture (DoA, AP Govt.) guided the villagers to identify and locate check-dams and other S&WC structures. The physical structures were built by the villagers under the guidance of engineers from the State Department of Govt. of AP, and payments were made from the DPAP fund.

This was a two-pronged strategy under which the impact of drought was to be minimized by supporting farmers by providing livelihood during drought and ensuring agricultural productivity through S&WC on the long-run. The entire village has 19 micro-watersheds (MWS) of which 4 are treated with S&WC structures. For the present study we have taken one treated (TMWS) and another untreated micro-watershed (UTMWS). The TMWS selected for this study has an area of 129.49 ha. Over 40 per cent of its area is irrigated, 51 per cent un-irrigated where rainfed agriculture is practiced and the rest is scrubland with the ownership of Govt. The UTMW selected for the study covers an area of 21 ha with 23 per cent under irrigated agriculture and the rest under rainfed cultivation. The study of these two MWS has brought out interesting results.

MATERIAL AND METHODS

Study was conducted in an integrated modular mode using Geomatics tools-GIS, GPS and Satellite data in addition to conventional techniques used in multi-disciplinary studies *viz.*, field survey using toposheets, transact walk, civil survey using Total Station and GPS, soil survey, sampling and physico-chemical analysis in the lab, socio-economic survey using questionnaires and open-ended interviews with farmers, Participatory Rural Appraisal (PRA) at the village and collection of secondary data from mandal and district head quarters etc.

Watershed hierarchy was identified and mapped using ArcGIS (Ver. 9.0). The catchments of 1st order stream were nested into that of 2nd order stream catchments which in turn were nested into the 3rd order stream catchments and so forth.

The National Watershed Atlas classifies the entire drainage network of India in a hierarchical manner consisting of 5 stages, namely, water resource region, river basin, catchments, sub-catchments and watershed; we have delineated the 3rd, 2nd and 1st order streams and up-linked these to the national watershed hierarchy in earlier studies. Watersheds in Pamana village were delineated in a similar fashion into sub-watersheds, mini-and micro-watersheds respectively. A Treated or Developed Micro-Watersheds (TMWS) where S&WC structures were located and one Untreated Micro-Watersheds (UTMWS) where no interventions were made, were selected for evaluation. The nomenclature of the selected treated micro-watershed is as follows: TMW - 4D1E8a4c which stands for 4 - Southern Water Region, D-Krishna River, 1 - Musa River, E - Himayatsagar sub-catchment, 8 - Watershed No. (4th order stream catchments), a sub-watershed code (3rd order stream catchments), 4 mini-watershed (2nd order stream catchments) and c micro-watershed (1st order stream catchments).

Socio-economic survey was conducted using a structured questionnaire that was created to measure sustainability indicators. Two databases - one for watershed information and another for village information-were created in MS-Access and were linked to GIS platform. Soil and water sampling and analysis for 12 physico-chemical and biological parameters were undertaken and the results were input into Watershed Database. Satellite imagery of IRS 1D LISS-III of 16 Nov. 1998 (pre-project period), 17 March 2001, 16 Oct. 2004 and IRS - P6 data of 4 Nov. 2005 (post-project period) were digitally interpreted using ERDAS Imagine Ver. 9.0 and land use, cover and degradation maps were prepared. The results were integrated for evaluation of WDP in Pamana.

CURRENT SITUATIONS FOR WATER DEMAND MANAGEMENT

In order to ensure water resources equitable distribution and allocation, to improve water use efficiency and to make up the cost in the operating, maintaining and renewing the water supply projects, the regulation of water pricing and water fee using for water supply projects was issued by the State Council in 1985, and it indicated that there is no more water supplied for free. In this regulation, it is stipulated that water users, whom extract water from water supply projects, such as reservoirs, cannels, etc., should be charged by the managing companies, regardless the purposes of water use.

The principle for drawing water tariffs as well as the ways of collecting water fees and using the money are also ruled in this regulation. In 1988, Water Law was published, it stipulated officially that water resources is also a kind of economic goods, those who take the water from lakes and rivers or ground aquifers, should get water usage licenses and be charged in some degree, so called water resources fee. In 1993, the State Council draw up the regulation of implementing procedure for water usage licenses, it is made clear that each unit or individual who take water directly from lakes, rivers or ground aquifers by constructing projects or pumping facilities etc., should apply water usage licenses, and be charged based on the amount of water taken, which be contracted in the license.

Anymore, the regulation of annual examining water usage was set up, it rules that the water administrative departments at all levels should examine all water users annually within its authority, in terms of the amount of water taken, the water quality of discharge, water saving measures taken as well as the amount of water applied for the next year. Anymore, the water administrative departments have the rights to examine all index mentioned above at anytime within the year, and if the amount of water taken in the year exceed that contracted in the license, it should be charged at higher rate, also several penalties are set up in case of no compliance with the regulation.

Current Economic Instruments

The current economic instruments which are being put into practice in Changjiang River Basin have three: water resources fee, water fee charged by water supply projects, and tape water charge.

Water Resources Fee

Except for Shanghai City and Hunan Province, other provinces in Changjiang River Basin have already set up the regulations of collecting water resources fee based on the local situation, all water users have been registered and paid for water taking. Those who construct the new projects or expand the scale for water taking should go to corresponding water administrative departments for fore-apply and applying for the licenses. The rates of water resources fee vary with the provinces, and being set up by provincial water administrative departments.

The standard for water resources fee setting are mainly dependent on the types of water use and water supply sources. At present, the rate of water resources fee is set too low (for surface water taking, it cost 0.02-0.05 RMB for 1 m3, while it cost 0.03-0.05 RMB for 1 m3 groundwater drawing), and not high enough to show the functions of economic instrument. Especially the rate between surface water taking and ground water drawing are too close, and led to ground water being over-developed in the regions whose surface water are highly polluted. For instants, in Changjiang delta plain, land subsidence have already occurred in some area, and threatened the safety of the highway from Shanghai to Nanjing. The maximiue depth of land subsidence even reached 1 m in some region. The reasons causing the problem are that the groundwater was over-taken by the companies and enterprises due to the surface water highly polluted and eutrophication.

The cost of taking, treating surface water is higher than that of ground water extraction (including paying higher water resources fee). To avoid the worse state occurring, Jiangsu provincial water administrative department adjusted the strategies for ground water management, and the water resources fee for ground water will be raised in a short period, and the applying procedure for digging new wells will be more stricter, in addition, the plan for reducing the amount of groundwater extracting annually have already been made and been implemented. It has proved that these measures have effects on the control of land subsidence. Stricter regulation for ground water extracting in those regions will be draw up soon.

Water Fee Charged by Water Supply Projects

It has been made clear in the Water Law that those who use water provided by water-supply projects shall pay water fee to the supplying unit. The activities charged include using facilities to take water from reservoirs, irrigation canals, manmade channels, etc. for different water use purposes.

At present, water fee is considered as a kind of administrative charge, and each year the government gave subsidies to those projects. To lighten the burden of farmers, some local governments even cancel the water fee for irrigation purpose. The standards for collecting water fee are also set far below the cost, and the non-block rate is commonly practiced. Therefore it is no good for encouraging efficient water use, and water supply units also can not receive sufficient payment for their services, consequently, they are not able to maintain their system adequately, hence led to system at the edge of break-down and inefficient water use.

Another problem occurring in the implementing procedure of this regulation is that agreement between different administrative regions is hard to be reached in case of that the water supply project and water users belong to different administrative regions. For example, the Danjiangkou project on Hanjiang River, which is in charge of by Changjiang Water Resource Commission, MWR, is a multiple purpose project. It has several functions such as: flood control, power generation, irrigation and water supply for industry. More than 30 enterprises and tap water supply companies from Hubei Province and Henan Province are drawing water from the reservoir without any payment, due to the agreement can not be reached between local government and the project managing body, until now (20 years after the regulation drawn), the affair is still under discussion.

Price for Tap Water

Tap water supplying industry is managed by government in China, and the charge for tap water is based on the amount of water to be used (usually to be metered). To ensure each resident can accesses to the tap water, the price is usually set lower than the cost, only considered past of the cost of taking and treating water. Each year the government should subsidise it in order to keep their operation. Although the low rate of price guarantee most of residents access to the tap water, but standing in other point, this price policy also encourage inefficient water use and meaningless for public environmental-friendly awareness arising.

Also the arrangement place too much financial burden on the government, and made the operation fund for water company is not so abundant, therefore the maintaining of the water transfer network will be lagged, and led more water lost before the water reach consumers tapes.

In recent years, some reform was made on the tap water price. The price of tape water is raising in some cities, and the sewage discharge, which occupy public sewer system, is also be charged and include into the tap water price based on the amount of water each household use.

But irrational pricing policy still exists. For industry using tap water, the price rate will be low down if the amount of water exceeds a certain quota.

In addition to the measures, water saving techniques is widely used. At present, the emphasis of water saving in Changjiang River Basin is put on the modification of irrigation projects and channel lining as well as the irrigation pattern changing. In cities, several water saving measures are also be taken, such as: water saving facilities used in public toilets; domestic recycling waste water for irrigation; recycling water using within enterprises, etc.

Furthermore, to minimize the water lost from the tape net, some provincial administrative departments give supports to the enterprises to do water balance testing work, and it contribute a lot to those enterprises for water saving.

DEMAND MANAGEMENT OF WATER RESOURCES

Rising the water price to promote efficient water use and sustainable development of water resources The current water prices, either water resources fee or tap water price or water charge for water supply projects, are set too low due to several causes, and the rate for same type of charge are set un-flexiblly, also the payment from users can not recover the cost.

All kinds of irrationals in water pricing can not promote the initiative of water supply sector, and it is no help for improving the public awareness.It is suggested that water prices for all types can be risen based on current water supply and managing system.

The price rates charged by water supply project can be set at different levels, such as: subsidised price, planned price and non-planned water price (water supply project contracts the amount of water used monthly with the users, and give a profit price to it. In case that the water used exceeds the contracted one, the higher price rate will be implemented); seasonal price (water price will be changed with the wet and dry seasons), etc. The water supply managing units will shift to cost-recovering and financial independence step by step.

For tap water price, it is suggested that full cost-recovery with low benefit pricing rate could be implemented in the economic well-developed regions. For water resource scare regions, the water resource fee should be risen up to some degree, especially for ground water with good quality withdrawing.

Educating people more frequently by multiple ways to improve public awareness. Water saving is always be encouraged in China, and it is considered as one of basic national developing strategies. In each 'Water Week of China' many educating activities are held and presented to the public through televisions, newspapers and broadcasting etc. by water management sectors.

But the education is not only the responsibility of water sectors; it should involve all stakeholders, including enterprises, companies, schools and each householder. Enhance current laws and regulations, and speedy up the step of stipulating of new related laws and regulations Due to the imperfect of some present laws and regulations, there are difficulties existing in implementing those laws and regulations in practice.

Now the Water Law is under amendment. It is suggested that regulations for water fee charged by water supply projects should be amended and enhanced soon according the implementing difficulties existing in practice.

Several regulations or laws, which is under consideration, should also be enhanced and published soon. Reform current water supply system, privatisation of water supply can be tried in some region.

Now private tap water supply companies, which were invested and operated by foreign companies, have already put into use in Guangdong Province and Shanghai City.

It seems that the water use efficiency of those companies is much better than the ones under the traditional operation. To ensure water consumers can get good quality service and protect the public health, the government and private companies make contracts on the guarantee degree of water supply and water price, moreover the government has the rights to check the water quality without informing the private companies at anytime. It is recommended that this kind of water supply system could be experienced in more cities and regions.

Favourable policy should give to the utilisation of water saving technique The government should stipulate favourable policy to encourage and support the utilisation of water saving technique. Grants and soft loans can be supplied to water users that wish to invest in water saving measures, such as: give subsidies to irrigation projects for water saving measures taking; low interest rate loans can be given to enterprises which are willing to invest in water circling use or other water saving measures; water saving facilities should be sale in low benefit or non-benefit.

Demand management has contributed a lot to integrated water resources management in the Changjiang River Basin, but it still has a long way to go. Water resources manager should help and encourage water users to use water saving measures and restructure water use pattern according to the local water resources conditions, while they implement economic and legal instruments for demand management.

6

Integrated Water Resources Management

Integrated water resources management can take different forms and is examined best in specific situations. In the water-supply field, the term "integrated resource planning" has come into use to express concepts of integration in supply development. Perhaps the most comprehensive concept for water supply is "Total Water Management."

According to a 1996 report of the American Water Works Research Foundation, Total Water Management is the exercise of stewardship of water resources for the greatest good of society and the environment. A basic principle of Total Water Management is that the supply is renewable, but limited and should be managed on a sustainable-use basis.

Taking into consideration local and regional variations, Total Water Management:

- Encourages planning and management on a natural water systems basis through a dynamic process that adapts to changing conditions;
- Balances competing uses of water through efficient allocation that addresses social values, cost effectiveness and environmental benefits and costs;
- Requires the participation of all units of government and stakeholders in decision-making through a process of coordination and conflict resolution;
- Promotes water conservation, reuse, source protection and supply development to enhance water quality and quantity;
- Fosters public health, safety and community goodwill.

This definition focuses on the broad aspects of water supply. Examples can be given for other situations, including water-quality management planning, water allocation and flood control.

BALANCING DIVERSE INTERESTS

Water is a natural resource critical to the environment. Water also is an economic resource critical to society. Unfortunately, people who champion water as an economic resource essential to society commonly see themselves in direct opposition to those who champion water as a critical component of the environment that must be conserved and protected. This creates a difficult situation for those who must manage the available water resources to best satisfy all of the diverse interests that depend on water.

It is, of course, impossible to successfully manage water resources solely from either of the two extremes. If public policy exclusively protected ecological interests at the expense of economic interests, then it could threaten society's ability to meet the basic need all people have for water. From an ecological perspective, this could weaken government and diminish the ability to protect the environment, whereas from an economic standpoint, jobs and essential services such as housing and communications could be lost. Likewise, if water management policies focus entirely on the economy, then the environment often is harmed. A diminished environment affects the public health, the quality of life and ultimately the ability to survive on planet Earth. Clearly, society is as dependent on a healthy environment as it is on a healthy economy.

LEGISLATION

In many Western Hemisphere countries, water resources are managed through legislation and regulations. In the United States, elected officials in Congress and the state legislatures set the policies that prioritize where water can or cannot be used and how much water must remain to function in the natural environment. These laws are then implemented through regulatory agencies at the federal, state and local levels of government. One example of this legislation is the federal Clean Water Act, which requires that the quality of surface-water bodies, such as rivers and lakes, be kept at a level that will assure the maintenance of both environmental and economic functions.

Public Opinion

The effectiveness of these policies to meet both environmental and economic interests is dependent, in part, on how well the laws are written and how effectively they are enforced. However, public opinion strongly affects the type of policies that get enacted. For example, in the 1930s, the United States was emerging from a severe economic depression, so the growth and protection of the economy were paramount in the minds of the public and policymakers alike. As a result, the national policy from roughly 1930 to 1970 was to use the water of major rivers to provide jobs and to allow cities to grow in order to expand the economy. This was often accomplished through the federal government's dam-building projects for hydroelectric power and water supply, particularly for irrigation.

Shifting Sentiment

The dam-building policy was beneficial to the economy, but by 1970 national policy and public sentiment had shifted towards the environmental health of rivers and lakes, many of which had been harmed by the dam projects. One outgrowth of this environmental pendulum shift was the Endangered Species Act (ESA) passed by the U.S. Congress in 1973. The ESA is an example of legislation that fundamentally changed water policy without directly addressing water issues. On its face, the law would not seem to be about water policy. When applied to fish species, however, it places requirements on water resource management to meet certain stream flow levels in order to protect a given species. Though this is clearly a good policy, it often requires extraordinary efforts in the regional management of water to ensure that the water demands of the society are met without further endangering the listed species. These efforts can be very costly. A balance must be found whereby the environment is protected to maintain the function of the rivers and lakes while still meeting the water demands of the community.

WATER MANAGEMENT

Even without the demands of environmental laws, minimizing impacts on streams and rivers while maintaining water supplies for cities and industry is a complex task because of natural constraints on water availability. Areas of the United States like the arid Southwest have limited amounts of available water such that any additional use has the potential to significantly harm natural systems. However, water resource management is difficult even in areas with substantial annual rainfall. Here the problem is often one of timing because water may be abundant only in the winter months when water demand is typically low. Conversely, satisfying water demands for irrigation, meeting minimum-streamflow regulations and providing water to cities is typically far greater in the summer months.

All of this complicates the job of the water resource manager. As with any problem where the timing of supply is not well matched with the timing of demand, the best solution is effective storage. For example, if the annual floods of rivers like the Mississippi River could be captured and stored for use later in the year, drought would be less of a problem. In this way, sufficient water is often available to meet both ecological and economic needs provided the problem is considered regionally and over a long enough period of time.

The world is now in an era where neither the economy nor the environment can absorb much negative impact from the mismanagement of water resources. Regional watershed management may help shape policy to store water from the high-flow periods of watersheds and use that water to maintain flows for fish and wildlife requirements and meet the demands of the community during low-flow periods. Everyone should continue to strive for balanced policies that allow for the use of water without inordinate harm to either the environment or the economy. The need to balance the various and diverse interests that depend on water is more essential and more complex than ever.

SOURCES OF FRESH WATER

SURFACE WATER

Surface water is water in a river, lake or fresh water wetland. Surface water is naturally replenished by precipitation and naturally lost through discharge to the oceans, evaporation, and sub-surface.

Although the only natural input to any surface water system is precipitation within its watershed, the total quantity of water in that system at any given time is also dependent on many other factors. These factors include storage capacity in lakes, wetlands and artificial reservoirs, the permeability of the soil beneath these storage bodies, the runoff characteristics of the land in the watershed, the timing of the precipitation and local evaporation rates. All of these factors also affect the proportions of water lost.

Human activities can have a large and sometimes devastating impact on these factors. Humans often increase storage capacity by constructing reservoirs and decrease it by draining wetlands. Humans often increase runoff quantities and velocities by paving areas and channelizing stream flow.

The total quantity of water available at any given time is an important consideration. Some human water users have an intermittent need for water. For example, many farms require large quantities of water in the spring, and no water at all in the winter. To supply such a farm with water, a surface water system may require a large storage capacity to collect water throughout the year and release it in a short period of time. Other users have a continuous need for water, such as a power plant that requires water for cooling. To supply such a power plant with water, a surface water system only needs enough storage capacity to fill in when average stream flow is below the power plant's need. Nevertheless, over the long term the average rate of precipitation within a watershed is the upper bound for average consumption of natural surface water from that watershed.

Natural surface water can be augmented by importing surface water from another watershed through a canal or pipeline. It can also be artificially augmented from any of the other sources listed here, however in practice the quantities are negligible. Humans can also cause surface water to be "lost" (i.e. become unusable) through pollution. Brazil is the country estimated to have the largest supply of fresh water in the world, followed by Russia and Canada.

UNDER RIVER FLOW

Throughout the course of the river, the total volume of water transported downstream will often be a combination of the visible free water flow together with a substantial contribution flowing through sub-surface rocks and gravels that underlie the river and its floodplain called the hyporheic zone.

For many rivers in large valleys, this unseen component of flow may greatly exceed the visible flow. The hyporheic zone often forms a dynamic interface between surface water and true ground-water receiving water from the ground water when aquifers are fully charged and contributing water to ground-water when ground waters are depleted. This is especially significant in karst areas where pot-holes and underground rivers are common.

GROUND WATER

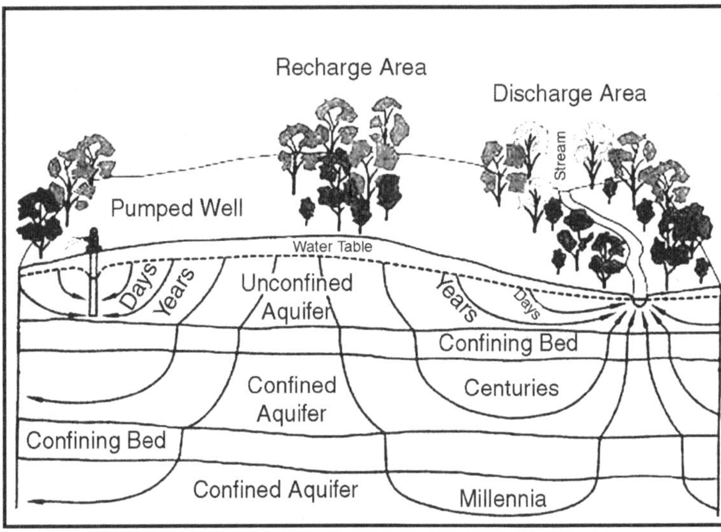

Fig. Sub-Surface Water Travel Time.

Sub-surface water, or groundwater, is fresh water located in the pore space of soil and rocks. It is also water that is flowing within aquifers below the water table. Sometimes it is useful to make a distinction between sub-surface water that is closely associated with surface water and deep sub-surface water in an aquifer (sometimes called "fossil water").

Sub-surface water can be thought of in the same terms as surface water: inputs, outputs and storage. The critical difference is that due to its slow rate of turnover, sub-surface water storage is generally much larger compared to inputs than it is for surface water. This difference makes it easy for humans to use sub-surface water unsustainably for a long time without severe consequences. Nevertheless, over the long term the average rate above a sub-surface water source is the upper bound for average consumption of water from that source.

The natural input to sub-surface water is seepage from surface water. The natural outputs from sub-surface water are springs and seepage to the oceans. If the surface water source is also subject to substantial evaporation, a sub-surface water source may become saline. This situation can occur naturally under endorheic bodies of water, or artificially under irrigated farmland. In coastal areas, human use of a sub-surface water source may cause the direction of ocean to reverse which can also cause soil salinization. Humans can also cause sub-surface water to be "lost" (i.e. become unusable) through pollution. Humans can increase the input to a sub-surface water source by building reservoirs or detention ponds.

Desalination

Desalination is an artificial process by which saline water (generally sea water) is converted to fresh water. The most common desalination processes are distillation and reverse osmosis. Desalination is currently expensive compared to most alternative sources of water, and only a very small fraction of total human use is satisfied by desalination. It is only economically practical for high-valued uses (such as household and industrial uses) in arid areas. The most extensive use is in the Persian Gulf.

Frozen Water

Several schemes have been proposed to make use of icebergs as a water source, however to date this has only been done for novelty purposes. Glacier runoff is considered to be surface water.

Uses of fresh water

Uses of fresh water can be categorized as consumptive and non-consumptive (sometimes called "renewable"). A use of water is consumptive if that water is not immediately available for another use. Losses to sub-surface seepage and evaporation are considered consumptive, as is water incorporated into a product (such as farm produce). Water that can be treated and returned as surface water, such as sewage, is generally considered non-consumptive if that water can be put to additional use.

Agricultural

It is estimated that 69% of worldwide water use is for irrigation, with 15-35% of irrigation withdrawals being unsustainable.

In some areas of the world irrigation is necessary to grow any crop at all, in other areas it permits more profitable crops to be grown or enhances crop yield. Various irrigation methods involve different trade-offs between crop yield, water consumption and capital cost of equipment and structures. Irrigation methods such as most furrow and overhead sprinkler irrigation are usually less expensive but also less efficient, because much of the water evaporates or runs off. More efficient irrigation methods include drip or trickle irrigation, surge irrigation, and some types of sprinkler systems where the sprinklers are operated near ground level. These types of systems, while more expensive, can minimize runoff and evaporation. Any system that is improperly managed can be wasteful. Another trade-off that is often insufficiently considered is salinization of sub-surface water.

Aquaculture is a small but growing agricultural use of water. Freshwater commercial fisheries may also be considered as agricultural uses of water, but have generally been assigned a lower priority than irrigation.

As global populations grow, and as demand for food increases in a world with a fixed water supply, there are efforts underway to learn how to produce more food with less water, through improvements in irrigation methods and technologies, agricultural water management, crop types, and water monitoring.

Industrial

It is estimated that 15% of worldwide water use is industrial. Major industrial users include power plants, which use water for cooling or as a power source (i.e. hydroelectric plants), ore and oil refineries, which use water in chemical processes, and manufacturing plants, which use water as a solvent.

The portion of industrial water usage that is consumptive varies widely, but as a whole is lower than agricultural use.

Water is used in power generation. Hydroelectricity is electricity obtained from hydropower. Hydroelectric power comes from water driving a water turbine connected to a generator. Hydroelectricity is a low-cost, non-polluting, renewable energy source. The energy is supplied by the sun. Heat from the sun evaporates water, which condenses as rain in higher altitudes, from where it flows down.

Three Gorges Dam is the largest hydro-electric power station Pressurized water is used in water blasting and water jet cutters. Also, very high pressure water guns are used for precise cutting. It works very well, is relatively safe, and is not harmful to the environment. It is also used in the cooling of machinery to prevent over-heating, or prevent saw blades from over-heating. Water is also used in many industrial processes and machines, such as the steam turbine and heat exchanger, in addition to its use as a chemical solvent. Discharge of untreated water from industrial uses is pollution. Pollution includes discharged solutes (chemical pollution) and discharged coolant water (thermal pollution). Industry requires pure water for many applications and utilizes a variety of purification techniques both in water supply and discharge.

Household

It is estimated that 15% of worldwide water use is for household purposes. These include drinking water, bathing, cooking, sanitation, and gardening. Basic household water requirements have been estimated by Peter Gleick at around 50 litres per person per day, excluding water for gardens. Drinking water is water that is of sufficiently high quality so that it can be consumed or used without risk of immediate or long term harm. Such water is commonly called potable water. In most developed countries, the water supplied to households, commerce and industry is all of drinking water standard even though only a very small proportion is actually consumed or used in food preparation.

Recreation

Recreational water use is usually a very small but growing percentage of total water use. Recreational water use is mostly tied to reservoirs. If a reservoir is kept fuller than it would otherwise be for recreation, then the water retained could be categorized as recreational usage. Release of water from a few reservoirs is also timed to enhance whitewater boating, which also could be considered a recreational usage. Other examples are anglers, water skiers, nature enthusiasts and swimmers.

Recreational usage is usually non-consumptive. Golf courses are often targeted as using excessive amounts of water, especially in drier regions. It is, however, unclear whether recreational irrigation (which would include private gardens) has a noticeable effect on water resources. This is largely due to the unavailability of reliable data. Some governments, including the Californian Government, have labelled golf course usage as agricultural in order to deflect environmentalists' charges of wasting water. However, using the above figures as a basis, the actual statistical effect of this reassignment is close to zero.

Additionally, recreational usage may reduce the availability of water for other users at specific times and places. For example, water retained in a reservoir to allow boating in the late summer is not available to farmers during the spring planting season. Water released for whitewater rafting may not be available for hydroelectric generation during the time of peak electrical demand.

INTEGRATED WATER RESOURCE MANAGEMENT MODELS

The water management literature is rich with IWRM models that have focused either on understanding how water flows through a watershed in response to hydrologic events or allocating the water that becomes available in response to those events. Hydrologic simulation attempts to capture the most important land–atmosphere components of the hydrologic cycle. One well-known hydrologic simulation tool is the United States Department of Agriculture's Soil Water Assessment Tool.

The SWAT model has sophisticated physical hydrologic watershed modules that describe, among other things, rainfall–run-off processes, irrigated agriculture processes, and point and non-point watershed dynamics.

The Danish Hydraulic Institute (DHI) offers a suite of models, including MIKE SHE, which is an integrated water resource modelling tool that can simulate all the major processes in the land phase of the hydrologic cycle. The United States Army Corp of Engineers Hydrologic Engineering Centre (HEC) developed the HEC-Hydrologic Modeling System (HMS), which simulates the precipitation–run–off processes of dendritic watershed systems. The Delft Hydraulics Laboratory developed the HYMOS model for surface and groundwater hydrology and includes rainfall–run–off simulation.

Important to mention, but perhaps of less importance in terms of water supply and demand management, are hydrodynamics models. These models are typically developed to track the propagation of water through a river system at very short time steps (*e.g.*, minutes to hours). Applications include flood inundation mapping and flood forecasting. From a climate change perspective, this sort of hydrodynamics model could be used to study the interacting effects of sea level rise and changes in freshwater discharge into bay–delta systems at the event scale.

Models of this type include Delft's DELFT3D, a sophisticated two- and three-dimensional hydrodynamics model that can simulate non-steady flow and transport resulting from tidal and meteorological forcing. Other hydrodynamics models are DHI's MIKE21 and MIKE3, which can simulate hydraulics, water quality and sediment transport in rivers, lakes and coastal areas, and can be used for local to regional watershed studies. The HEC's hydrodynamics models include HEC–RAS, which is a one-dimensional model for hydraulic calculations and water surface profiles.

This CGE training material focuses more attention on water resource management modelling, which can be used to investigate water supply and demand issues over long planning time horizons, consistent with climate change projections. Water resource management models include the RiverWare DSS, a state–of–the–art water planning and operations model that can be used to develop multiobjective simulations and optimizations of river and reservoir systems, such as and including storage and hydropower reservoirs, river reaches, diversions and water users.

The DHI modelling group provides a GIS-based planning model for studying water management options, referred to as MIKE BASIN. The HEC-ResSim is a reservoir simulation model that can describe operating rules, such as release requirements and constraints, hydropower requirements and multiple reservoir operations, but it too requires prescribed flows from other models. The MODSIM DSS is a generalized river basin network flow model that can simultaneously incorporate the complex physical, hydrological and institutional/ administrative aspects of river basin management, including water rights, but boundary flows must be prescribed.

The MULINO DSS is a multisectoral, integrated and operational decision support system for sustainable use of water resources at the catchment scale, with a focus on the DSS as a multicriteria decision aid. Similar to RiverWare, MULINO can accommodate a physical watershed hydrology model that is external to the system, linked through appropriate input–output procedures.

WaterWare is a sophisticated water resource DSS that includes dynamic simulation of physical models of water quality, allocation, rainfall–run–off, groundwater and water management elements, including demand/supply, cost–benefit analysis and multicriteria analysis. Although WaterWare integrates the physical hydrology and the management system, applying the model requires a rather sophisticated level of user and hardware support. The Delft Hydraulics River Basin Simulation Model (RIBASIM) is a generic water resource planning model for investigating the behaviour of river basins under various hydrologic conditions. The WEAP21 attempts to address the gap between water management and watershed hydrology, and the requirements that an effective IWRM be useful, easy to use, affordable and readily available to the broad water resource community. WEAP21 integrates a range of physical hydrologic processes with the management of demands and installed infrastructure in a seamless and coherent manner. It allows for multiple scenario analysis, including alternative climate scenarios and changing anthropogenic stressors, such as land use variations, changes in municipal and industrial demands, alternative operating rules and points of diversion changes. WEAP21's strength is in addressing water planning and resource allocation problems and issues, and, importantly, it is not designed to be a detailed water operations model that might be used to optimize hydropower based on hydrologic forecasts.

The management system in the WEAP21 DSS is described by a user-defined demand priority and supply preference set for each demand site used to construct an optimization routine that allocates available supplies. Demands are defined by the user, but typically include municipal and industrial demand, irrigated portions of subcatchments, and instream flow requirements. Demand analysis in WEAP that is not covered by the evapotranspiration-based irrigation demand follows a disaggregated, end-use-based approach for determining water requirements at each demand node. Economic, demographic and water use information is used to construct alternative scenarios that examine how total and disaggregated consumption of water evolve over time. These demand scenarios are computed in WEAP and applied deterministically to a linear-programme-based allocation algorithm. Demand analysis is the starting point for conducting integrated water planning analysis because all supply and resource calculations in WEAP are driven by the optimization routine that determines the final delivery to each demand node, based on the priorities specified by the user.

USING IWRM FOR ADAPTATION ASSESSMENT

Water managers have long had to cope with the challenges posed by climate and hydrologic variability, both intra–annually and inter-annually. Their adaptation strategies include responding to both seasonal variability and extended wet and drought periods using integrated reservoir and irrigation systems that allow for the capture of water during the wet season for use during dry seasons and extended drought periods. Other adaptations have been the use of levees and dams in concert to protect communities from heavy precipitation and high flood flows during extreme wet periods. Climate change might challenge these conventional adaptations, forcing more aggressive strategies, such as artificially recharging aquifers or developing integrative strategies that optimally operate reservoirs in conjunction with the artificial recharging of aquifers. Protecting growing communities from the risk of flooding also has increased in importance. Two adaptation strategies are flood control operating rules for large reservoirs and flood bypasses that move water away from human settlements. In many cases, flood conveyance restricts land use to not allow permanent structures, so during periods of high flow, large volumes of water can be diverted from the main river channels, thereby reducing the risk of flooding along the developed riverfront areas. Climate change adaptation could include the re–operation of reservoirs to maintain their important services and, in some cases, the construction of new facilities to help in flood protection or to secure water supplies. These adaptations would require careful consideration to ensure their usefulness in adapting to climate change, with an IWRM modelling process a key in assessing the benefits of alternative strategies for adaptation to climate change. Other water resource adaptations are designed to limit impacts on important aquatic ecosystems. Adaptations include establishing minimum instream flow requirements at important points in the water system. The physical rehabilitation of riverine ecosystems has taken on a priority because the watershed itself can act as a flow regulating system, buffering rapid stream flow response as water slowly migrates through the complex pathways of the watershed.

Water planners now realise that the extensive channelization of many watersheds around the world limits the amount of wetland and riparian habitat available. Setting communities back from the riverine corridor is an adaptation being considered together with the concept that flow-bypass structures can be managed as wetland complexes. There is also growing recognition that ecosystems require more than the minimum flows often prescribed for them.

Other factors, such as the temperature and quality of the water in rivers, are also important. Adaptations with regard to water temperature include the construction of temperature control devices in large dams which allow for the controlled management of cold and warm water pools that generally develop when large reservoirs stratify, which could be amplified with climate change. Water quality adaptation measures can include the development of discharge permitting requirements. To date these have been limited to point discharges, but they are now being contemplated for non–point sources as well. There has been a clear historical trend towards placing a higher priority on environmental security as societies place greater value on the role of ecosystems.

DATA

Water resource planning models require data on water demand and water supply. Water demand information usually needs to come from local sources–including water use per capita domestic rates, and industrial and commercial water use rates. Common water use rates can be extracted from literature. Irrigation demands can be determined from knowledge about crops and the climate. Data on demand for cooling water for thermal power plants and mainstream demands for navigation, recreation and hydropower are usually available from the users. Data on ecosystem demand may be available from environmental agencies. All the demands must be adjusted for climate change.

WATER RESOURCES MANAGEMENT SYSTEM ORIENTED

In China, river basin management has existed for hundreds of years. Currently, river basin management organizations have been created for important rivers and a system has taken shape that water resources of large rivers are managed within a basin framework. Changjiang (Yangtze) is the longest river in China. Execution of river basin management in a modern concept dated back to the 1920s.

By 70 years' efforts, especially through vigorous development since 1949, great achievements have been accomplished in every undertaking in the valley, and the strategies for river basin management have been improved substantially. Nevertheless, with social and economic development in the valley, the current river basin management system can no longer sufficiently fit the new situations. With a view to accommodate to the needs in the new millennium, it is necessary and urgent to establish a new management system on basis of the current one. This new system shall be a guarantee for preventing flood and drought disasters in a more efficient manner and promoting the integrated and sustainable development of water resources in the Changjiang valley.

CURRENT SITUATION OF CHANGJIANG RIVER BASIN MANAGEMENT

Currently, water management for Changjiang River valley applies such a structure, which is a combination of basin management by the central government and regional management by local governments. Changjiang Water Resources Commission (CWRC) is the river basin management organization, dispatched by the central government to execute water administration function in the Changjiang valley.

In accordance with the principle of unified management combined with departmental management, the CWRC has the responsibility to manage water resources and all river channels within the scope of the valley on basis of related laws and regulations. Its missions include: comprehensive harnessing of water resources, administration and management of backbone water projects, long-term river basin planning, water administration, water development coordination, supervision and service-providing and the integrated development, utilization and protection of water resources.

Local governments within the valley can carry out regional water management schemes tailored to the actual conditions under its administrative jurisdictions according to related regulations. It is an important component of river basin management and the materialization of unified management combined with regional management. At present, the main tasks assumed by the CWRC in harnessing, development and management of water resources in the Changjiang valley and related problems are as follows.

The CWRC has been Working For the Establishment of a Sound Water

Water administration department is the core department for river basin management in the valley. The main tasks in this field are the following: publicizing related laws, regulations and policies and supervising their execution; participating in the formulation of and amendment to related laws, regulations and policies; resolving inter-provincial water affair disputes; carrying out water resources management and river channel management; executing the law for water administration and other related activities. The primary problems involved in this field are as follows: Institutional and policy weaknesses concerning the legal position and administration functions of the river basin management authority, which needs to be strengthened; Shortage of efficient means for this authority to coordinate benefits between different regions and different sectors.

Flood Prevention and Disaster Reduction

Flood disaster is the most severe natural hazard in Changjiang valley, always with huge flooding losses. Flood prevention and disaster reduction have been the priority task for the CWRC. Through continual construction of flood control projects, flood control standards on Changjiang River have been raised significantly. Since the year of 1954, in which an extraordinary heavy basin–wide flood occurred, the main dykes have withstood all the heavy floods happened on the River ever since, the 1998 floods in particular, which has demonstrated the great achievements in flood control engineering constructions.

Safety for hundreds of millions of people' properties and lives has been ensured and the continual and stable growth of national economy guaranteed. Nevertheless, due to the fact that ground elevations in the plain areas on the middle and lower Changjiang are generally lower than flood stages of the River and that flood control standards are in general on the lower side, flood control situations on the Changjiang have always been severe.

Water and Soil Conservation has been Implemented With Force

Attention has also been paid to both ecological system protection and water and soil conservation. Up to now, more than 100,000 sq. km areas of water and soil loss regions have been brought under control. In these conservation areas, water and soil loss has basically halted and environment quality improved. However, water and soil loss in the valley has not been completely brought to an end.

It is estimated that the amount of area existing water and soil loss is about 560,000 sq. km in the valley. The areas are still increasing due to human activities such as deforestation. Sediment load discharged into the sea reaches 500 million tons each year.

Great Importance has been Attached to the Fundamental

Hydrologic and survey data collection and processing have provided basic data for planning, scientific researches, design, flood fighting and water administration and basis for decision making. Currently, there are more than 6400 hydrologic and meteorological stations in the valley with many survey and experimental units scattered all over the valley. However, great difficulties have always been encountered for these units to carry out their works due to institutional and market factors.

These difficulties include fund shortage, too heavy burdens of various kinds, difficulty in translating scientific and technological advances into production forces and competition without order. All this has severely constrained the smooth implementation of fundamental programmes in the valley.

River Basin Planning has been an Important Task of the CWRC

During the mid-1950s, the CWRC carried out overall river basin planning in the light of requirements for economic development at the time. In 1959 the CWRC formulated the Report on Main Points of Changjiang Valley Comprehensive Planning, which has been the guidance for the development, harnessing and management of the River. In thc ycars that follow, the CWRC has completed designs for Three Gorges Project, Danjiangkou Project and so on, planning for river reaches of the main stem and the primary tributaries and planning for South to North Water Transfer, flood control on the middle and lower Changjiang River and river training and so forth.

This report has been approved by the State Council in December 1990 and made the basis for the development, utilization and protection of water resources and flood prevention in the valley. However, there is a shortage of definite legislation for supervising the implementation of river planning so as to ensure the execution of the planning. It happened now and then events that violated the planning principles. There exist weaknesses in functions for the river basin management authority to execute macroscopical management and supervision.

The Execution of Water Management for Protection

Up to now, the CWRC has received 75 pieces of water withdraw register applications and granted 45 pieces of water withdraw licenses, the annual approved withdraw amount totaling 374.1 billion m^3. Through implementation of water quality monitoring and protection measures, the discharging of pollutants in the valley is being brought under control.

Great efforts have been made to realise unified management of water quality and water quantity so as to guarantee the sustainable development of water resources in the valley. However, due to the fact that water management operations have not been completely put into place and that water quality management system has not been tidied up yet, water management in the valley has been severely hampered.

CWRC has Further Provided Services to and Participated in Social and Economic

Upon the firm footing of carrying out survey and exploration, design and scientific researches for water resources and hydropower development, the CWRC has actively involved it in other fields, such as construction, transportation, information, commerce, trade and so on. It has made unique contributions to water resources and hydropower development, especially the construction of large–scale backbone projects in the valley, contributing a great deal to social and economic growth. However, the current market of survey and exploration, design and scientific researches is not adequately mature yet, and related regulations have not been made sound and complete, which has influenced the execution of these activities. In addition, for lack of fund and policy support from the government, the river basin management authority is hard to organize construction of backbone projects on the main stem and its primary tributaries and to carry out rolling development planning.

It is prescribed in a State Council approved responsibility-division scheme that river basin management authorities shall assume the responsibility to organize the construction and to manage the backbone water projects or key inter–provincial projects. Actually this provision is just idle theorizing, because the river basin management authorities have no means to develop their mainstay businesses, say no more of rolling developments.

WATER STORAGE AND MANAGEMENT

An intensified hydrological cycle could make reservoir management more challenging, because there is often a trade-off between storing water for dry period use and evacuating reservoirs before the onset of the flood season to protect downstream communities. Reservoirs have been usually sized to handle a certain amount of stream flow variability, determined from a relatively short historical record. If the variability increases, reservoirs may be undersized to meet demands or adequately serve as flood protection. Thus, it may become more difficult to meet delivery requirements during prolonged periods between reservoir refilling without also increasing the risk of flooding. Earlier spring run-off from snowmelt is a likely manifestation of global warming. To the extent that adequate reservoir space is available, changing the operation procedures of reservoirs could mitigate some of these effects.

GROUNDWATER CHANGES

In many communities, groundwater is the main source of water for both irrigation and municipal and industrial demands. Generally there are two types of groundwater resources–renewable and non-renewable. Renewable groundwater is directly tied to near-surface hydrologic processes; it is thus intricately tied to the overall hydrologic cycle and could be directly affected by climatic change.

In many places, the overdraft of renewable groundwater aquifers occurs because the rate of withdrawal exceeds the rate of recharge. In fact, renewable groundwater supplies are often thought of being the same resource as surface water because they are so intertwined.

Thus, climate changes could directly affect these recharge rates and the sustainability of renewable groundwater. Non-renewable groundwater supplies are usually derived from deep earth sediments deposited long ago and so have little climatic linkage.

WATER DEMAND CHANGES

Future climate change could affect municipal and industrial water demand. Municipal water demand–especially for garden, lawn, and recreational field watering–is affected by climate to a certain extent, but rates of water use are highly dependent on water resource regulations and local user education. Industrial use for processing purposes is relatively insensitive to climate change; it is conditioned by technologies and modes of use. Demand for cooling water would be affected by a warmer climate because increased water temperatures will reduce the efficiency of cooling, perhaps necessitating increased source water abstraction to meet cooling requirements (or, alternatively, changes in cooling technologies to make them more efficient).

REGIONAL CHANGES

Although the preceding sections postulate some expected hydrologic changes from global warming, these generalizations will not be applicable in all places and at all times. Watson *et al.* examined the regional impacts of climate change, with a particular focus on assessing vulnerability. The report noted that more than 1 billion people do not have access to adequate water supplies, and that some 19 countries, primarily in the Middle East and Northern and Southern Africa, face severe water shortfalls. This number could double by 2025, in large part because of the increased demand caused by economic and population growth. Climate change could exacerbate the situation.

Watson *et al.* noted that many developing countries are particularly vulnerable to climate change because they already experience water shortfalls, being in arid and semi-arid regions. Many people derive their water from single-point systems, such as boreholes or isolated reservoirs.

This lack of "water diversification" increases people's vulnerability to water shortage. These systems do not have the redundancy necessary to minimize the risks during times of shortage. Also, given the often limited technical, financial and management resources available to developing countries, adjusting to shortages or implementing adaptation measures can impose a burden on national economies.

These small water supply systems are found in many parts of the world. Persistent drops in water level in these systems could adversely affect the quality of water by increasing the concentrations of sewage waste and industrial effluents, thereby increasing the potential for outbreaks of disease and reducing the quantity of potable fresh water available for domestic use.

There is evidence that flooding is likely to become a larger problem in many temperate and humid regions, requiring adaptation not only to droughts and chronic water shortages but also to floods and associated damage, raising concerns about dam safety.

Trenberth *et al.* hypothesized that global warming due to enhanced GHGs could increase the intensity of precipitation and reduce its frequency, which would be particularly problematic in regions with rapid changes in land use and land cover, because this would mean changes in surface run-off and groundwater recharge characteristics.

Flooding could be worse, accompanied by rapid drying and less overall water resource availability. The effects on water resources could be sufficient to lead to conflicts among users, regions and countries.

WATER RESOURCES PLANNING

Most public utilities engage in some form of planning, although the extent and scope of planning vary greatly. Utility planning can be characterized by four general approaches: traditional supply planning, least-cost utility planning, integrated resource planning and total water management. Each iteration retains the tried-and-true methods of the preceding approach while expanding the scope of the planning horizon to include new issues and potential solutions.

TRADITIONAL SUPPLY PLANNING

Traditional planning for water utilities is not that different from traditional planning by electricity utilities, which can be characterized by its focus on utility ownership and control of all production resources (including centralstation power plants), its reliance on system and financial planning processes internal to the utility and its emphasis on the goals of minimizing electricity prices and maintaining a high level of system reliability. Risk avoidance also appears to be a paramount consideration in traditional utility planning. In the case of water, ownership and control of resources is more constrained (for example, by limits to groundwater withdrawals). However, the emphasis on utility ownership of the water delivery infrastructure (plants, pipes and so on) prevails much like the case of electricity distribution.

Shortcomings

Three principal concerns about the traditional approach have been advanced. First, forecast demand is taken as a given and virtually no attempt is made to integrate supply management and demand management options.

Second, the public-at-large, outside experts and government regulators generally have little or no involvement in traditional utility planning. Demand analysis and the assessment of supply alternatives takes place within the utility (or a single planning unit within the utility); only the final product is made available for review or regulatory approval. Often, major investment decisions are made with little or no oversight. Third, traditional planning also tends to be confined to individual utilities in virtual isolation. The decision-making process excludes parties who not only have a vested interest but also unique insights about resource options. In sum, there is a tendency for traditional planning to be narrowly focused and exclusionary. Once a utility has committed itself to a plan, little room is left for altering the chosen course.

Supply-Driven Focus

Like other types of public utilities, the prevailing planning processes undertaken by water utilities have been internally driven and dominated by supply considerations. The result has been an emphasis on maintaining reliable water supplies and, accordingly, the engineering of facilities for source development, treatment and storage and transmission and distribution of water. Water-supply planning generally takes the form of forecasting future demand and developing and analysing supply options to meet the projected demand level, plus a comfortable margin. The result is a disaggregated planning approach focusing only on new supply alternatives, while initiatives in the areas of demand management and conservation are consigned to separate programmes. Moreover, conservation effects often are not reflected in revised demand and revenue forecasts.

Delivery, not Demand

Engineering considerations have always been central to water utility planning, at times to the exclusion of other perspectives. Engineering does take into account the benefits and costs of supply projects. However, the emphasis on supply options can result in additions to capacity that outpace growth in demand, which is a problem familiar to the electricity industry.Water's natural abundance in many areas may explain why the central water supply issue is that of engineering water delivery (getting water to where it is needed) rather than managing water demand. Historically, it was easy to presume that there always would be enough water to go around and that plentiful amounts would generally be so inexpensive that investments in demand management would not be cost-effective.

The utility corporate culture, which understandably emphasizes selling more (not less) product, might also favour the supply side. At the very least, utilities traditionally have had little incentive to promote conservation.

LEAST-COST PLANNING

The shortcomings of traditional planning, along with significant external economic and political forces, gave rise to the current interest in least-cost planning, or integrated resource planning (IRP). Least-cost planning emerged in the context of the energy industries during the 1980s as a response to rising costs, a poor record of forecasting and growing concerns about environmental externalities. According to its proponents, planning allows regulators to be more proactive, that is, to actively affect utility decisions rather than simply react to them later on.

Least-cost planning emphasizes a balanced consideration of supply management and demand management options in identifying feasible least-cost alternatives for meeting future water needs. Compared with traditional planning, least-cost planning recognizes that water demand is malleable and that forecast demand does not have to simply be taken as a given in the planning process.

Different definitions emphasize the minimization of rates, customer bills, utility revenue requirements and production (both capacity and operating) costs. The variety of available perspectives leaves open the question of whose costs are supposed to be least: existing customers, future customers, utility shareholders, or society at large.

Another unfortunate implication of the concept of least cost is that it suggests a single, optimal solution. Regulators and utility managers do not necessarily have identical views about the meaning of least-cost planning. According to one survey, "regulators tend to view least-cost planning with an emphasis on conservation, whereas utilities tend to regard least-cost planning as an integrated supply-and-demand analysis."

A Broader Context

Least-cost planning has come to be understood as the comprehensive evaluation of all supply and demand alternatives with the end result, in an attempt to minimize costs, of creating a flexible plan allowing for uncertainty and a changing economic environment. Cost minimization, resource diversity, risk management and flexibility are the hallmarks of least-cost planning.

In practical terms, least-cost planning can be characterized by the consideration of a diverse set of resource options (including conservation, load management, pricing and purchases from other producers); coordination among several departments within the utility; and the use of multiple resource selection goals, including those that address prices, costs, revenue requirements, utility financial condition, risk reduction, technological diversity, environmental quality and economic development. Least-cost planning in no way abandons sound engineering practices, but it does place them in a wider context. It follows that least-cost planning can facilitate regulatory review of supply management and demand management practices and regulatory approval of capacity expansion projects prior to construction. Least-cost planning also can be used to educate policymakers about the critical issues in utility supply decisions and induce utilities to aggressively engage in long-term strategic planning. Least-cost planning can focus on a particular utility or take the form of a statewide assessment of all utilities in a given utility sector, the latter of which is typically performed by a state resource management agency.

Demand Versus Supply

In contrast to traditional supply planning, leastcost planning gives much weight to the distinction between demand management and supply management activities, both of which can be used to achieve reliability goals. Least-cost planning recognizes that demand is malleable rather than simply a fixed input to planning models. The demand side involves any strategy to eliminate or defer the need for an investment in new capacity by the utility, including load management, conservation and pricing strategies. The supply side involves determining the most efficient method of meeting growing demand, including investments in new capacity.

All demand management activities that decrease the demand for utility services tend to affect supply management since existing system capacity is released for other customers and other uses. That is, the freed or redirected utility capacity can be compared to that provided by more traditional means. Thus emerged the concept of "negawatts," meaning electricity "produced" through conservation and efficient use of existing electricity supply resources. A related idea is the trend to establish energy service companies, as compared with traditional electric utilities, who could market efficiency (or demand management) as well as electrical power.

Complexity, Risk and Cost

Least-cost utility and planning is complicated by the lack of familiarly with demand management, barriers to coordination with nearby utilities, the use of broad definitions of costs (such as those associated with externalities) and the inclusion of goals (such as resource protection) not directly attributable to the utility. Traditional planners tend to view least-cost planning as more risky, as least in terms of supply reliability. Advocates of least-cost planning would counter that planning actually reduces some forms of risk, such as the revenue recovery risk associated with excess capacity.

While highly pertinent to the debate, these disagreements can be overcome. One issue that merits especially careful attention, however, is that of the cost of planning itself. Certainly, the benefits of planning should outweigh the costs. This calculation itself poses a rational decision-making problem. The benefits of increased awareness and understanding and reduced ignorance and uncertainty can be substantial but are not easily quantified.

WATER RESOURCES IN INDIA

India is rich in water resources, being endowed with a network of great rivers and vast alluvial basins to hold groundwater. Conditions, however, vary widely from region to region. Whereas there are some chronically drought affected areas, there are others which are frequently subject to damage by floods.

On the whole, under the pressure of rapid population growth, the available resources of water are being developed and depleted at a fast rate and the situation seriously underlines the need for taking up integrated plans for water conservation and utilization for every agro-ecological area to meet the increasing demands of irrigation, water harvesting, human and livestock consumption,expanding industry, hydro-electric power generation, recreation,navigation and other uses.

Water resources of a country constitute one of its vital assets. India receives annual precipitation of about 4000 km^3. The rainfall in India shows very high spatial and temporal variability and paradox of the situation is that Mousinram near Cherrapunji, which receives the highest rainfall in the world, also suffers from a shortage of water during the non-rainy season, almost every year. The total average annual flow per year for the Indian rivers is estimated as 1953 km^3. The total annual replenishable groundwater resources are assessed as 432 km^3.

The annual utilizable surface water and groundwater resources of India are estimated as 690 km^3 and 396 km^3 per year, respectively. With rapid growing population and improving living standards the pressure on our water resources is increasing and per capita availability of water resources is reducing day by day. Due to spatial and temporal variability in precipitation the country faces the problem of flood and drought syndrome.

Overexploitation of groundwater is leading to reduction of low flows in the rivers, declining of the groundwater resources, and salt water intrusion in aquifers of the coastal areas.

Over canal-irrigation in some of the command areas has resulted in waterlogging and salinity. The quality of surface and groundwater resources is also deteriorating because of increasing pollutant loads from point and non-point sources.

The climate change is expected to affect precipitation and water availability. So far, the data collection, processing, storage and dissemination have not received adequate attention.

The efforts initiated under the Hydrology Project Phase-I and the development of the Decision Support System proposed under Hydrology Project Phase-II are expected to bridge some of the gaps between the developed advanced technologies of water resources planning, designing and management and their field applications.

The paper presents availability and demands of water resources in India as well as describes the various issues and strategies for developing a holistic approach for sustainable development and management of the water resources of the country.

It also highlights integration of the blue and green flows and concepts of virtual water transfer for sustainable management of the water resources for meeting the demands of the present, without compromising the needs of future generations.

Of all the planet's renewable resources, water has a unique place. It is essential for sustaining all forms of life, food production, economic development, and for general well being.

It is impossible to substitute for most of its uses, difficult to de-pollute, expensive to transport, and it is truly a unique gift to mankind from nature. Water is also one of the most manageable of the natural resources as it is capable of diversion, transport, storage, and recycling.

All these properties impart to water its great utility for human beings. The surface water and groundwater resources of the country play a major role in agriculture, hydropower generation, livestock production, industrial activities, forestry, fisheries, navigation, recreational activities, etc.

According to National Water Policy in the planning and operation of systems, water allocation priorities should be broadly as:

- Drinking water,
- Irrigation,
- Hydropower,
- Ecology,
- Agro-industries and non-agricultural industries,
- Navigation.

India receives annual precipitation of about 4000 km^3, including snowfall. Out of this, monsoon rainfall is of the order of 3000 km^3. Rainfall in India is dependent on the south-west and north-east monsoons, on shallow cyclonic depressions and disturbances and on local storms. Most of it takes place under the influence of south-west monsoon between June and September except in Tamil Nadu, where it is under the influence of north-east monsoon during October and November. India is gifted with a river system comprising more than 20 major rivers with several tributaries. Many of these rivers are perennial and some of these are seasonal. The rivers like Ganges, Brahmaputra and Indus originate from the Himalayas and carry water throughout the year. The snow and ice melt of the Himalayas and the base flow contribute the flows during the lean season. Lal mentioned that more than 50% of water resources of India are located in various tributaries of these river systems.

Average water yield per unit area of the Himalayan rivers is almost double that of the south peninsular rivers system, indicating the importance of snow and glacier melt contribution from the high mountains. Apart from the water available in the various rivers of the country, the groundwater is also an important source of water for drinking, irrigation, industrial uses, etc. It accounts for about 80% of domestic water requirement and more than 45% of the total irrigation in the country. As per the international norms, if per-capita water availability is less than 1700 m^3 per year then the country is categorized as water stressed and if it is less than 1000 m^3 per capita per year then the country is classified as water scarce. In India per capita surface water availability in the years 1991 and 2001 were 2309 and 1902 m3 and these are projected to reduce to 1401 and 1191 m^3 by the years 2025 and 2050 respectively.

Hence, there is a need for proper planning, development and management of the greatest assets of the country, viz. water and land resources for raising the standards of living of the millions of people, particularly in the rural areas.

MAN'S INFLUENCE ON HYDROLOGICAL CYCLE

The hydrological cycle is being modified quantitatively and qualitatively in most of the river basins of our country as a result of the developmental activities such as construction of dams and reservoirs, land use change, irrigation, etc. Such human activities affecting the hydrological regime can be classified into four major groups:

- Activities which affect river runoff by diverting water from rivers, lakes, and reservoirs or by groundwater extraction,
- Activities modifying the river channels, e.g. construction of reservoirs and ponds, levees and river training, channel dredging, etc.
- Activities due to which runoff and other water balance components are modified due to impacts of basin surface e.g. agricultural practices, drainage of swamps, afforestation or deforestation, urbanization, etc.

- Activities which may induce climate changes at regional or global scale, e.g. modifying the composition of atmosphere by increasing the 'greenhouse' gases or by increased evaporation caused by large scale water projects.

For understanding the effects appropriately, hydrological modelling approaches have to be adopted.

MONSOON AND ITS FORECASTING

The word monsoon is derived from 'mausim', an Arabic word, which means season and the word is applied to winds whose direction is reversed completely from one season to the next season. The largest precipitation accumulations for periods greater than 24 h are associated with the Asian monsoon. Normal duration of monsoon in India is about 100 to 120 days beginning from first June.

In India, the two monsoon seasons (the southwest monsoon in June to September and the northeast monsoon in November– December) bring forth rains.

An important feature affecting the rainfall in India is the change in the direction of wind currents that occurs in different months. In May when the weather is very hot, the south-east trade winds from the south Indian Ocean cross the equator and after deflecting, due to rotation of the earth, extend rapidly into the north Indian ocean, viz. the Bay of Bengal in early May and afterwards get established over both the sea areas.

This westerly current, which extends from the Arabic coast to the China sea across India is known as the southwest monsoon. In winter season, the wind currents over India blow from north to south. The winds over the country are mostly of continental origin and are dry during this season. This period is known as the winter in north-east monsoon. The weather disturbances moving from the west result in snowfall as well as rainfall over the Himalayas and rainfall over north India.

The north-east monsoon picks up moisture over the Bay of Bengal and produces rain over Tamil Nadu. Scientists of India Meteorological Department (IMD), New Delhi, have developed a new monsoon forecast model that is claimed to be more accurate than the earlier one. The model uses eight land, ocean and wind parametres to predict the extent of the monsoon. It replaces an earlier 16-parameter model, developed in 1988.

The new model enables a forecast to be made 40 days earlier than previously, and allows scientists to update their predictions halfway through the June–September monsoon season, a time that is crucial for Indian summer crops. In this model there is scope for correction, as by mid-July, the nature of advance of the monsoon becomes known, and any disturbing trends in El Niño (which can adversely influence the Indian monsoon performance) become apparent.

The new model has retained six of the parametres used in the previous model, which had a relatively stable link with the monsoon, and two additional parametres believed to influence the Indian monsoon: temperatures in northwest Europe in January and in the southern Indian Ocean in March. It was devised using 38 years of data up to 1995, and has been verified for the seven-year period from 1996 to 2002. The new model is claimed to be 95% accurate. Its true test lies ahead, but it is expected that India now has a more realistic and more statistically stable model for forecasting monsoons.

WATER RESOURCES MANAGEMENT IN INDIA

In view of the existing status of water resources and increasing demands of water for meeting the requirements of the rapidly growing population of the country as well as the problems that are likely to arise in future, a holistic, wellplanned long-term strategy is needed for sustainable water resources management in India. The water resources management practices may be based on increasing the water supply and managing the water demand under the stressed water availability conditions.

Data monitoring, processing, storage, retrieval and dissemination constitute the very important aspects of the water resources management. These data may be utilized not only for management but also for the planning and design of the water resources structures. In addition to these, now a days decision support systems are being developed for providing the necessary inputs to the decision makers for water resources management.

Also, knowledge sharing, people's participation, mass communication and capacity building are essential for effective water resources management. Some important aspects of such strategies are described as follows.

Flood Management

Among all natural disasters, floods are the most frequent to be faced in India. Floods in the eastern part of India, viz. Orissa, West Bengal, Bihar and Andhra Pradesh in the recent past, are striking examples. According to the information published by different government agencies, the tangible and intangible losses due to floods in India are increasing at alarming rate.

As reported by the Central Water Commission (CWC) under the Ministry of Water Resources, Government of India, the annual average area affected by floods is 7.563 Mha. This observation is based on the data for the period 1953–2000 published in IWRS, with variability ranging from 1.26 Mha in 1965 to 1.75 Mha in 1978.

On an average floods have affected about 33 million persons during 1953 to 2000. There is every possibility that this figure may increase due to rapid growth of population and increased encroachments of the flood plains for habitation, cultivation and other activities. The main causes of floods in India are inadequate capacity within river banks to contain high flows, river bank erosion and silting of river beds.

The additional factors are as land slides leading to obstruction of flow and change of the river course, retardation of flow due to tidal and backwater effects, poor natural drainage in the flood-prone area, cyclone and associated heavy rain storms or cloud bursts, snowmelt and glacial outbursts and dam break flows.

After the disastrous floods of 1954 a national programme of flood management was launched. The Government of India has taken a number of steps for flood management. As stated by Mohapatra and Singh, some of the important policies on flood management include: policy statement, high level committee on flood, policy statement, ministerial committee on flood control, ministers committee on flood and flood relief; working groups on flood control for five-year plans; Rashtriya Barh Ayog, National Water Policy, National Commission for Integrated Water Resource Development, Regional Task Force, and National Water Policy.

The committees and commissions constituted by the government have given valuable recommendations on different issues of flood management. Various types of structural and non-structural measures have been taken up to reduce the damages in the flood plains. The structural measures, such as the construction of embankments, levees, spurs, etc. have been implemented in some of the states. The total length of constructed embankments is 16,800 km and drainage channels are of 32,500 km. A total of 1040 towns and 4760 villages are currently protected against flood. Barring occasional breaches in embankments, these have provided reasonable protection to an area of about 15.07 Mha. A large number of reservoirs have been constructed and these reservoirs have resulted in reduction of intensity of floods. The non-structural measures such as flood forecasting and warning are also being adopted. The flood forecasting and flood warning in India commenced in 1958, for the Yamuna river in Delhi. It has evolved to cover most of the flood-prone interstate river basins in India. The CWC has established a flood forecasting system covering 62 major rivers with more than 157 stations for issuing flood forecasts covering almost all the flood-prone states. The response of state governments towards enactment of flood plain zoning bill is not encouraging. Though some of the states (e.g. Rajasthan and Manipur) have enacted the flood plain zoning legislation, the major flood-affected states (e.g. Assam, Himachal, Goa and Sikkim) have not considered such legislation.

A working group of National Natural Resources Management System standing committee on water resources for flood risk zoning of major flood-prone rivers considering remote sensing input was constituted by the Ministry of Water Resources in 1999. The working group recommended flood risk zoning using satellite-based remote sensing with a view to giving thrust towards implementation of flood plain zoning measures.

The flood management measures have to be more focused and targeted towards the decided objectives within a stipulated time frame. For flood plain zoning, methods have to be evolved in consultation with the local bodies so that the legislation on flood plain zoning is adopted. As suggested by the Working Group of tenth five-year plan that the possible apprehensions of difficulties in drafting a legislation should not become a bar to the idea of the approach of flood plain zoning itself.

Flood forecasting constitutes one of the most important actions of flood disaster preparedness. Technical advancement in a wellplanned flood forecasting and warning system can help in providing higher lead time for timely action. It is well recognized that long-term solution of flood problems lies in creating appropriate flood storage in reservoirs. The total live storage capacity of completed projects in India is about 174 km^3. A large flood storage space in reservoirs is required for a successful flood management programme. Flood management also calls for community participation.

Farmers, professional bodies, industries and voluntary organizations have to be aware about flood management. People's participation in preparedness, flood fighting and disaster response is required. Media like radio, TV, newspapers can also play an important role in flood management. As India shares river systems with six neighbouring countries, viz. Nepal, China, Bhutan, Pakistan, Bangladesh and Myanmar, bilateral cooperation for flood management is necessary for India and the concerned country. The government of India has taken some initiatives in this regard however, more active participation is required.

Drought Management

The drought-prone area assessed in the country is of the order of 51.12 Mha. The planning and management of the effects of drought appear to have a low priority due to associated randomness and uncertainty in defining the start and end of droughts. Further, most of the drought planning and management schemes are generally launched after persisting drought conditions. The traditional system of drought monitoring and estimating losses by crop cutting needs replacement with real time remote sensing, GIS, GPS and modelling techniques for ensuring transparency and quick response.

Scope of losses may be extended to groundwater depletion, damage to perennial trees, plantations, orchards and depletion in fertility of livestock. Food, fodder, agricultural inputs and water banks may be established in vulnerable areas instead of their storage in surplus regions to avoid transport bottlenecks during the drought. Robust and rainfall independent off-farm livelihood opportunities may be targeted in the drought mitigation strategy.

Conjunctive use of surface and groundwater, aquifer recharge and watershed management with community participation is another important policy paradigm shift to be internalized fully. After normal rainfall resumes there is a rapid decrease of government and public interest in drought-planning schemes. Most of the time the execution of the drought management scheme is based on the administrative units, while planning of water resources is based on basin scale.

Therefore, an integrated basin development approach is required to be developed and implemented for preparing the drought management plan before, during and after the occurrence of the drought. In this regard, there is a need for the development of the decision support systems (DSS) for the monitoring and management of the drought on basin scale utilizing the advanced capabilities of remote sensing, geographical information system and knowledgebased systems.

The DSS should also provide support to the decision makers for providing the information at different spatial and temporal scales. It would help them in taking the required management measures in the droughtprone areas for different administrative units. In the drought-prone areas, publication campaign may be launched for water conservation with the help of electronic and print media.

Necessary steps may be taken at political, administrative and technical levels to encourage people participation in the drought management for optimum utilization of the available water supply to meet the demands. Strengthening of RandD and capacity building in terms of emerging information technologies and issues of damages is also called upon to bring in resilience in the drought coping strategies.

Groundwater Management

To protect the aquifers from overexploitation, an effective groundwater management policy oriented towards promotion of efficiency, equity and sustainability is required. Agricultural holdings in India are highly fragmented and the rural population density is large. The exploitation of groundwater resources should be regulated so as not to exceed the recharging possibilities, as well as to ensure social equity.

The detrimental environmental consequences of over-exploitation of groundwater need to be effectively prevented by the Central and State Governments. Overexploitation of groundwater should be avoided, especially near the coasts to prevent ingress of seawater into freshwater aquifers. Clearly, a joint management approach combining government administration with active people participation is a promising solution.

In critically overexploited areas, bore-well drilling should be regulated till the water table attains the desired elevation. Artificial recharge measures need to be urgently implemented in these areas. Amongst the various recharge techniques, percolation tanks are least expensive in terms of initial construction costs. Many such tanks already exist but a vast majority of these structures have silted up. In such cases, cleaning of the bed of the tank will make them reusable.

Promotion of participatory action in rehabilitating tanks for recharging would go a long way in augmenting groundwater supply. Due to declining water table, the cost of extraction of groundwater has been increasing over time and wells often go dry. This poses serious financial burden on farmers. Hence, special programmes need to be designed to support these farmers. Finally, the role of government will have to switch from that of a controller of groundwater development to that of a facilitator of equitable and sustainable development. Shah mentions that three large-scale responses to groundwater depletion in India have emerged in recent years in an uncoordinated manner, and each presents an element of what might be its coherent strategy of resources governance as follows:

Energy–irrigation Nexus

Throughout South Asia, the 'groundwater boom' was fired during the 1970s and 90s by government support to tubewells and subsidies to electricity supplied by state-owned electricity utilities to farmers. The invidious energy–irrigation nexus that emerged as a result and wrecked the electricity utilities and encouraged waste of groundwater are widely criticized.

However, hidden in this nexus is a unique opportunity for groundwater managers to influence the working of the colossal anarchy that is India's groundwater socio-ecology. Even while subsidizing electricity, many state governments have begun restricting power supply to agriculture to cut their losses.

The International Water Management Institute Research has shown that with intelligent management of power supply to agriculture, energy–irrigation nexus can be a powerful tool for groundwater demand management in livelihood supporting socio-ecologies to create tradable poverty rights in groundwater. Mexico finally had to turn to electricity supply management to enforce its groundwater concessions.

Inter-basin Transfers to Recharge Unconfined Alluvial Aquifers

In western India's unconfined alluvial aquifers, it is being increasingly realised that groundwater depletion can be countered only by importing surface water, Arizonastyle. The Jiangsu province in eastern China has implemented its own little inter-basin water transfer from Yangzee to counter groundwater depletion in the Northern part. Similarly, one of the major uses Gujarat has found for water of the Sardar Sarovar Project on Narmada river is to recharge the depleted aquifers of North Gujarat and Kachchh. A key consideration behind

India's proposed mega-scheme to link its northern rivers with peninsular rivers too is to counter groundwater depletion in western and southern India.

Mass-based Recharge Movement

In many parts of hardrock India, groundwater depletion has invoked wildfire community-based mass movement for rainwater harvesting and recharge, which interestingly has failed to take off in unconfined alluvial aquifers. It is difficult to assess the social value of this movement partly because 'formal hydrology' and 'popular hydrology' have failed to find a meeting ground. Scientists want check dams sited near recharge zones; villagers want them close to their wells.

Scientists recommend recharge tubewells to counter the silt layer impeding recharge; farmers just direct floodwaters into their wells after filtering. Scientists worry about upstream–downstream externalities; farmers say everyone lives downstream. Scientists say the hard-rock aquifers have too little storage to justify the prolific growth in recharge structures; people say a recharge structure is worthwhile if their wells provide even 1000 m^3 of lifesaving irrigation/ha in times of delayed rain. Hydrologists keep writing the obituary of the recharge movement; but the movement has spread from eastern Rajasthan to Gujarat, thence to Madhya Pradesh and Andhra Pradesh. Protagonists think that with better planning of recharge structures and larger coverage, decentralized recharge movement can be a major response to India's groundwater depletion because it can ensure that water tables in pockets of intensive use rebound close to pre-development levels at the end of the monsoon season every year they have a good monsoon, which is at least twice in five years. They surmise that this is not impossible because even today, India's total groundwater extraction is barely 5% of its annual precipitation. Shah mentions the following workable solutions for management of groundwater resources:

- Banning private wells is futile; crowd them out by improving public water supply.
- Regulating final users is impossible; facilitate mediating agencies to emerge, and regulate them.
- Pricing agricultural groundwater use is infeasible; instead, use energy pricing and supply to manage agricultural groundwater draft.
- No alternative to improved supply side management: better rain-water capture and recharge, imported surface water in lieu of groundwater pumping.
- Grow the economy, take pressure off land, and formalize the water sector.

Conjunctive use of Surface and Groundwater

Large canal infrastructure network for providing irrigation has been the prime goal of the Government of India, since the first five-year plan, which continued up to seventh five-year plan. In some of the irrigation project commands such as Sarda Sahayak in UP, Gandak in Bihar, Chambal in Rajasthan, Nagarjuna Sagar in Andhra Pradesh, Ghataprabha and Malaprabha in Karnataka etc., problems of waterlogging are being faced.

The main reason for excessive use of surface water as compared to groundwater is its much lower price for irrigation as compared to the cost incurred in using groundwater. Waterlogging problems could be overcome if conjunctive use of surface and groundwater is made. Groundwater utilization for irrigation in waterlogged areas can help to lower the groundwater table and reclaim the affected soil.

Over exploitation of groundwater in areas like Mehsana, in Gujarat; parts of Meeurt and Varanasi districts in Uttar Pradesh, Coimbatore in Tamil Nadu and Karnal district in Haryana etc. have resulted in mining of groundwater. Many research workers have focused the causes of waterlogging. Several groundwater flow modelling studies have focused on assessing the waterlogged areas and measures to control problems of waterlogging and salinization.

It is desirable that the irrigation needs for fulfilling crop water requirements should be satisfied by judicious utilization of available canal water in conjunction with groundwater so as to keep the water table within the acceptable range. Thus, the optimal conjunctive use of the region's surface and groundwater resources would help in minimizing the problems of waterlogging and groundwater mining.

Water Conservation

Water conservation implies improving the availability of water through augmentation by means of storage of water in surface reservoirs, tanks, soil and groundwater zone. It emphasizes the need to modify the space and time availability of water to meet the demands. This concept also highlights the need for judicious use of water.

There is a great potential for better conservation and management of water resources in its various uses. On the demand side, a variety of economic, administrative and community-based measures can help conserve water. Also, it is necessary to control the growth of population since large population is putting massive stress on all natural resources. Since agriculture accounts for about 69% of all water withdrawn, the greatest potential for conservation lies in increasing irrigation efficiencies. Just a 10% improvement in irrigation efficiency could conserve enough water to double the amount available for drinking. In India, sprinkler irrigation is being adopted in Haryana, Rajasthan, Uttar Pradesh, Karnataka, Gujarat and Maharashtra. The use of sprinkler irrigation saves about 56% of water for the winter crops of bajra and jowar, while for cotton, the saving is about 30% as compared to the traditional gravity irrigation.

An important supplement to conservation is to minimize the wastage of water. In urban water supply, for example, almost 30% of the water is wasted due to leakages, carelessness, etc. while most metro cities face deficit in supply of water. It is, therefore, imperative to prevent wastage. In industries also, there is a scope for economy in the use of water. Prices of water for all uses should be fixed, keeping in mind its economic value, control of wastage, and the ability of users to pay. As water is becoming scarcer, pricing will be an important factor in avoiding wastage and ensuring optimal use.

Watershed Management

For an equitable and sustainable management of shared water resources, flexible, holistic approach of Integrated Water Resources Management (IWRM) is required, which can cater to hydrological variations in time and space and changes in socio-economic needs along with societal values.

Watershed is the unit of management in IWRM, where surface water and groundwater are inextricably linked and related to land use and management. Watershed management aims to establish a workable and efficient framework for the integrated use, regulation and development of land and water resources in a watershed for socio-economic growth. Local communities play a central role in the planning, implementation and funding of activities within participatory watershed development programmes.

In these initiatives, people use their traditional knowledge, available resources, imagination and creativity to develop watershed and implement community-centred programme. Currently, many programmes, campaigns and projects are underway in different parts of India to spread mass awareness and mobilize the general population in managing water resources.

Some of these are being implemented by the Central/State Governments, while others have been taken up by various Non-Governmental Organizations (NGOs). For example, Hariyali (meaning 'greenery') is a watershed management project, launched by the Central Government, which aims at enabling the rural population to conserve water for drinking, irrigation, fisheries and afforestation as well as generate employment opportunities.

The project is being executed by the Gram Panchayats (village governing bodies) with people's participation; the technical support is provided by the block (sub-district) administration. Another good example of water conservation efforts is the 'Neeru-Meeru' (Water and You) programme launched in May 2000 by the Government of Andhra Pradesh.

During the last three years, an additional storage space of more than 18,000 lakh m^3 has been created by constructing various water-harvesting structures such as percolation tanks, dugout ponds, check dams, etc. through peoples' participation. Tarun Bharat Sangh (Young India Association) or TBS is an NGO which promotes sustainable water management through rainwater harvesting in Rajasthan. Since 1986, TBS has helped in building or restoring nearly 10,000 water harvesting structures in Alwar and neighbouring districts in the Aravalli hills of northeastern Rajasthan.

The central message of TBS is that good water management requires good land management. Emphasis is also put on protecting forests. The efforts of villagers are visible in the form of rising water table and regenerated forests on the rocky slopes of Aravalli hills. Despite some of the above success stories, so far there is no appreciable improvement on watershed resources utilization at national level. Undoubtedly, coordinated watershed development programmes need to be encouraged and awareness about benefits of these programmes must be created among the people.

Rainwater Harvesting

Rainwater harvesting is the process to capture and store rainfall for its efficient utilization and conservation to control its runoff, evaporation and seepage.

Some of the benefits of rainwater harvesting are:

- It increases water availability
- It checks the declining water table
- It is environmentally friendly
- It improves the quality of groundwater through dilution, mainly of fluoride, nitrate, and salinity,
- It prevents soil erosion and flooding, especially in the urban areas.

Even in ancient days, people were familiar with the methods of conservation of rainwater and had practised them with success. Different methods of rainwater harvesting were developed to suit the geographical and meteorological conditions of the region in various parts of the country.

Traditional rainwater harvesting, which is still prevalent in rural areas, is done by using surface storage bodies like lakes, ponds, irrigation tanks, temple tanks, etc. For example, *Kul* (diversion channels) irrigation system which carries water from glaciers to villages is practised in the Spiti area of Himachal Pradesh. In the arid regions of Rajasthan, rainwater harvesting structures locally known as *Kund* (a covered underground tank), are constructed near the house or a village to tackle drinking water problem.

In Meghalaya, *Bamboo Rainwater Harvesting* for tapping of stream and spring water through bamboo pipes to irrigate plantations is widely prevalent. The system is so perfected that about 18–20 litres of water entering the bamboo pipe system per minute is transported over several hundred metres.

There is a need to recharge aquifers and conserve rainwater through water harvesting structures. In urban areas, rainwater will have to be harvested using rooftops and open spaces. Harvesting rainwater not only reduces the possibility of flooding, but also decreases the community's dependence on groundwater for domestic uses. Apart from bridging the demand–supply gap, recharging improves the quality of groundwater, raises the water table in wells/bore-wells and prevents flooding and choking of drains.

One can also save energy to pump groundwater as water table rises. These days rainwater harvesting is being taken up on a massive scale in many states in India. Substantial benefits of rainwater harvesting exist in urban areas as water demand has already outstripped supply in most of the cities.

Water Quality Conservation and Environment Restoration

Implementation of water pollution prevention strategies and restoration of ecological systems are integral components of all development plans. To preserve our water and environment, we need to make systematic changes in the way we grow our food, manufacture the goods, and dispose off the waste. In India, agriculture is the biggest user and polluter of water.

If pollution by agriculture is reduced, it would improve water quality and would also eliminate cost incurred for treatment of diseases. Like all other inputs, there is an optimal quantity of fertilizer for given conditions and excess application does not improve the crop yield. Pricing of fertilizers and pesticides as well as appropriate legislation to regulate their use will also go a long way in stopping indiscriminate use. Industries need to carefully treat their waste discharges.

Manufacturers may reduce water pollution by reusing materials and chemicals and switching over to less toxic alternatives. Industrial symbiosis, in which the unusable wastes from one product/firm become the input for another, is an attractive solution. Also, there is a need to encourage reductions or replacement of toxic chemicals, possibly through fiscal measures.

Pollution taxes in the Netherlands, for example, have helped the country slash discharges of heavy metals such as mercury and arsenic into waterways by up to 99% between 1976 and the mid-1990s. Many countries discourage use of equipment, such as thermometres that contain mercury. Such measures in India would also be helpful.

For this purpose, society and individuals should have a greater knowledge and ability to bring about the required changes. Widely and readily available technical help about 'how to do this' will accelerate the process. Environmental improvement and restoration should be planned and implemented such that the freshwater resources are protected and their quality is maintained and/or enhanced.

A broad perspective is needed that unites social, economic and environmental concerns in a landscape where upland forests and rangeland, wetlands, agricultural and urban areas are integrated. An understanding of watershed linkages allows long-term and sustainable solutions to a variety of natural resource problems.

Model efforts in this direction include the capture, storage and safe release of water and the prevention of accelerated soil erosion through the structures and vegetation. While utilizing water and land resources, their ability to serve other uses is often degraded either inadvertently or due to carelessness. Efforts should be made to restore landscapes and ecosystems to more efficiently protect water quality, aquatic and wildlife. On the legislative front, laws are required to check littering as well as to implement 'polluter pays' principle. More importantly, these laws should be strictly enforced.

Recycle and Reuse of Water

Another way through which we can improve freshwater availability is by recycle and reuse of water. It is said that in the city of Frankfurt, Germany, every drop of water is recycled eight times. Use of water of lesser quality, such as reclaimed wastewater, for cooling and fire fighting is an attractive option for large and complex industries to reduce their water costs, increase production and decrease the consumption of energy.

This conserves better quality waters for potable uses. Currently, recycling of water is not practised on a large scale in India and there is considerable scope and incentive to use this alternative. Estimates show that recyclable water is between 103 and 177 km^3/year for low and high population projections.

Interbasin Water Transfer

The vast variation, both in space and time, in the availability of water in different regions of India has created a food–drought–flood syndrome with some areas suffering from flood damages and other areas facing acute water shortage. Karnataka, Tamil Nadu, Rajasthan, Gujarat, Andhra Pradesh and Maharashtra are the worst drought-prone states. Uttar Pradesh, Bihar, West Bengal, Orissa and Assam face severe flood problems. Inter-basin transfer of water in India is a long-term option to partly overcome the spatial and temporal imbalance of availability and demand of water resources.

The transfer of water from surplus areas to deficit areas is not a new concept. Many such schemes have been implemented all over the world. In India too, projects like the Periyar–Vaigai system, Indira Gandhi canal and Telugu Ganga stand as classic examples of inter-basin water transfer. In the seventies, the Garland Canal proposal of Dastur and the Ganga–Cauvery Canal proposal of Rao were received with considerable attention. A National Perspective Plan (NPP) for water resources development was formulated by the Government of India in 1980s. The distinctive feature of the NPP is that the transfer of water is essentially by gravity and only in small reaches by lift pumping (not exceeding 120 m). This plan comprises two components:

- Himalayan Rivers Development,
- Peninsular Rivers Development.

While the second component will be an inter-state venture, the first will involve neighbouring countries too and thus will be an international venture. Some of the major benefits expected from inter linking of the rivers are:

- Irrigation potential is to increase from 140 to 175 Mha;
- Drinking water availability is to increase by about 12 km^3;
- Peak flood discharge to get reduced by about 30% due construction of reservoirs;
- Generation of 34,000 MW of electricity;
- Possibilities of inland navigation to provide cheap transport.

Vulnerability to Climate Change and Adaptation Strategies

Climate change is a human-induced stress (at least in part) that is generally not yet taken into account. An annual mean global warming of 0.4 to 0.8°C has been reported since the late 19th century27. In India, the analysis of seasonal and annual air temperatures, using the data for 1881 to 1997 has shown a warming trend of 0.57°C per hundred years.

Substantial increases in greenhouse gases are likely in the future as a consequence of which global mean surface temperature is expected to increase by between 1.4°C and 3°C for low emission scenarios and between 2.5°C and 5.8°C for high-emission scenarios by 2100 with respect to 1990. Lal states that globally averaged precipitation is projected to increase, but at the regional scale both increases and decreases are projected.

Global mean sea level is likely to rise by 0.14 to 0.80 m from 1990 to 2100. Under changed climatic scenarios, a number of chain events like melting of glaciers, sea level rise, submergence of islands/coastal areas and deviant rainfall patterns, are likely to occur. Likely impacts would include a greater annual variability in the monsoon's precipitation levels, leading to more intense floods and droughts. Thus, climate change in future is expected to have implications on river flows in South Asia including India.

Global climate change is likely to result in severe droughts and floods in India, with major impacts on human health and food supplies. Developing countries of temperate and tropical Asia already are highly vulnerable to the extreme climate events such as floods, droughts and cyclones. Climate change and variability would exacerbate these vulnerabilities.

Annual and seasonal changes in climate would alter the frequency and severity of major droughts. Changing temperature and evaporation rates would alter soil moisture conditions and the amount of runoff from the catchments into reservoirs. There are some evidences of increases in the intensity or frequency of some of these extreme events on regional scales throughout the 20th century. The abnormalities generated due to climate change are likely to trigger shifts in the existing biodiversity patterns and demands for totally new set of land uses. The growing frequency and magnitude of extreme environmental events worldwide has intensified research interest in natural disasters as well as regional vulnerability and response capabilities. Water resources assessment and planning assumes that the past records of variability are reflections of what will happen in the future. Climate change is likely to result in hydrologic conditions and extremes of a nature that will be different from those for which the existing projects were designed.

The approaches for effectively dealing with climate change will have to be different from those that have been employed to manage variability in the past. It is also likely that the variability due to climate change may be beyond the range for which current projects have been designed and are being operated. A review of current coping strategies of populations already affected by climate variability is needed.

The likely impacts of increased climate variability and climate change on the water resources are required to be assessed. The coping strategies need to be evolved considering major factors, viz. social, economic, institutional, etc. to reduce vulnerability and enhance adaptation to climate-related developments and events. Some part of the country facing the frequent drought are adopting the dry land farming practices to grow the crops which require less amount of water.

However, there is a need to take up such studies for assessment of available water resource for different agro-climatic regions of India and various adaptation practices under the changing climatic scenarios. Some recommendations to cope with the problems in a systematic and a planned manner are:

- A nation-wide climate monitoring programme should be developed;
- While formulating new projects that influence climate, it should be ensured that no action is taken which causes irreversible harmful impact on the climate;
- Improved methods for accounting of climate-related uncertainty should be developed and made part of decision making process;
- Existing systems should be examined to determine how they will perform under the climate situations that are likely to arise;
- Water availability and demands in all regions, particularly in water-scarce regions should be reassessed in the new climate scenario;
- A re-examination of the water allocation policies and operating rules should be taken up to see how these need to be updated to handle extremes that are likely to arise;
- There should be proper coordination among concerned organizations so as to freely share the data, technology and experience for capacity building.

7

Groundwater Management

GROUNDWATER

Groundwater is water located beneath the ground surface in soil pore spaces and in the fractures of rock formations. A unit of rock or an unconsolidated deposit is called an aquifer when it can yield a usable quantity of water. The depth at which soil pore spaces or fractures and voids in rock become completely saturated with water is called the water table. Groundwater is recharged from, and eventually flows to, the surface naturally; natural discharge often occurs at springs and seeps, and can form oases or wetlands. Groundwater is also often withdrawn for agricultural, municipal and industrial use by constructing and operating extraction wells. The study of the distribution and movement of groundwater is hydrogeology, also called groundwater hydrology. Typically, groundwater is thought of as liquid water flowing through shallow aquifers, but technically it can also include soil moisture, permafrost, immobile water in very low permeability bedrock, and deep geothermal or oil formation water. Groundwater is hypothesized to provide lubrication that can possibly influence the movement of faults. It is likely that much of the Earth's subsurface contains some water, which may be mixed with other fluids in some instances. Groundwater may not be confined only to the Earth. The formation of some of the landforms observed on Mars may have been influenced by groundwater. There is also evidence that liquid water may also exist in the subsurface of Jupiter's moon Europa.

AQUIFERS

An aquifer is a layer of porous substrate that contains and transmits groundwater. When water can flow directly between the surface and the saturated zone of an aquifer, the aquifer is unconfined. The deeper parts of unconfined aquifers are usually more saturated since gravity causes water to flow downward. The upper level of this saturated layer of an unconfined aquifer is called the water table or phreatic surface. Generally all pore spaces are saturated with water is the phreatic zone. Substrate with low porosity that permits limited transmission of groundwater is known as an aquitard. An aquiclude is a substrate with porosity that is so low it is virtually impermeable to groundwater.

A confined aquifer is an aquifer that is overlain by a relatively impermeable layer of rock or substrate such as an aquiclude or aquitard. If a confined aquifer follows a downward grade from its recharge zone, groundwater can become pressurized as it flows. This can create artesian wells that flow freely without the need of a pump and rise to a higher elevation than the static water table at the unconfined, aquifer. The characteristics of aquifers vary with the geology and structure of the substrate and topography in which they occur. Generally, the more productive aquifers occur in sedimentary geologic formations. By comparison, weathered and fractured crystalline rocks yield smaller quantities of groundwater in many environments. Unconsolidated to poorly cemented alluvial materials that have accumulated as valley-filling sediments in major river valleys and geologically subsiding structural basins are included among the most productive sources of groundwater.

The high specific heat capacity of water and the insulating effect of soil and rock can mitigate the effects of climate and maintain groundwater at a relatively steady temperature. In some places where groundwater temperatures are maintained by this effect at about 50°F/10°C, groundwater can be used for controlling the temperature inside structures at the surface. For example, during hot weather relatively cool groundwater can be pumped through radiators in a home and then returned to the ground in another well. During cold seasons, because it is relatively warm, the water can be used in the same way as a source of heat for heat pumps that is much more efficient than using air.

WATER CYCLE

Groundwater makes up about twenty per cent of the world's fresh water supply, which is about 0.61% of the entire world's water, including oceans and permanent ice. Global groundwater storage is roughly equal to the total amount of freshwater stored in the snow and ice pack, including the north and south poles. This makes it an important resource which can act as a natural storage that can buffer against shortages of surface water, as in during times of drought. Groundwater is naturally replenished by surface water from precipitation, streams, and rivers when this recharge reaches the water table. Groundwater can be a long-term 'reservoir' of the natural water cycle as opposed to short-term water reservoirs like the atmosphere and fresh surface water.

The Great Artesian Basin in central and eastern Australia is one of the largest confined aquifer systems in the world, extending for almost 2 million km^2. By analysing the trace elements in water sourced from deep underground, hydrogeologists have been able to determine that water extracted from these aquifers can be more than 1 million years old.

By comparing the age of groundwater obtained from different parts of the Great Artesian Basin, hydrogeologists have found it increases in age across the basin. Where water recharges the aquifers along the Eastern Divide, ages are young. As groundwater flows westward across the continent, it increases in age, with the oldest groundwater occurring in the western parts. This means that in order to have travelled almost 1000 km from the source of recharge in 1 million years, the groundwater flowing through the Great Artesian Basin travels at an average rate of about 1 metre per year.

ISSUES

Certain problems have beset the use of groundwater around the world. Just as river waters have been over–used and polluted in many parts of the world, so too have aquifers. The big difference is that aquifers are out of sight. The other major problem is that water management agencies, when calculating the 'sustainable yield' of aquifer and river water, have often counted the same water twice, once in the aquifer, and once in its connected river. This problem, although understood for centuries, has persisted, partly through inertia within government agencies. In Australia, for example, prior to the statutory reforms initiated by the Council of Australian Governments water reform framework in the 1990s, many Australian States managed groundwater and surface water through separate government agencies, an approach beset by rivalry and poor communication.

The time lags inherent in the dynamic response of groundwater to development have generally been ignored by water management agencies, decades after scientific understanding of the issue was consolidated. In brief, the effects of groundwater overdraft may take decades or centuries to manifest themselves. In a classic study in 1982, Bredehoeft and colleagues modelled a situation where groundwater extraction in an intermontane basin withdrew the entire annual recharge, leaving 'nothing' for the natural groundwater—dependent vegetation community. Even when the borefield was situated close to the vegetation, 30% of the original vegetation demand could still be met by the lag inherent in the system after 100 years. By year 500 this had reduced to 0%, signalling complete death of the groundwater-dependent vegetation.

The science has been available to make these calculations for decades; however water management agencies have generally ignored effects which will appear outside the rough timeframe of political elections. Marios Sophocleous argued strongly that management agencies must define and use appropriate timeframes in groundwater planning. This will mean calculating groundwater withdrawal permits based on predicted effects decades, sometimes centuries in the future.

As water moves through the landscape it collects soluble salts, mainly sodium chloride. Where such water enters the atmosphere through evapotranspiration, these salts are left behind. In irrigation districts, poor drainage of soils and surface aquifers can result in water tables coming to the surface in low-lying areas. Major land degradation problems of soil salinity and waterlogging result, combined with increasing levels of salt in surface waters. As a consequence, major damage has occurred to local economies and environments.

First, flood mitigation schemes, intended to protect infrastructure built on floodplains, have had the unintended consequence of reducing aquifer recharge associated with natural flooding. Second, prolonged depletion of groundwater in extensive aquifers can result in land subsidence, with associated infrastructure damage–as well as saline intrusion. Fourth, draining acid sulphate soils, often found in low-lying coastal plains, can result in acidification and pollution of formerly freshwater and estuarine streams.

Another cause for concern is that groundwater drawdown from over-allocated aquifers has the potential to cause severe damage to both terrestrial and aquatic ecosystems–in some cases very conspicuously but in others quite imperceptibly because of the extended period over which the damage occurs.

Overdraft

Groundwater is a highly useful and often abundant resource. However, over-use, or overdraft, can cause major problems to human users and to the environment. The most evident problem is a lowering of the water table beyond the reach of existing wells. Wells must consequently be deepened to reach the groundwater; in some places the water table has dropped hundreds of feet because of extensive well pumping. In the Punjab region of India, for example, groundwater levels have dropped 10 meters since 1979, and the rate of depletion is accelerating. A lowered water table may, in turn, cause other problems such as groundwater–related subsidence and saltwater intrusion. Groundwater is also ecologically important. The importance of groundwater to ecosystems is often overlooked, even by freshwater biologists and ecologists. Groundwaters sustain rivers, wetlands and lakes, as well as subterranean ecosystems within karst or alluvial aquifers.

Not all ecosystems need groundwater, of course. Some terrestrial ecosystems—for example, those of the open deserts and similar arid environments—exist on irregular rainfall and the moisture it delivers to the soil, supplemented by moisture in the air. While there are other terrestrial ecosystems in more hospitable environments where groundwater plays no central role, groundwater is in fact fundamental to many of the world's major ecosystems.

Water flows between groundwaters and surface waters. Most rivers, lakes and wetlands are fed by, and feed groundwater, to varying degrees. Groundwater feeds soil moisture through percolation, and many terrestrial vegetation communities depend directly on either groundwater or the percolated soil moisture above the aquifer for at least part of each year. Hyporheic zones and riparian zones are examples of ecotones largely or totally dependent on groundwater.

Aquifer drawdown or overdrafting and the pumping of fossil water increases the total amount of water within the hydrosphere subject to transpiration and evaporation processes, thereby causing accretion in water vapour and cloud cover, the primary absorbers of infrared radiation in the Earth's atmosphere. Adding water to the system has a forcing effect on the whole earth system, an accurate estimate of which hydrogeological fact is yet to be quantified.

A Solution to Over-use of Groundwater

Irrigated agriculture is a big business in Asia. It accounts for 70 per cent of the world's irrigated land and 73 per cent of water used each year by the farming industry. As ageing large-scale surface irrigation schemes have become increasingly inefficient, and farmers have begun growing a wider range of crops requiring water on demand, the number of groundwater wells in India has exploded. In 1960, there were fewer than 100,000 such wells; by 2006 the figure had risen to nearly 12 million. In India, a possible solution to over-use of groundwater is emerging, known as 'groundwater recharge'. It involves capturing rainwater that would otherwise run-off, and using it to refill aquifers.

Since 2000, the International Water Management Institute has been working with the Indian authorities to help improve the availability of water for agriculture in India. In 2006, India's finance minister invited IWMI to submit policy recommendations based on its research on groundwater depletion.

One of the key recommendations was to instigate a programme of recharging groundwater across the 65 per cent of India that has hard-rock aquifers. As a result, the Indian government allocated ₹1800 crore to fund dug–well recharge projects in 100 districts within seven states where water stored in hard–rock aquifers has been over-exploited.

These geological formations have a much lower capacity to store rainwater than alluvial areas with porous sand or clay rocks, hence being given priority. The money is sufficient to fund seven million structures to be installed on dug–wells to divert monsoon run-off. The structures include a de-siltation chamber, plus pipes to collect surplus rainwater and divert de-silted water from the chamber to the well. As of the end of November 2009, funds amounting to ₹216.98 crore had been released to the concerned states. Subsidies had been released to 566,637 beneficiaries.

Subsidence

Subsidence occurs when too much water is pumped out from underground, deflating the space below the above–surface, and thus causing the ground to actually collapse. The result can look like craters on plots of land. This occurs because in its natural equilibrium state, the hydraulic pressure of groundwater in the pore spaces of the aquifer and the aquitard supports some of the weight of the overlying sediments. When groundwater is removed from aquifers by excessive pumping, pore pressures in the aquifer drop and compression of the aquifer may occur. This compression may be partially recoverable if pressures rebound, but much of it is not.

When the aquifer gets compressed it may cause land subsidence, a drop in the ground surface. The city of New Orleans, Louisiana, is actually below sea level today, and its subsidence is partly caused by removal of groundwater from the various aquifer/aquitard systems beneath it. In the first half of the 20th century, the city of San Jose, California, dropped 13 feet from land subsidence caused by overpumping; this subsidence has been halted with improved groundwater management.

Seawater Intrusion

Generally, in very humid or undeveloped regions, the shape of the water table mimics the slope of the surface. The recharge zone of an aquifer near the seacoast is likely to be inland, often at considerable distance. In these coastal areas, a lowered water table may induce sea water to reverse the flow towards the land. Sea water moving inland is called a saltwater intrusion. Alternatively, salt from mineral beds may leach into the groundwater of its own accord.

Mining

Sometimes the water movement from the recharge zone to the place where it is withdrawn may take centuries. When the usage of water is greater than the recharge, it is referred to as mining water. Under those circumstances it is not a renewable resource.

Pollution

Water pollution of groundwater, from pollutants released to the ground that can work their way down into groundwater, can create a contaminant plume within an aquifer. Movement of water and dispersion within the aquifer spreads the pollutant over a wider area, its advancing boundary often called a plume edge, which can then intersect with groundwater wells or daylight into surface water such as seeps and springs, making the water supplies unsafe for humans and wildlife. The interaction of groundwater contamination with surface waters is Analysed by use of hydrology transport models.

The stratigraphy of the area plays an important role in the transport of these pollutants. An area can have layers of sandy soil, fractured bedrock, clay, or hardpan. Areas of karst topography on limestone bedrock are sometimes vulnerable to surface pollution from groundwater. Earthquake faults can also be entry routes for downward contaminant entry. Water table conditions are of great importance for drinking water supplies, agricultural irrigation, waste disposal, wildlife habitat, and other ecological issues.

In the US, upon commercial real estate property transactions both groundwater and soil are the subjects of scrutiny, with a Phase I Environmental Site Assessment normally being prepared to investigate and disclose potential pollution issues. In the San Fernando Valley of California, Real estate contracts for property transfer below the Santa Susana Field Laboratory and eastward have clauses releasing the seller from liability for groundwater contamination consequences from existing or future water pollution of the Valley Aquifer.

Love Canal was one of the most widely known examples of groundwater pollution. In 1978, residents of the Love Canal neighbourhood in upstate New York noticed high rates of cancer and an alarming number of birth defects. This was eventually traced to organic solvents and dioxins from an industrial landfill that the neighbourhood had been built over and around, which had then infiltrated into the water supply and evaporated in basements to further contaminate the air. Eight hundred families were reimbursed for their homes and moved, after extensive legal battles and media coverage.

Another example of widespread groundwater pollution is in the Ganges Plain of northern India and Bangladesh where severe contamination of groundwater by naturally occurring arsenic affects 25% of water wells in the shallower of two regional aquifers. The pollution occurs because aquifer sediments contain organic matter that generates anaerobic conditions in the aquifer. These conditions result in the microbial dissolution of iron oxides in the sediment and thus the release of the arsenic, normally strongly bound to iron oxides, into the water. As a consequence, arsenic-rich groundwater is often iron-rich, although secondary processes often obscure the association of dissolved arsenic and dissolved iron.

GROUNDWATER QUALITY

Just because you have a well that yields plenty of water doesn't mean you can go ahead and just take a drink. Because water is such an excellent solvent it can contain lots of dissolved chemicals. And since groundwater moves through rocks and subsurface soil, it has a lot of opportunity to dissolve substances as it moves. For that reason, groundwater will often have more dissolved substances than surface water will.

Even though the ground is an excellent mechanism for filtering out particulate matter, such as leaves, soil, and bugs, dissolved chemicals and gases can still occur in large enough concentrations in groundwater to cause problems. Undergroundwater can get contaminated from industrial, domestic, and agricultural chemicals from the surface. This includes chemicals such as pesticides and herbicides that many homeowners apply to their lawns.

Contamination of groundwater by road salt is of major concern in northern areas of the United States. Salt is spread on roads to melt ice, and, with salt being so soluble in water, excess sodium and chloride is easily transported into the subsurface groundwater. The most common water–quality problem in rural water supplies is bacterial contamination from septic tanks, which are often used in rural areas that don't have a sewage-treatment system. Effluent from a septic tank can percolate down to the water table and maybe into a homeowner's own well. Just as with urban water supplies, chlorination may be necessary to kill the dangerous bacteria.

The U.S. Geological Survey is involved in monitoring the Nation's ground-water supplies. A national network of observation wells exists to measure regularly the water levels in wells and to investigate water quality.

PESTICIDES IN GROUNDWATER

If you ask your grandparents what life was like when they were kids, the answer will probably be that things were simpler, slower, less automated, and that people did not move so often.

But since your grandparent's time two major things have happened:

1. The population of the United States has increased greatly, and
2. Technology and scientific innovations have come to play a major role in our lives.

Pesticide use has grown because not only must our exploding population be supplied with food, but crops and food are grown for export to other countries.

The United States has become the largest producer of food products in the world, partly owing to our use of modern chemicals to control the insects, weeds, and other organisms that attack food crops. But, as with many things in life, there's a hidden cost to the benefit we get from pesticides. We've learned that pesticides can potentially harm the environment and our own health.

Water plays an important role here because it is one of the main ways that pesticides are transported from the areas where they are applied to other locations, where they may cause health problems.

PESTICIDES CAN CONTAMINATE GROUNDWATER

Pesticide contamination of ground water is a subject of national importance because ground water is used for drinking water by about 50 per cent of the Nation's population. This especially concerns people living in the agricultural areas where pesticides are most often used, as about 95 per cent of that population relies upon ground water for drinking water.

Before the mid–1970s, it was thought that soil acted as a protective filter that stopped pesticides from reaching ground water. Studies have now shown that this is not the case. Pesticides can reach water–bearing aquifers below ground from applications onto crop fields, seepage of contaminated surface water, accidental spills and leaks, improper disposal, and even through injection waste material into wells.

Chemicals can take a Long Time to Appear in Groundwater

The effects of past and present land-use practices may take decades to become apparent in ground water. When weighing management decisions for protection of ground–water quality, it is important to consider the time lag between application of pesticides and fertilizers to the land and arrival of the chemicals at a well.

This time lag generally decreases with increasing aquifer permeability and with decreasing depth to water. In response to reductions in chemical applications to the land, the quality of shallow ground water will improve before the quality of deep ground water, which could take decades.

Pesticides are mostly modern chemicals. There are many hundreds of these compounds, and extensive tests and studies of their effect on humans have not been completed. That leads us to ask just how concerned we should be about their presence in our drinking water. Certainly it would be wise to treat pesticides as potentially dangerous and, thus, to handle them with care. We can say they pose a potential danger if they are consumed in large quantities, but, as any experienced scientist knows, you cannot draw factual conclusions unless scientific tests have been done.

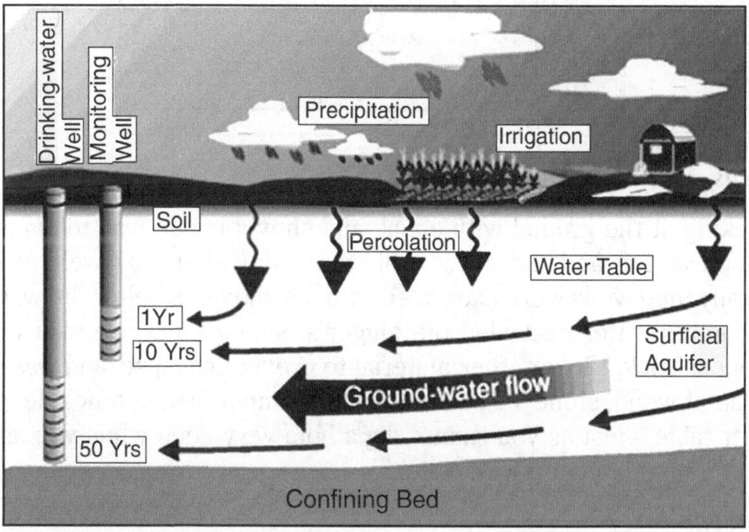

Some pesticides have had a designated Maximum Contaminant Limit in drinking water set by the U.S. Environmental Protection Agency but many have not. Also, the effect of combining more than one pesticide in drinking water might be different than the effects of each individual pesticide alone. It is another situation where we don't have sufficient scientific data to draw reliable conclusions.

GROUNDWATER: WELLS

There's a good chance that the average Joe who had to dig a well in ancient Egypt probably did the work with his hands, a shovel, and a bucket. He would have kept digging until he reached the water table and water filled the bottom of the hole. Some wells are still dug by hand today, but more modern methods are available. It's still a dirty job, though! Wells are extremely important to all societies. In many places wells provide a reliable and ample supply of water for home uses, irrigation, and industries. Where surface water is scarce, such as in deserts,people couldn't survive and thrive without ground water.

Types of Wells

Digging a well by hand is becoming outdated today. Modern wells are more often drilled by a truck-mounted drill rig. Still, there are many ways to put in a well—here are some of the common methods.

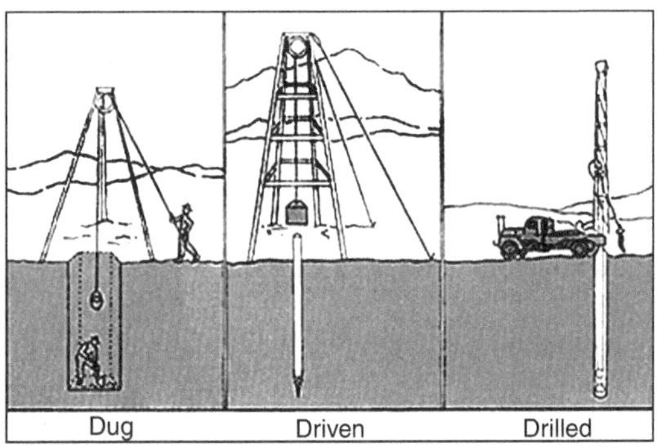

Dug Wells

Hacking at the ground with a pick and shovel is one way to dig a well. If the ground is soft and the water table is shallow,then dug wells can work. Historically, dug wells were excavated by hand shovel to below the water table until incoming water exceeded the digger's bailing rate. The well was lined with stones, brick, tile, or other material to prevent collapse, and was covered with a cap of wood, stone, or concrete. They cannot be dug much deeper than the water table—just as you cannot dig a hole very deep when you are at the beach... it keeps filling up with water!

Driven Wells

Driven wells are still common today. They are built by driving a small-diameter pipe into soft earth, such as sand or gravel. A screen is usually attached to the bottom of the pipe to filter out sand and other particles. Problems? They can only tap shallow water, and because the source of the water is so close to the surface, contamination from surface pollutants can occur.

Drilled Wells

Most modern wells are drilled, which requires a fairly complicated and expensive drill rig. Drill rigs are often mounted on big trucks. They use rotary drill bits that chew away at the rock, percussion bits that smash the rock, or, if the ground is soft,large auger bits. Drilled wells can be drilled more than 1,000 feet deep. Often a pump is placed at the bottom to push water up to the surface.

Water Levels in Wells

Ground-water users would find life easier if the water level in the aquifer that supplied their well always stayed the same. Seasonal variations in rainfall and the occasional drought affect the "height" of the underground water level. If a well is pumped at a faster rate than the aquifer around it is recharged by precipitation or other underground flow, then water levels around the well can be lowered.

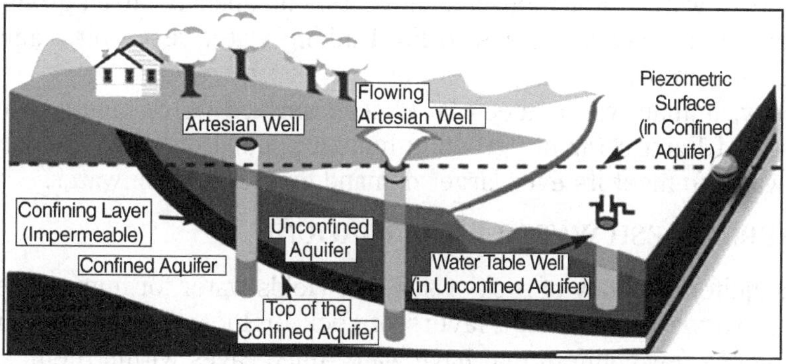

Fig. Aquifers and Wells

The water level in a well can also be lowered if other wells near it are withdrawing too much water. When water levels drop below the levels of the pump intakes, then wells will begin to pump air—they will "go dry."

FORMATION OF GROUNDWATER MANAGEMENT

Groundwater is fresh water in the rock and soil layers beneath Earth's land surface. Some of the precipitation (rain, snow, sleet, and hail) that falls on the land soaks into Earth's surface and becomes groundwater. Water-bearing rock layers called aquifers are saturated (soaked) with groundwater that moves, often very slowly, through small openings and spaces.

This groundwater then returns to lakes, streams, and marshes (wet, low-lying land with grassy plants) on the land surface via springs and seeps (small springs or pools where groundwater slowly oozes to the surface). Groundwater makes up more than one-fifth (22%) of Earth's total fresh water supply, and it plays a number of critical hydrological (water-related), geological and biological roles on the continents.

Soil and rock layers in groundwater recharge zones (a entry point where water enters an aquifer) reduce flooding by absorbing excess run-off after heavy rains and spring snowmelts. Aquifers store water through dry seasons and dry weather, and groundwater flow carries water beneath arid (dry) deserts and semi-arid grasslands. Groundwater discharge replenishes streams, lakes, and wetlands on the land surface and is especially important in arid regions that receive limited rainfall. Flowing groundwater interacts with rocks and minerals in aquifers, and carries dissolved rock-building chemicals and biological nutrients. Vibrant communities of plants and animals (ecosystems) live in and around groundwater springs and seeps.

Almost all of the fresh liquid water that is readily available for human use comes from underground. (The bulk of Earth's fresh water is frozen in ice in the North and South Pole regions. Water in streams, rivers, lakes, wetlands, the atmosphere, and within living organisms makes up only a tiny portion of Earth's fresh water.) For thousands of years, humans have used groundwater from springs and shallow wells to fill drinking water reservoirs, and water livestock and crops.

Today, human water needs far exceed surface water supplies in many regions, and Earth's rapidly-growing human population relies heavily upon groundwater to meet its ever larger demand for clean, fresh water.

AQUIFERS: FRESH WATER UNDERGROUND

An aquifer is a body of rock or soil that yields water for human use. Most aquifers are water-saturated layers of rock or loose sediment. With the exception of a few aquifers that have water-filled caves within them, aquifers are not underground lakes or holding tanks, but rather rock "sponges" that hold groundwater in tiny cracks, cavities, and pores (tiny openings in which a liquid can pass) between mineral grains (rocks are made of minerals).

The total amount of empty pore space in the rock material, called its porosity, determines the amount of groundwater the aquifer can hold. Materials like sand and gravel have high porosity, meaning that they can absorb a high amount of water.

Rocks like granite, marble, and limestone have low porosity, and make poor groundwater reservoirs. Aquifers must have high permeability in addition to high porosity. Permeability is the ability of the rock or other material to allow water to pass through it. The pore space in permeable materials is interconnected throughout the rock or sediment, allowing groundwater to move freely through it.

Some high–porosity materials, like mud and clay, have very low permeability. They soak up and hold water, but don't release it easily to wells or other groundwater discharge points, so they are not good aquifer materials. Sandstone, limestone, fractured granite, glacial sediment, loose sand, and gravel are examples of materials that make good aquifers. Water enters aquifers by seeping into the land surface at entry points called recharge zones and leaves at exit points called discharge zones. (Some aquifers discharge into the ocean.)

Influent or "water-losing" streams, ponds, or lakes are bodies of surface water in recharge zones that contribute groundwater from their water supply. Groundwater flows into effluent or "watergaining" streams and ponds in discharge zones. For the water level in an aquifer to remain constant, the amount of water entering at recharge zones must equal the amount leaving at discharge zones. (Imagine a bucket punched with holes under a dripping faucet. If water drips in at the same rate that it drips out, the water level stays the same.)

If water discharges or is pumped from an aquifer more quickly than it recharges, the groundwater level will fall. The time an average water molecule spends within an aquifer is called its residence time. Water in some fast–flowing aquifers spends only a few days underground, while other rock layers can hold water for ten thousand years. Average aquifers have residence times of about two hundred years.

The Water Table and Unconfined Aquifers

Water enters aquifers by moving slowly down through a layer of surface rocks and soil whose pore spaces are partially filled with air (zone of infiltration). The water continues moving downwards until it reaches a level where all the pore spaces are completely filled with water (zone of saturation).

The top of the zone of saturation is called the water table. In some wet, lowland regions, southern Florida for example, the water may be only a few feet (meters) below the surface. In others, like the American Southwest, water–saturated rocks may be hundreds of feet below the land surface. Groundwater reservoirs that have uniform rock or soil properties (porosity and permeability) throughout are called unconfined aquifers. The water table forms the upper surface of an unconfined aquifer. The shape of the water table in an unconfined aquifer mirrors the shape of the land surface, but its slopes are gentler.

In temperate (moderate) climates that receive moderate amounts of groundwater–replenishing rainfall, water infiltrates into unconfined aquifers in hilltop recharge zones and discharges into effluent streams and ponds in low areas where the water table intersects the land surface. Water will only rise to the level of the water table in a well, so a pump or bucket is required to extract water from an unconfined aquifer.

Confined Aquifers and Artesian Flow

Confined aquifers are pressurized groundwater reservoirs that lie beneath layers of non-permeable rock (granite, shale) or sediment (clay). Groundwater enters a confined aquifer in recharge zones beyond the uphill edges of the confining layer and discharges beyond the downhill edges. Groundwater trapped beneath an impermeable barrier cannot rise to the height of the water table, so pressure builds up in confined aquifers. Artesian wells are wells drilled in confined aquifers where the pressure is great enough to make water flow at the surface.

Lakes are large inland bodies of fresh or saline (salty) water. Lakes form in places where water collects in low areas or behind natural or man-made dams (barriers constructed to contain the flow of water). Some lakes are fed by streams (natural bodies of flowing freshwater), and some form where groundwater (water flowing in rock layers beneath the land surface) discharges onto the land surface. Water leaves lakes by flowing into outlet streams, infiltrating (soaking in) into groundwater reservoirs called aquifers, and by evaporating into the atmosphere (mass of air surrounding Earth). Lakes vary in size from large lakes such as the Great Lakes of North America, to small mountain lakes. Lakes are larger than ponds, which are small bodies of fresh water that are shallow enough for rooted plants to grow.

The study of ecology (relationships between living organisms and their environment) in lakes, inland seas, and wetlands is called limnology. Lakes store only a tiny percentage of Earth's fresh water. They are, however, an extremely important water resource for humans.

Freshwater lakes provide water for agricultural irrigation (watering), industrial processes, municipal uses, and residential water supplies. People who live in the continental interiors use lakes for fishing and recreation, and very large lakes have important shipping and transportation routes.

Humans also construct artificial lakes, called reservoirs, by building dams across rivers. In addition to providing the benefits of natural lakes, reservoirs also store water for specific communities, control floods, and generate hydroelectricity (electricity generated from water power).

HOW LAKES FORM AND DISAPPEAR

Earth scientists who study water on the continents (hydrologists and hydrogeologists) see lakes as temporary reservoirs within stream and groundwater systems. All water that falls as precipitation (rain, snow, sleet, hail) on the land surface of continents eventually makes its way to the ocean or evaporates back into the atmosphere. Water collects in lakes because it enters more rapidly than it escapes, but it is never permanently trapped there. As in a tub with a running faucet and an open drain, individual water molecules (smallest unit of water, each containing two hydrogen atoms and one oxygen atom) are constantly entering and escaping.

After arriving in a lake, an average water molecule spends about one hundred years before moving to a new reservoir. (The time that an average water molecule spends in a reservoir is called it residence time. Water resides for about two weeks in rivers, forty years in glaciers (slow moving mass of ice), and between two hundred and ten thousand years in groundwater reservoirs.)

To geologists (Earth scientists), lakes are temporary features. Stream-fed lakes within stream systems are destined for destruction. Every stream seeks to create a constant slope, called a graded profile, between where the stream's waters begin and ends by eroding (wearing away) and depositing sediment (particles of sand, silt, and clay) along its course. When a natural or man-made obstruction blocks a stream, such as a river, streams deposit sediment in the lake or reservoir behind the obstruction and erode away in front of it. Eventually, the dam will collapse, and the lake will empty. Lakes that fill depressions and have no outlets fill when the regional climate becomes wetter or when warm periods melt mountain snows and glacial ice. They evaporate away during periods of dry weather and dryer climate. It may take thousands, or even tens of thousands of years, but lakes eventually drain, collapse, or dry up.

LAKE LAYERS AND OVERTURNS

Contrary to their common image as evenly mixed pools of unmoving water, lakes are complex, dynamic bodies of moving surface water. Lake water varies within the lake; its temperature, chemical content, light infiltration, and biological habitats vary from top to bottom and side to side.

Furthermore, the vertical layering (stratification), horizontal variations, and circulation patterns within lakes change over time. Waves, currents (a moving mass of water), and even tides affect circulation of water within lakes. Lakes are thermally stratified (layered just as to temperature); they have layers of warm and cool water that are separated by layers where the temperature changes (thermoclines). Like the oceans, many lakes have a thin layer of warm surface water, and a thicker layer of cool deep water that is separated by a thermocline layer. Wind generates currents on lake surfaces and creates some mixing. Unlike the oceans, however, many lakes have seasonal overturns that mix their waters. water is denser than solid water (ice). Water reaches its maximum density at 39°F (4°C). Because of this odd property, the warm less-dense water rises, the cool denser water sinks, ice floats, and lakes overturn.

Lakes that are ice-covered for part of the year undergo overturns that partially or completely mix their waters. Many lakes in temperate (moderate temperatures) regions like the northern United States overturn and mix completely twice a year (dimictic lakes). During the warm summer months, these lakes have a usual temperature profile with warm surface waters, a thermocline, and cool bottom water. In the fall, when the surface water cools down to 39°F (4°C), it becomes denser than the water underneath it and the surface layer sinks to the bottom. The bottom water rises to the surface, and the lake overturns. Over the winter, the bottom water is the warmest, and the frozen surface water is the coldest. (Plants and animals survive the winter on the lake floor in the chilly, but not frozen, bottom water.) In the spring, when the ice melts, and the water warms to 39°F (4°C), it sinks, and the lake overturns again. Limnologists classify lakes just as to the number of mixing events they undergo each year.

Lake type classifications have the root term mictic, meaning "to mix," and include:

- *Oligomictic*: Warm, ice-free lakes that rarely mix. They are warmest at the top, and coolest at the bottom. Tropical, oligomictic lakes have warm bottom water and very warm surface water. They rarely overturn because their water does not near 39°F (4°C).
- *Meromictic*: Warm, ice–free lakes that mix incompletely. These are deep lakes that are warmest at the top, and coolest at the bottom.
- *Monomictic/dimictic/polymictic*: Lakes with seasonal ice covers that overturn and mix completely once (monomictic), twice (dimictic), or many times per year (polymictic). Lake overturns are the norm in temperate regions, but local conditions affect the timing and number of overturns in specific lakes.
- *Amictic*: Lakes that never overturn because they are icecovered throughout the year. These lakes exist near the North and South Poles and atop very high mountains. They have cold bottom water that hovers near 39°F (4°C) and frozen surface water.

LAKE CHEMISTRY: SALINE LAKES

Many of Earth's largest and most important lakes contain salt water. All surface water contains some dissolved chemicals, called salts. Groundwater, streams, and freshwater lakes all contain the chemical components of rocks and minerals. Humans can drink fresh water because our bodies can use or at least tolerate the types and concentrations of dissolved chemicals it contains. Salt water, on the other hand, has a very high concentration of dissolved salts, and is undrinkable. The Dead Sea, on the border between Israel and Jordan, is Earth's saltiest body of water. It is truly a dead sea because it is too salty to support life. Saline lakes generally form in arid (dry) regions where surface water evaporates quickly.

When water evaporates, the salts stay behind. Over time, the lake water becomes saltier. Some saline lakes, such as the Great Salt Lake, are all that remains of a much larger fresh water lake that has evaporated over time. Others, like the Caspian Sea in central Asia, began as saltwaterfilled ocean basins that have since closed. Saline lakes are often temporary features that fill during periods of wetter climate and then dry up when stream flow or groundwater discharge slows. Playa lakes are flat desert basins that occasionally fill with water. Desert oases (watering holes) form and disappear with such regularity that thirsty travellers think they imagined them. The Great Salt Lake, Caspian Sea, Aral Sea, and Dead Sea are all presently evaporating. Over time, the dissolved chemicals become so concentrated in drying lakes that they bond together and form solid salt crystals. Thick layers of salt cover dry lake beds.

LAKE BIOLOGY

Lakes support rich communities of plants and animals (ecosystems) that have adapted to live within ever-changing conditions on lake beds, within the water column (water running from the surface to the lake floor, often showing differences in temperature, nutrients, etc.), and along lake shores. Lakes, like islands, are often closed systems that only rarely gain new species or individuals from other lakes.

Many lakes host groups of rare species that have evolved (changed over time) together in their specific lake. These ecosystems are rich and unique, but fragile. They have little defence against foreign predators or diseases. Human alterations and water pollution have threatened many lake species. Environmental groups and government agencies are presently attempting to protect and revive threatened lake species such as cichlids (rare doublejawed fish) that inhabit the lakes of the Great Rift Valley in east Africa. Lake organisms live in zones that are determined by the physical structure of their lakes such as the amount of available light, water depth, and distribution of nutrients. Most lake plants and animals live in shallow, well-lit surface waters called the euphotic zone.

Most plants depend on the Sun's energy to produce food by the chemical process of photosynthesis, and they cannot grow in water that is too deep or too cloudy for light to penetrate. Lake animals such as fish need oxygen that plants give off during photosynthesis, so they live mostly in the euphotic zone as well. Plants with roots grow in shallow water along edges of lakes where light reaches the lake floor (littoral zone) and floating plants perform photosynthesis in the open surface waters (limnetic zone). Oxygen-consuming bacteria inhabit the deepest, darkest parts of lakes (benthic zone) where dead plant and animal materials accumulate. Limnologists also classify lakes by the balance of organisms and nutrients in their waters.

Types include lakes that are described as oligotrophic, eutrophic, and mesotrophic:

- *Oligotrophic*: Nutrient poor lakes that support very few plants and animals. Oligotrophic lakes are typically cool, deep, and have very clear water. Very little organic (relating to or from living organisms) mud accumulates in oligotropic lakes, and they often have sand and gravel beds.
- *Eutrophic*: Lakes rich in plant nutrients that support abundant plant life in their surface waters. Their water is often clouded by

microscopic plants, and their beds covered with thick layers of decaying plant material. Bacteria that live on the organic mud use up oxygen, and eutrophic lakes often have oxygen–poor deep water. Plants and bacteria eventually take over eutrophic lakes. They become oxygen-poor bogs and marshes where fish cannot live. Some chemicals that humans use, including fertilizers and detergents, cause a process called eutrophication when they run off into lakes, which causes the population of plants to increase to such an extent that eventually oxygen-starved fish die.

- *Mesotrophic*: Lakes with moderate amounts of nutrients and healthy, balanced communities of plants, animals and bacteria. Mesotrophic lakes receive adequate amounts of fresh water and nutrients, and seasonal overturns allow nutrient–poor and nutrient–rich layers to mix. Mesotrophic lakes are intermediate between crystal-clear, lifeless oligothrophic lakes and cloudy, muddy eutrophic lakes.

WHERE LAKES FORM: LAKE BASINS

Lakes form where water collects in depressions, or basins. Many lakes fill low areas created by plate tectonic movements (tectonic basins) and volcanic activity. (Plate tectonics is the movement of large, rigid pieces of Earth's outer rock shell called the lithosphere.) Retreating glaciers and ice sheets leave behind large basins and small depressions that fill with meltwater. Though flowing streams and rivers generally act to fill in and drain lake basins, other sedimentary processes can create landscape depressions and natural dams that confine water in lakes.

Lakes in Tectonic Basins

Rift valley lakes fill long, linear valleys within rift zones. (Rifts are areas where the continental lithosphere is stretching and beginning to break into pieces. They are the precursors of ocean basins.) A chain of large lakes including Tanganyika, Naivete, and Malawi follows the Great Rift Valley through eastern Africa. Lake Victoria, the world's second-largest lake, lies between two branches of the rift valley. The Red Sea, Sea of Galilee, Dead Sea, and Gulf of Ababa fill the northern branches of the rift where it crosses the Arabian Peninsula in the Middle East. Russia's Lake Baikal, the world's deepest lake, fills an ancient, inactive rift valley in central Asia. Lakes also form in places where continents are moving towards each other. The Black Sea, Caspian Sea, and Mediterranean Seas fill a closing ocean basin between Africa and Europe. When continents collide, water fills depressions in the landscape over folded and broken (faulted) rock layers that were caught between the land masses. Slopes that are too steep collapse and block rivers with natural dams. Blocks of uplifted, erosion-resistant rock form bedrock that holds back mountain lakes.

Volcanic Lakes

Volcanoes are mountains that form from eruptions of molten rock (lava) on the land surface. When a volcanic peak collapses into its emptied magma chamber (a pool or room of magna held under tremendous pressure within a volcano prior to a volcanic eruption), it forms a large circular basin called a caldera. (Craters, the small basins near the top of active volcanoes, sometimes also contain small lakes, but most significant volcanic lakes, including inaccurately-named Crater Lake, fill calderas.) Yellowstone Lake in Wyoming and Crater Lake in Oregon are examples of caldera lakes. Volcanic ash, mud, and lava flows also create natural dams in river valleys. A dam of volcanic rock confines Lake Tahoe in a high valley of the Sierra Mountains on the California–Nevada border.

Glacial Lakes

The thick continental ice sheets that covered northern North America, Europe, and Asia during the Pleistocene ice ages (a division of geologic time that lasted from two million to ten thousand years ago) left behind thousands of lake and ponds when they retreated about twenty thousand years ago.

The weight of the ice sheets pushed down on the continents, leaving broad basins that filled with melt water when they retreated. The Great Lakes of North America (Superior, Huron, Michigan, Erie, and Ontario) formed this way. Hundreds of lakes, such as the Winnipeg, Athabasca, Great Slave, and Great Bear cover the central and eastern provinces and territories of Canada that are still rebounding from their heavy ice load. Advancing glaciers also pile tall ridges of sediment, called moraines, at their toes (the end of extensions of glaciers along the ground). When glaciers retreat, moraines hold back meltwater. Small lakes and ponds also form in glacial depressions called kettles that form when blocks of ice buried in glacial sediment melt. Melting mountain glaciers feed many mountain lakes and glacial sediment traps streams and meltwater.

Groundwater Discharge Lakes

Water moving through pore spaces in rock and soil layers discharges on the land surface in places where the water table (level below which pore spaces are saturated with water) intersects the land surface. In regions with wet climates, the water table is near the land surface and ground water discharges in low spots. Groundwater chemically erodes limestone and other rocks and creates caves, cavities, sink holes, and collapse basins called karst features. Florida's many lakes, including Lake Okeechobee, are groundwater filled karst features.

ECONOMIC USES OF GROUNDWATER

Groundwater is one of human's most valuable natural resources. Groundwater is the water contained in the rock and soil layers beneath Earth's surface, and it makes up most of Earth's supply of fresh, liquid water. (The oceans and ice in the North and South Poles contain 99% of Earth's total water supply. Groundwater accounts for almost all of the remaining 1%.) Throughout history, humans have settled in areas with plentiful and pure groundwater, and have fought to own and protect wells and springs. Today, human water needs in many arid (dry) or heavily populated regions far exceed surface water supplies. Earth's rapidly–growing human population is becoming increasingly reliant on groundwater. Groundwater fills wells and city water supplies. Groundwater irrigates (waters) crops, feeds livestock, and produces farm-raised fish. Groundwater is used to cool nuclear reactors that generate electricity, mix concrete, and manufacture millions of consumer products. In short, groundwater plays a vital role in almost every facet of people's lives, from drinking water, foods, and products people buy to roads and the buildings in which people live and work.

GROUNDWATER RESERVOIRS: AQUIFERS

Water enters underground reservoirs by soaking in through soils, stream beds, and ponds in areas termed recharge zones. Water flows, often very slowly, through interconnected pore (tiny opening) spaces and then remerges onto the land surface at natural discharge points called springs and seeps. When discharge from natural springs and/or human wells exceeds the rate of recharge, the groundwater level falls, shallow wells and springs dry, and eventually, the reservoir empties. Many groundwater reservoirs, particularly those beneath arid deserts and semi-arid grasslands, filled with water many centuries ago when regional climate was wetter.

Groundwater reservoirs that yield water for human use are called aquifers. In part, human economics determine which water-bearing units are exploited as aquifers. In regions where clean surface water is plentiful and inexpensive, groundwater may go unused. In arid regions with scarce or polluted surface water, and in places where human water needs exceed the water supply in streams and lakes, groundwater extraction and purification become economically worthwhile. When conditions change, as during periods of drought (prolonged dry weather) or increased population growth, new groundwater supplies are tapped, thereby elevating them to aquifer status.

WELLS

In addition to collecting groundwater from springs, humans extract water from aquifers by digging or drilling wells that extend from the ground surface to the water table, the level below which all the empty space in the rocks and soil are completely full of water (saturated). When a well reaches the water table, groundwater fills the hole like water filling a hole dug in beach sand. In wet regions, the water table may lie only a few feet (meters) below the surface.

In arid regions, groundwater wells are often hundreds of feet (meters) deep. Most wells require a bucket system or pump to raise the water to the land surface. Some aquifers, however, contain pressurized ground-water that flows to the land surface on its own. Such free-flowing groundwater discharges are called artesian wells and springs. There are a number of ways to construct wells.

Some common types of wells are hand-dug, driven, and drilled wells:

- *Hand-dug wells*: Historically, wells were dug into soil and even rock by hand. Well diggers with shovels or picks would dig a hole below the water table by bailing water faster than it flowed into the well. Once a well was complete, its builders reinforced its walls and fitted it with a bucket system or pump to bring water to the surface. Hand-dug wells are still regularly constructed in many parts of the world, but they are uncommon in developed nations like the United States.
- *Driven wells:* Driven wells are constructed by forcing or hammering a narrow pipe into soft ground. These wells are inexpensive and can reach very deep aquifers, but can only be used in areas that have loose soil or sediment (particles of sand, gravel, and silt).
- *Drilled wells*: Today, most water wells are drilled using rotary (turning) or percussion (hammering) machines that are mounted on large trucks. Drilled wells that penetrate loose material are lined with plastic or metal pipe called casing, which keeps the sides of the hole from collapsing. An electric pump is placed at the bottom of the well to bring the water to the surface.

HISTORICAL GROUNDWATER USE

Humans in arid regions such as northern Africa, the Middle East, and central Asia have relied on groundwater to provide drinking water and irrigate crops for thousands of years.

DOWSING

Groundwater can be hard to find. Today, hydrogeologists use scientific methods to locate aquifers and productive water wells. Aquifers can be extremely complex and groundwater flow patterns difficult to predict, and it is not uncommon for hydrogeologists to drill dry wells. In the past, water–seekers consulted with spiritually-guided water prospectors called dowsers or water witches.

Dowsers profess special powers that allow them to sense or divine water beneath the ground. While a hydrogeologist searches for groundwater by taking measurements, making observations, and drawing maps, a dowser strolled across the client's land holding a metal or wooden Y-or L–shaped divining rod or a pendulum. When water was present, the rod or pendulum was said to be attracted to the water beneath. Some dowsers even claimed that their divining rods would locate groundwater on maps of the land surface.

The practice of dowsing has its roots in ancient Egypt and China, and its first published reference appeared in 1430. Early dowsers and water witches probably relied on a combination of spiritual guidance and astute scientific observations of groundwater discharge features such as springs, seeps, and vegetation patterns to locate underground water. Like witch doctors in ancient cultures, dowsers used all their available tools, including scientific knowledge, to help their clients solve problems. As such, modern hydrogeologists are perhaps their closest professional descendants.

Modern-day dowsers claim to find water entirely with their spiritually enhanced extrasensory powers. They assert that ground-water has a magnetic field that pulls on their dowsing rods, a theory that has never been scientifically proven. Dowsers do successfully locate groundwater, but without clues to the local groundwater system, their results are statistically no better than random well drilling.

Archeologists have discovered the remains of hand-dug wells, oasis (areas in the desert with a source of water) settlements, and groundwater distribution systems throughout the ancient world. Humans have drunk from groundwater springs at the Oasis of Bahariya in the Sahara desert of western Egypt since the early stone age (Paleolithic Age) more than one million years ago.

Knowledge of groundwater supplies and extraction technologies was critical information for ancient desert empires such as Mesopotamia, Sumeria, and Egypt. Nomads (wandering tribes) in the Saharan and Arabian deserts relied upon fiercely guarded knowledge of groundwater springs and seeps to survive. Egyptians, Mesopotamians, and Chinese who first practiced agriculture dug wells to provide irrigation for water–intensive crops such as rice and cotton, and drinking water for permanent settlements. Groundwater availability affected patterns of conquest and settlement in Greek and Roman Empires. European explorers sought groundwater and white settlers excavated wells that supported settlement and farming throughout North and South America.

MODERN GROUNDWATER USE

Today, people use groundwater for agricultural irrigation, industrial processes, municipal (city) and residential (home) water supplies. In the United States, groundwater accounted for about one quarter (26%) of total water use in the year 2000. (Surface freshwater made up the other 74%.) Groundwater use, however, varies by location, and many U.S. residents and industries depend almost completely upon water drawn from regional aquifers. More than one-third of U.S.' 100 largest cities, including Miami Beach, San Antonio, Memphis, Honolulu, and Tucson get all their water from aquifers. Almost all rural households (98%) draw their water from private wells.

Farmers and ranchers in Midwestern and Western states make heavy use of groundwater for irrigation of crops. In the eastern and southern U.S., most drinking and agricultural water comes from lakes and streams, but industries use vast quantities of groundwater for such activities as refining petroleum, aluminum, and other ores; manufacturing steel and chemicals; producing plastics; and mining. Aquaculture (fish farming) is big business and a significant groundwater consumer in Southeastern states like Mississippi, Alabama, and Louisiana. In the United States, groundwater is particularly important in arid and semi-arid agricultural states in the western half of the nation. Heavily agricultural states such as California, Oregon, and Texas use large quantities of groundwater for irrigation of food crops. The livestock industry also draws heavily upon groundwater supplies in states such as Texas, Nebraska, Kansas, and Colorado. Water drawn from wells not only fills watering troughs, but also irrigates vast tracts of midwestern cropland that produce material for cattle, poultry, pig, and fish feed. Meat processing plants also require water. (It takes about 13 gallons [49 liters] of water to produce 1 pound (0.45 kilogram) of beef, and about 4 gallons [15 liters] of water go into producing 1 gallon [3.8 liters] of milk!)

8

Rainwater Management: Harvesting and Utilisation

In most urban areas, population is increasing rapidly and the issue of supplying adequate water to meet societal needs and to ensure equity in access to water is one of the most urgent and significant challenges faced by decision-makers. With respect to the physical alternatives to fulfil sustainable management of freshwater, there are two solutions: finding alternate or additional water resources using conventional centralised approaches; or better utilising the limited amount of water resources available in a more efficient way.

To date, much attention has been given to the first option and only limited attention has been given to optimising water management systems. Among the various alternative technologies to augment freshwater resources, rainwater harvesting and utilisation is a decentralised, environmentally sound solution, which can avoid many environmental problems often caused in conventional large-scale projects using centralised approaches.

In most urban areas, population is increasing rapidly and the issue of supplying adequate water to meet societal needs and to ensure equity in access to water is one of the most urgent and significant challenges faced by decision-makers. With respect to the physical alternatives to fulfil sustainable management of freshwater, there are two solutions: finding alternate or additional water resources using conventional centralised approaches; or better utilising the limited amount of water resources available in a more efficient way. To date, much attention has been given to the first option and only limited attention has been given to optimising water management systems. Among the various alternative technologies to augment freshwater resources, rainwater harvesting and utilisation is a decentralised, environmentally sound solution, which can avoid many environmental problems often caused in conventional large-scale projects using centralised approaches.

Rainwater harvesting, in its broadest sense, is a technology used for collecting and storing rainwater for human use from rooftops, land surfaces or rock catchments using simple techniques such as jars and pots as well as engineered techniques. Rainwater harvesting has been practiced for more than 4,000 years, owing to the temporal and spatial variability of rainfall.

It is an important water source in many areas with significant rainfall but lacking any kind of conventional, centralised supply system. It is also a good option in areas where good quality fresh surface water or groundwater is lacking. The application of appropriate rainwater harvesting technology is important for the utilisation of rainwater as a water resource.

GLOBAL POPULATION GROWTH

Global population has more than doubled since 1950 and reached six billion in 1999. The most recent population forecasts from the United Nations indicate that, under a medium fertility scenario, global population is likely to peak at about 8.9 billion in 2050. Given that many natural resources (such as water, soil, forests and fish stocks) are already being exploited beyond their limits in some regions, significant effort will be required to meet the needs of an additional three billion people in the next 50 years.

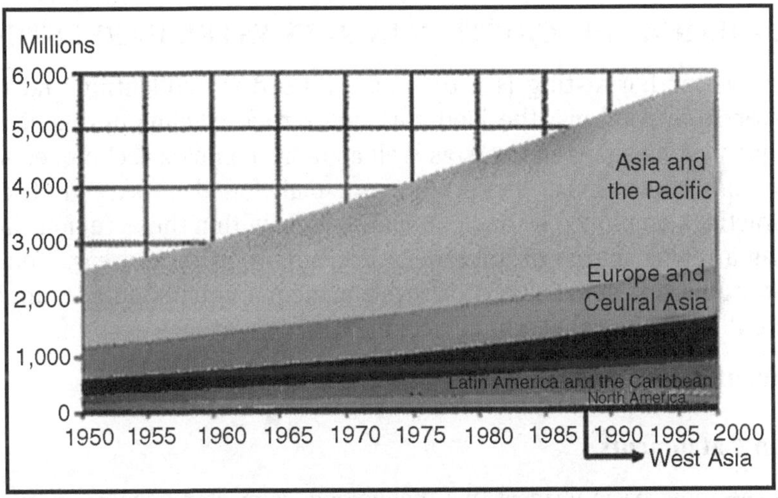

Fig. World Population Reached 6 Billion in 1999.

In parallel with these changes, there have been profound demographic shifts as people continue to migrate from rural to urban areas in search of work and new opportunities. Since 1950, the number of people living in urban areas has jumped from 750 million to more than 2.5 billion people. Currently, some 61 million people are added to cities each year through rural to urban migration, natural increase within cities, and the transformation of villages into urban areas.

Urbanisation creates new needs and aspirations, as people work, live, move and socialise in different ways, and require different products and services. Urban environmental impacts and demands are also different.

By 2025, the total urban population is projected to double to more than five billion, and 90 per cent of this increase is expected to occur in developing countries.

THE GLOBAL WATER CRISIS

Rapid population growth, combined with industrialisation, urbanisation, agricultural intensification and water-intensive lifestyles is resulting in a global water crisis. About 20 per cent of the population currently lacks access to safe drinking water, while 50 per cent lacks access to a safe sanitation system. Falling water tables are widespread and cause serious problems, both because they lead to water shortages and, in coastal areas, to salt intrusion.

Both contamination of drinking water and nitrate and heavy metal pollution of rivers, lakes and reservoirs are common problems throughout the world. The world supply of freshwater cannot be increased. More and more people are becoming dependent on limited supplies of freshwater that are becoming more polluted. Water security, like food security, is becoming a major national and regional priority in many areas of the world.

TECHNICAL DESCRIPTION IN RAINWATER HARVESTING

Rainwater harvesting is a technology used for collecting and storing rainwater from rooftops, the land surface or rock catchments using simple techniques such as jars and pots as well as more complex techniques such as underground check dams. The techniques usually found in Asia and Africa arise from practices employed by ancient civilizations within these regions and still serve as a major source of drinking water supply in rural areas. Commonly used systems are constructed of three principal components; namely, the catchment area, the collection device, and the conveyance system.

Catchment Areas

Rooftop Catchments

In the most basic form of this technology, rainwater is collected in simple vessels at the edge of the roof. Variations on this basic approach include collection of rainwater in gutters which drain to the collection vessel through down-pipes constructed for this purpose, and/or the diversion of rainwater from the gutters to containers for settling particulates before being conveyed to the storage container for the domestic use. As the rooftop is the main catchment area, the amount and quality of rainwater collected depends on the area and type of roofing material.

Reasonably pure rainwater can be collected from roofs constructed with galvanized corrugated iron, aluminium or asbestos cement sheets, tiles and slates, although thatched roofs tied with bamboo gutters and laid in proper slopes can produce almost the same amount of runoff less expensively.

However, the bamboo roofs are least suitable because of possible health hazards. Similarly, roofs with metallic paint or other coatings are not recommended as they may impart tastes or colour to the collected water. Roof catchments should also be cleaned regularly to remove dust, leaves and bird droppings so as to maintain the quality of the product water. Figure shows a schematic of a rooftop collection system.

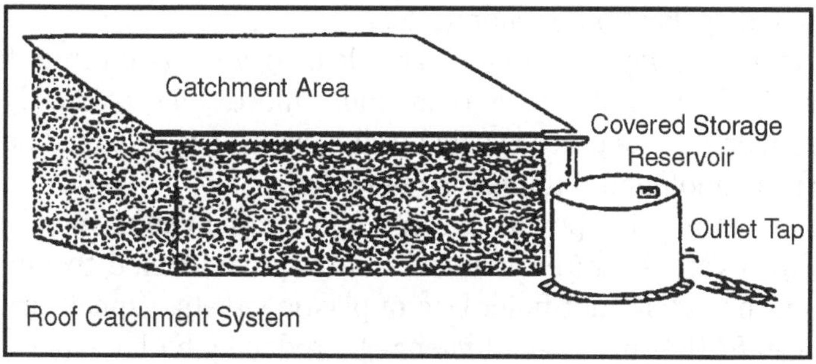

Fig. Rooftop Catchment System.

Land surface catchments: Rainwater harvesting using ground or land surface catchment areas is less complex way of collecting rainwater. It involves improving runoff capacity of the land surface through various techniques including collection of runoff with drain pipes and storage of collected water.

Compared to rooftop catchment techniques, ground catchment techniques provide more opportunity for collecting water from a larger surface area. By retaining the flows (including flood flows) of small creeks and streams in small storage reservoirs (on surface or underground) created by low cost (e.g., earthen) dams, this technology can meet water demands during dry periods.

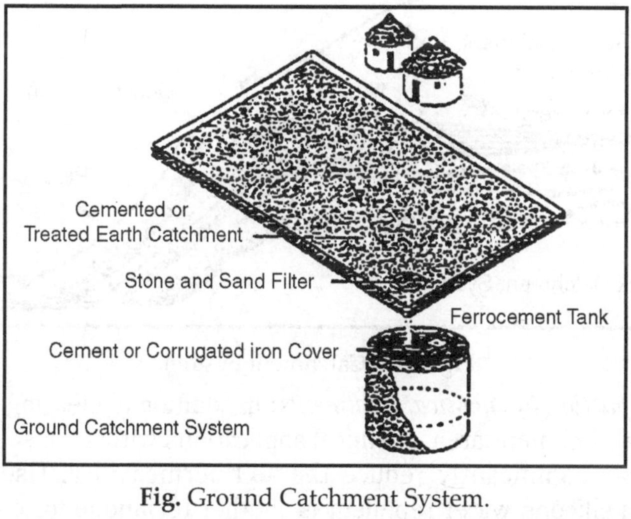

Fig. Ground Catchment System.

There is a possibility of high rates of water loss due to infiltration into the ground, and, because of the often marginal quality of the water collected, this technique is mainly suitable for storing water for agricultural purposes. Various techniques available for increasing the runoff within ground catchment areas involve: i) clearing or altering vegetation cover, ii) increasing the land slope with artificial ground cover, and iii) reducing soil permeability by the soil compaction and application of chemicals.

Clearing or altering vegetation cover: Clearing vegetation from the ground can increase surface runoff but also can induce more soil erosion. Use of dense vegetation cover such as grass is usually suggested as it helps to both maintain an high rate of runoff and minimize soil erosion.

Increasing slope: Steeper slopes can allow rapid runoff of rainfall to the collector. However, the rate of runoff has to be controlled to minimise soil erosion from the catchment field. Use of plastic sheets, asphalt or tiles along with slope can further increase efficiency by reducing both evaporative losses and soil erosion. The use of flat sheets of galvanized iron with timber frames to prevent corrosion was recommended and constructed in the State of Victoria, Australia, about 65 years ago.

Soil compaction by physical means: This involves smoothing and compacting of soil surface using equipment such as graders and rollers. To increase the surface runoff and minimize soil erosion rates, conservation bench terraces are constructed along a slope perpendicular to runoff flow. The bench terraces are separated by the sloping collectors and provision is made for distributing the runoff evenly across the field strips as sheet flow. Excess flows are routed to a lower collector and stored.

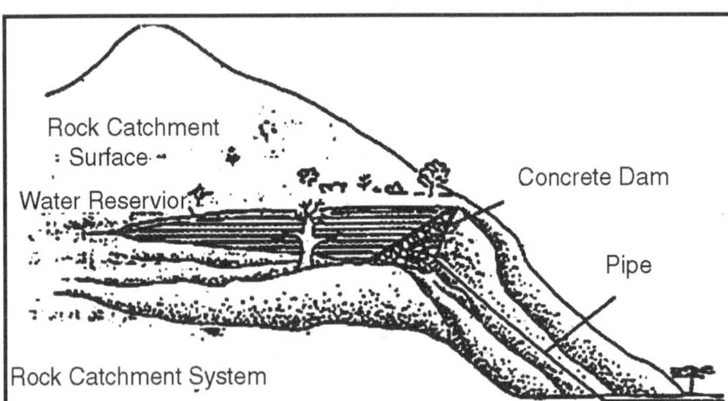

Fig. Rock Catchment System.

Soil compaction by chemical treatments: In addition to clearing, shaping and compacting a catchment area, chemical applications with such soil treatments as sodium can significantly reduce the soil permeability. Use of aqueous solutions of a silicone-water repellent is another technique for enhancing soil compaction technologies. Though soil permeability can be reduced through chemical treatments, soil compaction can induce greater rates of soil erosion and may be expensive. Use of sodium-based chemicals may increase the salt content in the collected water, which may not be suitable both for drinking and irrigation purposes.

Rock catchments systems: The presence of massive rock outcrops provides suitable catchment surfaces for freshwater augmentation. In these systems, runoff is channelled along stone and cement gutters, constructed on the rock surface, to reservoirs contained by concrete dams. The collected water then can be transported through a gravity fed pipe network to household standpipes.

Collection Devices

Storage Tanks

Storage tanks for collecting rainwater harvested using guttering may be either above or below the ground. Precautions required in the use of storage tanks include provision of an adequate enclosure to minimise contamination from human, animal or other environmental contaminants, and a tight cover to prevent algal growth and the breeding of mosquitos.

Open containers are not recommended for collecting water for drinking purposes. Various types of rainwater storage facilities can be found in practice. Among them are cylindrical ferrocement tanks and mortar jars. The ferrocement tank consists of a lightly reinforced concrete base on which is erected a circular vertical cylinder with a 10 mm steel base. This cylinder is further wrapped in two layers of light wire mesh to form the frame of the tank. Mortar jars are large jar shaped vessels constructed from wire reinforced mortar.

The storage capacity needed should be calculated to take into consideration the length of any dry spells, the amount of rainfall, and the per capita water consumption rate. In most of the Asian countries, the winter months are dry, sometimes for weeks on end, and the annual average rainfall can occur within just a few days. In such circumstances, the storage capacity should be large enough to cover the demands of two to three weeks. For example, a three person household should have a minimum capacity of 3 (Persons) × 90 (l) × 20 (days) = 5 400 l.

Rainfall water Containers

As an alternative to storage tanks, battery tanks (i.e., interconnected tanks) made of pottery, ferrocement, or polyethylene may be suitable. The polyethylene tanks are compact but have a large storage capacity (ca. 1 000 to 2 000 l), are easy to clean and have many openings which can be fitted with fittings for connecting pipes.

In Asia, jars made of earthen materials or ferrocement tanks are commonly used. During the 1980s, the use of rainwater catchment technologies, especially roof catchment systems, expanded rapidly in a number of regions, including Thailand where more than ten million 2 m3 ferrocement rainwater jars were built and many tens of thousands of larger ferrocement tanks were constructed between 1991 and 1993. Early problems with the jar design were quickly addressed by including a metal cover using readily available, standard brass fixtures.

The immense success of the jar programme springs from the fact that the technology met a real need, was affordable, and invited community participation. The programme also captured the imagination and support of not only the citizens, but also of government at both local and national levels as well as community based organizations, small-scale enterprises and donor agencies.

The introduction and rapid promotion of Bamboo reinforced tanks, however, was less successful because the bamboo was attacked by termites, bacteria and fungus. More than 50 000 tanks were built between 1986 and 1993 (mainly in Thailand and Indonesia) before a number started to fail, and, by the late 1980s, the bamboo reinforced tank design, which had promised to provide an excellent low-cost alternative to ferrocement tanks, had to be abandoned.

The design considerations vary according to the type of tank and various other factors have to be considered while designing the rainwater tanks which are:

- A solid, secure cover to keep out insects, dirt and sunlight which will act to prevent the growth of algae inside the tank.
- A coarse inlet filter for excluding coarse debris, dirt, leaves, and other solid materials.
- An overflow pipe. - A manhole, sump and drain for cleaning.
- An extraction system that doesn't contaminate the water (e.g., a tap or pump).
- A lock on the tap. - A soakaway to prevent spilled water from forming puddles near the tank.
- A maximum height of 2 m to limit the water pressure acting on the container to minimize burst tanks.
- A device to indicate the level of water in the tank.
- A sediment trap, tipping bucket or other fouled flush mechanism.
- A second, clear water storage tank if the rainwater has to be subjected to some form of water treatment, such as desalination using a density stratification process in the first tank.

Conveyance systems are required to transfer the rainwater collected on the rooftops to the storage tanks. This is usually accomplished by making connections to one or more down-pipes connected to the rooftop gutters.

When selecting a conveyance system, consideration should be given to the fact that, when it first starts to rain, dirt and debris from the rooftop and gutters will be washed into the down-pipe. Thus, the relatively clean water will only be available some time later in the storm. There are several possible choices to selectively collect clean water for the storage tanks. The most common is the down-pipe flap. With this flap it is possible to direct the first flush of water flow through the down-pipe, while later rainfall is diverted into a storage tank.

When it starts to rain, the flap is left in the closed position, directing water to the down-pipe, and, later, opened when relatively clean water can be collected. A great disadvantage of using this type of conveyance control system is the necessity to observe the runoff quality and manually operate the flap. An alternative approach would be to automate the opening of the flap as described below.

A simple and effective method of diverting rainwater without the need for supervision is depicted in Figure. A funnel-shaped insert is integrated into the down-pipe system. Because the upper edge of the funnel is not in direct contact with the sides of the down-pipe, and a small gap exists between the down-pipe walls and the funnel, water is free to flow both around the funnel and through the funnel.

When it first starts to rain, the volume of water passing down the pipe is small, and the "dirty" water runs down the walls of the pipe, around the funnel and is discharged to the ground as is normally the case with rainwater guttering.

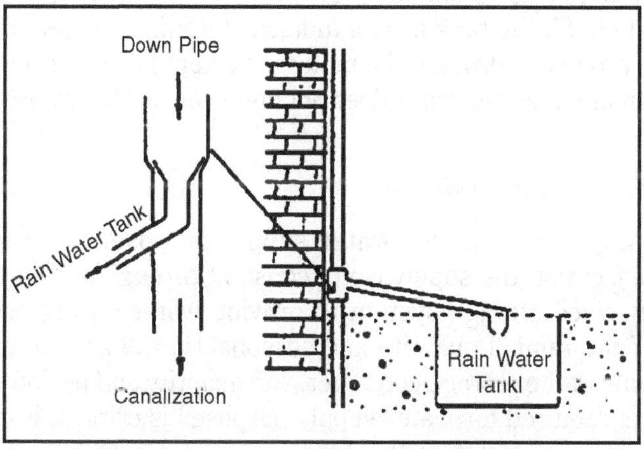

Fig. Typical Conveyance System.

However, as the rainfall continues, the volume of water increases and "clean" water fills the down-pipe. At this higher volume, the funnel collects the clean water and redirects it to a storage tank. The pipes used for the collection of rainwater, wherever possible, should be made of plastic, PVC or other inert substance, as the pH of rainwater can be low (acidic) and could cause corrosion, and mobilization of metals, in metal pipes.

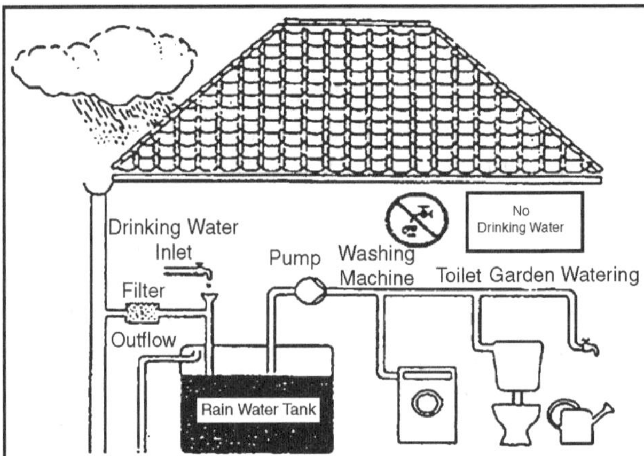

The collection of rainwater in a tank with an overflow,transmission to the several users.

Fig. Typical Distribution System.

In order to safely fill a rainwater storage tank, it is necessary to make sure that excess water can overflow, and that blockages in the pipes or dirt in the water do not cause damage or contamination of the water supply. The design of the funnel system, with the drain-pipe being larger than the rainwater tank feed-pipe, helps to ensure that the water supply is protected by allowing excess water to bypass the storage tank. A modification of this design is shown in Figure, which illustrates a simple overflow/bypass system. In this system, it also is possible to fill the tank from a municipal drinking water source, so that even during a prolonged drought the tank can be kept full. Care should be taken, however, to ensure that rainwater does not enter the drinking water distribution system.

Calculating the Amount Available

When using rainwater for water supply purposes, it is important to recognize the fact that the supply is not constant throughout the year and plan an adequately-sized storage system to provide water during dry periods. A knowledge of the rainfall quantity and seasonality, the area of the collection area and volume of the storage container, and quantity and period of use during which water is required for water supply purposes is critical. For example, in Tokyo, the average annual rainfall is 1 800 mm, and, assuming that the effective collection area of a house is equal to its roof area, the typical collection area is about 100 m^2. Thus, the average annual volume of rainwater falling on the roof may be calculated as the product of the collection area, 100 m2, and rainfall amount, 1 800 mm, or 180 m3. However, in practice, this volume can never be achieved since a portion of the rainwater evaporates from the rooftop and a portion, including the first flush, may be lost to the drainage system. Additional rainwater volume may be lost as overflow from the storage container if the storage tank is of insufficient volume to contain the entire volume of runoff. Thus, the net usable or available amount of rainwater from a tiled roof would be approximately 70% to 80% of the gross volume of rainfall, or about 130 m3 to 140 m3 if the water container is big enough to hold that quantity of rainwater available. Such a volume would be sufficient to save a significant amount of freshwater and money.

ADVANTAGES OF RAINWATER HARVESTING

Rainwater harvesting systems can provide water at or near the point where water is needed or used. The systems can be both owner and utility operated and managed. Rainwater collected using existing structures (i.e., rooftops, parking lots, playgrounds, parks, ponds, flood plains, etc.), has few negative environmental impacts compared to other technologies for water resources development.

Rainwater is relatively clean and the quality is usually acceptable for many purposes with little or even no treatment. The physical and chemical properties of rainwater are usually superior to sources of groundwater that may have been subjected to contamination.

Some Other Advantages of Rainwater Harvesting Include:

- Rainwater harvesting can co-exist with and provide a good supplement to other water sources and utility systems, thus relieving pressure on other water sources.
- Rainwater harvesting provides a water supply buffer for use in times of emergency or breakdown of the public water supply systems, particularly during natural disasters.
- Rainwater harvesting can reduce storm drainage load and flooding in city streets.
- Users of rainwater are usually the owners who operate and manage the catchment system, hence, they are more likely to exercise water conservation because they know how much water is in storage and they will try to prevent the storage tank from drying up.
- Rainwater harvesting technologies are flexible and can be built to meet almost any requirements. Construction, operation, and maintenance are not labour intensive.

GENERAL DESCRIPTION OF THE TECHNOLOGY

Historical Development of Rainwater Harvesting and Utilisation

Rainwater harvesting and utilisation systems have been used since ancient times and evidence of roof catchment systems date back to early Roman times. Roman villas and even whole cities were designed to take advantage of rainwater as the principal water source for drinking and domestic purposes since at least 2000 B.C. In the Negev desert in Israel, tanks for storing runoff from hillsides for both domestic and agricultural purposes have allowed habitation and cultivation in areas with as little as 100mm of rain per year.

The earliest known evidence of the use of the technology in Africa comes from northern Egypt, where tanks ranging from 200-2000m3 have been used for at least 2000 years – many are still operational today. The technology also has a long history in Asia, where rainwater collection practices have been traced back almost 2000 years in Thailand.

The small-scale collection of rainwater from the eaves of roofs or via simple gutters into traditional jars and pots has been practiced in Africa and Asia for thousands of years. In many remote rural areas, this is still the method used today. The world's largest rainwater tank is probably the Yerebatan Sarayi in Istanbul, Turkey. This was constructed during the rule of Caesar Justinian. It measures 140m by 70m and has a capacity of 80,000 cubic metres.

TYPES OF RAINWATER HARVESTING SYSTEMS

Typically, a rainwater harvesting system consists of three basic elements: the collection system, the conveyance system, and the storage system. Collection systems can vary from simple types within a household to bigger systems where a large catchment area contributes to an impounding reservoir from which water is either gravitated or pumped to water treatment plants. The categorisation of rainwater harvesting systems depends on factors like the size and nature of the catchment areas and whether the systems are in urban or rural settings. Some of the systems are described below.

Simple Roof Water Collection Systems

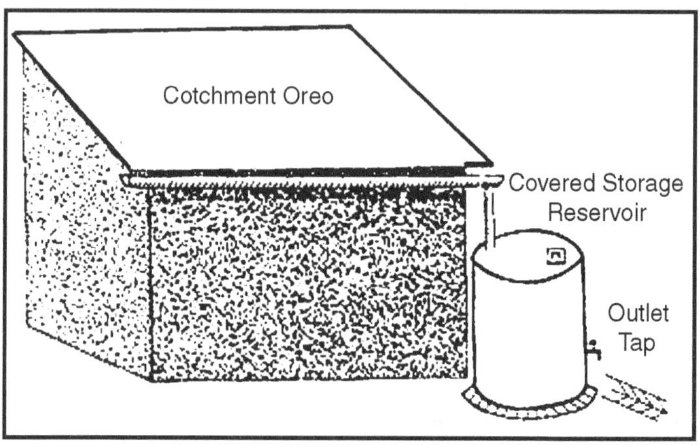

Fig. Example of a roof catchment system.

While the collection of rainwater by a single household may not be significant, the impact ofthousands or even millions of household rainwater storage tanks can potentially be enormous. The main components in a simple roof water collection system are the cistern itself, the piping that leads to the cistern and the appurtenances within the cistern. The materials and the degree of sophistication of the whole system largely depend on the initial capital investment. Some cost effective systems involve cisterns made with ferrocement, etc. In some cases, the harvested rainwater may be filtered. In other cases, the rainwater may be disinfected.

Larger Systems for Educational Institutions, Stadiums, Airports, and other Facilities

When the systems are larger, the overall system can become a bit more complicated, for example rainwater collection from the roofs and grounds of institutions, storage in underground reservoirs, treatment and then use for non-potable applications.

Roof Water Collection Systems for High-rise Buildings in Urbanised Areas

In high-rise buildings, roofs can be designed for catchment purposes and the collected roof water can be kept in separate cisterns on the roofs for non-potable uses.

Land Surface Catchments

Rainwater harvesting using ground or land surface catchment areas can be a simple way of collecting rainwater. Compared to rooftop catchment techniques, ground catchment techniques provide more opportunity for collecting water from a larger surface area.

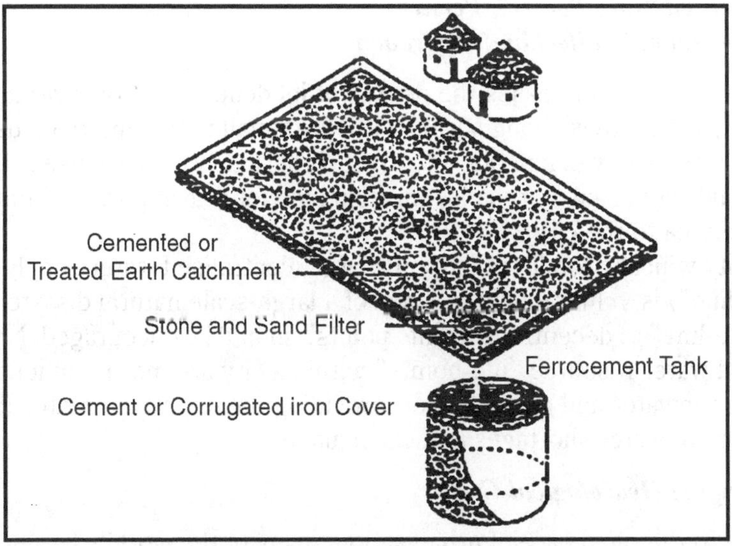

Fig. Example of a Ground Catchment System

By retaining the flows (including flood flows) of small creeks and streams in small storage reservoirs (on surface or underground) created by low cost (e.g., earthen) dams, this technology can meet water demands during dry periods. There is a possibility of high rates of water loss due to infiltration into the ground, and because of the often marginal quality of the water collected, this technique is mainly suitable for storing water for agricultural purposes.

Collection of Stormwater in Urbanised Catchments

The surface runoff collected in stormwater ponds/reservoirs from urban areas is subject to a wide variety of contaminants. Keeping these catchments clean is of primary importance, and hence the cost of water pollution control can be considerable.

Rainwater Harvesting and Utilisation Contribute to a Sustainable Water Strategy

Self-Sufficiency in Water Supply, Without Being Dependent on Remote Water Sources

Many cities around the world obtain their water from great distances - often over 100km away. But this practice of increasing dependence on the upper streams of the water resource supply area is not sustainable. Building dams in the upper watershed often means submerging houses, fields and wooded areas.

It can also cause significant socio-economic and cultural impacts in the affected communities. In addition, some existing dams have been gradually filling with silt. If not properly maintained by removing these sediments, the quantity of water collected may be significantly reduced.

Decentralised "Life-Points", Versus the Conventional "Life-Line" Approach

When the city increases the degree of its dependence on a remote water resource, and there is a long period without rainfall in the upstream dam sites, the ability of the city to function effectively is seriously compromised. The same can be said about a city's reliance on a pipeline for drawing water from a water resource area to the city.

A city which is totally reliant on a large, centralised water supply pipeline (or "lifeline") is vulnerable in the face of a large-scale natural disaster. A shift from "life-line" to decentralised "life points" should be encouraged. Numerous scattered water resource "life-points" within a city are more resilient and can draw on rainwater and groundwater, providing the city with greater flexibility in the face of water shortages and earthquakes.

Restoring the Hydrological Cycle

Due to the rapid pace of urbanisation, many of the world's large cities are facing problems with urban floods. The natural hydrological cycle manifests itself at different scales, depending upon climatic, geographic and biological factors. As rain falls over time and seeps underground to become groundwater, it feeds submerged springs and rivers.

The concrete and asphalt structures of cities have tended to disrupt the natural hydrological cycle, and reduce the amount of rainwater permeating underground.

A decrease in the area where water can penetrate speeds up the surface flow of rainwater, causing water to accumulate in drains and streams within a short time. Every time there is concentrated heavy rain, there is an overflow of water from drains, and small and medium sized rivers and streams repeatedly flood. These conditions can often lead to an outpouring of sewage into rivers and streams from sewer outlets and sewer pumping stations, thus contaminating the quality of urban streams and rivers.

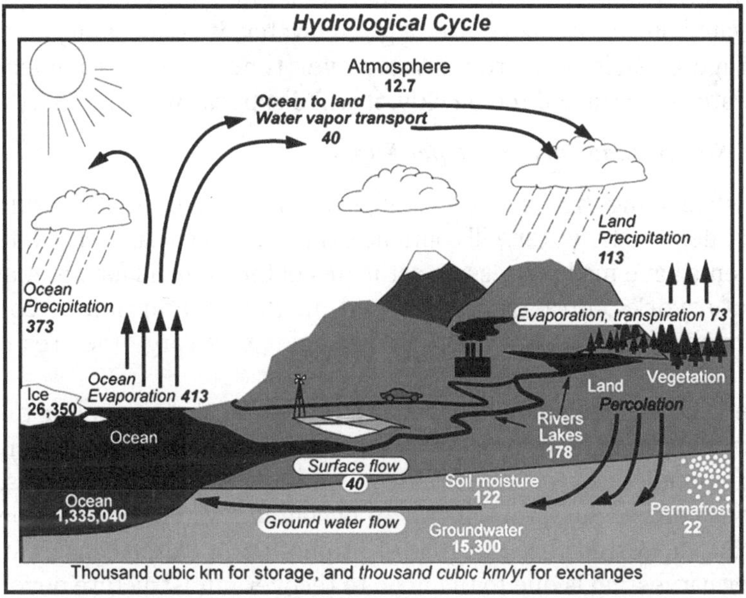

Concrete and asphalt have a profound impact on the ecology of the city. These include:

- Drying of the city: This happens as rivers and watercourses are covered, natural springs dry up, and greenery is cut down.
- Heat pollution: In some cities during the hot summer, an asphalt road at midday can reach temperatures of over 60°C. The heat expelled from air conditioners can further aggravate this.

This dramatically alters the city's natural hydrological cycle and ecological environment. In order to achieve a comprehensive solution to this problem, new approaches to urban development are required emphasising sustainability and the restoration of the urban hydrological cycle. Traditionally, storm sewer facilities have been developed based on the assumption that the amount of rainwater drained away will have to be increased. From the standpoint of preserving or restoring the natural water cycle, it is important to retain rainwater and to facilitate its permeation by preserving natural groundcover and greenery.

Introducing the Concept of "Cycle Capacity"

In thinking about sustainable development, one must view environmental capacity from a dynamic perspective and consider the time required for the restoration of the hydrological cycle. "Cycle capacity" refers to the time that nature needs revive the hydrological cycle. The use of groundwater should be considered from the point of view of cycle capacity.

Rain seeps underground and over time becomes shallow stratum groundwater. Then, over a very long period of time, it becomes deep stratum groundwater. For sustainable use of groundwater, it is necessary to consider the storage capacity for groundwater over time. If this is neglected and groundwater is extracted too quickly, it will disappear within a short time.

Demand Side Management of Water Supply

In establishing their water supply plans, cities have usually assumed that the future demand for water will continue to increase. Typically, city waterworks departments have made excessive estimates of the demand for water and have built waterworks infrastructure based on the assumption of continued development of water resources and strategies to enlarge the area of water supply.

The cost of development is usually recovered through water rates, and when there is plenty of water in the resource area, conservation of the resource is not promoted. This tends to create a conflict when drought occurs, due to the lack of policies and programmes to encourage water conservation. It has even been suggested that the lack of promotion of water conservation and rainwater harvesting is due to the need to recover infrastructure development costs through sales of piped water.

The exaggerated projection of water demand leads to the over-development of water resources, which in turn encourages denser population and more consumption of water. Sustainability of urban water supply requires a change from coping with water supply without controlling demand, to coping with supply by controlling demand. The introduction of demand side management encourages all citizens to adopt a water conservation approaches, including the use of freely available, locally supplied rainwater.

QUALITY AND HEALTH ASPECTS IN UTILISING RAINWATER

In the past, it was believed that rainwater was pure and could be consumed without pre-treatment. While this may be true in some areas that are relatively unpolluted, rainwater collected in many locations contains impurities. Particularly during the last three decades, "acid rain" has affected the quality of the collected water, to the point where it now usually requires treatment.

Rainwater quality varies for a number of reasons. While there are widely accepted standards for drinking water, the development of approved standards for water when it is used for non-potable applications would facilitate the use of rainwater sources. In terms of physical-chemical parametres, collected roof water, rainwater and urban storm water tend to exhibit quality levels that are generally comparable to the World Health Organisation (WHO) guideline values for drinking water.

However, low pH rainwater can occur as a result of sulphur dioxide, nitrous oxide and other industrial emissions, hence air quality standards must be reviewed and enforced. In addition, high lead values can sometimes be attributed to the composition of certain roofing materials – thus it is recommended that for roof water collection systems, the type of roofing material should be carefully considered.

A number of collected rainwater samples have exceeded the WHO values in terms of total coliform and faecal coliform. The ratios of faecal coliform to faecal streptococci from these samples indicated that the source of pollution was the droppings of birds, rodents, etc. Currently, water quality control in roof water collection systems is limited to diverting first flushes and occasional cleaning of cisterns.

Boiling, despite its limitations, is the easiest and surest way to achieve disinfection, although there is often a reluctance to accept this practice as taste is affected. Chlorine in the form of household bleach can be used for disinfection, however the cost of UV disinfection systems are usually prohibitive. One promising area of research is the use of photo-oxidation based on available sunlight to remove both the coliforms and streptococci.

DESIGN AND MAINTAIN FACILITIES FOR RAINWATER UTILISATION

Catchment Surface

The effective catchment area and the material used in constructing the catchment surface influence the collection efficiency and water quality. Materials commonly used for roof catchment are corrugated aluminium and galvanized iron, concrete, fibre-glass shingles, tiles, slates, etc. Mud is used primarily in rural areas. Bamboo roofs are least suitable because of possible health hazards. The materials of catchment surfaces must be non-toxic and not contain substances which impair water quality.

For example, asbestos roofs should be avoided; also, painting or coating of catchment surfaces should be avoided if possible. If the use of paint or coating is unavoidable, only non-toxic paint or coating should be used; lead, chromium, and zinc-based paints/coatings should be avoided. Similarly, roofs with metallic paint or other coatings are not recommended as they may impart tastes or colour to the collected water.

Catchment surfaces and collection devices should be cleaned regularly to remove dust, leaves and bird droppings so as to minimize bacterial contamination and maintain the quality of collected water. Roofs should also be free from over-hanging trees since birds and animals in the trees may defecate on the roof. When land surfaces are used as catchment areas, various techniques are available to increase runoff capacity, including:

- Clearing or altering vegetation cover,
- Increasing the land slope with artificial ground cover,
- Reducing soil permeability by soil compaction.

Specially constructed ground surfaces (concrete, paving stones, or some kind of liner) or paved runways can also be used to collect and convey rainwater to storage tanks or reservoirs. In the case of land surface catchments, care is required to avoid damage and contamination by people and animals. If required, these surfaces should be fenced to prevent the entry of people and animals.

Large cracks in the paved catchment due to soil movement, earthquakes or exposure to the elements should be repaired immediately. Maintenance typically consists of the removal of dirt, leaves and other accumulated materials. Such cleaning should take place annually before the start of the major rainfall season.

Conveyance Systems

Conveyance systems are required to transfer the rainwater collected on catchment surfaces (e.g. rooftops) to the storage tanks. This is usually accomplished by making connections to one or more down-pipes connected to collection devices (e.g. rooftop gutters). The pipes used for conveying rainwater, wherever possible, should be made of plastic, PVC or other inert substance, as the pH of rainwater can be low (acidic) and may cause corrosion and mobilization of metals in metal pipes.

When selecting a conveyance system, consideration should be given to the fact that when it first starts to rain, dirt and debris from catchment surfaces and collection devices will be washed into the conveyance systems (e.g. down-pipes). Relatively clean water will only be available sometime later in the storm. The first part of each rainfall should be diverted from the storage tank.

There are several possible options for selectively collecting clean water for the storage tanks. The common method is a sediment trap, which uses a tipping bucket to prevent the entry of debris from the catchment surface into the tank. Installing a first flush (or foul flush) device is also useful to divert the initial batch of rainwater away from the tank.

Gutters and down-pipes need to be periodically inspected and carefully cleaned. A good time to inspect gutters and down-pipes is while it is raining, so that leaks can be easily detected. Regular cleaning is necessary to avoid contamination.

Storage Tanks

Storage tanks for collected rainwater may be located either above or below the ground. They may be constructed as a part of the building, or may be built as a separate unit located some distance away from the building. The design considerations vary according to the type of tank and other factors. Various types of rainwater storage facilities can be found in practice. Storage tanks should be constructed of inert material. Reinforced concrete, fibreglass, polyethylene, and stainless steel are suitable materials.

Ferrocement tanks and jars made of mortar or earthen materials are commonly used. As an alternative, interconnected tanks made of pottery or polyethylene may be suitable. The polyethylene tanks are compact but have a large storage capacity (1,000 to 2,000 litres). They are easy to clean and have many openings which can be fitted with connecting pipes. Bamboo reinforced tanks are less successful because the bamboo may become infested with termites, bacteria and fungus.

Precautions are required to prevent the entry of contaminants into storage tanks. The main sources of external contamination are pollution from debris, bird and animal droppings, and insects that enter the tank. Sometimes, human, animal and other environmental contaminants, which happen to fall into tanks, can cause contamination. Open containers are not recommended for storing water for drinking purposes.

A solid and secure cover is required to avoid breeding of mosquitoes, to prevent insects and rodents from entering the tank, and to keep out sunlight to prevent the growth of algae inside the tank. A coarse inlet filter is also desirable for excluding coarse debris, dirt, leaves, and other solid materials. The storage tank should be checked and cleaned periodically. All tanks need cleaning and their designs should allow for thorough scrubbing of the inner walls and floors.

A sloped bottom and the provision of a sump and a drain are useful for collection and discharge of settled grit and sediment. An entrance hole is required for easy access for cleaning. The use of a chlorine solution is recommended for cleaning, followed by thorough rinsing. Chlorination of the cisterns or storage tanks is necessary if the water is to be used for drinking and domestic uses.

Dividing tanks into two sections or dual tanks can facilitate cleaning. Cracks in the storage tanks can create major problems and should be repaired immediately. The extraction system (e.g., taps/faucets, pumps) must not contaminate the stored water. Taps/faucets should be installed at least 10 cm above the base of the tank as this allows any debris entering the tank to settle on the bottom, where if it remains undisturbed, will not affect the quality of the water.

Rainwater pipes must be permanently marked in such a way that there is no risk of confusing them with drinking water pipes. Taps must also be clearly labelled for the user both in the local language and in clear graphic images. The handle of taps might be detachable to avoid the misuse by children. Periodic maintenance should also be carried out on any pumps used to lift water to selected areas in the house or building. The following devices are also desirable.

- An overflow pipe leading into either infiltration plants, drainage pipes with sufficient capacity or the municipal sewage pipe system.
- An indicator of the amount of water in the storage tank
- A vent for air circulation (often the overflow pipe can substitute)
- Protection against insects, rodents, vermin, etc. may also be required.

Calculation of Required Storage Size

When using rainwater, it is important to recognize that the rainfall is not constant throughout the year; therefore, planning the storage system with an adequate capacity is required for the constant use of rainwater even during dry periods. Knowledge of the rainfall quantity and seasonality, the area of the catchment surface and volume of the storage tank, and quantity and period of use required for water supply purposes is critical.

For example, in Tokyo, the average annual rainfall is about 1,400 mm. Assuming that the effective catchment area of a house is equal to the horizontal line of its roof surface area, and given that that the roof surface area is 50 m^2, the average annual volume of rainwater falling on the roof may be calculated as 70 m3. However, in practice, this volume can never be achieved since a portion of the rainwater evaporates from the roof surface and a portion may be lost to the drainage system, including the first flush. Furthermore, a portion of collected rainwater volume may be lost as overflow from the storage container if the storage tank has insufficient capacity to store the entire collected volume even in a heavy rain. Thus, the net usable or available amount of rainwater from the roof surface would be approximately 70% to 80% of the gross volume of rainfall. In the above example, the actual usable amount of rainwater would be about 49 m3 to 56 m3 in a year.

Selecting Rainwater as a Water Supply Source

The disadvantages of the rainwater harvesting and utilisation systems are:

- The catchment area and storage capacity of a system are relatively small. There is a great variation in weather. During a prolonged drought, the storage tank may dry up.
- Maintenance of rainwater harvesting systems, and the quality of collected water, can be difficult for users.

- Extensive development of rainwater harvesting systems may reduce the income of public water systems.
- Rainwater harvesting systems are often not part of the building code and lack clear guidelines for users/developers to follow.
- Rainwater utilisation has not been recognized as an alternative of water supply system by the public sector. Governments typically do not include rainwater utilisation in their water management policies, and citizens do not demand rainwater utilisation in their communities.
- Rainwater storage tanks may be a hazard to children who play around it.
- Rainwater storage tanks may take up valuable space.
- Some development costs of larger rainwater catchment system may be too high if the costs are not shared with other systems as part of a multi-purpose network.

Learning from these advantages and disadvantages, the decision to use rainwater as a new water source should be discussed among citizen/user groups and government water officials. Topics of such discussion might include:

- What are the alternatives for new water supply sources?
- What are the advantages and disadvantages of each alternative of new water source?
- How is rainwater utilisation ranked among the alternatives of new water supply sources, taking into account the viewpoints of private citizens and governmental officials?
- What are the responsibilities of users and communities for the participation in new water source development?

After these discussions, if rainwater utilisation is selected for development, then a detailed engineering feasibility study can be undertaken.

Promotion and Further Development of Rainwater Utilisation

A Systematic Approach

Rainwater utilisation, together with water conservation and wastewater reclamation, should be incorporated into municipal ordinances and regulations. Some standardisation of materials, at least at regional level, may be desirable from a maintenance and replacement point of view. It may be also appropriate to standardise the design of the rainwater utilisation system, at least at the regional level.

Implementation Policy

Various implementation policies should be established to make rainwater utilisation and other measures a part of the social system. Leadership is very important and local governments must take the initiative to promote the concept of water resource independence and restoration of the natural hydrological cycle. Consideration should be given to subsidising facilities for rainwater utilisation.

Technology Development and Training

Encouraging technology and human resources development to support rainwater utilisation is very important. It is also important to promote the development of efficient and affordable devices to conserve water, facilities to use rainwater and devices to enhance the underground seepage of rainwater. Together with this, there is a need to train specialists with a thorough grasp of these technologies and devices.

Networking

To promote rainwater harvesting and utilisation as an environmentally sound approach for sustainable urban water management, a network should be established involving government administrators, citizens, architects, plumbers and representatives of equipment manufacturers. It is essential to encourage regional exchanges amongst public servants, citizens and industry representatives involved in rainwater storage, seepage and use, as well as the conservation and reclamation of water.

Examples of Rainwater Harvesting and Utilisation Around the World

Singapore

Singapore, which has limited land resources and a rising demand for water, is on the lookout for alternative sources and innovative methods of harvesting water. Almost 86% of Singapore's population lives in high-rise buildings. A light roofing is placed on the roofs to act as catchment. Collected roof water is kept in separate cisterns on the roofs for non-potable uses.

A recent study of an urban residential area of about 742 ha used a model to determine the optimal storage volume of the rooftop cisterns, taking into consideration non-potable water demand and actual rainfall at 15-minute intervals. This study demonstrated an effective saving of 4% of the water used, the volume of which did not have to be pumped from the ground floor. As a result of savings in terms of water, energy costs, and deferred capital, the cost of collected roof water was calculated to be S$0.96 against the previous cost of S$1.17 per cubic metre.

A marginally larger rainwater harvesting and utilisation system exists in the Changi Airport. Rainfall from the runways and the surrounding green areas is diverted to two impounding reservoirs. One of the reservoirs is designed to balance the flows during the coincident high runoffs and incoming tides, and the other reservoir is used to collect the runoff. The water is used primarily for non-potable functions such fire-fighting drills and toilet flushing. Such collected and treated water accounts for 28 to 33% of the total water used, resulting in savings of approximately S$ 390,000 per annum.

Tokyo, Japan

In Tokyo, rainwater harvesting and utilisation is promoted to mitigate water shortages, control floods, and secure water for emergencies. The Ryogoku Kokugikan Sumo-wrestling Arena, built in 1985 in Sumida City, is a well-known facility that utilises rainwater on a large scale. The 8,400 m2 rooftop of this arena is the catchment surface of the rainwater utilisation system.

Collected rainwater is drained into a 1,000 m3 underground storage tank and used for toilet flushing and air conditioning. Sumida City Hall uses a similar system. Following the example of Kokugikan, many new public facilities have begun to introduce rainwater utilisation systems in Tokyo.

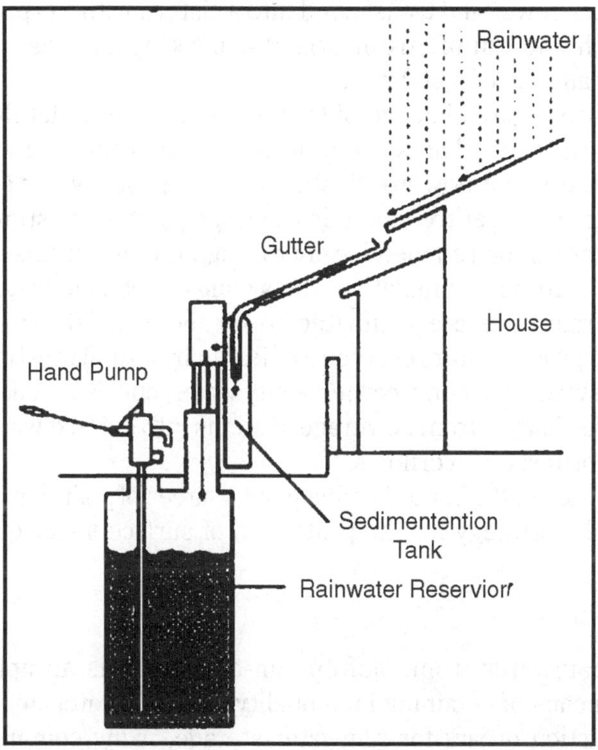

Fig. Rojison, a Simple and Unique RainWater Utilisation Facility at the Community Level in Tokyo, Japan.

At the community level, a simple and unique rainwater utilisation facility, "Rojison", has been set up by local residents in the Mukojima district of Tokyo to utilise rainwater collected from the roofs of private houses for garden watering, fire-fighting and drinking water in emergencies. To date, about 750 private and public buildings in Tokyo have introduced rainwater collection and utilisation systems. Rainwater utilisation is now flourishing at both the public and private levels.

Berlin, Germany

In October, rainwater utilization systems were introduced in Berlin as part of a large scale urban redevelopment, the DaimlerChrysler Potsdamer Platz, to control urban flooding, save city water and create a better micro climate. Rainwater falling on the rooftops (32,000 m^2) of 19 buildings is collected and stored in a 3500 m^3 rainwater basement tank.

It is then used for toilet flushing, watering of green areas (including roofs with vegetative cover) and the replenishment of an artificial pond. In another project at Belss-Luedecke-Strasse building estate in Berlin, rainwater from all roof areas (with an approximate area of 7,000 m^2) is discharged into a separate public rainwater sewer and transferred into a cistern with a capacity of 160 m^3, together with the runoff from streets, parking spaces and pathways (representing an area of 4,200 m^2).

The water is treated in several stages and used for toilet flushing as well as for garden watering. The system design ensures that the majority of the pollutants in the initial flow are flushed out of the rainwater sewer into the sanitary sewer for proper treatment in a sewage plant. It is estimated that 58% of the rainwater can be retained locally through the use of this system.

Based on a 10- year simulation, the savings of potable water through the utilisation of rainwater are estimated to be about 2,430 m^3 per year, thus preserving the groundwater reservoirs of Berlin by a similar estimated amount. Both of these systems not only conserve city water, but also reduce the potential for pollutant discharges from sewerage systems into surface waters that might result from stormwater overflows.

This approach to the control of non point sources of pollution is an important part of a broader strategy for the protection of surface water quality in urban areas.

Thailand

Storing rainwater from rooftop run-off in jars is an appropriate and inexpensive means of obtaining high quality drinking water in Thailand. Prior to the introduction of jars for rainwater storage, many communities had no means of protecting drinking water from waste and mosquito infestation. The jars come in various capacities, from 100 to 3,000 litres and are equipped with lid, faucet, and drain.

The most popular size is 2,000 litres, which costs 750 Baht, and holds sufficient rainwater for a six-person household during the dry season, lasting up to six months. Two approaches are used for the acquisition of water jars. The first approach involves technical assistance and training villagers on water jar fabrication. This approach is suitable for many villages, and encourages the villagers to work cooperatively.

Added benefits are that this environmentally appropriate technology is easy to learn, and villagers can fabricate water jars for sale at local markets. The second approach is applicable to those villages that do not have sufficient labour for making water jars. It involves access to a revolving loan fund to assist these villages in purchasing the jars. For both approaches, ownership and self-maintenance of the water jars are important. Villagers are also trained on how to ensure a safe supply of water and how to extend the life of the jars. Initially implemented by the Population and Community Development Association (PDA) in Thailand, the demonstrated success of the rainwater jar project has encouraged the Thai government to embark on an extensive national programme for rainwater harvesting.

Indonesia

In Indonesia, groundwater is becoming more scarce in large urban areas due to reduced water infiltration. The decrease of groundwater recharge in the cities is directly proportional to the increase in the pavement and roof area. In addition, high population density is has brought about high groundwater consumption. Recognising the need to alter the drainage system, the Indonesian government introduced a regulation requiring that all buildings have an infiltration well.

The regulation applies to two-thirds of the territory, including the Special Province of Yogyakarta, the Capital Special Province of Jakarta, West Java and Central Java Province. It is estimated that if each house in Java and Madura had its own infiltration well, the water deficit of 53% by the year of 2000 would be reduced to 37%, which translates into a net savings of 16% through conservation.

Capiz Province, the Philippines

In the Philippines, a rainwater harvesting programme was initiated in 1989 in Capiz Province with the assistance of the Canadian International Development Research Centre (IDRC). About 500 rainwater storage tanks were constructed made of wire-framed ferro-cement, with capacities varying from 2 to 10 m3. The construction of the tanks involved building a frame of steel reinforcing bars (rebar) and wire mesh on a sturdy reinforced concrete foundation.

The tanks were then plastered both inside and outside, thereby reducing their susceptibility to corrosion relative to metal storage tanks. The rainwater harvesting programme in Capiz Province was implemented as part of an income generation initiative. Under this arrangement, loans were provided to fund the capital cost of the tanks and related agricultural operations. Loans of US$200, repayable over a three-year period, covered not only the cost of the tank but also one or more income generating activities such as the purchase and rearing of pigs, costing around US$25 each. Mature pigs can sell for up to US$90 each, providing an income opportunity for generating that could provide sufficient income to repay the loan. This type of innovative mechanism for financing rural water supplies can help avoid the requirement for water resources development subsidies.

Bangladesh

In Bangladesh, rainwater collection is seen as a viable alternative for providing safe drinking water in arsenic affected areas. Since 1997, about 1000 rainwater harvesting systems have been installed in the country, primarily in rural areas, by the NGO Forum for Drinking Water Supply and Sanitation. This Forum is the national networking and service delivery agency for NGOs, community-based organisations and the private sector concerned with the implementation of water and sanitation programmes in unserved and underserved rural and urban communities. Its primary objective is to improve access to safe, sustainable, affordable water and sanitation services and facilities in Bangladesh. The rainwater harvesting tanks in Bangladesh vary in capacity from 500 litres to 3,200 litres, costing from Tk. 3000-Tk.8000 (US$ 50 to US$ 150). The composition and structure of the tanks also vary, and include ferro-cement tanks, brick tanks, RCC ring tanks, and sub-surface tanks.

The rainwater that is harvested is used for drinking and cooking and its acceptance as a safe, easy-to-use source of water is increasing amongst local users. Water quality testing has shown that water can be preserved for four to five months without bacterial contamination. The NGO Forum has also undertaken some recent initiatives in urban areas to promote rainwater harvesting as an alternative source of water for all household purposes.

Gansu Province, China

Gansu is one of the driest provinces in China. The annual precipitation is about 300 mm, while potential evaporation amounts to 1500-2000 mm. Surface water and groundwater is limited, thus agriculture in the province relies on rainfall and people generally suffer from inadequate supplies of drinking water. Since the 1980s, research, demonstration and extension projects on rainwater harvesting have been carried out with very positive results.

In 1995/96, the "121" Rainwater Catchment Project implemented by the Gansu Provincial Government supported farmers by building one rainwater collection field, two water storage tanks and providing one piece of land to grow cash crops. This project has proven successful in supplying drinking water for 1.3 million people and developing irrigated land for a courtyard economy.

As of 2000, a total of 2,183,000 rainwater tanks had been built with a total capacity of 73.1 million m^3 in Gansu Province, supplying drinking water for

1.97 million people and supplementary irrigation for 236,400 ha of land. Rainwater harvesting has become an important option for Gansu Province to supply drinking water, develop rain-fed agriculture and improve the ecosystem in dry areas. Seventeen provinces in China have since adopted the rainwater utilization technique, building 5.6 million tanks with a total capacity of 1.8 billion m3, supplying drinking water for approximately 15 million people and supplemental irrigation for 1.2 million ha of land.

Africa

Although in some parts of Africa rapid expansion of rainwater catchment systems has occurred in recent years, progress has been slower than Southeast Asia. This is due in part to the lower rainfall and its seasonal nature, the smaller number and size of impervious roofs and the higher costs of constructing catchment systems in relation to typical household incomes.

The lack of availability of cement and clean graded river sand in some parts of Africa and a lack of sufficient water for construction in others, add to overall cost. Nevertheless, rainwater collection is becoming more widespread in Africa with projects currently in Botswana, Togo, Mali, Malawi, South Africa, Namibia, Zimbabwe, Mozambique, Sierra Leone and Tanzania among others. Kenya is leading the way. Since the late 1970s, many projects have emerged in different parts of Kenya, each with their own designs and implementation strategies.

These projects, in combination with the efforts of local builders called "fundis" operating privately and using their own indigenous designs, have been responsible for the construction of many tens of thousands of rainwater tanks throughout the country. Where cheap, abundant, locally available building materials and appropriate construction skills and experience are absent; ferro-cement tanks have been used for both surface and sub-surface catchment.

Dar es Salaam, Tanzania

Due to inadequate piped water supplies, the University of Dar es Salaam has applied rainwater harvesting and utilisation technology to supplement the piped water supply in some of the newly built staff housing. Rainwater is collected from the hipped roof made with corrugated iron sheets and led into two "foul" tanks, each with a 70-litre capacity. After the first rain is flushed out, the foul tanks are filled up with rainwater. As the foul tanks fill up, settled water in the foul tanks flows to two underground storage tanks with a total capacity of 80,000 litres. Then, the water is pumped to a distribution tank with 400 litres capacity that is connected to the plumbing system of the house. The principles for the operation of this system are:

- Only one underground tank should be filled at a time;
- While one tank is being filled, water can be consumed from the other tank,

- Rainwater should not be mixed with tap water;
- Underground storage tanks must be cleaned thoroughly when they are empty;
- In order to conserve water, water should only be used from one distribution tank per day.

Botswana

Thousands of roof catchment and tank systems have been constructed at a number of primary schools, health clinics and government houses throughout Botswana by the town and district councils under the Ministry of Local Government, Land and Housing (MLGLH).

The original tanks were prefabricated galvanized steel tanks and brick tanks. The galvanized steel tanks have not performed well, with a short life of approximately 5 years.

The brick tanks are unpopular, due to leakage caused by cracks, and high installation costs. In the early 1980s, the MLGLH replaced these tanks in some areas with 10-20 m3 ferro-cement tanks promoted by the Botswana Technology Centre. The experience with ferro-cement tanks in Botswana is mixed; some have performed very well, but some have leaked, possibly due to poor quality control.

Brazil

Over the past decade, many NGOs and grassroots organisations have focused their work on the supply of drinking water using rainwater harvesting, and the irrigation of small-scale agriculture using sub-surface impoundments. In the semi-arid tropics of the north-eastern part of Brazil, annual rainfall varies widely from 200 to 1,000 mm, with an uneven regional and seasonal rainfall pattern. People have traditionally utilised rainwater collected in hand-dug rock catchments and river bedrock catchments.

To address the problem of unreliable rural drinking water supply in north-eastern Brazil, a group of NGOs combined their efforts with government to initiate a project involving the construction of one million rainwater tanks over a five year period, with benefits to 5 million people. Most of these tanks are made of pre-cast concrete plates or wire mesh concrete. Rainwater harvesting and utilisation is now an integrated part of educational programmes for sustainable living in the semi-arid regions of Brazil.

The rainwater utilisation concept is also spreading to other parts of Brazil, especially urban areas. A further example of the growing interest in rainwater harvesting and utilisation is the establishment of the Brazilian Rainwater Catchment Systems Association, which was founded in 1999 and held its 3rd Brazilian Rainwater Utilisation Symposium in the fall of 2001.

Fig. A Tank Made of Pre-cast Concrete Plates.
A Tank Made of Wire Mesh Concrete.

Bermuda

The island of Bermuda is located 917 km east of the North American coast. The island is 30 km long, with a width ranging from 1.5 to 3 km. The total area is 53.1 km2. The elevation of most of the land mass is less than 30 m above sea level, rising to a maximum of less than 100 m. The average annual rainfall is 1,470 mm.

A unique feature of Bermuda roofs is the wedge-shaped limestone "glides" which have been laid to form sloping gutters, diverting rainwater into vertical leaders and then into storage tanks. Most systems use rainwater storage tanks under buildings with electric pumps to supply piped indoor water.

Storage tanks have reinforced concrete floors and roofs, and the walls are constructed of mortar-filled concrete blocks with an interior mortar application approximately 1.5 cm thick. Rainwater utilisation systems in Bermuda are regulated by a Public Health Act which requires that catchments be whitewashed by white latex paint; the paint must be free from metals that might leach into water supplies.

Owners must also keep catchments, tanks, gutters, pipes, vents, and screens in good repair. Roofs are commonly repainted every two to three years and storage tanks must be cleaned at least once every six years.

St. Thomas, US Virgin Islands

St. Thomas, US Virgin Islands, is an island city which is 4.8 km wide and 19 km long. It is situated adjacent to a ridge of mountains which rise to 457 m above sea level. Annual rainfall is in the range of 1,020 to 1,520 mm. A rainwater utilisation system is a mandatory requirement for a residential building permit in St. Thomas. A single-family house must have a catchment area of 112 m^2 and a storage tank with 45 m3 capacity. There are no restrictions on the types of rooftop and water collection system construction materials. Many of the homes on St. Thomas are constructed so that at least part of the roof collects rainwater and transports it to storage tanks located within or below the house. Water quality test of samples collected from the rainwater utilisation systems in St. Thomas found that contamination from faecal coliform and Hg concentration was higher than EPA water quality standards, which limits the use of this water to non-potable applications unless adequate treatment is provided.

Island of Hawaii, USA

At the U.S. National Volcano Park, on the Island of Hawaii, rainwater utilisation systems have been built to supply water for 1,000 workers and residents of the park and 10,000 visitors per day. The Park's rainwater utilisation system includes the rooftop of a building with an area of 0.4 hectares, a ground catchment area of more than two hectares, storage tanks with two reinforced concrete water tanks with 3,800 m3 capacity each, and 18 redwood water tanks with 95 m^3 capacity each. Several smaller buildings have their own rainwater utilisation systems as well. A water treatment and pumping plant was built to provide users with good quality water.

OPEN SKY RAINWATER HARVESTING MANAGEMENT

The open sky rainwater catchment is the least sophisticated form of rainwater harvesting, requiring minimal levels of investment to install, maintain and operate. For this reason, open sky rainwater harvesting is usually practised by relatively poor people who cannot afford appropriately-sized gutters or motkas in which to store water.

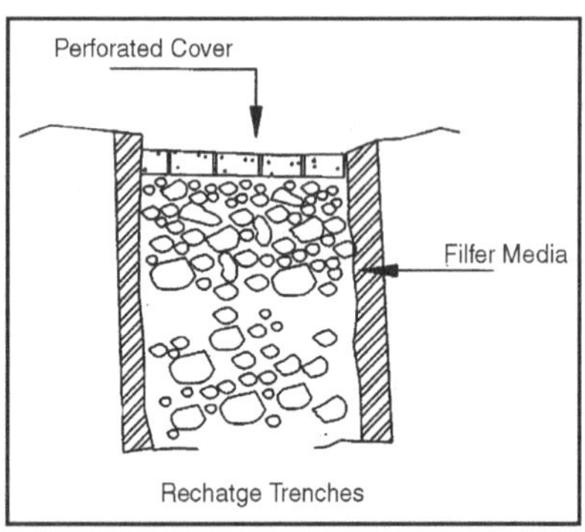

Fig. Open Sky Rainwater Harvesting.

In Bangladesh, a number of variants on this technology have been observed, ranging in cost and design from two corrugated iron sheets supported by four bamboo posts and slanted in such a way as to collect and direct rainwater into pots, motkas, etc., to plastic sheeting, suspended on four bamboo sticks, with an hole in the centre, weighted with a brick chip, to direct rainwater into a pot placed below the hole, as shown in Figure. When applied for agricultural use, the polyethylene sheeting may be placed in the open and slanted so that rainwater collecting on the plastic flows off the sheeting and downslope to the agricultural. Mosquito nets, bed sheets or even sarees (women's garments), inverted umbrellas, and open drums have been used as catchments to harvest rainwater, while fishermen and mariners living offshore for a considerable periods have traditionally harvested rainfall to replenish potable water supplies on their boats.

Operation and Maintenance

This technology requires little maintenance, except that devoted to the periodic cleaning of water storage pots, and few skills to operate.

Level of Involvement

This technology may be implemented at the household level.

Costs

Use of this technology can be had for a minimal investment in materials. In its relatively sophisticated version, that constructed of corrugated iron sheeting, typical costs would be between \$5 and \$9 for two corrugated iron sheets. In its least expensive form, that constructed of plastic sheeting, the cost would be about \$0.50. Likewise, the cost of storing the harvested rainwater depends on the type of storage vessel used. Typical costs would range from about \$0.25 to over \$500: pitchers would cost about \$0.25 each; small earthen jars (motkas), \$1.20; medium-sized earthen jars, \$5.00; large earthen jars, \$10.00; cement underground storage tanks, \$50 to \$500; and, cement above ground storage tanks, \$100 to \$300.

Effectiveness of the Technology

This technology is effective in meeting the short term water requirements of people living in boats and of small families lacking access to other water supplies.

Suitability

This technology is limited to very small scale uses. Advantages This technology is simple to use, requiring few skills and minimal materials.

Fig. Woman Taking Fresh Water from a Pond on Hatya Island.

Disadvantages

It may be difficult to securely anchor the rainwater catchment materials during windy conditions or during storms, limiting the ability of the technology to harvest rainwater. Because of the limited surface area of the rainwater catchment, this technology does not provide a reliable source of water, and its use is restricted to the wet season.

Cultural Acceptability

There are no known cultural problems associated with the use of this technology.

9

Soil, Water and Forest Conservation Methods

SOIL CONSERVATION

Soil conservation is a set of management strategies for prevention of soil being eroded from the Earth's surface or becoming chemically altered by overuse, acidification, salinization or other chemical soil contamination.

It is a component of environmental soil science. Decisions regarding appropriate crop rotation, cover crops, and planted windbreaks are central to the ability of surface soils to retain their integrity, both with respect to erosive forces and chemical change from nutrient depletion.

Crop rotation is simply the conventional alternation of crops on a given field, so that nutrient depletion is avoided from repetitive chemical uptake/ deposition of single crop growth.

EROSION PREVENTION

Practices

There are also conventional practices that farmers have invoked for centuries. These fall into two main categories: contour farming and terracing, standard methods recommended by the U.S. Natural Resources Conservation Service, whose Code 330 is the common standard.

Contour farming was practiced by the ancient Phoenicians, and is known to be effective for slopes between two and ten percent. Contour plowing can increase crop yields from 10 to 50 percent, partially as a result from greater soil retention.

There are many erosion control methods that can be used such as conservation tillage systems and crop rotation. Keyline design is an enhancement of contour farming, where the total watershed properties are taken into account in forming the contour lines. Terracing is the practice of creating benches or nearly level layers on a hillside setting. Terraced farming is more common on small farms and in underdeveloped countries, since mechanized equipment is difficult to deploy in this setting. Human overpopulation is leading to destruction of tropical forests due to widening practices of slash-and-burn and other methods of subsistence farming necessitated by famines in lesser developed countries. A sequel to the deforestation is typically large scale erosion, loss of soil nutrients and sometimes total desertification.

Perimeter Runoff Control

Trees, shrubs and groundcovers are also effective perimeter treatment for soil erosion prevention, by insuring any surface flows are impeded. A special form of this perimeter or inter-row treatment is the use of a "grassway" that both channels and dissipates runoff through surface friction, impeding surface runoff, and encouraging infiltration of the slowed surface water.

SOIL EROSION AND ITS CONSERVATION

Soil is one of the most important natural resources of man. Soils are essential for man for growing crops, fodder and limber. Once the fertile portion of the earth's surface is lost, it is very difficult to replace it. In India, the destruction of the top-soil has already reached an alarming proportion. Land degradation problems have resulted in increasing depletion of the productivity of the basic land stock through nutrient deficiencies. In addition to the direct loss of crop producing capacity, soil erosion increases the destructiveness of floods and decreases the storage capacity of water in reservoirs. It is therefore essential that the soils should not be allowed to wash or blow-away more rapidly than they can be regenerated, their fertility should not be exhausted and their physical structure should remain suited to continued production of desired plant materials. Protection of land from further degradation, adoption of various conservation measures, including reclamation and scientific manage-ment of available land stock is very important for a country like India to achieve higher productivity of food, fodder, fuel and industrial raw materials on a substantial basis. Besides, demand for land for providing social priorities such as shelter, roads, industrial activities is increasing at a very fast rate with the rise in population and very often good agricultural and forest lands are being diverted to such use. It is, therefore, necessary to keep soil in place and in a state favourable to its highest productive capacity.

Soil Erosion

The process of destruction of soil and the removal of the destroyed soil material constitute soil erosion. According to Dr. Bennett "the vastly accelerated process of soil removal brought about by the human interference, with the normal disequilibrium between soil building and soil removal is designated as soil erosion".

Types of Soil-Erosion

Erosion of soil by water is quite significant and takes place chiefly in two ways (a) Sheet erosion, (b) Gully erosion.

Sheet Erosion

Sheet movement of water causes sheet erosion and depends on the velocity and quantity of pronounced surface runoff and the erodability of the soil itself. In such cases, the soil is eroded as layers from the hill slopes, sometimes slowly and in-sidiously and sometimes more rapidly. Sheet erosion is more or less universal on:-

- all bare follow land,
- all uncultivated land whose plant cover has been thinned out by over grazing, fire or other misuse, and
- all sloping cultivated fields and on sloping forest, scrub jungles where natural porosity of soil has been removed by heavy grazing, felling of trees or burning etc.

The particles loosened and shifted by the rain drops are carried down slope by a very thin sheet of water which moves along the surface. The impacts of the raindrops increases the turbulance and transporting capacity of this unchannelized sheetwash which results in the uniform skimming of the top soil. Sheet erosion is considered as dangerous as it may continue for years but may or may not leave any trace of the damage. Sheet erosion is common in the Himalayan foot-hills, in Assam, Western ghats and Eastern ghats. When sheet erosion continues unchecked, the silt laden run-off forms well-defined minute finger shaped grooves over the entire field. Such thin channeling is known as 'rill-erosion', which is active over wide areas in Bihar, Uttar Pradesh, Madhva Pradesh and in semiarid areas of Maharashtra, Karnataka, Andhra Pradesh and Tamil Nadu.

Gully Erosion

On a gentle slope, adequately covered by vege-tation, clay soil will resist erosion to a great extent and the water forms small rivulets which can then erode deeper. The rivulets in turn join together to form larger channels until gullies are formed gradually deep gullies cut into the soil and then spread and grow until all the soil is removal from the sloping ground. This phenomenon once started and if not checked, goes on extending and ultimately the whole land is converted into a bad-land topography. Gully erosion is more common in areas where the river system has cut down into elevated plateaus so that feeders and branches carve out an intricate pattern of gullies.

Apart from this, it also takes place in relatively level country whenever large blocks of cultivation give rise to con-centration of field run-off.

Wind Erosion

It occurs in dry climatic areas having a sparse and low vegetation cover on mechanically weathered, loosened surficial material. Dust storms are the principal agents of wind erosion. The top soil is often blown off from the surface rendering it infertile. Besides, with the decrease in the wind velocity coarse sand particles get deposited in some areas covering the existing soil and rendering it unproductive.

SOIL NATURAL RESOURCES AND CONSERVATION SERVICE

The Natural Resources Conservation Service (NRCS), formerly known as the Soil Conservation Service (SCS), is an agency of the United States Department of Agriculture (USDA) that provides technical assistance to farmers and other private landowners and managers.

Its name was changed in 1994 during the Presidency of Bill Clinton to reflect its broader mission. It is a relatively small agency, currently comprising about 12,000 employees. Its mission is to improve, protect, and conserve natural resources on private lands through a cooperative partnership with local and state agencies. While its primary focus has beenagricultural lands, it has made many technical contributions to soil surveying, classification and water qualityimprovement. One example is the Conservation Effects Assessment Project (CEAP), set up to quantify the benefits of agricultural conservation efforts promoted and supported by programmes in the Farm Security and Rural Investment Act of 2002 (2002 Farm Bill). NRCS is the leading agency in this project.

PROGRAMMES AND SERVICES

As of November 2011 the NRCS consists of 42 programmes and activities. The NRCS also offers services to private land owners, conservation districts, tribes, and other types of organizations.

Farm Bill

The conservation provisions in the Food, Conservation, and Energy act of 2008. This bill provides conservation opportunities for farmers. Services also include financial assistance which makes sure money is allocated and used properly in providing conservation for various natural resources, technical assistance which is given through the Conservation Technical Assistance programme (CTA). This service is available to anyone interested in conservation of natural resources and easements. This includes:

Farm and Ranch Land Protection Programme

(FRPP) The purpose of this programme is to work with land owners to purchase development rights to current farm and ranch land, in order to keep said land from being developed for other uses. The programme matches funds from property owners, and can be applied whether potential buyers are private or from state or local government, as well as Native American tribes. In order to receive funds from the programme, the land must be privately owned, and have an offer for sale pending. The land must be large enough to support substantial agricultural yield, and be surrounded by land with a similar nature. If there is a danger for soil erosion, a conservation plan must be included.

Grasslands Reserve Programme

(GRP) Volunteer programme to increase animal and plant biodiversity, and to protect grasslands. Participants limit use of grassland for commercial and agricultural development. The land may still be grazed or seeded, with the exception of the nesting seasons of bird species that are protected under law. A grazing management plan must be submitted for participation.

Healthy Forests Reserve Programme

(HFRP) Landowners volunteer to restore and protect forests in 30 or 10 year contracts. This programme hands assisting funds to participants.

The objectives of HFRP are to:

- Promote the recovery of endangered and threatened species under the Endangered Species Act (ESA)
- Improve plant and animal biodiversity
- Enhance carbon sequestration.

Wetlands Reserve Programme

(WRP) Volunteer programme for landowners to protect or restore wetlands on properties they own. The programme offers both financial and technological support to these landowners in order to help cultivate long term wetland health with optimal biodiversity per acre.

NRCS National Ag Water Management Team

(AGWAM) Serves 10 states in the Midwest United States in helping to reduce Nitrate levels in soil due to run-off from fertilized farmland. The project began in 2010 and initially focused on the Mississippi Basin area. The main goal of the project is to implement better methods of managing water drainage from agricultural uses, in place of letting the water drain naturally as it had done in the past. In October 2011, the The National "Managing Water, Harvesting Results" Summit was held to promote the drainage techniques used in hopes of people adopting them nationwide.

Snow Survey and Water Supply Forecasting

Includes water supply forecasts, reservoirs, and the Surface Water Supply Index (SWSI) for Alaska and other Western states. NRCS agents collect data from snowpack and mountain sites to predict spring run-off and summer streamflow amounts. These predictions are used in decision making for agriculture, wildlife management, construction and development, and several other areas. These predictions are available within the first 5 days of each month from January to June.

Wildlife Habitat Incentive Programme

(WHIP) Is a volunteer programme for improving habitats for wildlife on farmlands, private lands, and Indian land. The programme was renewed in 2008 under the Food, Conservation, and Energy Act. WHIP provides up to 75 per cent cost share and technical assistance, and includes both terrestrial and freshwater aquatic habitats. The programme aims to protect seven threatened species in particular:

- Lesser Prairie Chicken
- New England Cottontail
- Southwestern Willow Flycatcher
- Greater Sage-Grouse
- Gopher Tortoise
- Bog Turtle
- Golden-winged Warbler

Conservation Technical Assistance Programme

(CTA) Is a blanket programme which involves conservation efforts on soil and water conservation, as well as management of agricultural wastes, erosion, and general longterm sustainability. NRCS and related agencies work with landowners, communities, or developers to protect the environment. Also serve to guide people to comply with acts such as the Highly Erodible Land, Wetland (Swampbuster), and Conservation Compliance Provisions acts. The CTA can also cover projects by state, local, and federal governments.

Gulf of Mexico Initiative

(GoMI)Is a programme to assist gulf bordering states (Alabama, Florida, Louisiana, Mississippi, and Texas) improve water quality and use sustainable methods of farming, fishing, and other industry. The programme will deliver up to 50 million dollars over 2011-2013 to apply these sustainable methods, as well as wildlife habitat management systems that do not hinder agricultural productivity, and prevent future over use of water resources to protect native endangered species.

International programmes

The NRCS (formerly SCS)has been involved in soil and other conservation issues internationally since the 1930s. The main bulk of international programmes focused on preventing soil erosion by sharing techniques known to the United States with other areas. NRCS sends staff to countries worldwide to conferences to improve knowledge of soil conservation. There is also international technical assistance programmes similar to programmes implemented in the United States. There are long term technical assistance programmes in effect with one or more NRCS staff residing in the country for a minimum of one year. There are currently long term assistance programmes on every continent. Short term technical assistance is also available on a two week basis.

These programmes are to encourage local landowners and organizations to participate in the conservation of natural resources on their land, and lastly landscape planning has a goal to solve problems dealing with natural resource conservation with the help of the community in order to reach a desired future outcome.

TECHNICAL RESOURCES

Water

Pollution of water due to a number of different pollutants has driven the NRCS to take action. Not only do they offer financial assistance but they also provide the equipment needed for private land owners to protect our water resources. Water gets polluted by nitrogen and phosphorus which causes algae to grow proliferously causing the oxygen concentrations to decline rapidly, life is no longer supported in this habitat. Excessive sedimentation is also another concern along with pathogens threats that can find their way into water systems and cause detrimental effects. NRCS works in a way to help both the land owner and the water systems that need prevention or restoration.

Water Management

Water management strives to manage and control the flow of water in a way that is efficient while causing the least amount of damage to life and property. This helps provide protection in high risk areas from flooding. Irrigation water management is the most efficient way to use and recycle water resources for land owners and farmers. Drainage management is the manipulation of sub surface drainage networks in order to properly disperse the water to the correct geographical areas. The NRCS engineering division is constantly making improvements to irrigation systems in a way that incorporates every aspect of water restoration.

Water Quality

A team of highly trained experts on every aspect of water is employed by the NRCS to analyze water from different sources. They work in many areas such as: hydrology and hydraulics, stream restoration, wetlands, agriculture, agronomy, animal waste management, pest control, salinity, irrigation, and nutrients in water.

Watershed Programme

Under watershed programmes the NRCS works with states, local governments, and tribes by providing funding and resources in order to help restore and also benefit from the programmes. They would like to provide: watershed protection, flood mitigation, water quality improvement, soil erosion reduction, irrigation, sediment control, fish and wildlife enhancement, wetland and wetland function creation and restoration, groundwater recharge, easements, wetland and floodplain conservation easements, hydropower, watershed dam rehabilitation.

Plants and Animals

Plants and animals play a huge role in the health of our ecosystems. A delicate balance exists between relationships of plants and animals. If an animal is introduced to an ecosystem that is not native to the region that it could destroy plants or animals that should not have to protect itself from this particular threat. As well as if a plant ends up in a specific area where it should not be it could have adverse effects on the wildlife that try to eat it. NRCS protects the plants and animals because they provide us with food, materials for shelter, fuel to keep us warm, and air to breathe. Without functioning ecosystems we would have none of the things mentioned above. NRCS provides guidance to assist conservationists and landowners with enhancing plant and animal populations as well as helping them deal with invasive species.

Fish and Wildlife

NRCS for years has been working towards restoration, creation, enhancement, and maintenance for aquatic life on the nearly 70 per cent of land that is privately owned in order to keep the habitats and wildlife protected. NRCS with a science based approach, provides equipment to wildlife and fish management. They also do this for landowners who qualify to benefit from these technologies.

Insects and Pollinators

Pollination via insects plays a huge role in the production of food crop and flowering plants. Without pollinators searching for nectar and pollen for food the plants would not produce a seed that will create another plant. NRCS sees the importance of this process so they are taking measures to increase the declining number of pollinators. There are many resources provided from the NRCS that will help any individual do their part in conservation of these important insects. Such as Backyard Conservation which tells an individual exactly how to help by just creating a small habitat in minutes There are many others such as: Plants for pollinators, pollinators habitat in pastures, pollinator value of NRCS plant releases in conservation planting, plant materials publications relating to insects and pollinators, PLANTS database: NRCS pollinator documents. All of these are valuable resources that any individual can take advantage of.

Invasive Species and Pests

Many adverse effects are present due to invasive species. Plants and animals both inhabit areas that they are not intended to be. The kudzu vine for example covers miles of foliage. These invasive species cause America's reduction in economic productivity and ecological decline. Humans are unknowingly transporting these invasive species via ships, planes, boats, and their own bodies.

NRCS works in collaboration with the plant materials centers scattered throughout the country in order to get a handle on the invasive species of plants.These centers scout out the plants and take measures to control and eradicate them from the particular area.Invasive animals such as feral hog, european gypsy moth, and the sirex woodwasp pose a significant threat to America's wildlife as well as to the health of human beings. The hog was introduced as a food source for humans, but now the swine pandemic is a serious threat to humans.

They gypsy moth destroys natural forests that are habitat to many beneficial species. The Woodwasp feeds on pine trees as well as providing a means of transportation for a fungus that kills pine trees.

Livestock

Livestock management is an area of interest for the NRCS because if not maintained valuable resources such as food, wools, and leather would not be available.

The proper maintenance of livestock can also improve soil and water resources by providing a waste management system so that run off and erosion is not a problem. The NRCS provides financial assistance to land owners with grazing land and range land that is used by livestock in order to control the run off of waste into fresh water systems and prevent soil erosion.

Plants

Plants are a huge benefit to the health of ecosystems. NRCS offers significant amounts of resources to individuals interested in conserving plants. From databases full of information to financial assistance the NRCS works hard to provide the means needed to do so. The plant materials programme, Plant materials centers, Plant materials specialists, PLANTS database, National Plant Data Team (NPDT) are all used together to keep our ecosystems as healthy as possible. This includes getting rid of unwanted species and building up species that have been killed off that are beneficial to the environment. The NRCS utilizes a very wide range of interdisciplinary resources.

The NRCS also utilizes the following disciplines in order to maximize efficiency:

- Agronomy
- Erosion
- Air Quality and Atmospheric Change
- Animal Feeding Operations and Confined Animal Feeding Operations
- Biology
- Conservation Innovation Grants
- Conservation Practices
- Cultural Resources
- Economics
- Energy
- Engineering
- Environmental Compliance
- Field Office Technical Guide
- Forestry,
- Maps
- Data and Analysis
- Nutrient Management
- Pest Management
- Range and Pasture
- Social Sciences
- Soils, and Water Resources

These Science-Based technologies are all used together in order to provide the best conservation of natural resources possible.

WATER CONSERVATION

Conservation, in relation to a water resource, is defined in the Act as being the efficient use and saving of water, achieved through measures such as water saving devices, water-efficient processes, water conservation and demand management and water rationing (s1(1)(v)). The Water Conservation and Demand Management National Strategy Framework (DWAF, 1999a) interprets water conservation as being the minimisation of loss or waste, the preservation, care and protection of water resources and the efficient and effective use of water (p 12). This includes an additional concept, related to the care and protection of water resources, which is not referred to in the definition in the Act.

WATER CONSERVATION AND DEMAND MANAGEMENT

Water conservation and demand management is not defined in the Act. The Water Conservation and Demand Management National Strategy Framework (DWAF, 1999a) tentatively defines the concept as comprising the adaptation and implementation of a strategy (policies and initiatives) by a water institution to influence the water demand and usage of water in order to meet any of the following objectives: economic efficiency, social development, social equity, environmental protection, sustainability of water supply and services, and political acceptability.

RELATIONSHIP BETWEEN THE CONCEPTS

Water conservation, in terms of the efficient and effective use of water, can therefore be seen as an overall policy objective. Water conservation and demand management, through the implementation of a coordinated strategy, provides the means through which this policy objective can be met.

WATER CONSERVATION AND DEMAND MANAGEMENT IMPORTANT

Water scarcity, unpredictability and uneven distribution

The average annual rainfall is 500mm compared with the global average of 800mm, and is unevenly distributed geographically and seasonally. It is also highly variable over time, resulting in unpredictable and often lengthy droughts (McKenzie et al, 1999). The high evaporation rates that prevail mean that much of the rain that does fall is soon returned to the atmosphere before it can be effectively utilised. South Africa is also poorly endowed with groundwater.

Constant increasing demand

Water demand in South Africa has been growing at around 4.5 per cent per annum since the 1930s (McKenzie et al, 1999). Within 20 to 25 years, if current consumption patterns continue, the water scarcity problem in South Africa could be extremely severe (Schreiner, 1999). An estimated 41 per cent of the total mean annual run-off in South Africa is already allocated.

Significant potential cost savings

Meeting South Africa's growing water demand through increasing supply is becoming more and more expensive, as cost-effective water augmentation options are being fully exploited. WC&DM can delay the need for additional water supply schemes by many years, with very significant financial savings. For example, McKenzie et al (1999) estimated that if a 10 per cent reduction in water demand was achieved in the Vaal River Supply Area, this would result in a 6-year delay in the need for a new water augmentation scheme with savings of around R6 000 million. These savings could reduce the cost of water to commercial and domestic water users.

STRATEGY FOR THE FOREST SECTOR

Scope and purpose

The WC&DM Strategy covers plantation forestry. This includes community forests. It excludes:

- The wood processing sector, which is included in the WC&DM Strategy for Industry
- Conservation forestry, which is included in the WC&DM Strategy for the Environment.

The definition of 'conservation' in the Act does not refer to water quality. Water conservation and demand management in the National Strategy Framework includes the protection of water resources and thus the management of water quality. Water quality also affects the usability of water downstream and thus has an indirect effect on water use efficiency. However, this Strategy focuses on water quantity, and will need to address water quality later.

The Purpose of Forest Sector WC&DM Strategy

The WC&DM Strategy for the forest sector seeks to achieve the following:

- Identify opportunities to reduce unnecessary water use and improve efficiency
- Provide guidance to stakeholders in the forest sector on achieving conservation and demand managemnet
- Define roles and responsibilities of institutions and stakeholders in the forest sector with regards to WC&DM efforts
- Facilitate co-operation between stakeholders within the forest sector and with those from other water-use sectors
- Provide a framework for implementing WC&DM within the forest sector (a scheduled Stream Flow Reduction Activity) as set out in Section 36(1)(a) of the NWA, through appropriate water management planning.

The Strategy sets out a broad approach to achieving WC&DM in the forest sector. It does not contain a detailed implementation plan.

PROCESS FOR THE STRATEGY DEVELOPMENT

The consultative process followed to develop this Strategy is described fully in Section 6. It involved the preparation and circulation of a Discussion Document in September 1999, a stakeholder workshop held in October 1999 and the preparation of a Draft Strategy in January 2000, which was circulated to stakeholders for comment, before finalisation. This, the updated draft strategy, will be used as the basis for discussion of a second workshop, to be held on the 5th of April 2000.

Progress towards Water Management in Forestry

There has been considerable progress in water management in South African forestry over the past several decades. This has been achieved at two levels, planning and allocation of water for the sector and improved forest management practices. The historical developments have been integrated into DWAF.

The relevant initiatives must all be seen as parts of the overall system for managing water in the forest sector. These parts include catchment management water use licensing, the SEA for SFRA, the water pricing policy, and sustainable forest management.

Water Allocation Planning and Control: SFRA Licensing

Allocation of water to plantation forests has been regulated by means of the afforestation permit system since 1972. This is now to be replaced by the new system of registering and licensing stream flow reduction activities (SFRAs) through the provisions of NWA. The DWAF has formulated a detailed policy and procedure for stream flow reduction licensing. This integrates with other statutory requirements for SFRAs, such as Environmental Impact Assessment, giving proposers a single channel for the processing of their applications for authorisation of such activities.

PLANTATION FOREST SECTOR

Plantation forestry has developed in South Africa because South Africa is a wood-scarce country, because it has a developing economy with escalating wood product requirements, because it has favourable growing conditions (*e.g.* climate etc.), and because it has world-class forestry knowledge and expertise. It is now a significant contributor to the national economy. Currently, the impact of the Forest sector can be summarized as follows (FIA, 2000):

- The area planted is 1,518,138 hectares (1,2 per cent of SA total land area)
- Approximately 400,000 hectares owned by the Forestry Industry remains unplanted (APS restricted), being managed primarily for the conservation of flora and fauna (including water)
- The turnover of the Forest sector is R2 billion per annum which equates to + 7 per cent of Agricultural GDP
- Sustainable annual production is over 18 million m^3 per year
- It employs almost 70,000 people, mainly in rural areas, and has an employment multiplier of almost 6 in downstream activities
- It is a major catalyst for rural development
- It can produce wood sufficient to meet 95 per cent of the country's wood products demand
- It is ranked 4th in the world in terms of the number of forest management units with FSC certificates
- Only 10 per cent of its output is exported in unbeneficiated form
- It produces enough timber to enable the timber processing sector to achieve the following:

- A turnover of in excess of R12 billion p.a.
- The export of 35 per cent of its value added production to the value of R5,6 billion p.a. (net trade surplus of R3,0 billion p.a.)
- A contribution of 7,4 per cent to S.A.'s total manufacturing GDP

DEMAND MANAGEMENT IMPORTANT FOR THE FOREST SECTOR?

Forest sector is a significant water user

Research on water use within the forest sector has mainly been focussed on commercial forestry. Community forestry has a local effect and this has not been quantified. The forest sector consumes 1,500 million m3 of water per year. This is the increment in evaporative losses that arises when natural veld is converted to plantation. This is 2.7 per cent of the total mean annual run-off for the country. This is equivalent to the amount of water used by industry, slightly less than the amount of water used for urban and domestic purposes, although much less than the amount used by agriculture (CSIR, 1999a). Low flows in rivers are decreased by 7.8 per cent (Scott et al (1998)). The forest sector in South Africa is clearly a significant user of water.

Improved ability to secure water allocation and licences

Commercial afforestation is identified as a stream flow reduction activity (SFRA) under the Act and is subject to licensing. Although forestry is at the moment the only SFRA, DWAF is currently in the process of identifying other land use activities with a view to declaration as SFRAs. One of the considerations when issuing licences is the efficient use of water (s27(1)(c)). Therefore, efforts by SFRAs, such as forestry, to implement WC&DM are likely to improve their ability to secure licences for water use.

Security of supply to forests

As water demands increase, WC&DM should prove to be a useful tool for ensuring security of water supply and sustainable forest production.

Improved marketability of forest produce

Efficient water use will help the forestry industry meet market requirements for sustainable forestry, as specified by certification systems such as that of the Forest Stewardship Council (FSC).

WATER CONSERVATION METHODS AND PRACTICES

It is estimated that about 46 per cent of the water received through rainfall is lost through surface run-off. Now it is visualized that if the rainfall water is obstructed and stored in soil at the place where it is received (in situ) it can help to reduce not only soil erosion but siltation of river beds and to tanks and ultimately control floods in plain. In addition to ! this, the water stored in soil can support good crops and increase the production markedly.

Table. Land Capability Classification.

Sl. NO	Class of land	Slope %	Adopted land use and soil conservation meausres
A. Land Suitable for Cultivation			
1	Class I	0-1	Any crop can be grown with proper crop rotation and green manuring to maintain soil fertility
2	Class II	1-3	Contour farming, contour strip cropping and cover cropping contour-bunding.
3	Class III	3-5	Intensive agronomical measures such as contour cropping, contour strip cropping, terracing or contour bunding
4	Class IV	5-8	Contour bunds or terraces and intense agronomic measures. Mostly soil building and soil maintenance crops are to be sown.
B. Land not suitable for cultivation			
5	Class V	8-12	Permanent pasture with controlled grazing
6	Class VI	12-18	Pasture, grasses and forestry. Grazing should be restricted
7	Class VII	18-25	Forest with restricted felling. Contour trenching as conservation measure.
8	Class VIII	>25	Forest with complete closure to grazing and felling of trees.

The term conservation means preservation of something against loss or deterioration. Water can be well-preserved by utilizing the lands appropriately and erecting some structures. The concept of using the lands according to their capacity in order to conserve soil and water is termed as 'land capability classification.

Using lands according to their capability, ensures use of land without its damage and sustains crop production on a pennanent basis.

Some of the very useful water and soil conservation techniques which can be adopted at the individual watershed level, according to their suitability to the local agro-climatic conditions are put under (A) agronomic measures, (B) agrostological measures, (C) mechanical or engineering measures, and (D) afforestation measures.

Agronomic Measures

Following agronomic measures can be adopted for con- serving water and soil.

Contour Farming

Contour farming is practiced in sloppy or hilly regions. In such areas, the rain water is absorbed in very little amount because of its quick downward movement on the slopes. If these areas are ploughed up and down the slope, tile heavy rainfall may cause gully development. Taking into consideration this effect, the sloppy areas are ploughed and seeded across the slope *i.e.* in circular furrows around the slope. This process is termed as contour farming. The contours (circular or spherical furrows) catch the downward moving water until it is absorbed in the soil. The ridges reduce the flow of water. The circular rows of the crop plants across the slope, reduce the speed of moving water. Greater amount of water is soaked by the soil. Reduction in amount and speed of run-off results in considerable reduction in soil and water loss.

Contour is an imaginary line which connects the points located on the land surface at the same heights. Before raising a furrow or ridge, contour line should be marked with the help of wooden sticks or small brick pieces/pebbles. Furrows should be opened parallel to this marked contour soil. These furrows or ridges should be made sloppy towards the main waterways. Tillage should then be done parallel to the contour line on both sides. On small fields of uniform slope, one guideline may be sufficient, on large and more regular fields, several lines may be required. On a hillside, first contour should ordinarily be laid about 1 to 1.5 m vertically below the top of the hill. Additional contour lines are located with the same spacing as the first. In ploughing, the best plan is to start back furrows on the guidelines and work around them.

Tillage Operation

Tillage operation includes ploughing, discing, harrowing and cultivating. The effect of tillage on water conservation may be both useful and harmful. Tillage is useful when it increases infiltration rate of water into the soil. It is harmful when it destroys soil structure, seals soil surface consequently decreasing infiltration and increasing run-off. The concept of minimum tillage can be advantageously applied for soil and water conservation. In this process the land surface is left least disturbed. As a measure of tillage operation, surface mulches are also used to prevent water and soil against draining away. These mulches reduce evaporation, increase infiltration capacity of soil, keep down weeds, improve soil structure and virtually increase crop yields. Crop residues like the stubbles, leaves, twigs etc. are used for mulching.

Crop Rotation

Crop rotation involves incorporation of legumes with cereals in a sequence in order to take advantage of different feeding zones of soil, both for, nutrients and water and to off-set disadvantages of mono-cropping in controlling insect pests and diseases. In an experiment at Dehloadun it was found that maize - pea rotation gives a net return of ₹ 1622/ha as compared to maize - fallow ₹ 988/1111 or maize - wheat ₹ I079/ ha. At another place, two year rotation of green manured bidi tobacco - kodo millet (I year) and pigeon pea mixture of Sundia sorghum (II year) under rainfed conditions has been found suitable for rainfed condition. Another rotation *i.e.* pearl millet mixed with green gram rotated with green manured bidi tobacco, is also found suitable for dryland regions.

Crop rotation helps in water conservation by improving soil structure. It improves soil aggregation which results in increased soil permeability and increased water retention.

Besides crop rotation, mixed cropping is also useful from the point of view of conserving moisture and soil. Advantages of this type of croppings are good crop cover, feeding of crops from different soil layers and under fainted condition ensures the farmers against a total crop failure. In medium black soils of Kota, cultivation of sorghum mixed with pigeon pea has been found useful in reducing run-off.

Strip Cropping

This system of cropping involves growing of a few erosion resisting and erosion permitting crops in alternate strips on contour or across the slope with the objective of breaking long slopes on farm and preventing water and soil loss.

Crops that can be grown with minimum stirring of soil are, in varying degrees, erosion resisting or soil conserving crops. These crops are often close-growing, and nutrient enriching. Most of the legume crops and grasses are erosion resisting, whereas the tall growing, widely spaced crops like maize, cotton, jowar, bajra etc. are erosion permitting crops.

Strip cropping is quite often used in conjunction with other water conservation measures like crop rotation, contour farming, cover cropping, terracing, bunding etc. The following are the four general types of strip cropping.

1. *Contour strip cropping:* In contour strip cropping, the crops are arranged in strips or bands laid on the contour line, just across the natural slope of land. In one strip, erosion resisting crop is grown and in next strip erosion permitting crop is grown. Usually the strips are cropped in a definite sequence.
2. *Field strip cropping:* Field strip cropping consists of strips of uniform width running generally perpendicular to the direction of the erosive force. For the control of erosion by water, the strips run across the general slope, but do not necessarily curve to follow any contour line. This practice is recommended only in areas where the topography is too irregular or undulating to make strip cropping practical.
3. *Wind strip cropping:* It is a farming system in which the strips of crop are raised across the direction of wind.
4. *Buffer strip cropping:* In buffer strip cropping, some grasses or legume crops are laid-out between contour strips of crops in the regular rotations. They may also be used as correction strips where the slope is irregular. The buffer strips may be wide or narrow. They may be even or may have variable depths. They may be placed only on the steep, badly eroded parts of a slope or they may be at more or less

regular interval on the slope. The buffer strips are used to give more protection against water erosion than is afforded by a solid planting of grain or inter- tilled crop.

Addition 'If Organic Matter

Organic matter can be added to the soil in the 101m of farmyard manure, compost and green manure. Organic manures not only supply plant food elements but also help in improving the soil physical condition. They improve the rate of water infiltration by bringing about desirable change in soil structure and its permeability.

Organic matter helps in retaining moisture in the soil and greater amount of run-off water infiltrates into the soil. This infiltrating water contributes to the underground reserves of water. These reserves can be tapped in times of need.

Agrostological Methods

The following are the important agrostological practices that check water erosion.

- *Lay farming:* This method consists of growing grasses in rotation with agricultural crops. This practice improves water holding capacity and fertility of soil, helps in binding the soil particles and reducing loss of water and soil.
- *Retiring the land:* This practice helps in generating grass cover on the soil. Under favourable climatic conditions grazing should also be restricted. Numerous researchers have shown that grasses have good soil binding capacity and they greatly help the soil to absorb a large amount of rainwater. In different places, doobgrass (*Cynodon dacrylon*), *Dacrylis glome rata*, *Eragrostis amabitis* and *Eragrostis cerbula* have proved their worth in conserving soil and water.
- *Afforestation and reforestation:* Tree plantations help a great deal in conserving rain water. The stems of the growing plants create a hindrance for moving water thereby allowing greater infiltration. Percolating water helps further vegetation to come up in the soil. Roots of vegetation hold the soil and water. After their death and decay, empty cavities are left which accelerate water retention in the soil. A large amount of organic matter is contributed by the trees too, which helps in moisture conservation.

  Extensive plantation strengthens ecology and the hydrogen cycle of the region. The chances of rainfall and consequent acceleration of further vegetative growth are greatly in- creased.
- *Restricted grazing:* Excessive grazing not only removes vegetation from the soil but also scratch and loosens the soil surface. In such a

situation, rainwater finds easy way to run-off along with valuable upper soil. Since grazing cannot be completely avoided a system of restricted or rotational grazing must be adopted. In this system an area open to grazing for sometimes should be closed for the following years to facilitate regeneration of trees and grasses and restore a thick ground vegetation.

TECHNOLOGY OF WATER CONSERVATION

Water conservation technologies cover all methods of conserving water through increasing water use efficiency, enhancing capacity to retain runoff water, and eliminating water pollution. Water use efficiency largely depends on availability and adoption of water saving devices and willingness of the consumers to reduce their total water consumption volumes. Furthermore, existing rules and regulations such as pricing mechanisms, reduce the total volume used, while economic incentives largely affect the choice and adoption of technology for water conservation technologies.

Water conservation processes can broadly be categorized into pre consumer and post consumer based approaches. Pre consumer based approaches involve increasing the efficiency of water extraction, storage and conveyance. Usually a large amount of water is lost either through evapotranspiration or seepage during transfer from the abstraction point to the point of use. It is estimated that, of the total rainfall in Thailand, about 70% returns to the atmosphere through the process of evaporation and transpiration. Using technologies that can minimize losses such as reducing evaporative losses from reservoirs, seepage losses from canals and water application losses prior to the water being used for economic purposes, can conserve a vast amount of water. In contrast, post consumer based approaches include the use of marginal quality waters, such as slightly saline water from the sea, untreated groundwater from shallow tubewells and rainwater collected from thatched roofs, for washing, toilet flushing purposes, etc.

In Asia, the agricultural sector consumes more than 75% of the total water withdrawn from all sources. About 60% of this water is lost during conveyance and distribution. Engineering technologies to reduce these losses, and to enhance utilization of water in irrigation schemes, are well studied and established practices which are beyond the scope of this book. In contrast, agronomic technologies such as efficient and modern methods of irrigation (including drip irrigation, sprinkler irrigation and surge irrigation) are less well-known and may be considered water conservation technologies. These technologies are documented in standard textbooks on agricultural and water resources engineering, and are briefly reviewed herein.

Recycling is also an alternative, post consumer technology for conserving and augmenting water supplies. It involves the reuse of water previously used for one purpose for a particular use in another application, before it reaches a natural waterway or aquifer. By using water several times, farms, urban areas and industries can increase the productivity of each litre of water consumed. Industries can conserve water by changing production processes from open to closed systems. In many industrial plants it is possible to recycle the cooling water. Some industries process water several times, and treat it at the end of its period of usefulness, prior to discharging the water to a natural water course. Reuse conserves raw water and, at the same time, reduces the volume of wastewater as well as wastewater treatment costs substantially. Several case studies on water conservation practices in India are described. In terms of particular technologies, there are no specific technologies involved, but rather a way of managing conservation practices in individual households and industries. Some of the technologies typically being practised in the Asian Region also are presented herein.

DUAL WATER DISTRIBUTION SYSTEM

Technical Description

Water reuse, and the reuse of wastewater in particular, is receiving increasingly wide attention, even though it is often considered to be of marginal quality. Use of treated wastewater through dual water distribution and plumbing systems can provide a secondary source of water for purposes such as irrigating private gardens and toilet flushing. The provision of waters of lesser quality through a separate distribution system for non-potable purposes from alternative sources of supply can help lower the demand for potable freshwater. Application of this technology is largely a matter of cost, acceptance and practice, as the distribution technology involved is not significantly different in dual distribution systems compared to conventional single distribution systems.

In the Kathmandu Valley, where water scarcity is increasing, conjunctive use of shallow groundwater sources for toilet flushing and washing of clothes, together with potable water supplied through the municipal water supply system for other purposes, is being practised in residential areas. A rower pump (hand pump) is fitted to a 3.8 cm diameter polyvinylchloride pipe ranging from 6 m to 15 m in length which is driven to the ground. Water from the groundwater source thus tapped is pumped manually whenever needed.

Extent of Use

This technology is widely used in the Kathmandu Valley in locations where the groundwater table is within 15 m of the ground surface. It is also popular in locations where the municipal water supply is intermittent. People of low income are increasingly using this technology in preference to the higher cost municipal supply.

Operation and Maintenance

The operation and maintenance of dual distribution systems is simple, and involves keeping the pipe and the pump clean. Maintenance consists of changing the pump washer once a year or whenever it starts leaking. No additional maintenance of the municipal supply system is required, and no changes in municipal distribution system operation are necessary.

Level of Involvement

Providing dual distribution systems at the household level requires no external involvement relative to the groundwater sourced portion of the system. The municipal sourced portion of the system is generally constructed and operated by the local governmental unit.

Costs

The total cost of the groundwater sourced portion of the system is about $55 for a 10 m deep well.

Effectiveness of the Technology

This technology has helped alleviate the problem of water scarcity in Kathmandu. For an average household, more than 60% of the annual household water requirements is met by using shallow groundwater, which is of lower quality than the municipal water, for non potable purposes.

Suitability

Water supplied from the rower pump can be used for toilets, bathing, gardening, car washing, and similar purposes. The dual distribution system is most suitable for use in areas where the groundwater is within 15 m of the ground surface; otherwise, a mechanical pump will be necessary, adding to the cost of the groundwater sourced portion of the system.

Advantages

This technology is inexpensive and can be constructed using locally-available technology. Water is made available whenever needed, and use of the dual sourced system eases the water scarcity problem not only at the household level but also throughout the entire city.

Disadvantages

Conjunctive use of dual sourced water may be limited as a result of poor water quality. Water drawn from alternative sources may not be used for drinking even after boiling because of odours and tastes associated with groundwater. Further, such water may pose severe health hazards if the abstraction point is located too close to septic tank outflows. The possible high nitrate concentrations and bacterial levels that may be present in surfacial groundwaters may also lead to health hazards when used by poor people and children for drinking purposes. Widespread use may contribute to a decline in the groundwater table (due to over exploitation). Also, water logging and mosquito breeding in the pump area may occur if proper drainage is not provided.

Cultural Acceptability

No cultural problems have been noted, although use may be limited due to odours associated with the groundwater.

Further Development of the Technology

This technology will be more attractive and useful if simple and inexpensive electric motors are attached to the tubewell and the groundwater sourced portion of the system is fully incorporated into the household water supply system.

EVAPORATION REDUCTION

Water Evaporation Retardants

In India, the use of Water Evaporation Retardants (WER) is being investigated as a water conservation measure in surface waters. Control of evaporative losses is being effected using Ceto-Stearyl alcohol, a blend of saturated fatty alcohols, previously imported at high cost and not readily available in India. India's first fatty alcohol plant was commissioned in 1981 at Jalgaon, Maharashtra, by Aegis Chemical Industries Ltd., using an exclusive technology based on an high pressure hydrogenation technology developed in collaboration with Haldor Topsoe, Denmark. The plant is one of the few in the world and the only one in India, producing alcohols to international specifications. In 1983, Aegis successfully developed an effective water evaporation retardant, Acilol TA 1618 WER, an emulsion based on fatty alcohols manufactured from natural vegetable oils. Acilol TA 1618 WER was developed in the laboratory after extensive research aimed at identifying a product compatible with the climatic conditions of the country. Field trials were conducted in March 1984 with the help of Gujarat Engineering Research Institute. These trials confirmed the effectiveness of Acilol TA 1618 WER.

A dispensing technique for applying Acilol TA 1618 WER to water surfaces, consisting of barrel tanks with a drip feed arrangement mounted on "Floating Rafts" anchored at different points on the lakes or reservoirs, was also developed to suit Indian conditions. The first major project using this technique to conserve water was undertaken by the Public Health Engineering Department (PHED), Jaipur, at Ramgarh Lake. About 50 mg/m2/d of the chemical is required and can result in a savings of about 30% of the daily loss of water due to evaporation.

Technical Description

Evaporative losses can be controlled using various technologies. For example, the use of mono molecular organic surface films has been shown to be an efficient technology for reducing such losses. The mono molecular film is applied to an open surface water storage area and allowed to over the water surface. Typical mono molecular films are comprised of long-chain fatty alcohols such as cetyl alcohol (hexadecanol) and stearyl alcohol (octadecanol). These chemical not only suppress evaporation but also prevent mosquito breeding in the water. The use of stearyl alcohol in doses of up to 70 g/cm2 can reduce evaporative losses by up to 55% of the loss due to evaporation from a free water surface. However, the economics and extent of use of this technology are yet to be explored and established.

Extent of Use

Use of surface films to reduce evaporative losses is principally in arid and semi-arid regions.

Operation and Maintenance

The operation and maintenance requirements of this technology are negligible. Maintenance is required only for the rafts and boats, which may be locally constructed, used during the application of the evaporation retardants. No specialized skill is required.

Level of Involvement

The implementation of this technology is generally carried out by government departments, primarily the public health engineering and water supply departments. In India, it is now being promoted by various state government agencies and local authorities. Generally, control of evaporation is focused at the government level having prime responsibility for water resources management.

Costs

No cost data were available as this technology remains largely experimental.

Effectiveness of the Technology

Of the various substances capable of forming mono molecular layers on a water surface, fatty alcohols in their pure form have been found to be most suitable and effective in retarding evaporation with no side effects. Savings from the prevention of water loss due to evaporation have been reported to be as high as 0.70 million cubic metres of water (equivalent to one month's water supply for Jaipur City, India) using Cetyl and Stearyl Alcohol as an evaporation retardant.

Suitability

The technology is most suitable in small surface water storages where there are no strong winds to disrupt the retardant layer.

Advantages

Use of evaporation control techniques requires a small capital investment. Locally constructed rafts can be used in its application, and skilled labour is not required, except for operation of motorized boats.

Fatty alcohols present no hazards in handling, and are non-inflammable, non-toxic, and non-irritating. There are no known harmful effects, making this technology safe for application on drinking water lakes and reservoirs. There are also no known ecological ramifications, as the alcohols contain straight chain carbon compounds which are biodegradable and permeable to oxygen.

Disadvantages

The fatty alcohols used as WERs are not readily available and are costly. Historically, fatty alcohols were produced only by sperm whales or by sodium reduction of animal oils and fats. It was only after the development of high pressure hydrogenation process that good quality fatty alcohols are now commercially available. However, this is a very advanced technology, and requires trained and skilled staff to operate.

Cultural Acceptability

There are no known problems with cultural acceptability.

Further Development of the Technology

More research is necessary in the area of stabilising the chemical film in the face of high wind velocities. Properties such as rate of spreading, specific resistance to evaporation and surface viscosity are required to be measured in evaluating the efficiency of the retardant.

COCONUT PICK-UPS

Technical Description

In South India, coconut pick-ups is a name popularly used for weirs constructed exclusively to provide water to coconut gardens. These weirs or pick-ups are small structures built across the seasonal or perennial streams to slow the flow of water at an appropriate location. This results in surface water storage, groundwater recharge, reduction of soil erosion and availability of water for other purposes.

The bunds that form the puck-ips are constructed of locally available materials such as stones, boulders or mud turfed with grass. The bunds are usually built within the water course almost to the height of the surrounding ground level, depending upon the width and steepness of the stream.

When stream flows occur, the coconut plantation, situated within the floodplain on either side of the water course, is temporarily flooded. The water impounded by the structures recedes within 3 to 4 days, with the excess water frequently diverted into a tank or cistern. Sometimes there will be several coconut pick-ups within a catchment, and several tanks which may flow from one tank to the other.

Extent of Use

This technology has been used in many places in South India.

Operation and Maintenance

The pick-up is constructed by the farmers and hence both operation and maintenance is the responsibility of the user. The principle maintenance requirement is keeping the pick-up sealed to prevent loss due to leakage.

Level of Involvement

Usually, the pick-ups are managed by the users who build them. Repair and maintenance are also carried out by the user. Government may be involved in the funding of the pick-ups, and in the initial permitting of the project site. This function is commonly performed by the local self-governing body that functions as a farmers/users association and manage their activities.

Costs

Construction of a typical coconut pick-up for an area of 10 ha in India would cost about $2 000.

Effectiveness of the Technology

The technology is successful in providing adequate water to many coconut farmers for agricultural purposes.

Suitability

The technology is suitable for use in tropical areas with moderately rolling topography and small streams.

Advantages

The use of pick-ups encourages groundwater recharge by promoting infiltration and vertical percolation. This recharge helps to sustain yields to percolation tanks and tube wells supplying open tanks. The recharge of open wells is almost immediate, even at a distance of up to 0.5 km depending on soil structure and gradients.

Ponds created by the pick-ups can serve also as a drinking water source for livestock from up to 10 villages.

Further, the floodwaters deposit a few millimetres of silt behind the pick-up structure and enrich the soils of the floodplains behind the pick-up with nutrients associated with materials like manure, leaves and other terrestrial debris carried in the runoff flows. These minerals and nutrients enrich the soil particularly during the monsoon season without the use of fertilizer supplements.

Disadvantages

The presence of the temporary ponds behind the pick-ups can promote mosquito growth and exacerbate human health risks.

FORESTS AND WATER CONSERVATION

The availability and quality of water in many regions of the world are more and more threatened by overuse, misuse and pollution, and it is increasingly recognized that both are strongly influenced by forests. Moreover, climate change is altering forest's role in regulating water flows and influencing the availability of water resources (Bergkamp, Orlando and Burton, 2003). Therefore, the relationship between forests and water is a critical issue that must be accorded high priority.

Forested catchments supply a high proportion of the water for domestic, agricultural, industrial and ecological needs in both upstream and downstream areas. A key challenge faced by land, forest and water managers is to maximize the wide range of multisectoral forest benefits without detriment to water resources and ecosystem function. To address this challenge, there is an urgent need for a better understanding of the interactions between forests/trees and water, for awareness raising and capacity building in forest hydrology, and for embedding this knowledge and the research findings in policies. Similarly, there is a need to develop institutional mechanisms to enhance synergies in dealing with issues related to forests and water as well as to implement and enforce action programmes at the national and regional levels.

In the past, forest and water policies were often based on the assumption that under any hydrological and ecological circumstance, forest is the best land cover to maximize water yield, regulate seasonal flows and ensure high water quality. Following this assumption, conserving (or extending) forest cover in upstream watersheds was deemed the most effective measure to enhance water availability for agriculture, industrial and domestic uses, as well as for preventing floods in downstream areas.

Forest hydrology research conducted during the 1980s and 1990s (summarized by Bruijnzeel, 2004; Calder, 2005, 2007; Van Dijk and Keenan, 2007) suggests a rather different picture. Although the important role of upstream forest cover in ensuring the delivery of high-quality water has been confirmed, earlier generalizations about the benefits of upstream forest cover on downstream annual and seasonal flows were generally fallacious and misleading. Studies have shown instead that, especially in arid or semi-arid ecosystems, forests are not the best land cover to increase downstream water yield. Moreover, solid evidence has shown that in tropical ecosystems the protective role of upstream forest cover against seasonal downstream floods has often been overestimated. This is especially true in connection with major events affecting large-scale watersheds or river basins (FAO and CIFOR, 2005).

The International Year of Freshwater 2003 and the third World Water Forum (Kyoto, Japan, 2003) helped drive the incorporation of this understanding of biophysical interactions between forests and water into policies. The International Expert Meeting on Forests and Water, held in Shiga, Japan in November 2002 in preparation for these events, highlighted the need for more holistic consideration of interactions between water, forest, other land uses and socio-economic factors in complex watershed ecosystems. During the past five years, the Shiga Declaration has become a key reference for the development of a new generation of forest and water policies.

This article summarizes the state of current knowledge about forest and water interactions in watershed ecosystems. It summarizes some key issues that have emerged from discussion among forest hydrologists, other water-sector experts and policy-makers in the years since the Shiga Declaration, the third World Water Forum and the International Year of Freshwater.

STATE OF KNOWLEDGE ON FORESTS AND WATER

Recent forest hydrology has focused on three topics that are particularly relevant for policy-making: the comparative advantages and disadvantages of forest cover in maximizing downstream water yields; the role of upstream forests in maintaining water flows during the dry season; and water-quality preservation. This section summarizes findings in these three areas (based on Hamilton, 2005).

In the past, policy-making was often based on the assumption that the more trees, the more water. Current forest hydrology research challenges this assumption. The forest ecosystem is in fact a major user of water. Tree canopies reduce groundwater and stream flow, through interception of precipitation and evaporation and transpiration from the foliage. As both natural and human-established forests use more water than most replacement land cover (including agriculture and forage), there is no question that forest removal (even partial) increases downstream water yields.

Consequently, removal of heavy water-demanding forest cover has sometimes been suggested, especially in semi-arid areas, as a means of preventing or mitigating drought. However, such a policy should be weighed against the consequent loss of the many other services and goods that forests supply, including erosion control, improved water quality, carbon fixation, recreation and aesthetic appeal, timber, fuelwood, other forest products and biodiversity. Such a practice should definitely be avoided in saline-prone areas, where forest removal would bring salts closer to the soil surface; and in mountain cloud forests, where tree foliage, epiphytic vegetative surfaces, twigs, branches, stems and shrubs provide a "net" to capture "horizontal precipitation" from fog or cloud.

It is also well established that partial or complete removal of tree cover may accelerate water discharge and increase flood risk during the rainy season and may reduce river flow or even cause river beds to dry out in the dry season. However, the importance of forest cover in regulating hydrological flows has often been overestimated. Impacts of forest cover removal are evident only at the micro level and in association with short-duration and low-intensity rainfall events (which are usually the most frequent). As rainfall duration or intensity increases, or as distance of the rainfall area from the watershed increases, the influence of tree cover on flow regulation decreases.

At the macro scale, natural processes in the upper watershed are more important than land management practices in the development of large floods. For instance, strong scientific evidence refutes the myth that deforestation in the Himalayas causes big floods in the lowlands of the Ganges and Brahmaputra; the large-scale floods result rather from a combination of simultaneous discharge peaks of the large rivers, high run-off from hills adjacent to the floodplains, heavy rainfall, high groundwater tables and spring tides, lateral river embankments and the disappearance of storage areas in the lowlands (Hofer and Messerli, 2006). Hence, although there are many good reasons for reforesting watersheds (*e.g.* reducing soil loss, keeping sediments out of streams, maintaining agricultural production, wildlife habitat and so forth), flood risk reduction or even control is not one of them. Reforestation to prevent or reduce floods is effective only at a local scale of a few hundred hectares. The complex relationships between forests and water in large river basins continue to be a matter of debate, and it is clear that more work is needed for full understanding of these relationships.

It is in maintaining high water quality that forests make their most significant contribution to the hydrological characteristics of watershed ecosystems. This is achieved through minimization of soil erosion on site, reduction of sediment in water bodies (wetlands, ponds, lakes, streams, rivers) and trapping or filtering of other water pollutants in the forest litter, particularly through the following mechanisms.

- On sloping land, soil moves downhill mainly because of gravity and displacement by the splash action of raindrops. Natural forest cover provides the most effective barrier to splash-induced soil erosion, largely because of the contribution of the lower canopy leaves and the ground litter in reducing the force of splashing. Forest removal and replacement with other land use systems leads in most cases to higher and accelerated erosion unless great care in soil conservation is practised.

- Erosion is generally associated with a higher sediment concentration in run-off and with siltation of watercourses. Good forest cover is more effective than any other kind of land cover in keeping the water as sediment free as possible. The surface cover, debris and tree roots trap sediments and stop their downslope movement. Moreover, deep tree roots stabilize slopes and help prevent shallow landslides.
- In addition to sediment, various types of pollution – depending on nearby land use and drainage to the watercourse – can also impair water quality. Potential pollutants include excessive concentrations of organic matter (leading to water eutrophication) and agricultural or industrial chemicals. Forest is certainly an appropriate ground cover for drinking-water–supply watersheds, because forestry activities (with the exception of intensively managed plantations) generally use no fertilizers or pesticides and avoid pollution from domestic sewage or industrial processes. In addition, non-point source pollution (*i.e.* pollution from many diffuse sources) from domestic, industrial and agricultural use can be greatly reduced or even eliminated by maintaining adequate riparian forest buffer zones along watercourses. Such zones, however, will not prevent groundwater contamination. Moreover, where atmospheric pollutants are captured by trees because of their height and aerodynamic resistance, watershed forests will not protect water quality. This problem is most prevalent in mountain forests in industrialized countries.

ISSUES IN CURRENT FOREST AND WATER POLICIES

Forest hydrologists, other water sector experts and policy-makers has focused on three core issues: incorporation of forest hydrology knowledge in water policies; inclusion of forest-sector contributions in integrated water resource management policies; and payment for forest- and water-related environmental services.

Incorporation of forest hydrology knowledge in water policies

Despite the significant advances in scientific understanding of forest and water interactions, the role of forests in relation to the sustainable management of water resources remains, as elaborated in the previous section, a contentious issue. Uncertainty, and in some cases confusion, persists because of difficulties in transferring research findings to different countries and regions, different watershed scales, different forest types and species and different forest management regimes. Another difficulty is a gap between research and policy, which persists at least in part because of a general failure to communicate results of hydrological research effectively to policy-makers and to challenge conventional assumptions with scientific evidence. To address these issues, in 2006 the International Union of Forest Research Organizations (IUFRO) created a Task Force on Forests and Water Interactions. Its aim is to promote consensus in the forest hydrology community on the key issues concerning forest and water interactions, and to identify areas of scientific uncertainty on which to focus policy-relevant research. Seeking to generate and disseminate information that non-specialists can easily and safely use, the task force has produced a one-page fact sheet to convey key concepts in forest hydrology to policy-makers. For the linking of research and policy related to forest hydrology, education has an important role. Scientific and technical education is generally highly sectoral. Education across disciplines is necessary to improve knowledge of forest and water interactions, *e.g.* to improve capacity to assess effects of afforestation and reforestation programmes on water quality and quantity, flood control and soil protection.

Inclusion of forestry in integrated water resource management

Development of integrated water resource management plans at the watershed and/or river-basin level was one of the targets set by the World Summit on Sustainable Development in 2002. These multisectoral plans should be aimed at ensuring "water for people, food, nature, and industry and other uses". The need to include the "nature for water" dimension in these plans is increasingly recognized. The concept of nature for water takes into account the role of terrestrial ecosystems in enhancing water yields and water quality. For instance, the Lange Erlen forested area in Switzerland is flooded a dozen days a month with water from the Rhine to allow forest soil to filter the water to improve its quality and recharge the groundwater of the nearby city of Basel.

As foresters are increasingly committed to the development of national forest programmes (NFPs) to implement sustainable forest management, there is scope for them to join forces with water experts to develop integrated water resource management plans and forestry programmes as part of a more comprehensive watershed/river-basin planning process. Similarly, management of transboundary watersheds and river basins should give greater consideration to the relationship between upstream forest cover and downstream water flows. For instance, the Programme for the Sustainable Development of the Rhine (ICPR, 2001), a transboundary initiative, adopts afforestation and forest conservation measures to facilitate water retention and to prevent floods in nearby downstream areas. Protected forest area in the basin was 1 200 km2 in 2005 and is expected to reach 3 500 km2 by 2020.

Many countries have begun to develop integrated water resource management plans at the national and/or watershed level. Their implementation is complicated by the number and variety of stake-holders within and beyond a watershed and their different and sometimes contrasting interests, as well as by overlap of the administrative responsibilities of different regional authorities in many countries. A step-by-step planning process is advisable to ensure buy-in for effective implementation of the plan.

Payments for environmental services

In many countries, forest and water policies, plans and programmes are coming together through the increased popularity of payment for environmental services schemes (also called incentive-based cooperative agreements, stewardship payments, compensation schemes or performance payments) as financing mechanisms for watershed management, sustainable forest management and other sustainable development processes. Payments do not necessarily involve money; often they take the form of services a community has been lacking, such as new or better roads, a school bus or weekly transport for farm produce.

Forest stewardship by upstream populations, for instance, can be compensated by downstream water users through direct payment for the provision of forest hydrological services such as discharge regulation or protection of water quality. In developing countries, the ensuing "hydrosolidarity" between upstream forest managers and downstream water users is often mediated by public agencies. For instance, since 1996 the Government of Costa Rica has sponsored schemes to create economic incentives for conserving forests and to compensate those whose land or land uses generate environmental services.

More sophisticated mechanisms involving subsidies generated by income taxes and other public-sector sources are being put in place in industrialized countries. The United Nations Economic Commission for Europe (UNECE) Convention on the Protection and Use of Transboundary Watercourses and International Lakes (2007) recently endorsed the concept of payments for ecosystem services including the conservation and development of forest cover.

APPROACHES TO ACHIEVE EFFICIENT ALLOCATION OF WATER TO PLANTATION FORESTRY

The allocation element refers to the quantity of water to which a sector or user within a sector has received entitlement through a water-use allocation plan, authorisation or license. Allocation management involves allocating water to the sector and between users within the sector, to achieve maximum efficiency. Several policy instruments are relevant here.

Identifying 'restricted' catchments

This activity is specific to regulation approaches. Specific catchments could be identified as 'restricted' and therefore unsuitable for afforestation, due to specific criteria, such as critical contribution to the water supply of a town or urban area. The class of water resources within a catchment, and water quality objectives, would also help in identifying restricted catchments. The catchment specific studies proposed by the SFRA SEA would also help to inform such an approach. In support of this, the Mountain Catchment Act (No 63 of 1970) gives the minister the right to declare any area as a mountain catchment area. This has, however, been done since the inception of the APS in 1972.

Promoting new plantation forests in areas where competing demand is low

This activity is specific to regulation approaches. Incentives could be provided for afforestation to locate in catchments where water demand is low, and to move out of catchments where water demand is high. This would apply in instances where new afforestation is contemplated but probably not to existing afforestation, as it will be virtually impossible to simply move an industry, with its infrastructure and processing facilities.

Registration and licensing of commercial afforestation

This replaces the old APS. Conditions requiring water conservation measures may be attached to licenses (s29(1)(b)(i)).

Water pricing in accordance with a pricing strategy

Water pricing may be used to implement demand management. Its likely impact on the forest sector, in terms of its water efficiency and international competitiveness, needs to be investigated further. The pricing policy for water use in SFRA is outlined in " The pricing policy for water use charges". However, a proper market must be established to ensure that trading is effective in achieving efficient allocation.

This require (a) proper conferring of water-use entitlements, which, which the NWA provides for (b) adequate security, eg. Through sufficiently long entitlement periods (c) a large number of willing buyers and sellers in the market, and (d) market equity, so that all buyers and sellers are on an equal footing.

Trading of water licences

The Act allows for trading in water-use licences. Incentives for both inter-sectoral and intra-sectoral trading would depend on the need for water downstream and the value attached to the water, and therefore the opportunity cost of not afforesting/deforesting certain parts of the land.

Full Assessment of Value Added to Water

This requires assessment of looks at the entire industrial water-use system, from raw materials acquisition through the manufacturing, use, reuse, recycling and waste management activities. The growth of timber, extraction and production of pulp, paper and other materials (*e.g.* rayon, viscose) would be a focus of this technique. This approach could be important to the allocation of water to forestry, as most of the value addition to forest products occurs down stream in the supply chain.

Equity Through Criteria-Based Allocation

As noted above, the considerations in the NWA have been formulated as criteria to apply in any allocation decision. If these criteria are applied transparently, and alternatives for the use of water weighed, consistently according to them, then equitable allocation should follow.

APPROACHES TO IMPROVE THE APPLICATION OF WATER AND TO COMPENSATE FOR STREAM FLOW REDUCTION

This requires measures to minimise waste, *i.e.* water that is consumed unproductively in the forest management unit.

Efficient riparian zone management

Research has indicated that trees within the 'riparian zone' use about twice as much or more than the quantity of water used by upslope plantations (Scott, 1999). As a result, for several years, foresters have been prohibited from planting adjacent to stream banks or perennial streams through conditions attached to afforestation permits. Forest managers in most areas have cleared and continue to clear its riparian zones. Forest managers are required to apply riparian zone management by the conditions on permits and licences, which are reinforced by the "Forest Industry Guidelines on Environmental Management", and the requirements for forest certification. The organised forest industry has also worked with stakeholders to develop improved methods to define the boundaries of riparian zones and other wetlands.

The greatest challenge ahead will be to achieve sustainable management of the natural habitats in these areas.

Controlling Alien Invasive Plants

Alien invaders waste significant amounts of water. Certain alien species are often associated with plantation forestry and can infest riparian areas and other open habitats (Nel et al. 1999). The spread of these species needs to be minimised. Forest industry guidelines and certification requirements require invasives to be controlled. Forest managers have made substantial progress in controlling the problem, and participate actively in the Working for Water

Programme. The two major companies, Sappi and Mondi, have recently signed an accord with the Minister which approves their commitment to this objective.

Appropriate forest management practices

Wasteful water use in plantations could be significantly reduced through effective weed management within plantations. Weeds transpire significant amounts of water, which could otherwise be available for tree growth.

Striving for normal age classes in Catchments

Even distribution of age classes within quaternary catchments will ensure more evenly distribution of the impact of tree water use over time.

Improving water quality

High quality run-off from areas under well-managed harvesting operations and well-constructed and maintained forestry roads has the effect of increasing the proportion of water which is utilisable. Research commissioned by the DWAF from the CSIR has shown that forest plantations generally enhance water quality (Lesch, 1995).

METHODS FOR CONSERVING FOREST GENETIC RESOURCES

A wide range of methods, from protected reserves to intensive management of breeding populations for production systems, can be used to conserve FGR. The choice of methods depends on available genetic material, selected time scale and specified aims. The method selected and the subsequent implementation of a conservation strategy also depend on the availability of both human and financial resources. The two most commonly considered methods for conserving FGR are *in situ* and *ex situ* conservation. The term *in situ* refers to the continued maintenance of tree populations at their natural sites, in the environment to which they have adapted. *Ex situ* conservation takes place outside the natural habitat of a tree species, and may consist of activities such as establishing live collections or *ex situ* conservation stands, or storing seeds, pollen or tissue. FGR can also be conserved and maintained by using tree species in forestry or other land-use systems such as agroforestry. It is likely, however, that forest management interventions reduce genetic variation in tree populations. Not even carefully planned and implemented forest management activities, therefore, can replace more active conservation measures with clearly specified objectives. The same caveat also applies to tree domestication and the use of trees in agroforestry systems.

IN SITU CONSERVATION

There is a general consensus among scientists and practitioners that no single conservation method is adequate, and that different methods should be applied in a complementary manner. *In situ* conservation, however, has a number of benefits and so often forms the basis of conservation programmes. It allows evolutionary processes to be maintained, including the adaptation of tree populations to changing environmental conditions. This is particularly important for breeding programmes, since future human needs and environmental conditions are difficult to predict. The reproductive biology and overall survival of many tropical forest species are dependent on complex ecological interactions. Thus long-term genetic conservation of such species is difficult, if not impossible, without *in situ* conservation. In addition, recalcitrant seed behaviour (*i.e.* inability to tolerate desiccation) also complicates long-term *ex situ* conservation efforts for many tropical tree species. *In situ*conservation can also contribute to the conservation of biological diversity at higher levels, *i.e.* species and ecosystems.

Protected areas have often been established on the basis of ecosystem or species conservation, rather than gene conservation. Thus the design of *in situ* conservation programmes has been considered primitive. In tropical forests in particular, the complexity of interactions and lack of scientific information have hampered the development of *in situ* conservation strategies. Uncertainty surrounds the adequate size of *in situ* conservation areas, the number of individuals to be included, how to select locations, and how genetic variation is distributed within selected areas. Undisturbed tropical forest ecosystems are often taken as a starting point when planning *in situ* conservation programmes. Today, however, rural landscapes are a mosaic of disturbed and less disturbed patches of forest, ranging from seemingly natural and secondary forests to seriously degraded forests and other wooded fragments. The most obvious genetic effects of fragmentation are a loss of genetic diversity at both population and species levels, changes in the genetic structure of a population and increased inbreeding. Clearly, *in situ* efforts cannot always rely on intact natural forests, and so it is essential to understand how the processes of genetic drift, gene flow, selection and mating affect genetic diversity in fragmented forests.

IPGRI's partners at the Universities of Costa Rica, Alberta and Massachusetts have been studying the effects of fragmentation on the genetic diversity of *Enterolobium cyclocarpum* in Costa Rica. Studies of the reproductive biology of *E. cyclocarpum*, a tropical dry forest species, in continuous forests and forest fragments in pastures indicate that pasture trees are less likely to receive pollen and set fruit, and that their fruits bear less seed, than trees located in continuous forests. Also, outcrossing rates within the two groups of trees have been found to be similar, but progeny vigour among seedlings in continuous forest is higher than in pastures. These results have immediate implications for the conservation and management of *E. cyclocarpum* and other species in similar habitats. Trees in pastures can aid the movement of pollinators between intact forest fragments and so contribute to gene flow and maintenance of genetic diversity among forest fragments. However, because seedlings in pastures have less vigour, seeds from these areas cannot be recommended for establishing plantations or rehabilitating degraded natural forests.

In southern India, sandal (*Santalum album*) forests have long been exposed to selective logging, poaching and changes in land use. The effects of disturbance on the genetic diversity of sandal have been investigated by the University of Boston, together with the Ashoka Trust for Research in Ecology and the University of Agricultural Sciences in Bangalore. Results from two protected areas indicate that genetic diversity of sandal is highest in the core undisturbed park zone, whereas allelic diversity is reduced in the outer buffer and disturbed zones. These findings suggest that present protection measures are adequate and that excessive logging will cause genetic deterioration in natural sandal populations. Allelic diversity, however, is similar in the two disturbed zones, which suggests that, contrary to general assumptions, no significant genetic segregation has resulted from different degrees of disturbance. This finding can be attributed to the fact that sandal is insect-pollinated and animal-dispersed, *i.e.* substantial gene flow still occurs despite varying degrees of disturbance.

EX SITU CONSERVATION

In situ and *ex situ* conservation should be used in a complementary fashion to conserve FGR. Both are an integral part of the conservation process, and both can only be effective after genetic diversity has been located and conservation priorities have been set. The main purpose of *ex situ* conservation is to capture and maintain a representative sample of the existing genetic diversity of a species. For highly endangered tree species, *ex situ* conservation may be the only approach in the short to medium term. The main pitfalls of collecting germplasm samples for *ex situ* conservation are: i) limited coverage of genetic variation; ii) biases in the collected plant material; and iii) samples that are too large to deal with. Because *ex situ* conservation is more costly than *in situ*conservation, it is particularly important that sampling of populations and germplasm within populations is given special attention to maximize the use of limited financial and human resources.

The traditional approach to *ex situ* conservation of FGR is to establish conservation stands of a species outside its native habitat to facilitate gene management. However, long-term maintenance of the collected genetic variation in *ex situ* stands tends to be complicated by genetic drift and potential contamination by external gene flow. Another commonly used method of *ex situ* conservation is to store seeds collected from a range of natural populations. In the case of many tropical tree species, however, this method is limited by recalcitrant seed behaviour. More than 70% of commercially valuable tropical tree species are estimated to have recalcitrant or intermediate seeds. In recent years, therefore, considerable effort has been expended in developing *in vitro* techniques for *ex situ* conservation of recalcitrant tree species. A notable example is cryopreservation. Cryopreservation, the storage of cells or tissue at ultra-low temperatures, offers great opportunities for longer-term *ex situ* gene preservation. Its applicability, however, has been limited by difficulties in identifying protocols to reduce the water content of tissue before freezing. Tissue water content must be reduced to avoid lethal ice formation in cells. Different results from different laboratories engaged in drying the same species of seed are an additional obstacle. Although it is likely that further research will ease these problems, the main application of cryopreservation seems to be in supporting tree improvement programmes and conserving biotechnically derived germplasm, rather than as a widely applied *ex situ* conservation method to support *in situ* conservation of FGR.

Micropropagation, the use of tissue and organ cultures for organogenesis and somatic embryogenesis, can also be applied to maintain genetic variation in germplasm collected for *ex situ* conservation. Practical propagation applications are already available for several tropical trees, based on shoot tissue culture in broadleaved tree species and on somatic embryogenesis in conifers. Micropropagation does not necessarily require expensive laboratory facilities, and can therefore be used in less-developed conditions. Maintaining juvenile material, however, can be problematic. At present, the technology used in somatic embryogenesis is in most cases too expensive for cost-effective *ex situ* conservation.

Since 1997, the Danida Forest Seed Centre (DFSC) and IPGRI have cooperated in enhancing *ex situ* conservation methods for recalcitrant tropical forest trees. Project activities have focused on determining whether seeds are recalcitrant, intermediate or orthodox, and have included seed development research to assess optimal conditions for seed collecting, germination and storage. An international Forest Tree Seed Research Network has been established under the project to facilitate information exchange among scientists developing protocols for collecting, handling, testing and screening of tolerance to desiccation and optimal storage conditions. At present more than 20 countries worldwide are involved in the project. More than 50 tropical forest species have been screened so far. Activities also include publications and training workshops to increase research capacity, particularly in developing countries.

10

Domestic Water Supply, Hygiene and Sanitation

EXPLOITATION OF WATER SUPPLY

The Vrana Lake is situated on the island of Cres, belonging to the group of Croatian islands of the Adriatic Sea - a marginal sea of the Mediterranean (Southern Europe). With its average area of approximately 5,75 sq.km. and volume of approximately 220 million cu.m. of water of exceptionally high quality on otherwise dry area of the island of Cres (the total area of the island is only 405,78 sq. km.), it represents an invaluable resource in both the environmental and economic sence.

The lake is a kryptodepression, with the water level between 16,70 m a.s.l. and 9,11 m a.s.l. on the average 13,13 m a.s.l. in the period from 1929 to 1995. The lake bottom is at 61.3 m below the mean sea level. The average annual rainfall in the area of the Vrana lake is 1064 mm, the mean annual air temperature is +14.8°C, and the annual evaporation from free water surface is 1161 mm. The falling trend of the water level in the lake in the eighties, never recorded before, caused a great concern among proffesuinals and the public regarding the future of the lake, and initiated the beginning of complex research work. In the recent years this trend has been stopped; however the need for protection of the lake is still present in the sense of defining the regime of water pumping from the lake. Because of its position and size, the issue of the origin of the lake water has been attracting the attention of scientists for a lond time. Already in the past century contrary assumptions appeared regarding its recharging - from the mainland or the local island catchment area. The results of all hydrological investigations carried out so far, both earlier and recent, althought not identical in figures and conclusions, speak in favour of the latter assumption. Mechanism of lake's aquifer functioning in way of hydraulic relation between salt and fresh water was analysed in Ozanic and Rubinic. In Bonacci hypotetical hydraulic model with assumption Lake's recharging from the mainland was analysed. The results of these hydraulical investigations confirm hydrological conclusions, so the problem of functioning and protection of Vrana Lake must be consider as part of island karst aquifer *i.e.* balance relation between salt and fresh water in according to the Ghyben-Hertzberg Low.

PROPERTIES OF THE VRANA LAKE SYSTEM

However, due to the specific properties of the Vrana Lake which has no directly measurable imflow nor run-off, the hydrological analyses of functioning of the lake system based on measuring of water balance parameters of the lake system (water level monitoring, precipitation regime, water pumping from the lake, evaporation from lake surface) have made a considerable contribution to the general level of knowledge on this natural phenomenon and its protection.

Due to its size compared to the comparatively small island enviroment, the lake containing 220 million cu.m. of potable water of exceptionally high quality affects significantly the dynamics of functioning of the entire aquifer. Except its position and size, the Vrana Lake is specific due to the fact that inflow into the lake, as well as the outflow, is accomplished by so far unidentified underground ways. No significant permanent springs have been noticed on the lake, except two temporary springs with the yield up to 0.005 cu.m./sec. Compared to the mater in the mainlend area beyond the direct influence of the sea, salinity of the lake water is somewat higher, ranging between 62 and 92 mgl-1. In the wider zone of the Vrana Lake - on the coast of the island of Cres several springs, vrulja and coastal sources have been noticed, as well as a zone of diffused fresh water outflow. Due to the constant outflow regime, some of these phenomena may be related to the Vrana Lake, or its aquifer, as possible privilleged directions of its discharging. Water level observations have been carried out on a daily basis since 1928, completed by rainfall observations on the catchment area and directly along the shore.

An expressed trend of water level decrease in the lake is noticed, in particular in the eighties. The trend of water level decrease in the entire period of analysis, 1929 to 1995, was 0,04 m per annum, while in the period from 1985 to 1990 it was even 0,48 m per annum. This trend caused the concern of the public and of the professionals for the destiny of the lake and possible disturbance of its balance, and possible breakthrough of sea water into its system. On the other hand, it may be seen that water pumping from the lake, which started in 1952, shows a clear growing trend, with the annual average for the 1964 to 1995 period of about 65 000 cu.m. per annum. During the recent decade, the average pumping rate from the lake is 0,072 cu.m./sec., with the maximum during the summer season, up to 0,160 cu.m./ sec. Fortunately, such drastic trend of water level decrease that could have endangered the balance of the fresh water aquifer of the Vrana Lake, was not continued - the rainfall conditions wereb improved, and due to the war situation in Croatia in the early nineties, the touristic traffic was reduced, resulting in reduced water pumpings from the lake, compared to pre-war maximum values.

RESULTS OF HYDROLOGICAL ANALYSIS

Multiple regression analysis of the annual changes of the lake status, in dependance on the magnitude of relevant hydrological parameters for the period from 1980 to 1995, when the most complete input data were available, gave a very acceptable regression dependance with the linear correlation coefficient k=0,96, wich may be seen. The resulting equation is: Hn=2,7369 On+1,12836 In–4,0069 Cn+0,23208 Gn-0,31284 H(n–1)+0,3718 (1) Hn - annual water level change, On - annual rainfall, In-annual evaporation, Cn-annual pumping, Gn-calculated losses through sinking determinated on the basis of the sinking curve and H(n-1)-mean annual water levels in the previous year–all expressed in (m) with regard to the mean lake level. Such analyses, along with detailed analyses of sinking from the lake system and, provided the preconditions for elaboration of the complex mathematical model of functioning of the lake system of RANA which was used to compute the mean monthly inflows into the Vrana Lake. According to the computations, in the period from 1929 to 1995, the mean annual inflow into the Vrana Lake system was 0,588 cu.m./sec., and its value varied from 1,144 cu.m./sec. and 0,273 cu.m./sec.

The average value of inflow from the direct catchment area was calculated as 0,393 cu.m./sec., and figure of 0,195 cu.m./sec. refers to the rain falling directly on lake surface. The area of the orographic catchment area sourrounding the Vrana Lake oscillations and to the analysis of regional run-off, it comes out that the average catchment area satisfying the Vrana Lake recharging balance is only about 24 sq.km. This size of catchment area is not clearly determinable, changing due to the karst character of the terrain in dependance on hydrological conditions.

LAKE PROTECTION FROM OVERPUMPING

As already mentioned, the Vrana Lake is the only source of water supply of the islands of Cres and Loiknj, and at the present requirements the annual quantity of water pumped out of the lake reaches 2,3 million cu.m. As the calculated annual average inflows are 18.5 million, and the evaporation losses at the mean water level are of the order of 6,7 million cu.m., and the losses through sinking from the lake system are 11,7 cu.m. it is obvious that pumping, although globally the smallest element of the water balance, disturbs the balance of the Vrana Lake system and influence lowering of the water level. This lowering of the mean lake level occurs to the case when the sinking losses are reduced in the magnitude of the increase of the pumped quantity. Namely, a functional relation has been determined between the quantity of sinking and the water level in the lake, and its gradient in domain of the observed water levels per each meter is approx. 0,028 cu.m./sec.

Until 1995, the total quantity of water pumped out of the lake reached 42 million m^3 which would, at the mean water level account for 7.3 m. The analysis showed that such water consumption, in spite of the expressed trend of water level lowering, caused, instead of the said 7.3 m, the actual lowering of the lake level by approximately 2 m. Therefore, it is obvious that this water loss was compensated by the change of hydrological conditions in the lake-first of all by reduction of the losses from the aquifer due to his lower level in relation to the sea, and partly due to the increased recharging from the underground part of the aquifer, caused by lowering of the lake level. The trend of recorded annual water levels in the Vrana Lake, and of values, obtained by mathematical simulation on the model of RANA, assuming there was no pumping, but also under the assumption that in the period of analysis pumping was even more intensive than the actual mean annual rate of 0,072 cu.m./sec., *i.e.* that they were double - 0,150 cu.m./sec., and 0,250 cu.m./sec., which is equal to the earlier forecasts of possible maximum allowed pumpings rates.

Althought the simulations of the Vrana Lakeb behaviour in cases of its intensified use have carried out on the basis of extrapolation of the determined regularities of behaviour in the real - higher water levels in the lake, and are therefore largely approximative, they still show that more intensive pumping of water from the lake may result in excessive consumption which, in turn, could cause disturbance of its dynamic balance with the sea. According to analysis minor planned increases of the pumping rate of the order of 20 to 30 per cent for the needs of the island population are not yet alarming. The formed fresh water lense of the island aquifer, by its higher pressure, on the principles of the Ghyben-Hertzberger Low, maintains balance with the sea and prevents its breakthrough into the lake. As the bottom of the Vrana Lake is even 61 m below the mean sea level, and with respect to the theoretical balance ratio (1m of fresh water lense above the sea level corresponds to 40 m of fresh water below the sea level) in that case the breakthrough of sea into the lake would occur at the lake level of 1,5 m a.s.l.

Such breakthrough into the lake would be a disaster for the lake system because the thermal currents in the lake, as well as winds, would cause salination of the entire lake, without any possibility of desalination later on. However, in reality, as the Vrana Lake is in the karst environment the limit of the contact of fresh water and the sea is not distinct, but involves a wider fresh and sea water mixing zone, which is considerably closer to the lake. Therefore, the above-mentioned theoretically possible lowering of the lake level should not be allowed, and increased pumping of water from the lake must be subject to constant control, and limited to the intensity that will not endanger the balance of the lake.

Vrana Lake is part of the complex system of island's karst aquifer, which functions in accordance with the principals of dynamical balance of the fresh water and the sea. In this paper are given the main characteristic of its hydrological system as also the analysis of problems of pumping from the lake.

This paper shows that we can analysed aquifer behaviour by hydrological modeling when their natural hydraulic give limitation of excessively exploitation. It has been determined that the observed lowering of the water level in the Lake during the eighties was the result of the coincidence of extremely dry hydrological conditions and increased consumption of water from the Lake (pumping). Existing pumping of average 0,072 m^3/s does not disturb Vrana Lake to its exhaustion. Such development, in perspective, with unavoidable increase of water consumption standards, results in new requirements for water pumping out of the lake, thereby bringing new risks of disturbing the existing water quality.

HYDRAULIC PROCESSES ANALYSIS SYSTEM

HyPAS builds on the inherent power of GIS while supplying easier tools for facilitation of hydraulic process analysis and reducing learning time typical with GIS implementation. HyPAS is an extension to ArcView, a commercially available software package marketed by Environmental Systems Research Institute (ESRI), and requires an additional extension from ESRI, 3D Analyst. HyPAS was designed for the non-GIS expert with ease of use as a priority. The HyPAS was designed to perform all major functions after collection of data to report writing.

HyPAS's velocity analysis tools cover three basic applications: contouring an area in plan view from a user-defined constituent and depth range, generating cross sections from a transect, and plotting vector magnitude and direction in plan view from a user-specified depth range. HyPAS's sediment sample analysis tools allow the user to generate frequency weight plots, calculate composite sample plots, and perform varied analysis routines. HyPAS's project management tools allow the user to import photographs for project enhancement and import time series data to manage and plot.

GENERATING PLAN VIEW CONTOURS

HyPAS provides the capability of generating contours in plan view for the different constituents collected from the Acoustic Doppler Current Profiler (ADCP) instrument. HyPAS will create colour-shaded contours and contour lines. This tool allows the user to calculate the depth average of the specific values from the entire water column or a specific depth range. The user selects the survey data to contour by drawing a box or polygon around them. A depth range is specified, and the user must choose which constituent to contour.

HyPAS then calculates the contour from the depth range specified. An example plan view contour of total velocity magnitude was created from ADCP data in the Columbia River, Oregon. The yellow dots represent actual velocity profiles collected by the ADCP as the boat moves along the line. The legend for the colour-shaded contours represents velocity magnitude in ft/sec. The units for velocity magnitude depend on how the data were processed. Often, velocity magnitude is represented in cm/sec.

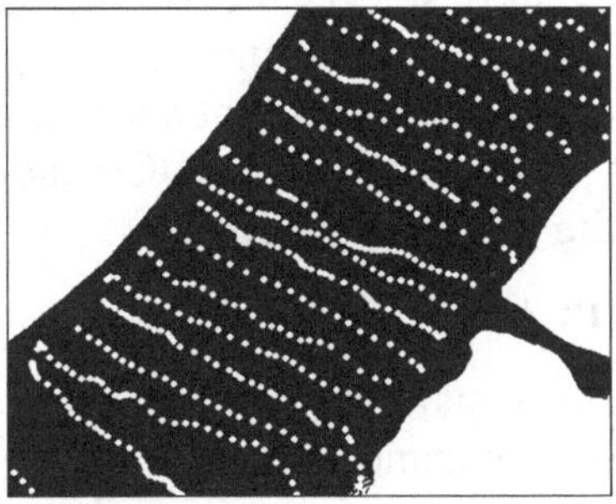

Fig. Plan View Contour of the Total Velocity Magnitude from an ADCP Survey in the Columbia River

GENERATING PLAN VIEW VECTOR

HyPAS provides the capability of generating a vector plot of magnitude and direction in plan view for the velocity data collected from the Acoustic Doppler Current Profiler (ADCP) instrument. HyPAS will create a plot with vectors pointing in the direction of flow and scaled in size by magnitude. This tool allows the user to calculate the depth average of velocity magnitude and direction from the entire water column or from a specific depth range. The user selects the survey data points to plot by drawing a polygon around them. A depth range is specified. HyPAS then calculates and plots the depth-averaged magnitude and direction for those survey points. Figure is an example of depth averaged velocity magnitude and direction vectors from ADCP data at Shinnecock Inlet, New York.

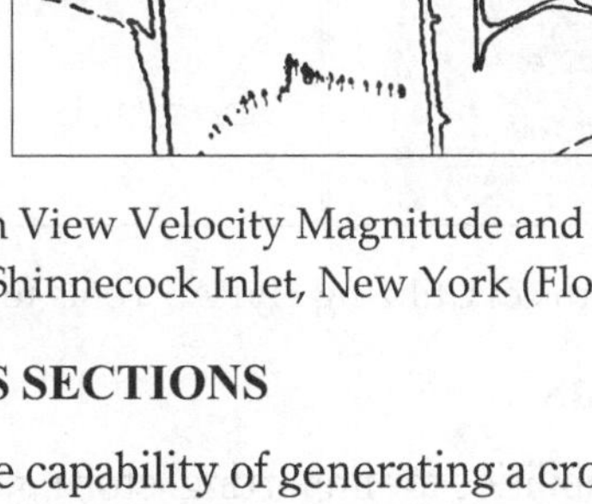

Fig. Plan View Velocity Magnitude and Direction Plot from Shinnecock Inlet, New York (Flood Current)

GENERATING CROSS SECTIONS

HyPAS provides the capability of generating a cross section from a specific transect or points along multiple transects from velocity survey data. This tool allows the user to calculate a cross section from any constituent in the data. This includes the north, east, and vertical components of velocity as well as acoustic backscatter. The user selects the survey data points by drawing a polygon around the individual points and selecting a starting point. The constituent to contour is selected. HyPAS then interpolates and plots the cross section. A cross section was created from ADCP data collected from an area called Victoria Bend in the Mississippi River.

IMPORTING AND DISPLAYING IMAGES

HyPAS provides the capability of importing and displaying digital photographs and images to enhance project management. This tool is not designed for image processing, but rather as an end product aid for representing analysis results and methods. This tool allows the user to import digital photographs and images and attach them to specific spatial locations throughout the study area.

The images are stored using a separate image theme as shown in Figure. On the image theme, a small solid filled circle with an "i" denotes the locations of the images. Presently, a maximum of ten digital images can be stored at each spatial location. This tool is useful for recording conditions at a site or progress of a construction site. Images allow the user the opportunity to store and display instruments, flow conditions, historic photos, and other visual information quickly and easily for reference. Several photographs were added to a GIS project for Shinnecock Inlet, New York. Two photographs are displayed showing the inlet at previous times in its history.

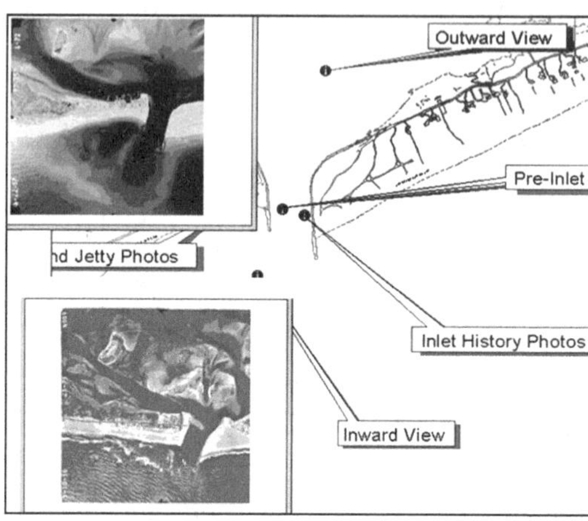

Fig. Shinnecock Inlet GIS Project Utilizing HyPAS Tools for Displaying Photographs

TIME SERIES ANALYSIS

HyPAS provides capabilities for importing, storing, analyzing, and exporting time-series data. This is a project management tool that allows the user to have time-series data flags throughout his project. The user create a location for time–series data and import the data for that location. Later the user can choose that location and HyPAS will display all the data types, which have been imported. HyPAS will plot the data on an X, Y plane using the plot and axis information given by the user. HyPAS automatically exaggerates the Y axis to fit an 8.5 x 11 landscape plot. Figure shows a time-series plot of wind speed information.

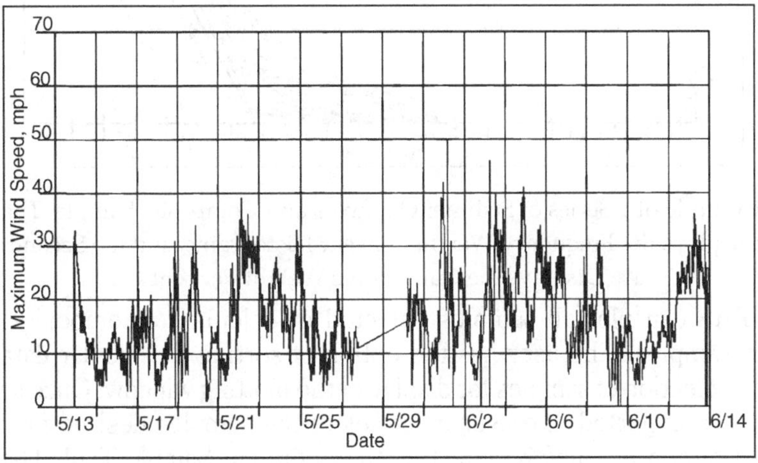

Fig. Maximum Wind Speed Time-Series Data Plot

PLOTTING GRAIN SIZE DISTRIBUTION

HyPAS provides the capability of plotting grain-size distribution for sediment sample data. The user can plot cumulative frequency weight or frequency weight per cent histograms.

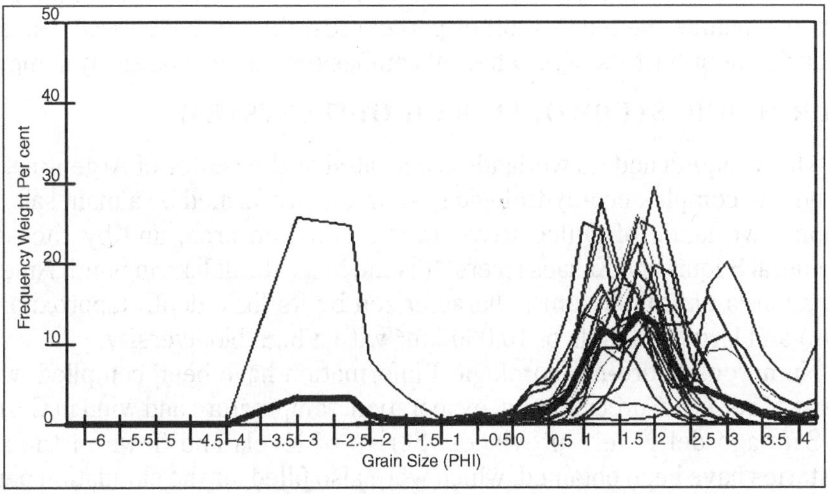

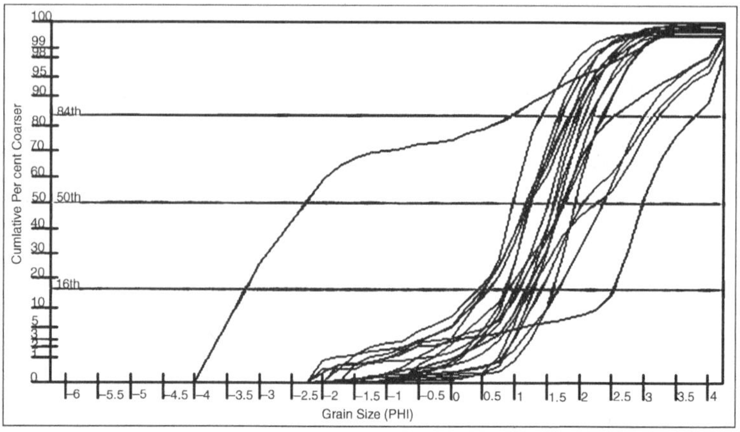

Fig. Example of a Series of Sediment Samples and Composite Sample. The First Plotdisplays the Frequency Weight Per cent Histograms, and the Second Plot Displays the Cumulative Weight Per cent

HyPAS can plot all samples selected or calculate a composite for the selected samples. The user has the option of sorting the tabular data before making a selection of samples for display in the plotting window. Once sediment samples are imported, the user must select the samples desired for a grain-size distribution plot before selecting the Sediment Sample Tool. The option to plot the cumulative frequency weight percents, the frequency weight per cent histogram, or a composite sample plot is provided. HyPAS then generates the distribution plot. Figure shows frequenc weight per cent histograms with a composite histogram from a subset of

A cumulative frequency weight per cent plot of the same sample is also shown. The thicker line delineates the composite sample. Various statistical parameters describing this composite sample are stored to a table. These statistics include the median, other percentiles, the Fill Factor (RA), and the Renourishment Factors (RJ). Different composites can then be easily compared.

HYDROLOGIC STUDY OF MAR CHIQUITA SYSTEM

Mar Chiquita and its wetlands are located at the center of Argentina. It is a large and complex eco-hydrologic system mainly formed by a main salt lake, lagoons, wetlands of Dulce River in the Northen area, and by the semi-ephemeral Suquía and Xanaes rivers. It is the biggest salt lake in South America, with an area near 6.000 km^2, characterized by its little depth (approximately 10 m.) and large wetlands of 10,000 km^2 with a high biodiversity.

Numerous hydro-meteorological information have been compiled, which consist of series on precipitation, evaporation, temperature and wind in Córdoba and Santiago del Estero provinces. Series of levels and flows in the main tributaries have been obtained, which were also filled for the simulation period.

The water level series of Mar Chiquita lake were obtained at Miramar City (south coast).

The geometric functions of the lake (curves height-area-volume) were computed using previous bathymetric data up to 66 m over sea level and a set of 8 satellite images over such level. In this way, a set of consistent information has been completed, allowing a six-month step hydrologic balance within the last 30 years covering three types of climatic periods (dry, medium and wet). The results of the numeric simulation allow a better knowledge of this complex system supporting a solid basis for the water resources management in this region.

Being of special utility to analyse the effects that can generate the increase of irrigation intakes from Dulce River upstream wetlands and lake, in order to prevent reduction effects such as the Aral sea case.

HYDROLOGIC SIMULATION OF MAR CHIQUITA SYSTEM

The conceptual model of Mar Chiquita System updates previous studies including the following hydrologic components: Mar Chiquita lake body, Dulce river wetlands area, three tributaries: Dulce, Suquía and Xanaes rivers from field measurements, Precipitation, Evaporation and flow extractions in the tributaries. The numerical model of the hydrologic balance solve the conservation of mass equation applied the system,

$$\Delta V = \sum Q_i \,_{\Delta}T + A_L\,(P\text{-}E)\,\Delta T - Q_{ext}\,\Delta T$$

Being Δ V volume variation of the lake, Q_i flow contribution of the tributaries, P media areal precipitation over the lake, E evaporation, A_L lake area, Q_{ext} flow extraction to the system and ΔT time step. The model was initially calibrated by adjusting the series of the tributary contributions, measured upstream the lake to the balance results assuming as data the series of precipitation, evaporation and lake levels.

The extraction flows to the system were assumed to be void during the process of model calibration, and variables between 4 y 60 m^3/s during the simulations. The time step was, according to the simulated case, 6 or 12 months. The results shown herein are with a 6 months interval. The calibration was performed for the 1967-1997 period, due to the availability of 30 years with all basic data for the calibration of model (mainly mean water levels).

Evaporation

As evaporation estimators, Lungeon, Meyer and Rohwer were compared with measurements, selecting the first one (ec. 2), to which a correction for the occurrence of variable salinity was added:

$$Em = 0.398.\ D.\ (es\text{–}ed).\ (\ (273\text{–}T)/\ 273\ ).\ 760/\ (Pa\text{–}es)$$

Being: Em monthly evaporation, D number of days per month, es and ed: monthly steam saturation pressure average and monthly steam pressure average respectively (mmHg), T monthly average value of the maximum daily temperatures (°C), Pa mean atmospheric pressure (mmHg). The saturation steam pressure was calculated as es = ew-0.00066.Pa.(Ta-Tw).(1+0.00115.Tw), with ew, steam pressure corresponding to the average temperature with humid bulb thermometer,Ta air temperature and Tw average temperature with humid bulb thermometer.

The monthly average steam pressure was estimated as ed= HR.es/100, being HR the relative humidity (%). The results of vertical balance of mass in the lake and wetlands have been published by Pagot el al. The volume variations have been obtained from the measured series of water levels and the corresponding geometric functions Area (level) and Volume (level).

Levels of Mar Chiquita Lake

The water levels were measured in the south coast of the lake in Miramar City. These series were previously corrected by datum changes. In this research monthly levels were adopted to avoid the influence of the wind effects ("wind set up" that can affect in more than 0.5 m). As it was mentioned before, the availability of measured levels from 1967 to 1997 has allowed the pre-calibration of the model in this period, when closing the equation for the volume balance because all its terms were known.

Salinity Variations

As mentioned before, the evaporation was obtained from direct measures taken in Miramar tank (with a correction factor = 0.7), and the calculus by Lungeon expression using meteorological data measured in the periods without direct evaporation measures. In the intervals without meteorological measures equivalent series were used, generated from the monthly average values measured in Miramar. The correction of the evaporation due to salinity variations was determined by,

$$EVPc=EVP\ (2-\rho)$$

where is the lake water density, which is calculated by the following empiric expression obtained from the measured data:

$$\rho = 0.0007\ S + 1$$

where S is the total content of salt dissolved in the water of the lake expressed in gr/l. This content of total dissolved salt S was obtained from a experimental relation that combines direct measures of S and the volumes V corresponding to the sampling dates. These functions were included in the model to automatically carry out the direct and inverse transformations.

RIVER FLOWS

The monthly flows near Mar Chiquita lake for Xanaes and Suquía rivers have been obtained from series of water levels and some discharge measurements. The rating curves were determined near the lake, extrapolating experimental values with the Manning formula, assuming steady and uniform flows. Dulce river discharges into the lake are one of the main results of the model, due to they can not be measured near the Mar Chiquita because of the wetlands existence and the very difficult access conditions. Then the closer data have been measured in Los Quiroga dam, near 300 km upstream the lake, where the main present and future extractions for irrigation are located.

Numerical Simulations

The numerical model is a simple dynamic one, developed in Fortran to solve equation 1, that applies a time discretization in finite differences and solves the non linear terms by means of an interactive standard procedure until reaching the convergence (*e.g.* the evaporation due to salinity, which is dependent of the volume that is unknown in each temporal step). The empiric functions of direct geometry A(H), V(H) and the inverses H(A) and H(V), and those of salinity S(V) and V(S) were conveniently adjusted as variable degree polynomials by sections, being evaluated in high precision in order to reduce the numeric error. The simulations were carried out with the model (previously pre-calibrated for the period between 1967 and 1997), assuming constant flow extraction in each one.

This can be seen in the reduction of lake volumes and the increase of salinity levels. However, for these small extractions, the lake-wetlands system demonstrates the capacity to quickly increase its dimensions if the hydrological conditions change, when increasing the precipitations and surface contributions, like it happened from 1976 when the lake overcame the average levels (66 m o.s.l.). For extractions of major flows -*e.g.* 10 m^3/s - the critical interval of the lake increases in almost one year. This critical period occurs when salinity level is greater than 50 gr/l -considered the first threshold of salinity for fish reproduction-. It is also observed that with these extraction flows, at the beginning of the 90s and during more than 3 years the levels of salinity overcome the 50 gr/l. For extractions of 20 m^3/s the recovery of the lake would take 3 more years, up to 1981. Also, from 1988 salinity values would severely increase, overcoming a second threshold of salinity of 100 gr/l (a limit for fish survival). At the end of the period the level of salinity would stay above of the critical value without never ending up recovering to smaller values or similar to 50 gr/l. For major extractions the effects would be extremely severe. The lake would dry off in more than half of the period simulated of 30 years, and salinity, would always stay above the first threshold and in approximately 80% of the time above the second threshold.

The modelling of Dulce river discharge showed a flow reduction near 40% from Los Quiroga dam to the lake, 300 Km downstream, due to the effects of the wetlands which act as a natural reservoir increasing evapo-transpiration.

MODELLING THE WATER BALANCE OF NATURAL LAKE

In the Southern part of Rift Valley Region of Ethiopia there are two natural Lakes, namely Abaya and Chamo Lakes, and little information is available about these Lakes. The watershed of the Lakes is about 18,000km^2 including water area and currently inhabited by more than 3 million people with growth rate of about 3% per annum. These Lakes are important shallow Lakes and among others importance, to inhabit a number of aquatic animals and to modify the climate of the area.

Yet there are evidences that they are heavily influenced by human activities and endangered Lakes unless proper precautionary measures are undertaken in the Lake's watersheds. In order to investigate the available water resources quantity in the lakes as well as impacts and influences of natural and man-induced factors a water balance model of the two Lakes have been developed. The knowledge of water balance of lakes and reservoirs is an essential component of water management. Water management decision as far as possible should be based on a thorough quantitative understanding of the hydrologic cycle of the lakes/reservoirs in the basin. In developing country like Ethiopia, the quantitative understanding of individual components of the hydrological system themselves is difficult. This paper focuses on developing a water balance model, and describe shortly methods employed to obtain the physical characteristics of the watersheds and the lakes as well as the components of hydro-meteorological elements of the water balance components under limited data situation.

The developed information is used for the simulation of lake water level. Furthermore, impacts of various influences such as sediment and water use are described and expected life of the Lakes under sediment load are discussed and measures to reverse the deteriorating situation are briefly discussed.

MODEL EQUATIONS AND SOULTION PROCEDURE

Basic Equations

The input and output components of the water balance of a lake or reservoir depend not only on the physical dimension of the water body, but also on the climatic, hydrological and geological factors affecting the water body and its surrounding areas. The water balance equation can be written, from continuity equation at any time, which is governed by the conditions that the water volume remains constant. The continuity equation intern governed by conservation of matter, which described by equilibrium between added water volume or depth, lost water volume or depth and change in volume or depth as:

$$V_{in} - V_{ou} + P - E - \Delta S = 0$$

Where Vin is surface and subsurface inflow; Vou is surface and subsurface outflow; P is precipitation volume; E is evaporation volume; S is change in storage. Alternatively, parameters can also be similarly defined in terms of depth of water. In ideal situation variables of the water balance equation are computed separately, and providing closed result. In practice however, the computation leads to a discrepancy or residual error. Considering the error term, d, the above equation can be re-written as:

$$V_{in} - V_{ou} + P - E - \Delta S \pm \delta = 0$$

In the above equations parameters can be distributed as:

$$V_{in} = V_{si} + V_{ssi}$$

$$V_{si} = \sum_{i-1}^{ngw} V_g + \sum_{i-1}^{nuw} V_{ug}$$

$$V_{ou} = V_{so} + V_{sso}$$

Where respectively, V_{si} and V_{so} are sums of surface inflow and outflow; V_{ssi} and V_{sso} are sub-surface inflow and outflow; V_g are V_{ug} are gauged and ungauged inflows; ngw and nuw are number of gauged and ungauged watersheds. The error term, δ, is treated component wise.

Solution Procedure

The water balance model equations written in the above form, using various water balance components can be used to compute and simulate the water volume, area, depth or alternatively unmeasured water balance components. The intention of the water balance in here is to simulate the water level and compute volume, area and their temporal variability on monthly or yearly time spans. In order to simulate the water level, volume based or depth-based equations, which have equal applicability, can be employed.

The depth based simulation procedure has been employed for results in this paper and described by the following steps:

- Compute initial parameters such as area and volume from the initial depth as boundary conditions,
- Assume, mean area in time period i, $A_{mi} = A_{1,i}$, where A1,i initial lake area,
- Compute change in depth, ΔZi,, from

$$\Delta Z_i = \frac{(PF \cdot p - EF \cdot e) \cdot A_{inj} + V_{inj} - V_{ouj}}{A_{mj}}$$

$A_{1,i}$ is area of the lake for evaporation and rainfall computation, with p and e are rainfall and evaporation depths respectively. PF and EF are rainfall and evaporation correction factors, which are used to adjust rainfall and evaporation on the lakes.

Depth at the end of the simulation interval is:

$$Z_{2,i} = Z_{ij} + \Delta Z_i$$

- Compute $A_{2,i,}$ the area at the end of time interval i from area elevation curve,

  Compute $A_{m,i,}$ from:

$$A_{m,i} = \frac{A_{1,i} + A_{2,j}}{2}$$

- Repeat steps 3 & 4 until reasonable agreement in Z obtained,
- Compute, volume $V_{2,i}$,at the end of time interval, i, using capacity curve,
- For the next time interval $Z_{1,i+1}$, $A_{1,i+1}$, $V_{1,i+1}$ are described by $Z_{2,i}$, $A_{2,i}$, $V_{2,i}$.

INPUT DATA PROCESS, STRUCTURE AND DATA

Structure of Data Elements

The programme for water balance named, LAKEBAL, has been developed and the modelling process constitutes three stages:

- Pre-processing of input data and selection of model parameters
- Simulation and computation of water balance components by executing the simulation programme
- Post processing of output from simulation result

Data of Water Balance Components

The components of the water balance, such as run-off, rainfall and evaporation, lake morphometry and etc., were not existing and these components have been developed in the wider scope of a research associated. The data can be stated as watershed data, lakes morphometric data, meteorological data, run-off data and peculiarities in hydrology of the watersheds.

The composed data for hydro-meteorology totals 27 years of Abaya and 22 years of Chamo Lake on monthly basis. The watersheds of the two lakes drainage basin have been modelled combining ArcView GIS and Watershed Modelling System (WMS) hydrological model. While the former has been employed for Digital Elevation Modelling (DEM) the latter has been used for Digital Terrain Modelling (DTM) in derivation of extensive hydrological parameters, such as slope, basin area, perimeter, etc.

After refining the sub watersheds capturing the locations of interest such as gauge stations and lake outlets, the entire basin was subdivided in to 52 sub-watersheds. The watershed data under the GIS environment masks the Lake morphometry due to data unavailability. In order to close this gap, a bathymetry surveys of the two Lakes have been undertaken combining Global Positioning System (GPS) and Echo-sounder. Most of the area in the two Lakes basin is ungauged (only 43.9% of land area is gauged). While the data of gauged areas have been used, a rainfall-run-off model based on monthly water balance concept was developed, to estimate ungauged portion of the watersheds as well as the missing elements of data in the simulation period.

Components of the subsurface flows are accounted via surface modelling and direct accounts are disregarded. Certain peculiar characteristics regarding the hydrology of the watersheds such as intensive evaporation due to wet land and inundation areas, hot springs, water uses in irrigation are accounted as these elements affect the magnitude of inflow components. Furthermore, surface outflows are accounted in the simulation model from the gauged information or by trial and error where such information is unavailable. The existing Lake level records constitute three gauge stations on Abaya and one station on Chamo Lake. While the Abaya Lake data could be filtered, corrected and missing values are filled by comparing the stations, in the case of Chamo Lake data certain years of monthly uninterrupted records at the beginning and end of simulation periods could be used, because the intermediate values are associated with shift of stations and change of recording mechanisms.

CALIBRATION OF PARAMETERS AND SIMULATION RESULTS

Calibration

The EF and PF parameters are used as calibration parameters. Optimum values of these parameters can be selected by minimising the error terms between measured and simulated Lake water level using ordinary least square procedures or by visual inspection of plotted results combined with regression equations. The optimum values of the calibration parameters can be set for various scenarios of investigating impacts on the lakes.

Simulation Result Using Lakebal

Due to uncertainty on the data of the water balance components on one hand and the need to obtain acceptable accuracy between the simulated and measured parameters on the other hand, the simulation and comparison of results were carried out for various scenarios.

Initial Simulation Without Considering Outflow

The first simulations have been made for both Lakes without considering outflows. After a number of trial simulation, it is shown in Figures 8.4 and 8.5

with respective description the simulation run of Abaya and Chamo for no outflow conditions, under the best selected parameters which suites simulation of level before commencement of outflows.

Simulation Considering Outflow

The simulation considering outflows are converged with EF parameters of 1.83 and 1.75 and PF parameters of 0.85 and 0.90 respectively for Abaya and Chamo Lakes. The higher evaporation factor for Abaya Lake is caused by higher heat absorption capacity of the Lake, underestimation of the method of evapotranspiration as well as uncertainty of the data derived from lake periphery. The lower rainfall factor is due to possible pluviometric depression effect of the rainfall falling on the Lakes.

The coefficient of determination of the regression of measured and gauged values for Abaya and Chamo Lakes under these conditions are 0.87 and 0.99 respectively. Analysis of error shows, the simulation result is highly sensitive to local error, and as such if an error due to data occurs at a particular point, the error propagates in the subsequent simulation periods and shows apparent errors.

Simulation Considering Estimated Sediment

The effect of deposited sediment on the lake is clear and is detrimental to the water carrying capacity of the Lakes. The sediment delivered in to the Lakes has no outlets and fully deposited. Sediment load entering the Lakes particularly that of Abaya is high in magnitude. The causes of the large quantity of sediment are associated to intensified erosion in the catchment area due to deforestation, overgrazing and poor farming practice.

In terms of Lake level simulation, the effect of inclusion of sediment deposition is to loose the bottom capacity of the Lakes and thereby an increased water level. In order to quantify the effects of sediment, unfortunately data of neither monitoring of sediment transported and delivered in to the Lakes nor adequate sediment measurement at some points in the rivers systems is available. In order to assess impact of sediment on the Lakes, 2 pairs of three various conditions of sediment inputs were evaluated. These are yield or concentration based under tolerable sediment, moderate and high sediment rates. These rates are based on watershed yield based to be 0.1, 2 and 25 t/ha per year respectively and the concentration based to be 0.02, 4 and 25 kg/m^3 respectively (scenarios II-1, II-2, II-3). Based on the various scenarios of sediment input the water level simulation and the life expectancy of the Lakes were evaluated.

Under this case, the existence to complete disappearance of Abaya Lake is estimated at 207 years and that of Chamo is estimated at 467 years. The latter would be dramatically reduced once Abaya is filled with sediment and the existence of Chamo would be then few decades after Abaya's disappearance. Investigation of research catchments located outside the watershed of the Lakes, see Dawit and other rivers in Ethiopia which have similar watersheds and climatic characteristics as well as evidences of the sediment load (short period sampled data) in the tributary rivers of the Lake show the sediment input in the two Lakes is rated medium to high rate. As a result the two shallow Lakes are threatened by the large deposition of sediment.

SANITATION, SEWERAGE AND WASTEWATER MANAGEMENT

The benefits from improved sanitation, and therefore the appropriate financing arrangements, are complex. At the lowest level, households place high value on sanitation services that provide them with a private, convenient and odour-free facility which removes excreta and wastewater from the property or confines it appropriately on-site. However, there are clearly benefits which accrue at a more aggregate level and are, therefore, "externalities" from the point of view of the household. Willingness-to-pay studies have shown consistently that households are willing to pay for the first category of service benefits, but have little or no interest in paying for external (environmental) benefits that they consider beyond their concern.

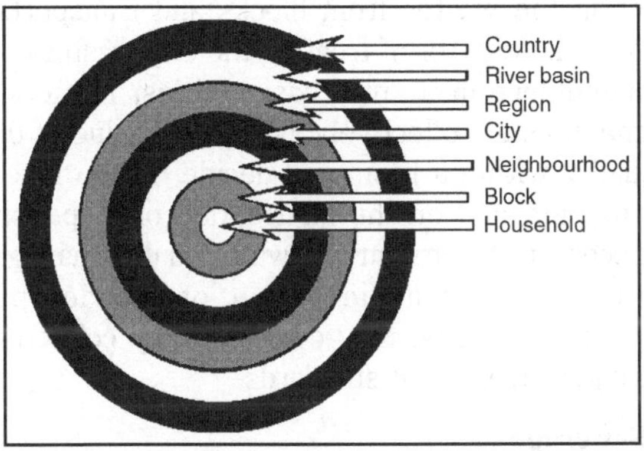

Fig. Levels of Dicision-making on Water and Sanitation.

At the next level (i.e. the block) households in a particular block value services which remove excreta from the block as a whole. Moving up a level, to that of the neighbourhood, residents value services which remove excreta and wastewater from the neighbourhood, or which render these wastes innocuous through treatment. Similarly, at the level of the city, the removal and/or treatment of wastes from the city and its surroundings are valued. Cities, however, do not exist in isolation - wastes discharged from one city pollute the water supply of downstream cities and of other users.

Accordingly, groups of cities (as well as farms and industries and others) in a river basin can perceive the collective benefit of environmental improvement. Finally, because the health and well-being of a nation as a whole may be affected by environmental degradation in one particular river basin, there are sometimes additional national economic, health and environmental benefits from wastewater management in that basin. The example of typhoid in Santiago illustrates the latter point. The fundamental principle of public finance is that costs should be assigned to different levels in this hierarchy according to the benefits accruing at the different levels.

This suggests that the financing of sanitation, sewerage and wastewater treatment should be allocated approximately as follows:

- Households pay the cost incurred in providing on-site facilities (bathrooms, toilets, sewerage connections).
- The residents of a block collectively pay the additional cost incurred in collecting the wastes from individual homes and transporting these to the boundary of the block.
- The residents of a neighbourhood collectively pay the additional cost incurred in collecting the wastes from blocks and transporting these to the boundary of the neighbourhood (or of treating the neighbourhood wastes).
- The residents of a city collectively pay the additional cost incurred in collecting the wastes from blocks and transporting these to the boundary of the city (or of treating the city wastes).
- The stakeholders in a river basin (cities, farmers, industries and environmentalists) collectively assess the value of different levels of water quality within a basin and decide on the level of quality they wish to pay for, and on the distribution of responsibility for paying for the necessary treatment and water quality management activities.
- The nation, for the achievement of broader public health or environmental benefits, may decide to pay collectively for meeting more stringent treatment standards.

Sanitation and Sewerage

Although there are complicating factors to be taken into account (including transaction costs of collection of revenues at different levels and the interconnectedness of several of the benefits), the principles discussed above are reflected both in the way some industrialised countries finance sewerage investments and in the most innovative and appropriate forms of subsector financing observed in developing countries. In many communities in the USA, for example, households and commercial organisations pay for sewer connections, primary sewer networks are financed by a sewer levy charged to all property owners along the streets served, and secondary sewers and major collectors and interceptors are often financed by improvement levies on all property owners in the serviced areas.

Innovative sewerage financing schemes are now being observed in developing country cities. In Orangi, an informal urban settlement in Karachi, a hierarchical scheme for financing sewerage services has developed in which households pay the costs of their "on-lot" (i.e. on-site) services (e.g. latrines and septic tanks), the primary sewers are paid for by the households along the "lane" (public passageway between rows of houses), contiguous "lanes" pool their resources to pay for neighbourhood sewers, and the city (via the Municipal Development Authority) pays for trunk sewers.

The arrangements for financing condominial sewers by the urban poor in Brazil follow a remarkably similar pattern; households pay for the on-site costs, blocks pay for the block sewers (and decide what level of service they want from these), with the water company or municipality paying for the trunk sewers. Lack of access to credit may impede investment in sanitation, drainage and other essential urban environmental services, especially in small cities and towns. This problem has been overcome in some cases by creating special municipal development funds or rotating funds to finance environmental investments. For example, the World Bank has supported the creation of municipal development funds in the State of Minas Gerais, Brazil, for environmental improvements in small cities and towns, and in Mexico for municipal water supply, sewerage and solid waste investments in intermediate cities.

Similarly, poor urban households need mechanisms to finance sewer connections and in-home sanitary facilities. Some cities provide credit to poor households for these investments that can be paid off in instalment payments (not subsidised) over periods of three to five years. Where there are well-managed water and sewerage utilities, the instalment payments can be collected as part of the monthly water bill. In some cases, households can provide "sweat equity" (labour inputs provided by the community for self-help construction schemes) or even make partial payment in the form of construction materials.

A special sanitation credit fund has been established in Honduras for poor urban households, fashioned along the lines of the well-known Grameen rural credit bank in Bangladesh. Such experiences show that the urban poor will invest in a healthier environment if they can spread the initial costs over time. Similarly, innovative schemes for providing urban households access to credit for sanitation investments have been demonstrated in Lesotho and in Burkina Faso.

SEWAGE TREATMENT

Sewage treatment, or domestic wastewater treatment, is the process of removing contaminants from wastewater and household sewage, both runoff and domestic. It includes physical, chemical, and biological processes to remove physical, chemical and biological contaminants. Its objective is to produce a waste stream and a solid waste or sludge suitable for discharge or reuse back into the environment. This material is often inadvertently contaminated with many toxic organic and inorganic compounds.

ORIGINS OF SEWAGE

Sewage is created by residences, institutions, hospitals and commercial and industrial establishments. Raw influent includes household waste liquid from toilets, baths, showers, kitchens, sinks, and so forth that is disposed of via sewers. In many areas, sewage also includes liquid waste from industry and commerce.

The separation and draining of household waste into greywater and blackwater is becoming more common in the developed world, with greywater being permitted to be used for watering plants or recycled for flushing toilets. A lot of sewage also includes some surface water from roofs or hard-standing areas.

Municipal wastewater therefore includes residential, commercial, and industrial liquid waste discharges, and may include stormwater runoff. Sewage systems capable of handling stormwater are known as combined systems or combined sewers. Such systems are usually avoided since they complicate and thereby reduce the efficiency of sewage treatment plants owing to their seasonality.

The variability in flow also leads to often larger than necessary, and subsequently more expensive, treatment facilities. In addition, heavy storms that contribute more flows than the treatment plant can handle may overwhelm the sewage treatment system, causing a spill or overflow. It is preferable to have a separate storm drain system for stormwater in areas that are developed with sewer systems.

As rainfall runs over the surface of roofs and the ground, it may pick up various contaminants including soil particles and other sediment, heavy metals, organic compounds, animal waste, and oil and grease. Some jurisdictions require stormwater to receive some level of treatment before being discharged directly into waterways. Examples of treatment processes used for stormwater include sedimentation basins, wetlands, buried concrete vaults with various kinds of filters, and vortex separators.

PROCESS OVERVIEW

Sewage can be treated close to where it is created or collected and transported via a network of pipes and pump stations to a municipal treatment plant. Sewage collection and treatment is typically subject to local, state and federal regulations and standards. Industrial sources of wastewater often require specialized treatment processes. Conventional sewage treatment involves three stages, called primary, secondary and tertiary treatment. First, the solids are separated from the wastewater stream. Then dissolved biological matter is progressively converted into a solid mass by using indigenous, water-borne micro-organisms.

Finally, the biological solids are neutralized then disposed of or re-used, and the treated water may be disinfected chemically or physically. The final effluent can be discharged into a stream, river, bay, lagoon or wetland, or it can be used for the irrigation of a golf course, green way or park. If it is sufficiently clean, it can also be used for groundwater recharge or agricultural purposes.

PRE-TREATMENT

Pre-treatment removes the materials that can be easily collected from the raw wastewater and disposed of. The typical materials that are removed during pre treatment include fats, oils, and greases, sand, gravels and rocks, larger settleable solids and floating materials. In modern plants serving large populations, sophisticated equipment with remote operation and control are employed whilst in smaller or less modern plants manually cleaned screen may be used.

SCREENING

The influent sewage water is strained to remove all large objects carried in the sewage stream, such as rags, sticks, tampons, cans, fruit, etc. This is most commonly done with a manual or automated mechanically raked bar screen. The raking action of a mechanical bar screen is typically paced according to the accumulation on the bar screens and/or flow rate. The bar screen is used because large solids can damage or clog the equipment used later in the sewage treatment plant. The large solids can also hinder the biological process. The solids are collected and later disposed in a landfill or incinerated. Pre treatment also typically includes a sand or grit channel or chamber where the velocity of the incoming wastewater is carefully controlled to allow sand grit and stones to settle, while keeping the majority of the suspended organic material in the water column. This equipment is called a de-gritter or sand catcher.

Sand, grit, and stones need to be removed early in the process to avoid damage to pumps and other equipment in the remaining treatment stages. Sometimes there is a sand washer followed by a conveyor that transports the sand to a container for disposal. The contents from the sand catcher may be fed into the incinerator in a sludge processing plant, but in many cases, the sand and grit is sent to a landfill.

PRIMARY TREATMENT

Sedimentation

In the primary sedimentation stage, sewage flows through large tanks, commonly called "primary clarifiers" or "primary sedimentation tanks". The tanks are large enough that sludge can settle and floating material such as grease and oils can rise to the surface and be skimmed off. The main purpose of the primary sedimentation stage is to produce both a generally homogeneous liquid capable of being treated biologically and a sludge that can be separately treated or processed. Primary settling tanks are usually equipped with mechanically driven scrapers that continually drive the collected sludge towards a hopper in the base of the tank from where it can be pumped to further sludge treatment stages.

Secondary Treatment

Secondary treatment is designed to substantially degrade the biological content of the sewage such as are derived from human waste, food waste, soaps and detergent. The majority of municipal plants treat the settled sewage liquor using aerobic biological processes. For this to be effective, the biota require both oxygen and a substrate on which to live. There are a number of ways in which this is done. In all these methods, the bacteria and protozoa consume biodegradable soluble organic contaminants and bind much of the less soluble fractions into floc.

Secondary treatment systems are classified as:

- Fixed-film or
- Suspended-growth.

Fixed-film treatment process including trickling filter and rotating biological contactors where the biomass grows on media and the sewage passes over its surface. In suspended-growth systems, such as activated sludge, the biomass is well mixed with the sewage and can be operated in a smaller space than fixed-film systems that treat the same amount of water. However, fixed-film systems are more able to cope with drastic changes in the amount of biological material and can provide higher removal rates for organic material and suspended solids than suspended growth systems. Roughing filters are intended to treat particularly strong or variable organic loads, typically industrial, to allow them to then be treated by conventional secondary treatment processes. Characteristics include typically tall, circular filters filled with open synthetic filter media to which wastewater is applied at a relatively high rate. They are designed to allow high hydraulic loading and a high flow-through of air. On larger installations, air is forced through the media using blowers. The resultant wastewater is usually within the normal range for conventional treatment processes.

SURFACE-AERATED BASINS

Most biological oxidation processes for treating industrial wastewaters have in common the use of oxygen and microbial action. Surface-aerated basins achieve 80 to 90% removal of Biochemical Oxygen Demand with retention times of 1 to 10 days. The basins may range in depth from 1.5 to 5.0 metres and use motor-driven aerators floating on the surface of the wastewater.

In an aerated basin system, the aerators provide two functions: they transfer air into the basins required by the biological oxidation reactions, and they provide the mixing required for dispersing the air and for contacting the reactants. Typically, the floating surface aerators are rated to deliver the amount of air equivalent to 1.8 to 2.7 kg O_2/kW·h. However, they do not provide as good mixing as is normally achieved in activated sludge systems and therefore aerated basins do not achieve the same performance level as activated sludge units. Biological oxidation processes are sensitive to temperature and, between 0 °C and 40 °C, the rate of biological reactions increase with temperature. Most surface aerated vessels operate at between 4 °C and 32 °C.

Filter Beds

In older plants and plants receiving more variable loads, trickling filter beds are used where the settled sewage liquor is spread onto the surface of a deep bed made up of coke, limestone chips or specially fabricated plastic media. Such media must have high surface areas to support the biofilms that form. The liquor is distributed through perforated rotating arms radiating from a central pivot. The distributed liquor trickles through this bed and is collected in drains at the base.

These drains also provide a source of air which percolates up through the bed, keeping it aerobic. Biological films of bacteria, protozoa and fungi form on the media's surfaces and eat or otherwise reduce the organic content. This biofilm is grazed by insect larvae and worms which help maintain an optimal thickness. Overloading of beds increases the thickness of the film leading to clogging of the filter media and ponding on the surface.

Biological Aerated Filters

Biological Aerated Filter or Biofilters combine filtration with biological carbon reduction, nitrification or denitrification. BAF usually includes a reactor filled with a filter media. The media is either in suspension or supported by a gravel layer at the foot of the filter.

The dual purpose of this media is to support highly active biomass that is attached to it and to filter suspended solids. Carbon reduction and ammonia conversion occurs in aerobic mode and sometime achieved in a single reactor while nitrate conversion occurs in anoxic mode. BAF is operated either in upflow or downflow configuration depending on design specified by manufacturer.

Membrane Bioreactors

Membrane bioreactors combines activated sludge treatment with a membrane liquid-solid separation process. The membrane component uses low pressure microfiltration or ultra filtration membranes and eliminates the need for clarification and tertiary filtration. The membranes are typically immersed in the aeration tank. One of the key benefits of a membrane bioreactor system is that it effectively overcomes the limitations associated with poor settling of sludge in conventional activated sludge processes. The technology permits bioreactor operation with considerably higher mixed liquor suspended solids concentration than CAS systems, which are limited by sludge settling.

The process is typically operated at MLSS in the range of 8,000–12,000 mg/L, while CAS are operated in the range of 2,000–3,000 mg/L. The elevated biomass concentration in the membrane bioreactor process allows for very effective removal of both soluble and particulate biodegradable materials at higher loading rates. Thus increased Sludge Retention Times—usually exceeding 15 days—ensure complete nitrification even in extremely cold weather. The cost of building and operating a MBR is usually higher than conventional wastewater treatment, however, as the technology has become increasingly popular and has gained wider acceptance throughout the industry, the life-cycle costs have been steadily decreasing. The small footprint of MBR systems, and the high quality effluent produced, makes them particularly useful for water reuse applications.

Secondary Sedimentation

The final step in the secondary treatment stage is to settle out the biological floc or filter material and produce sewage water containing very low levels of organic material and suspended matter.

ROTATING BIOLOGICAL CONTACTORS

Fig. Schematic Diagram of a Typical Rotating Biological Contactor.

Rotating biological contactors are mechanical secondary treatment systems, which are robust and capable of withstanding surges in organic load. RBCs were first installed in Germany in 1960 and have since been developed and refined into a reliable operating unit. The rotating disks support the growth of bacteria and micro-organisms present in the sewage, which breakdown and stabilise organic pollutants.

To be successful, micro-organisms need both oxygen to live and food to grow. Oxygen is obtained from the atmosphere as the disks rotate. As the micro-organisms grow, they build up on the media until they are sloughed off due to shear forces provided by the rotating discs in the sewage. Effluent from the RBC is then passed through final clarifiers where the micro-organisms in suspension settle as a sludge. The sludge is withdrawn from the clarifier for further treatment.

A functionally similar biological filtering system has become popular as part of home aquarium filtration and purification. The aquarium water is drawn up out of the tank and then cascaded over a freely spinning corrugated fiber-mesh wheel before passing through a media filter and back into the aquarium. The spinning mesh wheel develops a biofilm coating of microorganisms that feed on the suspended wastes in the aquarium water and are also exposed to the atmosphere as the wheel rotates. This is especially good at removing waste urea and ammonia urinated into the aquarium water by the fish and other animals.

TERTIARY TREATMENT

The purpose of tertiary treatment is to provide a final treatment stage to raise the effluent quality before it is discharged to the receiving environment. More than one tertiary treatment process may be used at any treatment plant. If disinfection is practiced, it is always the final process. It is also called "effluent polishing".

Filtration

Sand filtration removes much of the residual suspended matter. Filtration over activated carbon removes residual toxins.

Lagooning

Lagooning provides settlement and further biological improvement through storage in large man-made ponds or lagoons. These lagoons are highly aerobic and colonization by native macrophytes, especially reeds, is often encouraged. Small filter feeding invertebrates such as Daphnia and species of Rotifera greatly assist in treatment by removing fine particulates.

CONSTRUCTED WETLANDS

Constructed wetlands include engineered reedbeds and a range of similar methodologies, all of which provide a high degree of aerobic biological improvement and can often be used instead of secondary treatment for small communities. One example is a small reedbed used to clean the drainage from the elephants' enclosure at Chester Zoo in England.

NUTRIENT REMOVAL

Wastewater may contain high levels of the nutrients nitrogen and phosphorus. Excessive release to the environment can lead to a build up of nutrients, called eutrophication, which can in turn encourage the overgrowth of weeds, algae, and cyanobacteria. This may cause an algal bloom, a rapid growth in the population of algae. The algae numbers are unsustainable and eventually most of them die.

The decomposition of the algae by bacteria uses up so much of oxygen in the water that most or all of the animals die, which creates more organic matter for the bacteria to decompose. In addition to causing deoxygenation, some algal species produce toxins that contaminate drinking water supplies. Different treatment processes are required to remove nitrogen and phosphorus.

Nitrogen removal

The removal of nitrogen is effected through the biological oxidation of nitrogen from ammonia (nitrification) to nitrate, followed by denitrification, the reduction of nitrate to nitrogen gas. Nitrogen gas is released to the atmosphere and thus removed from the water. Nitrification itself is a two-step aerobic process, each step facilitated by a different type of bacteria.

The oxidation of ammonia to nitrite is most often facilitated by Nitrosomonas spp. Nitrite oxidation to nitrate, though traditionally believed to be facilitated by Nitrobacter spp. is now known to be facilitated in the environment almost exclusively by Nitrospira spp.

Denitrification requires anoxic conditions to encourage the appropriate biological communities to form. It is facilitated by a wide diversity of bacteria. Sand filters, lagooning and reed beds can all be used to reduce nitrogen, but the activated sludge process can do the job the most easily. Since denitrification is the reduction of nitrate to dinitrogen gas, an electron donor is needed.

This can be, depending on the wastewater, organic matter, sulfide, or an added donor like methanol. Sometimes the conversion of toxic ammonia to nitrate alone is referred to as tertiary treatment.

Phosphorus Removal

Phosphorus removal is important as it is a limiting nutrient for algae growth in many fresh water systems. It is also particularly important for water reuse systems where high phosphorus concentrations may lead to fouling of downstream equipment such as reverse osmosis.

Phosphorus can be removed biologically in a process called enhanced biological phosphorus removal. In this process, specific bacteria, called polyphosphate accumulating organisms, are selectively enriched and accumulate large quantities of phosphorus within their cells. When the biomass enriched in these bacteria is separated from the treated water, these biosolids have a high fertilizer value.

Phosphorus removal can also be achieved by chemical precipitation, usually with salts of iron, aluminum, or lime. This may lead to excessive sludge productions as hydroxides precipitates and the added chemicals can be expensive. Despite this, chemical phosphorus removal requires significantly smaller equipment footprint than biological removal, is easier to operate and is often more reliable than biological phosphorus removal. Once removed, phosphorus, in the form of a phosphate rich sludge, may be land filled or, if in suitable condition, resold for use in fertilizer.

DISINFECTION

The purpose of disinfection in the treatment of wastewater is to substantially reduce the number of microorganisms in the water to be discharged back into the environment. The effectiveness of disinfection depends on the quality of the water being treated, the type of disinfection being used, the disinfectant dosage, and other environmental variables.

Cloudy water will be treated less successfully since solid matter can shield organisms, especially from ultraviolet light or if contact times are low. Generally, short contact times, low doses and high flows all militate against effective disinfection. Common methods of disinfection include ozone, chlorine, or ultraviolet light. Chloramine, which is used for drinking water, is not used in wastewater treatment because of its persistence. Chlorination remains the most common form of wastewater disinfection in North America due to its low cost and long-term history of effectiveness. One disadvantage is that chlorination of residual organic material can generate chlorinated-organic compounds that may be carcinogenic or harmful to the environment. Residual chlorine or chloramines may also be capable of chlorinating organic material in the natural aquatic environment. Further, because residual chlorine is toxic to aquatic species, the treated effluent must also be chemically dechlorinated, adding to the complexity and cost of treatment.

Ultraviolet light can be used instead of chlorine, iodine, or other chemicals. Because no chemicals are used, the treated water has no adverse effect on organisms that later consume it, as may be the case with other methods. UV radiation causes damage to the genetic structure of bacteria, viruses, and other pathogens, making them incapable of reproduction.

The key disadvantages of UV disinfection are the need for frequent lamp maintenance and replacement and the need for a highly treated effluent to ensure that the target microorganisms are not shielded from the UV radiation. In the United Kingdom, light is becoming the most common means of disinfection because of the concerns about the impacts of chlorine in chlorinating residual organics in the wastewater and in chlorinating organics in the receiving water. Edmonton and Calgary, Alberta, Canada also use UV light for their effluent water disinfection. Ozone O_3 is generated by passing oxygen O_2 through a high voltage potential resulting in a third oxygen atom becoming attached and forming O_3. Ozone is very unstable and reactive and oxidizes most organic material it comes in contact with, thereby destroying many pathogenic microorganisms. Ozone is considered to be safer than chlorine because, unlike chlorine which has to be stored on site, ozone is generated onsite as needed. Ozonation also produces fewer disinfection by-products than chlorination. A disadvantage of ozone disinfection is the high cost of the ozone generation equipment and the requirements for special operators.

Package Plants and Batch Reactors

In order to use less space, treat difficult waste, deal with intermittent flow or achieve higher environmental standards, a number of designs of hybrid treatment plants have been produced. Such plants often combine all or at least two stages of the three main treatment stages into one combined stage. In the UK, where a large number of sewage treatment plants serve small populations, package plants are a viable alternative to building discrete structures for each process stage. One type of system that combines secondary treatment and settlement is the sequencing batch reactor. Typically, activated sludge is mixed with raw incoming sewage and mixed and aerated. The resultant mixture is then allowed to settle producing a high quality effluent. The settled sludge is run off and re-aerated before a proportion is returned to the headworks. SBR plants are now being deployed in many parts of the world including North Liberty, Iowa, and Llanasa, North Wales, Southwestern United States.

The disadvantage of such processes is that precise control of timing, mixing and aeration is required. This precision is usually achieved by computer controls linked to many sensors in the plant. Such a complex, fragile system is unsuited to places where such controls may be unreliable, or poorly maintained, or where the power supply may be intermittent. Package plants may be referred to as high charged or low charged. This refers to the way the biological load is processed. In high charged systems, the biological stage is presented with a high organic load and the combined floc and organic material is then oxygenated for a few hours before being charged again with a new load. In the low charged system the biological stage contains a low organic load and is combined with flocculate for a relatively long time.

Sludge Treatment and Disposal

The sludges accumulated in a wastewater treatment process must be treated and disposed of in a safe and effective manner. The purpose of digestion is to reduce the amount of organic matter and the number of disease-causing microorganisms present in the solids. The most common treatment options include anaerobic digestion, aerobic digestion, and composting. Choice of a wastewater solid treatment method depends on the amount of solids generated and other site-specific conditions. However, in general, composting is most often applied to smaller-scale applications followed by aerobic digestion and then lastly anaerobic digestion for the larger-scale municipal applications.

ANAEROBIC DIGESTION

Anaerobic digestion is a bacterial process that is carried out in the absence of oxygen. The process can either be *thermophilic* digestion, in which sludge is fermented in tanks at a temperature of 55°C, or *mesophilic*, at a temperature of around 36°C. Though allowing shorter retention time, thermophilic digestion is more expensive in terms of energy consumption for heating the sludge. One major feature of anaerobic digestion is the production of biogas, which can be used in generators for electricity production and/or in boilers for heating purposes.

AEROBIC DIGESTION

Aerobic digestion is a bacterial process occurring in the presence of oxygen. Under aerobic conditions, bacteria rapidly consume organic matter and convert it into carbon dioxide. The operating costs are characteristically much greater for aerobic digestion because of the energy costs needed to add oxygen to the process.

SLUDGE DISPOSAL

When a liquid sludge is produced, further treatment may be required to make it suitable for final disposal. Typically, sludges are thickened to reduce the volumes transported off-site for disposal. There is no process which completely eliminates the need to dispose of biosolids. There is, however, an additional step some cities are taking to superheat the wastewater sludge and convert it into small pelletized granules that are high in nitrogen and other organic materials.

In New York City, for example, several sewage treatment plants have dewatering facilities that use large centrifuges along with the addition of chemicals such as polymer to further remove liquid from the sludge. The removed fluid, called centrate, is typically reintroduced into the wastewater process. The product which is left is called "cake" and that is picked up by companies which turn it into fertilizer pellets. This product is then sold to local farmers and turf farms as a soil amendment or fertilizer, reducing the amount of space required to dispose of sludge in landfills.

TREATMENT IN THE RECEIVING ENVIRONMENT

Many processes in a wastewater treatment plant are designed to mimic the natural treatment processes that occur in the environment, whether that environment is a natural water body or the ground. If not overloaded, bacteria in the environment will consume organic contaminants, although this will reduce the levels of oxygen in the water and may significantly change the overall ecology of the receiving water. Native bacterial populations feed on the organic contaminants, and the numbers of disease-causing microorganisms are reduced by natural environmental conditions such as predation or exposure to ultraviolet radiation. Consequently, in cases where the receiving environment provides a high level of dilution, a high degree of wastewater treatment may not be required. However, recent evidence has demonstrated that very low levels of certain contaminants in wastewater, including hormones and synthetic materials such as phthalates that mimic hormones in their action, can have an unpredictable adverse impact on the natural biota and potentially on humans if the water is re-used for drinking water.

In the US and EU, uncontrolled discharges of wastewater to the environment are not permitted under law, and strict water quality requirements are to be met. A significant threat in the coming decades will be the increasing uncontrolled discharges of wastewater within rapidly developing countries.

SEWAGE TREATMENT IN DEVELOPING COUNTRIES

There are few reliable figures on the share of the wastewater collected in sewers that is being treated in the world. In many developing countries the bulk of domestic and industrial wastewater is discharged without any treatment or after primary treatment only. In Latin America about 15% of collected wastewater passes through treatment plants. In Venezuela, a below average country in South America with respect to wastewater treatment, 97 percent of the country's sewage is discharged raw into the environment.

In a relatively developed Middle Eastern country such as Iran, Tehran's majority of population has totally untreated sewage injected to the city's groundwater. Israel has also aggressively pursued the use of treated sewer water for irrigation. In 2008, agriculture in Israel consumed 500 million cubic metres of potable water and an equal amount of treated sewer water. The country plans to provide a further 200 million cubic metres of recycled sewer water and build more desalination plants to supply even more water. chal Most of sub-Saharan Africa is without wastewater treatment.

Water utilities in developing countries are chronically underfunded because of low water tariffs, the inexistence of sanitation tariffs in many cases, low billing efficiency and poor operational efficiency. In addition, wastewater treatment typically is the process within the utility that receives the least attention, partly because enforcement of environmental standards is poor. As a result of all these factors, operation and maintenance of many wastewater treatment plants is poor. This is evidenced by the frequent breakdown of equipment, shutdown of electrically operated equipment due to power outages or to reduce costs, and sedimentation due to lack of sludge removal.

Developing countries as diverse as Egypt, Algeria, China or Colombia have invested substantial sums in wastewater treatment without achieving a significant impact in terms of environmental improvement. Even if wastewater treatment plants are properly operating, it can be argued that the environmental impact is limited in cases where the assimilative capacity of the receiving waters is high, as it is often the case.

IN DEVELOPING COUNTRIES

As of 2006, waterborne diseases are estimated to cause 1.8 million deaths each year. These deaths are attributable to inadequate public sanitation systems and it is clear that proper sewerage need to be installed. Appropriate technology options in water treatment include both community-scale and household-scale point-of-use designs. Military surplus water treatment units like the ERDLator are still seen in developing countries. Newer military style Reverse Osmosis

Water Purification Units are portable, self-contained water treatment plants are becoming more available for public use. In order for the decrease of waterborne diseases to have long term effects, water treatment programs implemented by research and development groups in developing countries must be sustainable by its own residents. This can ensure the efficiency of such programs after the departure of the research team as monitoring is difficult because of the remoteness of many locations.

WASTEWATER TREATMENT MANAGEMENT

Even when the appropriate financing and institutional principles are followed, very difficult issues can still arise with respect to the financing of wastewater treatment facilities. In industrial countries, two very different models are used. In many industrialised countries, the approach followed has been to set universal environmental standards and then to raise the funds necessary to finance the required investments. It is becoming increasingly evident that such an approach is proving to be very expensive and not financially feasible, even in the richest countries of the world.

In the UK, the target date for compliance with the water quality standards of the European Union (EU) is being reviewed as customers' bills rise astronomically to pay the huge costs involved. In the USA, US$ 56,000 million in federal construction grants were provided to local governments from 1972-89 to build mandated secondary treatment facilities, but these grants have now been eliminated (and replaced by State revolving funds for loans to municipalities) at the same time that increasingly stringent environmental standards are being proposed.

Many local governments are now refusing to comply with the unfunded mandates of the Federal Government. The city of San Diego, for example, has refused to spend US$ 5,000 million on federally-mandated secondary treatment, arguing that it is more cost-effective to use long, coastal outfalls for sewage disposal. San Diego brought suit against the Federal Government and recently won its case in the federal courts. The US National Research Council has advocated a change in which costs and benefits are both taken into account in the management of sewage, with a shift to a water quality-based approach at the coastal zone, watershed or basin level.

In a few countries, a different model has been developed. In these countries, river basin institutions have been put into place which:

- Ensure broad participation in the setting of standards, and in making the trade-offs between cost and water quality.
- Ensure that available resources are spent on those investments which yield the highest environmental return.
- Use economic instruments to encourage users and polluters to reduce the adverse environmental impacts of their activities.

These institutional arrangements are described more fully below. In river basins in Germany and France, and more recently in Brazil, river basin financing and management models are applied in order to raise resources for wastewater treatment and water quality management from users and polluters in the basin. The stakeholders, including users and polluters as well as citizens' groups, are involved in deciding the level of resources to be raised and the consequent level of environmental quality they wish to "purchase". This system has proved to be efficient, robust and flexible in meeting the financing needs of the densely industrialised Ruhr Valley for 80 years, and for the whole of France since the early 1960s. There is growing evidence that if such participatory agencies were developed, people would be willing to pay substantial amounts for environmental improvement, even in developing countries.

In the state of Espirito Santo in Brazil, a household survey showed that families were willing to pay 1.4 times the cost of sewage collection systems, but 2.3 times the higher cost of a sewage collection and treatment system. In the Rio Doce Valley, an industrial basin of nearly three million people in south-east Brazil, a river basin authority is in the process of being developed. Stakeholders have indicated that they are willing to pay about US$ 1,000 million over a five-year period for environmental improvement.

In the Philippines, recent surveys show that households are often prepared to make substantial payments for investments which will improve the quality of nearby lakes and rivers. For developing countries, the implications of the experience of industrialised countries are clear. Even rich countries manage to treat only a part of their sewage, e.g. only 52 per cent of sewage is treated in France and only 66 per cent in Canada. As in the USA, Japan and France, most countries have provided some form of environmental grants to municipalities in order to achieve their present levels of treatment. Given the very low initial levels in developing countries (e.g. only about 2 per cent of wastewater was treated in Latin America at the beginning of the decade) and the vital importance of improving the quality of the aquatic environment, an approach is needed that simultaneously makes the best use of available resources and provides incentives to polluters to reduce the loads they impose on surface and groundwaters.

An effluent tax is one form of incentive that is used in many countries, ranging from France, Germany and The Netherlands to China and Mexico. It can be applied to any dischargers, cities or industries, with two benefits; it induces waste reduction and treatment and can provide a source of revenue for financing wastewater treatment investments. The dramatic impact of the Dutch effluent tax on industrial discharges is described by Jansen. The overall industrial effluent loads decreased by two-thirds between 1969, when an effluent tax was first applied, and 1985 (falling from 33 million to 11 million population equivalents).

The experience of China in the application of an industrial effluent tax for financing industrial wastewater management improvements has been described by Suzhen. In France and Mexico, the effluent tax is applied equally to municipal and industrial effluents, thus encouraging local investment in municipal wastewater treatment plants. An effluent tax, however, should be used in combination with municipal sewer use charges in order to ensure that industries do not escape paying for their discharges by passing the cost on to the municipality, as well as to ensure that the municipal sewerage authority has sufficient revenues to build and to operate sewerage and treatment works.

COMMUNITY PARTICIPATION

The aspiration of most urban households, including the urban poor, is to have access to cost-effective and affordable sanitation services via public or private utilities. Consequently, they would be willing to participate, as responsible users, by paying the appropriate service charges. In the cities of many developing countries, however, such services are not yet universally accessible and poor communities must, themselves, get involved in the planning and delivery of sanitation and sewerage options.

The examples of the condominial sewer system in Brazil and the Orangi Pilot Project indicate an important institutional approach to community participation in which a productive partnership is formed between community groups and the municipal government or the utility. Often, such a system involves public provision of the external or trunk infrastructure, which may be operated by either the public or private sector, and the community providing and managing the internal or feeder infrastructure. The link between feeder and trunk infrastructure is essential for the evacuation and disposal of human waste collected by the community, but it is too easily overlooked. Many forms of community participation are possible for the provision of sanitation and sewerage services, such as:

- Information gathering on community conditions, needs and impact assessments.
- Articulation of, and advocacy for, local preferences and priorities.
- Consultations concerning programmes, projects and policies.
- Involvement in the selection and design of interventions.
- Contribution of "sweat equity" or management of project implementation.
- Information dissemination.
- Monitoring and evaluation of interventions.

Promoting and enabling community participation can take many forms. Where political will exists, governments may promote participation and create the conditions under which communities and households, as well as NGOs and the private sector, can play their appropriate roles. The World Bank-financed

PROSANEAR project in Brazil for example, provides a framework and the resources for municipalities and utilities to experiment with innovative technical and institutional arrangements for providing sanitation services to the urban poor. When such government support is absent, alternative approaches have commonly been used to stimulate community involvement and to build the necessary political will.

First, NGOs or community-based organisations (CBOs) often play a catalytic role in mobilising communities and forming partnerships. In one of the largest scale examples involving an NGO, Sulabh Shauchalaya International began, in 1970, promoting the construction of pour-flush latrines in Delhi and other Indian cities, and over a period of 20 years assisted in building over 660,000 private latrines and 2,500 public toilet complexes with community participation and government support.

Second, consultations and town meetings are increasingly used as a forum to discuss and agree on environmental priorities, and to propose participatory solutions. Finally, communities may engage in public protests or legal actions as a means of building a constituency of the urban poor, and applying pressure on local governments and utilities for dialogue and action. The Orangi Pilot Project had its origins in the discontent of local residents with excreta and wastewater overflowing in the streets as a result of the failure of the Karachi Development Authority to provide adequate sewerage.

A ROLE FOR THE PRIVATE SECTOR

Financial resources can also be mobilised through the private sector; poor service provision by the public sector often suggests a need for increasing partnerships with the private sector. Private sector participation, however, is only one possible opportunity; it is not a panacea. In situations in which existing sanitation service delivery is either too costly or inadequate, private sector participation should be examined as a means of enhancing efficiency and lowering costs, and of expanding the resources available for service delivery. In deciding whether to involve the private sector, it is important to assess several key factors which have been summarised by the *Infrastructure for Development: World Development Report, 1994*. Introducing competition is the most important step in creating conditions for greater efficiency by both private and public operators; some services can be split into separate operations to help create contestable markets. The principle of accountability to the public should be maintained through transparent contractual agreements that are open to public scrutiny and should help to minimise risks to public welfare, create real competition, ensure efficiency, and promote self-financing.

Paradoxically, public sector capacity may have to be strengthened in order to achieve effective private sector participation which requires public sector agencies with sufficient capacity to prepare bidding documents and performance indicators, assess proposed outputs and costs, administer the contracting process, and regulate contract performance. In Mexico, municipalities are granting concessions to the private sector to build and operate wastewater treatment plants, both as a means of financing investments in plants through the private sector and to overcome problems with weak local operating capacity.

The Puerto Vallarta wastewater treatment plant was the first of many new plants to come on line in the past few years. An important point to remember in cases such as Puerto Vallarta is that the private sector performs the necessary function of mobilising financing for needed investments, but the investments made together with operations, maintenance and depreciation costs will all have to be recovered through tariffs charged to domestic and industrial customers. Another innovative example is a concession to 26 industries in the Vallejo area of Mexico City to form a new enterprise, Aguas Industriales del Vallejo, to rehabilitate and expand with its own funds an old municipal wastewater treatment plant, treat up to 200l s-1 of sewage, and sell the treated water to shareholders at 75 per cent of the public utility water tariff.

Bibliography

A.K. Chakraborty and M.P. Singh: *Recent Techniques in Agroforestry*, Enkay Publishing House, Delhi, 2013.

A.K. Patra: *Agroforestry: Principles and Practices*, New India Publishing Agency, Delhi, 2013.

Antony Joseph Raj and S.B. Lal: *Agroforestry : Theory and Practices*, Scientific Publication, Delhi, 2014.

C.B.Pandey and O.P.Chaturvedi: *Agroforestry : Systems and Prospects*, New India Publishing Agency, Delhi, 2014.

Florencia Montagnini: *Environmental Services of Agroforestry Systems*, International Book Distributing Co, Delhi, 2007.

K.G. Tejwani: *Agroforestry in India*, Concept Publication, Delhi, 2002.

K.T. Parthiban, R. Umarani, S. Umesh Kanna, I. Sekar, P. Rajendran and P. Durairasu: *Industrial Agroforestry : Perspectives and Prospectives*, Scientific Publishers, Delhi, 2014.

L K Jha and P K Sen Sarma: *Agroforestry — Indian Perspective*, APH Publication, Delhi, 2008.

L K Jha: *Advances in Agroforestry*, APH Publication, Delhi, 2009.

M P Divya; K T Parthiban; K Vanangamudi; K Srinivasan and M Govinda Rao: *Social Forestry and Agroforestry*, Satish Serial Publishing House, Delhi, 2008.

M.G. Chitkara: *Agroforestry*, APH Publication, Delhi, 2012.

M.P. Singh and D.N. Tewari: *Agroforestry and Wastelands*, Anmol Publication, Delhi, 1996.

N.L. Sen, R.C. Dadheech, L.K. Dashora and T.S. Rawat: *Manual of Agroforestry and Social Forestry*, Agrotech Publication, Delhi, 2010.

O.P. Chaturvedi, A. Venkatesh, R.S. Yadav, Badre Alam, R.P. Dwivedi, Ramesh Singh and S.K. Dhyani: *Agroforestry : Natural Resource Sustainability, Livelihood and Climate Moderation*, Satish Serial Publication, Delhi, 2009.

P K Ramachandran Nair: *An Introduction to Agroforestry*, Springer, Delhi, 2008.

P.S. Pathak and Ram Newaj: *Agroforestry : Potentials and Opportunities*, Agrobios Publication, Delhi, 2003.

Pankaj Panwar, A.K. Tiwari and K.S. Dadhwal: *Agroforestry Systems for Resource Conservation and Livelihood Security in Lower Himalayas*, New India Publishing Agency, Delhi, 2012.

Ramesh Umrani and C.K. Jain: *Agroforestry : Systems and Practices*, Oxford Book Company, Delhi, 2010.

S.K. Dhyani, Ram Newaj, Badre Alam and Inder Dev: *Agroforestry Present Status and Way Forward*, Biotech Books, Delhi, 2016.

S.P. Singh: *Favourite Agroforestry Trees*, Agrotech Books, Delhi, 2010.

S.S Kundu, O.P. Chaturvedi, J.C.Dagar and S.K. Sirohi: *Environment, Agroforestry and Livestock Management*, International Book Distributing Co., Delhi, 2008.

S.S. Narwal, Pavle Pavlovic and Jacob John: *Research Methods in Plant Sciences: Vol. II : Forestry and Agroforestry*, Studium Press, Delhi, 2011.

Sanjeev K. Chauhan, S.S. Gill, H.N. Khajuria and Rajni Chauhan: *Production Technology and Management of Agroforestry Models*, Agrotech Publication, Delhi, 2006.

Satish Kumar Sinha: *Advances in Agroforestry*, Random Publication, Delhi, 2012.

Sunil Puri and Pankaj Panwar: *Agroforestry : Systems and Practices*, New India Publication, Delhi, 2007.

V.C. Srivastava: *Agroforestry a Sustainable Land Use System*, Agrobios Publication, Delhi, 2013.

Inex

F

G

H

I

L

M

N

O

P

Q

R

S

T